Brief Contents

Contents

RESEARCH MeTHODS
for the
Behavioral Sciences

FOURTH EDITION

Charles Stangor
University of Maryland

WADSWORTH
CENGAGE Learning

Australia • Brazil • Japan • Korea • Mexico • Singapore • Spain • United Kingdom • United States

WADSWORTH
CENGAGE Learning

Research Methods for the Behavioral Sciences, Fourth Edition
Charles Stangor

Publisher/Executive Editor: Jon-David Hague

Developmental Editor: Trina Tom

Editorial Assistant: Alicia McLaughlin

Media Editor: Mary Noel

Marketing Manager: Jessica Egbert

Marketing Coordinator: Anna Andersen

Marketing Communications Manager:
    Talis Wise

Content Project Management: Pre-Press
    PMG

Creative Director: Rob Hugel

Art Director: Vernon Boes

Print Buyer: Judy Inouye

Rights Acquisitions Account Manager, Text:
    Bob Kauser

Rights Acquisitions Account Manager, Image:
    Robyn Young

Production Service: Pre-Press PMG

Copy Editor: Pre-Press PMG

Cover Designer: Irene Morris

Cover Image: © Veer

Compositor: Pre-Press PMG

For product information and technology assistance, contact us at
Cengage Learning Customer & Sales Support, 1-800-354-9706

For permission to use material from this text or product,
submit all requests online at **cengage.com/permissions**
Further permissions questions can be emailed to
permissionrequest@cengage.com

Library of Congress Control Number: 2009942928

ISBN-13: 978-0-8400-3246-1

ISBN-10: 0-8400-3246-3

Wadsworth
20 Davis Drive
Belmont, CA 94002-3098
USA

Cengage Learning is a leading provider of customized learning solutions with office locations around the globe, including Singapore, the United Kingdom, Australia, Mexico, Brazil, and Japan. Locate your local office at **www.cengage.com/global**

Cengage Learning products are represented in Canada by Nelson Education, Ltd.

To learn more about Wadsworth, visit **www.cengage.com/Wadsworth**

Purchase any of our products at your local college store or at our preferred online store **www.CengageBrain.com**

Printed in the United States of America
1 2 3 4 5 6 7 14 13 12 11 10

3 Ethics in Research   **41**

6   Surveys and Sampling   106

7   Naturalistic Methods   127

10 Experimental Research: One-Way Designs   183

PART FOUR
DESIGNING AND INTERPRETING RESEARCH   205

11 Experimental Research: Factorial Designs   206

12   Experimental Control and Internal Validity   227

13 External Validity 254

14 Quasi-Experimental Research Designs 272

Preface

Research Methods for the Behavioral Sciences grew out of my perceived need for a textbook that covers a complete body of research approaches, is accessible for a first-year undergraduate methods or laboratory class, and yet is still detailed enough to serve as a reference book for students as they progress to higher-level courses. I think you will find this book to be easily understood by sophomores, yet comprehensive enough to serve as a useful handbook for students working as research assistants or writing theses. Indeed, I use the textbook as a test for my graduate students—if they know everything in it, I can trust that they will be able to fully and adequately analyze their data or be able to realize what other information they might need to do so.

Furthermore, I wanted a book that is balanced in emphasis between conducting and consuming research. For the consumer of research, I have incorporated many sections and much pedagogy on how to draw inferences from existing research (see for instance the Research Project Ideas in Chapters 11, 12, and 14). I have devoted two full chapters to the essential topics of internal and external validity and have endeavored to use these chapters to help develop students' critical thinking and interpretive skills. But I have also filled the book with practical advice for students who are conducting their own research, including:

- "Goals of an ethical research project" in Chapter 3
- "Guide to improving the reliability and validity of questionnaires" in Chapter 5
- Sections in Chapter 12 concerned with designing valid and powerful experiments
- Appendix A on writing research reports
- The section on data preparation and analysis in Appendix B
- Appendix F on using computers to collect data

A number of examples of IBM SPSS printouts have been placed in the chapters, allowing students to see how the statistics look when they are initially computed.

I have placed as much emphasis on nonexperimental research methods as I have on experimental ones, arguing that all three research approaches—descriptive, correlational, and experimental—have unique strengths and weaknesses (see Table 1.3). Although the focus is primarily on quantitative research, I have also pointed out the appropriate use of qualitative research, such as focus groups and case studies. I have devoted two full chapters (4 and 5) to the important concerns of creating measures and evaluating their effectiveness. My guess is that many of the students in this course will some day have to design a survey, and in order to do so they will have to know how to write effective, reliable, and valid items. Issues of measurement are frequently underdeveloped in research methods texts, and I have tried to correct this omission.

I believe that this book simultaneously serves the needs of even the most demanding instructor and yet can be enjoyed by students. I have tried to make it thorough, interesting, integrative, accessible, and to provide an effective pedagogy. From an instructor's perspective, I think this book will help students enjoy learning about research methods, understand them well, and think critically and creatively about research. From a student's perspective, the book is brief and succinct, concepts are easy to grasp, and there are several helpful examples. As one reviewer put it, "The book basically represents the most important concepts—what a student might highlight in a longer book."

Organization and Coverage

The book is divided into four sections. Part One covers the background of research.

Chapter 1 emphasizes the importance of research to citizens in contemporary society and the potential implications of using (or failing to use) research to make decisions. Chapter 2 explains how science is conducted—the scientific method and the use of the literature review to develop and refine the research hypothesis. Chapter 3 represents a broad overview of research ethics, including practical guides for conducting ethical research.

Part Two deals with measures and measurement. Chapter 4 teaches students how to develop both self-report and behavioral measures and reviews the strengths and weaknesses of each. Practical hints for constructing useful measures are given. Chapter 5 covers the important aspects of reliability and construct validity, and in more detail than any competing text. Chapter 6 presents the elements of surveys and sampling, and Chapter 7 introduces observational and archival methods. I have attempted to point out to students (and instructors might note this as well) that the methods covered in these chapters are both research designs (descriptive research), but also methods that can be used as measured variables in correlational and experimental research.

The chapters in Part Three present the basics of testing research hypotheses. Chapter 8 covers the principles of hypothesis testing and inferential statistics, while Chapters 9 and 10 cover the logic of correlational and experimental research, respectively. Chapter 9 includes sections on multiple regression, longitudinal designs, path analysis, and structural equation modeling.

Part Four considers the design and interpretation of complex experiments, including factorial experimental designs and means comparison tests (Chapter 11). Internal and external validity are covered in Chapters 12 and 13, respectively, and the Hands-On Experiences in these chapters provide a wealth of examples. Chapter 12 also gives practical advice for designing effective experiments. Chapter 14 reviews the strengths and difficulties of quasi-experimental research designs, with a focus on the many threats to internal validity that they contain and how these threats can be overcome.

The Appendices are designed to supplement the text. They can be assigned at any time during the course or used for reference afterward. Appendix A presents an overview of how scientists share their data with others, including a detailed description of how to write a research report following APA style. This appendix also includes an annotated example of a research report written in APA format. Appendices B and C provide the formulas for most of the univariate statistical tests contained in an introductory statistics text. Appendix B also includes practical advice for analyzing data using computer software programs, along with many examples of IBM SPSS outputs. Students who are collecting and analyzing their own data should therefore find Appendix B extremely useful in helping them understand how to interpret their results. Appendix D summarizes the most commonly used multivariate research techniques, along with sample computer output. Although it is not likely that a first-year methods student will need to conduct a factor or structural equation analysis, these techniques are so common in contemporary research reports that students should have a place to go to learn the basics of such techniques, and accomplished students (for instance, those writing theses) should be able to learn how to conduct them if necessary.

Statistical Issues

I assume that most students who are taking a research methods or laboratory course are familiar with univariate statistical procedures, but I have designed this book to function effectively even for courses in which the students are not familiar with statistics. Although I cover many statistical issues in the book itself (Chapter 6, "Surveys and Sampling"; Chapter 8, "Hypothesis Testing and Inferential Statistics"; Chapter 9, "Correlational Research Designs"; and Chapters 10 and 11 on ANOVA), students who need a refresher can be directed to Appendices B and C at any point in the semester. The text always references the Appendices that cover the calculations of the statistics under discussion. The placement of all calculations in the Appendices allows instructors to choose whether and when to assign this material. Because of the increasing importance of students' learning to use computers to conduct statistical analyses, Appendix B introduces this process, and Appendix F, "Using Computers to Collect Data," expands upon this topic. Many examples of computer output are presented in the text and in the Appendices. The discussion is framed around the Statistical Package for the Social Sciences—in my opinion the package with the most user-friendly platform. I also recommend the accompanying manual, *Using IBM SPSS for Windows,* described on page xx, for students who are going to be calculating statistics.

Pedagogical Features

To promote mastery of the broad array of concepts, terms, and applications central to the research methods course, each chapter of the book includes both standard pedagogical elements and several unique features:

- A chapter outline provides a basic orientation to the chapter.
- Unique chapter-opening Study Questions help students learn to formulate appropriate questions about the topics that are to come before reading the chapter. Students can review these questions again when preparing for exams.
- A new feature, *Current Research in the Behavioral Sciences* provides students with examples of recent research studies. These studies can be used as discussion points to help students learn about current trends in behavioral research, and may also be used as background readings for students who are looking for project ideas.
- Boldface Key Terms and an end-of-text Glossary are useful tools for learning and reviewing the vocabulary of the course.
- A chapter Summary highlights the key points of the chapter.
- Review and Discussion Questions help students assess their mastery of chapter concepts and provide productive points of departure for classroom discussion.
- Particularly useful Research Project Ideas supply a wealth of practical problems and exercises that complement and expand upon the examples given in the text.

New to This Edition

In addition to a number of updates, the fourth edition of *Research Methods for the Behavioral Sciences* has added a new feature, *Current Research in the Behavioral Sciences,* to provide students with examples of new research studies. These studies can be used as discussion points to help students learn about current trends in behavioral research, and may also be used as background readings for students who are looking for project ideas.

Chapter 1:

New Feature: Current Research in the Behavioral Sciences: Preferences for Brands That Contain the Letters of Our Own Name

Chapter 4:

New Feature: Current Research in the Behavioral Sciences: Using Multiple Measured Variables to Assess the Conceptual Variable of Panic Symptoms

Chapter 5:

New Feature: Current Research in the Behavioral Sciences: The Hillyer-Joynes Kinematics Scale of Locomotion in Rats With Spinal Injuries

Chapter 6:

New Feature: Current Research in the Behavioral Sciences: Assessing Americans' Attitudes Toward Health Care

Chapter 7:

New Feature: Current Research in the Behavioral Sciences: Detecting Psychopathy From Thin Slices of Behavior

Chapter 9:

New Feature: Current Research in the Behavioral Sciences: Moral Conviction, Religiosity, and Trust in Authority

Chapter 10:

New Feature: Current Research in the Behavioral Sciences: Does Social Exclusion "Hurt"?

Chapter 11:

New Feature: Current Research in the Behavioral Sciences: Using Feelings in the Ultimatum Game

Chapter 13:

New Feature: Current Research in the Behavioral Sciences: A Meta-Analysis of the Effectiveness of Current Treatment Approaches for Withdrawal From Tranquilizer Addictions

Chapter 14:

New Feature: Current Research in the Behavioral Sciences: Damage to the Hippocampus Abolishes the Cortisol Response to Psychosocial Stress in Humans

Appendix A:

The sample research report and reference formats have been updated to conform to the "sixth edition" of the American Psychological Association *Publication Guide*.

Supplements to the Text

The following supplementary materials are available with *Research Methods for the Behavioral Sciences*. Contact your local Cengage Learning representative for more information.

For Instructors:

Instructor's Manual With Test Bank.   Full answers to the Review and Discussion Questions and the Hands-On Experiences can be found in the instructor's resource manual (which is author-written). For the fourth edition, this resource has been revised to include Learning Objectives at the beginning of each chapter, and a research paper checklist that can be distributed as an in-class handout.

Companion Website. Instructors will find content for each chapter including glossary, flash cards, multiple-choice quizzing, and more. www.cengage.com/psychology/stangor

For Students:

Using IBM SPSS® for Windows®, **Fourth Edition.**   I have also written a manual called *Using IBM SPSS® for Windows®* that introduces students to the basics of IBM SPSS. This handbook, with step-by-step instructions, sample output, and student exercises based on data sets provided on CD-ROM, can be shrink-wrapped with the text. The fourth edition has been fully updated to reflect the current version of IBM SPSS software, including new screenshots, more practice exercises, and additional data sets.

IBM SPSS® for Windows®, Software.   The current student version of IBM SPSS software can be shrink-wrapped with the text and is available for sale to students whose schools don't license SPSS.

Companion Website. Students will find content for each chapter including glossary, flash cards, multiple-choice quizzing, and more. www.cengage.com/psychology/stangor

Acknowledgments

It is not possible for me to acknowledge all of the people who helped me write this book. The list would include my students, whose questions, comments, and complaints taught me how to better teach research methods, convinced me of the need for this book, and helped me make the book more useful. My wife, Leslie, supported me as only she can during and after the long hours in front of the word processor. I am grateful to those who gave me feedback and materials, including Lisa Aspinwall, Jude Cassidy, Jack Fyock, Paul Hanges, Madeline Heilman, Bill Hodos, John Jost, Dave Kenny, James Lange, and Gretchen Sechrist. I am particularly indebted to Jud Mills, who read just about every word at least once and who was my own best instructor in research methods. Thanks also to the Department of Psychology at the University of Maryland, to the members of the Society for Personality and Social Psychology, and to the editorial and production group at Cengage Learning, including Executive Editor Jon-David Hague, and Assistant Editor Trina Tom.

I would also like to acknowledge the helpful comments of the revision reviewers. They helped shape the book and make it even more user-friendly:

- Jay C. Brown, Texas Wesleyan University
- Amy Dombach Connelly, Felician College
- Julie Evey, University of Southern Indiana
- Ronald S. Friedman, University at Albany, SUNY
- Gary G. Ford, Stephen F. Austin State University
- Deana L. Julka, University of Portland
- Jennifer Trich Kremer, Penn State Erie, The Behrend College
- Sean Laraway, San José State University
- Don E. Lindley, Regis University
- Marianne Lloyd, Seton Hall University
- Donna Stuber-McEwen, Friends University
- Ann V. McGillicuddy-De Lisi, Lafayette College
- Terry F. Pettijohn, Ohio State University—Marion Campus
- Pamela Schuetze, Buffalo State College
- Brian C. Smith, Graceland University
- Laurie Sykes Tottenham, University of Regina
- Mary Moore Vandendorpe, Lewis University
- Rose Marie Ward, Miami University

I am always interested in receiving comments from instructors and students. You can write me at the Department of Psychology, University of Maryland, College Park, MD 20742 or contact me via e-mail: Stangor@psyc.umd.edu. I hope you find this book useful and enjoyable.

PART **ONE**

Getting Started

CHAPTER ONE
Introduction to Research

STUDY QUESTIONS

- What is behavioral research, and why is it conducted?

- What are the limitations of "everyday science" and intuition for understanding behavior?

- What is the scientific method, and why do scientists use it?

- What is the difference between a fact and a value, and how do a scientist's values influence his or her research?

- What are the goals of basic research and of applied research, and how do the two types of goals relate to each other?

- What are the goals of descriptive, correlational, and experimental research? What are the advantages and disadvantages of each research approach?

- What benefits are there to be gained from learning how to evaluate research, conduct it, and think critically about it?

Part of the excitement of contemporary life is observing the speed at which the world around us changes. It was only one hundred years ago that people first flew in an airplane. Today, astronauts spend months at a time in space. It was only a little over five hundred years ago that Johannes Gutenberg printed the first page of a book. Today, more printed text is sent via e-mail in a few seconds than could be published in a lifetime only a few years ago. A doctor who studied medicine one hundred years ago learned that most diseases were incurable—medicine could hope only to make the remaining life of a patient more comfortable. Today, doctors routinely give people new life by replacing the coronary arteries of the heart and preventing the growth of tumors through the use of chemical and radiation treatments.

Yet, despite the benefits that technological change has brought, many of the problems facing humanity appear to be as great as ever. There are still many children, in all parts of the world, who are hungry and who do not have adequate housing or health care. Physical violence is prevalent, including child and spousal abuse, gang violence in cities, ethnic conflicts within nations, and terrorism. Divorce continues to have an impact on the lives of thousands of children, and people continue to expose themselves to deadly viruses such as acquired immune deficiency syndrome (AIDS), even when there are ways to avoid contracting these diseases. Although people are living longer and enjoy many of the comforts of technological achievement, the dramatic technological advances that have occurred over the past few decades have not generally been paralleled by advances in the quality of our interpersonal and social behavior.

It is this behavior, among both humans and animals, and the scientific research designed to study it that are the focus of this book. Indeed, the purpose of behavioral research is to increase our understanding of behavior and, where possible, to provide methods for improving the quality of our lives. The results of such research are becoming increasingly relevant to our perception of such human problems as homelessness, illiteracy, psychological disorders, family instability, and violence. Thus, it is not surprising that research is being used more and more frequently to help guide public policy. For instance, behavioral research has been used to guide court rulings on racism, such as in the landmark *Brown* v. *Board of Education* (1954), and sexism (Fiske, Bersoff, Borgida, Deaux, & Heilman, 1991), as well as on the use of lie detectors in criminal trials (Saxe, Dougherty, & Cross, 1985). Behavioral research is also being used to help us understand which methods of educating children are most effective, and teachers are being trained to make use of the most effective techniques. The federal government has recently created a center at my university to study the behavorial aspects of terrorism.

Behavioral research also provides important information that complements other scientific approaches. For instance, in the field of medicine, infectious diseases such as measles and polio were once major causes of death. Today, people's own behavior is implicated in most of the leading killers, including homicide, lung cancer, heart disease, and AIDS. Furthermore, much of the productive capability of modern societies is now dependent not only on further technological advances but also on the availability of an educated and skilled work force.

In sum, behavioral research is used to study important human problems and provide solutions to them. Because research has such a significant impact on scientific decisions and public policy, informed citizens, like you, are wise to understand it.

Behavioral Research

Behavioral research is conducted by scientists in such fields as behavioral medicine, communication, criminology, human development, education, psychology, and sociology. The goal of **behavioral research** is to discover, among other things, how people perceive their world, how they think and feel, how they change over time, how they learn and make decisions, and how they interact with others. Behavioral scientists study behavior both because they want to understand it and also because they want to contribute to creating solutions to the everyday problems that face human beings.

Of course, behavioral scientists aren't the only people who are concerned with human behavior or the only ones who propose solutions to social problems. Philosophers, religious leaders, and politicians, for instance, also attempt to provide explanations for social behavior. But, what sets behavioral scientists apart from many other people who are concerned with human behavior is their belief that, just as dramatic technological advances have occurred through scientific research, personal and social behavior can be understood, and potentially improved, through the application of scientific research methods. In contrast to many statements made by philosophers, politicians, and religious leaders, which are based only on their own personal beliefs, faith, or intuition, the statements made by social scientists are **empirical,** which means that they are based on systematic collection and analysis of data, where **data** are information collected through formal observation or measurement.[1] Behavioral scientists draw their conclusions about human behavior from systematic collection and analysis of data.

Behavioral scientists believe that research is the best tool for understanding human beings and their relationships with others. For instance, rather than accepting the claim of a religious leader that the adoption of traditional religious beliefs will change behavior, a behavioral scientist would collect data to empirically test whether highly religious people are more helpful and less aggressive toward others than are less religious people. Rather than accepting a politician's contention that creating (or abandoning) a welfare program will improve the condition of poor people, a behavioral scientist would attempt to empirically assess the effects of receiving welfare on the quality of

---

[1]Although the word *data* is technically a plural noun, scientists frequently treat it as a singular noun, and this practice is now accepted by linguists. Although it is thus correct to say either "the data were collected" or "the data was collected," this book uses the more traditional plural form.

life of welfare recipients. And, rather than relying on a school principal's beliefs about which teaching methods are most effective, behavioral scientists would systematically test and compare the effectiveness of different methods. In short, behavioral scientists believe in the value of scientific research to answer questions about human behavior.

The claim that human behavior is best known through the use of a scientific approach is not something that everyone believes or that is without controversy. Indeed, although I hope that you will become convinced of the utility of behavioral research for understanding people, I also hope that you will think critically about its value as you study this book. I hope that you will continually ask yourself what behavioral research methods offer in the way of understanding and improving our lives that other approaches do not. And, most important, I hope that you will learn how to evaluate behavioral research.

Finally, although behavioral research is conducted in large part to provide information about important social problems and to further scientific understanding about the principles of human behavior, I also hope that you will find it interesting in its own right—you might even discover that conducting research is fun! If you have ever wondered about how we learn and why we forget, what dreams are for and whether they influence us when we are awake, whether we can tell if others are lying to us, or even whether some people have extrasensory perception (ESP), you will find that behavioral research is the best way to provide answers to these interesting questions. Studying behavioral research and conducting it yourself is exciting, because it allows you to discover and understand new things. In sum, I hope you will enjoy this book, both because you like behavioral research, and also because you realize that it has a significant impact on human behavior, scientific decisions, and public policy.

Everyday Science Versus Empirical Research

Just like scientists, most of us have an avid interest in asking and answering questions about our world. We want to know why things happen, when and if they are likely to happen again, and how to reproduce or change them. Such knowledge enables us to predict our own behavior and that of others. We even collect data to aid us in this undertaking. Indeed, it has been argued that people are "everyday scientists" who conduct research projects to answer questions about behavior (Nisbett & Ross, 1980). When we perform poorly on an important test, we try to understand what caused our failure to remember or understand the material and what might help us do better the next time. When our good friends Eva and Joshua break up, despite what appeared to have been a relationship made in heaven, we try to determine what happened. When we contemplate the rise of terrorist acts around the world, we try to investigate the causes of this problem by looking at the people themselves, the situation around them, and the responses of others to them.

The results of these "everyday" research projects can teach us many principles of human behavior. We learn through experience that if we give someone bad news, she or he may blame us even though the news was not our fault. We learn that people may become depressed after they fail at a task. We see that aggressive behavior occurs frequently in our society, and we develop theories to explain why this is so. These insights are part and parcel of everyday social life. In fact, much behavioral research involves the scientific study of everyday behavior (Heider, 1958; Kelly, 1967).

Relying on Our Intuition

Many people believe that they can find answers to questions about human behavior by using their own intuition. They think that because they spend their whole lives with others, they should certainly have learned what makes people do what they do and why. As a result, many may believe that behavioral research is basically "common sense" and that, therefore, formal study of it is not necessary. Although there is no question that we do learn about other people by observing them, because our observations are conducted informally, they may lead us to draw unwarranted or incorrect conclusions. In fact, we are often incorrect in our intuition about why others do what they do and even (as Sigmund Freud so insightfully noted) why we ourselves do what we do!

The problem with the way people collect and interpret data in their everyday lives is that they are not always particularly thorough. Often, when one explanation for an event seems to make sense, we adopt that explanation as the truth even when other explanations are possible and potentially more accurate. To take a couple of examples, eyewitnesses to violent crimes are often extremely confident in their identifications of the perpetrators of these crimes. But evidence shows that eyewitnesses are no less confident of their identifications when they are incorrect than when they are correct (Wells, Leippe, & Ostrom, 1979). People also become convinced of the existence of extrasensory perception, or the predictive value of astrology, when there is no evidence for either. Accepting explanations without testing them thoroughly may lead people to think that they know things that they do not really know.

Behavioral scientists have also found that there are a variety of cognitive and motivational biases that frequently bias our perceptions and lead us to draw erroneous conclusions (Fiske & Taylor, 2007; Hsee & Hastie, 2006). As one example, the research by Brendl and his colleagues reported at the end of this chapter shows that people have a preference for the letters in their own name, even though it is unlikely that many people realize that they do. Because these biases occur out of our awareness, it is very difficult for us to correct for them.

Discovering the Limitations of Using Intuition

In one empirical demonstration of how difficult it can be to understand even our own behavior, Nisbett and Wilson (1977) had college students read a passage describing a woman who was applying for a job as a counselor in a crisis intervention center. Unknown to the students, the descriptions of the interview were varied so that different students read different information about what occurred during the interview. Some students read that the woman had superb academic credentials, whereas others did not learn this information. For some students the woman was described as having spilled a cup of coffee over the interviewer's desk during the interview, whereas for others no such event was mentioned. After reading the information, the students first judged the woman they had read about in terms of her suitability for the job on rating scales such as how much they liked her and how intelligent they thought she was. They also indicated how they thought each of the behaviors they had read about (for instance, being highly intelligent or spilling coffee over everything) influenced their judgments.

On the basis of these data, the researchers were able to determine how the woman's behaviors actually influenced the students' judgments of her. They found, for instance, that being described as having excellent academic credentials increased ratings of intelligence and that spilling coffee on the interviewer's desk actually *increased* how much the students liked her.[2] But, when the actual effects of the behaviors on the judgments were compared to the students' reports about how the behaviors influenced their judgments, the researchers found that the students were not always correct. Although the students were aware that information about strong academic credentials increased their judgments of intelligence, they had no idea that the applicant's having spilled coffee made them like her more.

Still another way that intuition may lead us astray is that, once we learn about the outcome of a given event (for instance, when we read about the results of a research project), we frequently believe that we would have been able to predict the outcome ahead of time. For instance, if half of a class of students is told that research concerning interpersonal attraction has demonstrated that "opposites attract" and the other half is told that research has demonstrated that "birds of a feather flock together," both sets of students will frequently report believing that they would have predicted this outcome before they read about it. The problem is that reading a description of the research finding leads us to think of the many cases that we know that support it, and thus, makes it seem believable. The tendency to think that we could have predicted something that we probably could not have predicted is called the **hindsight bias.**

In sum, although intuition is useful for getting ideas, and although our intuitions are sometimes correct, they are not infallible. Peoples' theories about how they make judgments do not always correspond well to how they actually make decisions. And people believe that they would have predicted events that they would not have, making research findings seem like they are just common sense. This does not mean that intuition is not important—scientists frequently rely on their intuition to help them solve problems. But, because they realize

---

[2]A person who seems "too good to be true" on the surface can sometimes endear him- or herself to observers by accidentally making a small, humanizing mistake (such as spilling coffee). Such a blunder is known as a *pratfall*.

that this intuition is frequently unreliable, they always back up their intuition empirically. Behavioral scientists believe that, just as research into the nature of electrons and protons guided the development of the transistor, so behavioral research can help us understand the behavior of people in their everyday lives. And these scientists believe that collecting data will allow them to discover the determinants of behavior and use this knowledge productively.

The Scientific Method

All scientists (whether they are physicists, chemists, biologists, sociologists, or psychologists) are engaged in the basic processes of collecting and organizing data and drawing conclusions about those data. The methods used by scientists to do so have developed over many years and provide a basis for collecting, analyzing, and interpreting data within a common framework in which information can be shared. We can label the set of assumptions, rules, and procedures that scientists use to conduct research the **scientific method.** Indeed, the focus of this book is the use of the scientific method to study behavior.

In addition to requiring that science be empirical—based on observation or measurement of relevant information—the scientific method demands that the procedures used be **objective,** or free from the personal bias or emotions of the scientist. The scientific method prescribes how scientists collect and analyze data, how they draw conclusions from data, and how they share data with others. These rules increase objectivity by placing data under scrutiny by other scientists and even by the public at large. Because data are reported objectively, other scientists know exactly how the scientist collected and analyzed the data. This means that they do not have to rely only on the scientist's own interpretation of the data; they may also draw their own, potentially different, conclusions. Of course, we frequently trust scientists to draw their own conclusions about their data (after all, they are the experts), and we rely on their interpretations. However, when conclusions are made on the basis of empirical data, a knowledgeable person can check up on these interpretations should she or he desire to do so. This book will demonstrate how.

The scientific method also demands that science be based on what has come before it. As we will discuss in Chapter 13, most new research is designed to *replicate*—that is, to repeat, add to, or modify—previous research findings. The scientific method results in an *accumulation* of scientific knowledge, through the reporting of research and the addition to and modifications of these reported findings through further research by other scientists.

Values Versus Facts in Scientific Research

Although scientific research is an important method of studying human behavior, not all questions can be answered using scientific approaches. Statements that cannot be objectively measured or objectively determined to be true or false are not within the domain of scientific inquiry. Scientists, therefore, draw a distinction between values and facts. **Values** are personal statements such as "Abortion should not be permitted in this country," "I will go to heaven when I die," or "It is important to study behavioral research." **Facts** are objective statements determined to be accurate through empirical study. Examples are "There were over 16,000 homicides in the United States in 2002," or "Behavioral research demonstrates that individuals who are exposed to highly stressful situations over long periods of time are particularly likely to develop health problems such as heart disease and cancer."

Facts and the Formation of Values.   Because values cannot be considered to be either true or false, science cannot prove or disprove them. Nevertheless, as shown in Table 1.1, behavioral research can sometimes provide facts that can help people develop their values. For instance, science may be able to objectively measure the impact of unwanted children on a society or the psychological trauma suffered by women who have abortions. The effect of capital punishment on the crime rate in the United States may also be determinable. This factual information can and should be made available to help people formulate their values about abortion and capital punishment, as well as to enable governments to articulate appropriate policies. Values also frequently come into play in determining what research is appropriate or important to conduct. For instance, the U.S. government has recently supported and provided funding for research on HIV and AIDS while at the same time limiting the possibility of conducting research using human stem cells.

Distinguishing Between Facts and Values.   Although scientists use research to help distinguish facts from values, the distinction between the two is not always as clear-cut as they might like. Sometimes statements that scientists consider to be factual later turn out to be partially or even entirely incorrect. This happens because there is usually more than one way to interpret data. As a result, scientists frequently disagree with each other about the meaning

TABLE 1.1 Examples of Values and Facts in Scientific Research

Personal Value	Scientific Fact
Welfare payments should be reduced for unmarried parents.	The U.S. government paid over $21 billion in unemployment insurance in 2002.
Handguns should be outlawed.	There were over 30,000 deaths caused by handguns in the United States in 2002.
Blue is my favorite color.	Over 35 percent of college students indicate that blue is their favorite color.
It is important to quit smoking.	Smoking increases the incidence of cancer and heart disease.

of observed data. One well-known example concerns the interpretation of race-related differences in IQ. Data show that, on average, African-American students score more poorly on standardized exams than do white students (Herrnstein & Murray, 1994). Some scientists argue that these data indicate inherent genetic differences in intelligence among racial groups, whereas others contend that these differences are caused by social effects, such as differences in nutrition, interests, and schooling. Still others maintain that the data demonstrate not that intelligence is unequal between races but that the tests themselves are culturally biased to favor some groups over others. In most cases such as this, the initial disagreement over the interpretation of data leads to further data collection designed to resolve the disagreements.

Although data must also be interpreted in the natural sciences, such as chemistry and physics, interpreting data is even more difficult in the behavioral sciences. Because people have their own hypotheses and beliefs about human behavior, they can easily make their own interpretations of the results of behavioral research, such as the meaning of differences on IQ tests between white and African-American students. Furthermore, the measures used by behavioral scientists, such as asking people questions and observing their behaviors, often appear less sophisticated than those used in other sciences. As a result, to many people behavioral science research does not appear to be as "scientific" as research in the natural sciences.

Even though behavioral research has not advanced as far as research in the natural sciences, behavioral scientists follow the same procedures as do scientists in other fields. These procedures involve creating a systematic set of knowledge about the characteristics of individuals and groups and the relationships among them. In this sense, behavioral science research is just as scientific as that in any other field. Furthermore, just because data must be interpreted does not mean that behavioral research is not useful. Although scientific procedures do not necessarily guarantee that the answers to questions will be objective and unbiased, science is still the best method currently known for drawing objective conclusions about the world around us. When old facts are discarded, they are replaced with new facts, based on newer and more correct data. Although science is not perfect, the requirements of empiricism, objectivity, and accumulation still result in a much greater chance of producing an accurate understanding of human behavior than is available through other approaches.

Values and Facts in the Research Report.   Although the goal of the scientific method is to be objective, this does not mean that values do not come into play in science. Scientists must make decisions about what to study, how to study it, whom to use as research participants, and how to interpret their data. Thus, the goal of science is not to make everything objective, but rather to make clear which parts of the research process are objective and which parts are not.

Scientific findings are made publicly available through the publication of *research reports*. The **research report** is a document that presents scientific findings using a standardized written format. Different research report formats are used in different fields of science, but behavioral science frequently uses the format prepared by the *American Psychological Association (APA)*. An overview of this approach is presented on the inside cover of this book, and a complete description of APA format can be found in Appendix A. If you are not familiar with it, you may wish to read Appendix A now.

One of the most important requirements of the research report is that the appropriate information goes in the appropriate section. In this regard, two of the sections—Introduction and Discussion—are relatively subjective, because they involve such questions as what topics are of importance to study and how the data should be interpreted. However, two other sections—Results and Discussion—are completely objective, describing the actual procedures of the experiments and the statistical analyses. Again, the point is that science has both objective and subjective components, and it attempts to clearly differentiate the two. One of the major things you will learn in this book is how to draw the important distinction between the values and facts (that is, between the subjective and the objective aspects) in behavioral research.

Basic and Applied Research

One way that the scientist's values influence research is in the types of research that he or she finds important to study. Some scientists conduct research primarily for the intellectual satisfaction of knowing something, whereas others conduct research for the purpose of gaining practical knowledge about a particular social issue or problem.

Basic research answers fundamental questions about behavior. For instance, cognitive psychologists study how different types of practice influence memory for pictures and words, and biological psychologists study how nerves conduct impulses from the receptors in the skin to the brain. There is no particular reason to study such things except to acquire a better knowledge of how these processes occur.

Applied research investigates issues that have implications for everyday life and provide solutions to everyday problems. Applied research has been conducted to study such issues as what types of psychotherapy are most effective in reducing depression, what types of advertising campaigns will reduce drug and alcohol abuse, how to predict who will perform well at managerial positions, and what factors are associated with successful college performance. One type of applied research is called **program evaluation research,** which is conducted to study the effectiveness of methods designed to make positive social changes, such as training programs, antiprejudice programs, and after-school learning programs. We will more fully discuss how to conduct program evaluation research in Chapter 14.

Although research usually has either a basic or an applied orientation, in most cases the distinction between the two types is not clear-cut. Scientists who conduct basic research are frequently influenced by practical issues in determining which topics to study. For instance, although research concerning the role of practice on memory for lists of words is basic in orientation, the results could someday be used to help children learn to read. Correspondingly, scientists who are interested in solving practical problems are well aware that the results of basic research can help them do so. Programs designed to reduce the spread of AIDS or to promote volunteering are frequently founded on the results of basic research concerning the factors that lead people to change their behaviors.

In short, applied research and basic research inform each other (Lewin, 1944). Basic research provides underlying principles that can be used to solve specific problems, and applied research gives ideas for the kinds of topics that basic research can study. Advances in the behavioral sciences occur more rapidly when each type of research is represented in the enterprise. Accordingly, we will discuss both approaches in this book.

The Importance of Studying Research Methods

I hope that you are now beginning to understand why instructors find it so important for students to take research methods or research laboratory courses as part of their behavioral science degree. To fully understand the material in a behavioral science course, you must first understand how and why the research you are reading about was conducted and what the collected data mean. A fundamental understanding of research methodology will help you read about and correctly interpret the results of research in any field of behavioral science.

Evaluating Research Reports

One goal of this book is to help you learn how to evaluate scientific research reports. We will examine how behavioral scientists develop ideas and test them, how they measure behavior, and how they analyze and interpret the data they collect. Understanding the principles and practices of behavioral research will be useful to you because it will help you determine the quality of the research that you read about. If you read that ibuprofen relieves headaches faster than aspirin, or that children learn more in private than in public schools, you should not believe it just because the findings are based on "research." As we will discuss in more detail in later chapters, research can mislead you if it is not valid. Thus, the most important skill you can gain from the study of research methods is the ability to distinguish good research from bad research.

Conducting Research

The second goal of this book is to help you learn how to conduct research. Such skills will obviously be useful to you if you plan a career as a behavioral scientist, where conducting research will be your most important activity. But the ability to design and execute research projects is also in demand in many other careers. For instance, advertising and marketing researchers study how to make advertising more effective, health and medical researchers study the impact of behaviors (such as drug use and smoking) on illness, and computer scientists study how people interact with computers. Furthermore, even if you are not planning a career as a researcher, jobs in almost any area of social, medical, or mental health science require that a worker be informed about behavioral research. There are many opportunities for college graduates who have developed the ability to conduct research, and you can learn about them by visiting the American Psychological Association website at **http://www. apa.org/students/brochure/.**

There is no question that conducting behavioral research is difficult. Unlike beakers full of sulfuric acid, the objects of study in the behavioral sciences—human beings and animals—differ tremendously from each other. No two people are alike, nor do they respond to attempts to study them in the same way. People are free to make their own decisions and to choose their own behaviors. They choose whether to participate in research, whether to take it seriously, and perhaps even whether to sabotage it. Furthermore, whereas the determinants of the pressure of a gas or the movement of a particle can be fairly well defined, the causes of human behavior are not at this time well understood. Although these difficulties represent real challenges, they also represent the thrill of conducting behavioral research. The path is difficult, but the potential rewards of understanding behavior are great.

Thinking Critically About Research

Progress in the behavioral sciences depends on people, like you, who have the skills to critically create, read, evaluate, and criticize research. As you read this book, you will acquire skills that allow you to think critically about research. Once you have learned these skills, you will be able to conduct sound research and to determine the value of research that you read about. In short, you will be able to ask the important questions, such as "How was the research conducted?" "How were the data analyzed?" and, more generally, "Are the conclusions drawn warranted by the facts?" In the remainder of this chapter, we will turn to these questions by considering the three major research approaches to studying human behavior.

Research Designs: Three Approaches to Studying Behavior

Behavioral scientists agree that their ideas and their theories about human behavior must be backed up by data to be taken seriously. However, although all scientists follow the basic underlying procedures of scientific investigation, the research of different scientists is designed with different goals in mind, and the different goals require different approaches to answering the researcher's questions. These different approaches are known as research designs. A **research design** is the specific method a researcher uses to collect, analyze, and interpret data. Although there are many variants of each, there are only three basic research designs used in behavioral research. These are descriptive research designs, correlational research designs, and experimental research designs.

Because these three research designs will form the basis of this entire book, we will consider them in some detail at this point. As we will see, each of the approaches has both strengths and limitations, and therefore all three can contribute to the accumulation of scientific knowledge. To fully understand how the research designs work, you need to be aware of the statistical tests that are used to analyze the data. If you are not familiar with statistical procedures (or if you feel that you need a bit of a brushup), you should read Appendix B and Appendix C before you continue.

Descriptive Research: Assessing the Current State of Affairs

The first goal of behavioral research is to describe the thoughts, feelings, and behavior of individuals. Research designed to answer questions about the current state of affairs is known as **descriptive research.** This type of research provides a "snapshot" of thoughts, feelings, or behaviors at a given place and a given time.

Surveys and Interviews. One type of descriptive research, which we will discuss in Chapter 6, is based on *surveys*. Millions of dollars are spent yearly by the U.S. Bureau of the Census to describe the characteristics of the U.S. population, including where people work, how much they earn, and with whom they live. Descriptive data in the form of surveys and interviews are regularly found in articles published in newspapers and magazines and are used by politicians to determine what policies are popular or unpopular with their constituents.

Sometimes the data from descriptive research projects are rather mundane, such as "Nine out of ten doctors prefer Tymenocin," or "The average income in Montgomery County is $36,712." Yet, other times (particularly in discussions of social behavior), descriptive statistics can be shocking: "Over 40,000 people are killed by gunfire in the United States every year," or "Over 45 percent of sixth graders at Madison High School report that they have used marijuana."

One common type of descriptive research, frequently reported in newspaper and magazine articles, involves surveys of the "current concerns" of the people within a city, state, or nation. The results of such a survey are shown in Figure 1.1. These surveys allow us to get a picture of what people are thinking, feeling, or doing at a given point in time.

Naturalistic Observation. As we will discuss more fully in Chapter 7, another type of descriptive research—known as *naturalistic observation*—is based on the observation of everyday events. For instance, a developmental psychologist who watches children on a playground and describes what they say to each other while they play is conducting descriptive research, as is a biological psychologist who observes animals in their natural habitats or a sociologist who studies the way in which people use public transportation in a large urban city.

FIGURE 1.1   Survey Research: U.S. Trusts the News but Sees Bias

A national survey conducted by the Missouri School of Journalism's Center for Advanced Social Research polled a sample of 495 adults during June–July 2004 regarding their opinions about fairness in news coverage. This chart indicates their responses to some of the questions that were asked. The survey has a margin of sampling error of plus or minus 3 percentage points.

Source: Hananel, S. (2005). Survey: U.S. Trusts the News but Sees Bias. Retrieved 4/27/2005 from **http://abcnews.go.com/US/WireStory?id=707810**

Qualitative Versus Quantitative Research.   One distinction that is made in descriptive research concerns whether it is *qualitative* or *quantitative* in orientation. **Qualitative research** is descriptive research that is focused on observing and describing events as they occur, with the goal of capturing all of the richness of everyday behavior and with the hope of discovering and understanding phenomena that might have been missed if only more cursory examinations had been used (Denzin & Lincoln, 2003). The data that form the basis of qualitative research are in their original rich form—for instance, descriptive narratives such as field notes and audio or video recordings. **Quantitative research** is descriptive research that uses more formal measures of behavior, including questionnaires and systematic observation of behavior, which are designed to be subjected to statistical analysis. The strength of qualitative research is that it vividly describes ongoing behavior in its original form. However, because it does not use statistical analysis, it is generally more subjective and may not fully separate the values of the researcher from the objectivity of the research process. In many cases, however, qualitative data are reported along with quantitative data to provide a fuller description of the observed behavior; this combination of approaches can be very informative.

Strengths and Limitations of Descriptive Research.   One advantage of descriptive research is that it attempts to capture the complexity of everyday behavior. For instance, surveys capture the thoughts of a large population of people, and naturalistic observation is designed to study the behavior of people or animals as it occurs naturally. Thus, descriptive research is used to provide a relatively complete understanding of what is currently happening. Nevertheless, descriptive research has a distinct disadvantage in that although it allows us to get an idea of what is currently happening, it is limited to providing static pictures. A study of the current concerns of individuals, for instance, cannot tell us how those concerns developed or what impact they have on people's voting behavior.

Correlational Research: Seeking Relationships Among Variables

In contrast to descriptive research, which is designed to provide static pictures, **correlational research** involves the measurement of two or more relevant variables and an assessment of the relationship between or among those variables. A **variable** is any attribute that can assume different values among different people or across different times or places. Sometimes variables are rather simple—for instance, measures of age, shoe size, or weight. In other cases (and as we will discuss fully in Chapters 4 and 5), variables represent more complex ideas, such as egomania, burnout, sexism, or cognitive development.

As we will see in Chapter 9, the goal of correlational research is to uncover variables that show systematic relationships with each other. For instance, the variables of height and weight are systematically related, because taller people generally weigh more than shorter people. In the same way, study time and memory errors are also related, because the more time a person is given to study a list of words, the fewer errors she or he will make. Of course, a person's score on one variable is not usually perfectly related to his or her score on the other. Although tall people are likely to weigh more, we cannot perfectly predict how tall someone is merely by knowing that person's weight.

The Pearson Product–Moment Correlation Coefficient. Because the size of the relationships of interest to behavioral scientists is usually very small, statistical procedures are used to detect them. The most common measure of relationships among variables is the **Pearson product–moment correlation coefficient,** which is symbolized by the letter r.

The correlation coefficient ranges from $r = -1.00$ to $r = +1.00$. Positive values indicate positive correlations, in which people who are farther above average on one variable (for instance, height) generally are also farther above average on the other variable (for instance, weight). Negative values of r indicate negative correlations, in which people who are farther above average on one variable (for instance, study time) generally are also farther below average on the other variable (memory errors). Values of the correlation coefficient that are farther from zero (either positive or negative) indicate stronger relationships, whereas values closer to zero indicate weaker relationships.

The Use of Correlations to Make Predictions.   One type of correlational research involves predicting future events from currently available knowledge. In this case, one or more variables of interest are measured at one time, and other variables are measured at a later time. To the extent that there is a correlation between what we know now and what will occur later, we can use knowledge about the things that we already know to predict what will happen later. For instance, Nettles, Thoeny, and Gosman (1986) used a correlational research design to predict whether college students would stay in school or drop out. They measured characteristics of 4,094 college students at thirty different colleges and universities and assessed the ability of these characteristics to predict the students' current college grade-point average (GPA). In addition to intellectual variables such as high school GPA and Scholastic Aptitude Test (SAT) scores, they also assessed social variables including socioeconomic status, the students' reports of interfering social problems such as emotional stress and financial difficulties, and the students' perceptions of the quality of faculty–student relations at their university. The last measure was based on responses to questions such as "It is easy to develop close relationships with faculty members," and "I am satisfied with the student–faculty relations at this university."

As shown in Table 1.2, the researchers found that students' ratings of the social problems they experienced on campus were as highly predictive of their grade-point average as were the standardized test scores they had taken before entering college. This information allows educators to predict which students will be most likely to finish their college education and suggests that campus experiences are important in this regard.

Strengths and Limitations of Correlational Research.   One particular advantage of correlational research is that it can be used to assess behavior as it occurs in people's everyday lives. Imagine, for instance, a researcher who finds

TABLE 1.2   Predictors of College Performance

Predictor Variable	r
SAT score	.31
High school GPA	.30
Socioeconomic status	.12
Study habits	.30
Interfering social problems	−.39
Feelings of faculty involvement	.19

The column labeled *r* indicates the observed Pearson correlation coefficient between the predictor variable and college GPA. Note that most of the variables are *positively* correlated with college GPA, whereas the presence of interfering social problems is *negatively* correlated with GPA.

a negative correlation between the row in which his students normally sit in his class and their grade on the final exam. This researcher's data demonstrate a very interesting relationship that occurs naturally for students attending college—those who sit nearer the front of the class get better grades.

Despite the ability of correlational studies to investigate naturally occurring behavior, they also have some inherent limitations. Most important, correlational studies cannot be used to identify causal relationships among the variables. It is just as possible that getting good grades causes students to sit in the front of the class as it is that sitting in the front of the class causes good grades. Furthermore, because only some of all the possible relevant variables are measured in correlational research, it is always possible that neither of the variables caused the other and that some other variable caused the observed variables to be correlated. For instance, students who are excited by the subject matter or who are highly motivated to succeed in school might both choose to sit in the front of the class and also end up getting good grades. In this case, seating row and grades will be correlated, even though neither one caused the other.

In short, correlational research is limited to demonstrating relationships between or among variables or to making predictions of future events, but it cannot tell us why those variables are related. For instance, we could use a correlational design to predict the success of a group of trainees on a job from their scores on a battery of tests that they take during a training session. But we cannot use such correlational information to determine whether the training caused better job performance. For that, researchers rely on experiments.

Experimental Research: Understanding the Causes of Behavior

Behavioral scientists are particularly interested in answering questions about the causal relationships among variables. They believe that it is possible, indeed necessary, to determine which variables cause other variables to occur. Consider these questions: "Does watching violent television cause aggressive behavior?", "Does sleep deprivation cause an increase in memory errors?", and "Does being in a stressful situation cause heart disease?" Because it is difficult to answer such questions about causality using correlational designs, scientists frequently use experimental research. As we will discuss more fully in Chapters 10 and 11, **experimental research** involves the active creation or *manipulation* of a given situation or experience for two or more groups of individuals, followed by a measurement of the effect of those experiences on thoughts, feelings, or behavior. Furthermore, experimental research is designed to create *equivalence* between the individuals in the different groups before the experiment begins, so that any differences found can confidently be attributed to the effects of the experimental manipulation.

Elements of Experiments. Let us look, for instance, at an experimental research design used by social psychologists Macrae, Bodenhausen, Milne, and Jetten (1994). The goal of this experiment was to test the hypothesis that suppressing the use of stereotypes may cause an unexpected "rebound" in which those stereotypes are actually used to a greater extent at a later time. In the experiment, college students were shown a picture of a "skinhead" and asked to write a short paragraph describing what they thought he was like. While doing so, half of the students were explicitly told not to let their stereotypes about skinheads influence them when writing their descriptions. The other half of the students were just asked to write a description.

After the students had finished writing their descriptions, they were told that they were going to be meeting with the person they had written about and were taken into a separate room. In the room was a row of nine chairs, with a jean jacket and a book bag sitting on the center one. The experimenter explained that the partner (the skinhead) had evidently left to go to the bathroom but that he would be right back and the students should take a seat and wait. As soon as the students sat down, the experiment was over. The prediction that students who had previously suppressed their stereotypes would sit, on average, farther away from the skinhead's chair than the students who had not suppressed their stereotypes was confirmed.

Strengths and Limitations of Experimental Research.   This clever experiment nicely demonstrates one advantage of experimental research. The experiment can be interpreted as demonstrating that suppressing stereotypes caused the students to sit farther away from the skinhead because there was only one difference between the two groups of students in this experiment, and that was whether they had suppressed their stereotypical thoughts when writing. It is this ability to draw conclusions about causal relationships that makes experiments so popular.

Although they have the distinct advantage of being able to provide information about causal relationships among variables, experiments, like descriptive and correlational research, also have limitations. In fact, experiments cannot be used to study the most important social questions facing today's society, including violence, racism, poverty, and homelessness, because the conditions of interest cannot be manipulated by the experimenter. Because it is not possible (for both practical and ethical reasons) to manipulate whether a person is homeless, poor, or abused by her or his parents, these topics cannot be studied experimentally. Thus, descriptive and correlational designs must be used to study these issues. Because experiments have their own limitations, they are no more "scientific" than are other approaches to research.

The Selection of an Appropriate Method

The previous sections have described the characteristics of descriptive, correlational, and experimental research designs. Because these three approaches represent fundamentally different ways of studying behavior, they each provide different types of information. As summarized in Table 1.3, each research design has a unique set of advantages and disadvantages. In short, each of the three research designs contributes to the accumulation of scientific knowledge, and thus, each is necessary for a complete study of behavior.

TABLE 1.3 Characteristics of the Three Research Designs

Research Design	Goal	Advantages	Disadvantages
Descriptive	To create a snapshot of the current state of affairs	Provides a relatively complete picture of what is occurring at a given time	Does not assess relationships among variables
Correlational	To assess the relationships between and among two or more variables	Allows testing of expected relationships between and among variables and making of predictions	Cannot be used to draw inferences about the causal relationships between and among the variables
Experimental	To assess the impact of one or more experimental manipulations on a dependent variable	Allows drawing of conclusions about the causal relationships among variables.	Cannot experimentally manipulate many important variables

To determine what research approach is best for a given research project, the researcher must look at several matters. For one, practical issues such as the availability of research participants, researchers, equipment, and space will determine the research approach. As we will see in Chapter 3, ethical principles of research will shape the researcher's choice. But the decision will also derive from the researcher's own ideas about research—what she or he thinks is important to study. It is to the development of research ideas that we will turn in the next chapter.

Furthermore, because each of the three research designs has different strengths and weaknesses, it is often effective to use them together. For instance, the impact of population density on mental health has been tested using naturalistic observation, correlational studies, and experimental research designs. Using more than one technique (such as more than one research design) to study the same thing, with the hope that all of the approaches will produce similar findings, is known as **converging operations.** As we will see, the converging-operation approach is common in the behavioral sciences.

Current Research in the Behavioral Sciences: Preferences for Brands That Contain the Letters of Our Own Name

A recent study reported in the *Journal of Consumer Research* (Brendl, Chattopadhyay, Pelham, & Carvallo, 2005) is an example of the kind of research that behavioral scientists conduct, and which demonstrates that people are frequently unaware of the causes of their own behavior. Their research demonstrated that, at least under certain conditions (and although they do not know it), people frequently prefer brand names that contain the letters of their own name to brand names that do not contain the letters of their own name.

The research participants were recruited in pairs, and were told that the research was about a taste test of tea. The experimenter created for each pair of participants two teas by adding the word stem "oki" to the first three letters of each participant's first name. For example, for Jonathan and Elisabeth these would have been Jonoki and Elioki. (Fortunately, the researchers did not encounter anyone named Kari!)

The participants were then shown 20 packets of tea that were supposedly being tested. Each packet was labeled with a made-up Japanese name (for instance "Mataku" or "Somuta"), with two of them being the brand names just constructed. The experimenter explained that each participant would taste only two teas and would be allowed to choose one packet of these two to take home.

One of the two participants was asked to draw slips of paper to select the two brands that would be tasted at this session. However, the drawing was rigged so that the two brands containing the participants' initials were always chosen for tasting. Then, while the teas were being brewed, the participants completed a task designed to heighten their needs for self esteem, and which was expected to increase the desire to choose a brand that had one's own initials. Specifically, the participants all wrote about an aspect of themselves that they would like to change.

After the teas were ready, the participants tasted them. The two teas were actually identical, except that a drop of lemon juice had randomly been added to one of them so that they did not taste exactly the same. After tasting, the participants chose to take a packet of one of the teas home with them. After they made their choice, the participants were asked why they chose the tea they had chosen, and then the true purpose of the study was explained to them.

The results of this study found that participants chose the tea that included the first three letters of their own name 64 percent of the time, whereas they chose the brand that included the first three letters of their partner's name only 36 percent of the time. Furthermore, the participants did not know why they chose the tea they chose. Over 90 percent of the students thought that they had chosen on the basis of taste, whereas only 5 percent of the respondents mentioned something about the brand names.

Can you determine what type of research design was used by the researchers? Does the fact that the participants were unable to explain why they chose the tea that they chose surprise you? The author's analysis of the study is available at the companion website to this book.

SUMMARY

Behavioral research is conducted by scientists who are interested in understanding the behavior of human beings and animals. These scientists believe that knowledge gained through personal intuition or the claims of others is not a sufficient basis for drawing conclusions about behavior. They demand that knowledge be gained through the accumulation of empirical data, as prescribed by the scientific method. Behavioral scientists understand that the scientific approach is not perfect, but it is better than any other known way of drawing conclusions about behavior.

Although science is designed to create a collection of facts, it is not entirely free of values. The values of scientists influence how they interpret their data, what and whom they study, and how they report their research. For instance, some scientists conduct basic research, whereas others conduct applied research. One of the important goals of the scientific method is to make clear to others which aspects of the research process are based on facts and which are based on values.

There are three major research designs in behavioral research. There are advantages and disadvantages to each of the approaches, and each provides an essential avenue of scientific investigation. Descriptive research, such as surveys and naturalistic observation, is designed to provide a snapshot of the current state of affairs. Descriptive research may be either qualitative or quantitative in orientation. Correlational research is designed to discover relationships among variables and to allow the prediction of future events from present knowledge. The relationships among variables are frequently described using the Pearson correlation coefficient. Because correlational research cannot provide evidence about causal relationships between variables, experimental research is often employed to do so. Experiments involve the creation of equivalence among research participants in more than one group, followed by an active manipulation of a given experience for these groups and a measurement of the influence of the manipulation. The goal is to assess the causal impact of the manipulation. Because each of the three types of research designs has both strengths and limitations, it is very important to learn to think critically about research. Such critical evaluation will allow you to select the appropriate research design and to determine what conclusions can and cannot be drawn from research.

KEY TERMS

applied research 11	objective 8
basic research 11	Pearson product–moment correlation coefficient (*r*) 16
behavioral research 4	
converging operations 20	program evaluation research 11
correlational research 16	quantitative research 15
data 4	qualitative research 15
descriptive research 14	research design 13
empirical 4	research report 10
experimental research 18	scientific method 8
facts 9	values 9
hindsight bias 7	variable 16

REVIEW AND DISCUSSION QUESTIONS

1. What is behavioral research? What are its fundamental goals and limitations? Why is learning about behavioral research important?

2. In what ways is behavioral research similar to and different from research in the natural sciences, such as chemistry, biology, and physics?

3. Why are behavioral scientists wary of using their intuition to understand behavior?

4. What is the scientific method, and how does it guide research?

5. Discuss the basic characteristics of scientific inquiry (empiricism, objectivity, and accumulation) and their value to science.

6. In what ways is science objective, and in what ways is it subjective? What prevents the subjectivity of science from compromising it as a discipline?

7. Consider the similarities and differences between basic research and applied research. What does each contribute to our knowledge about behavior?

8. Describe the characteristics of descriptive, correlational, and experimental research designs, and discuss the advantages and disadvantages of each.

RESEARCH PROJECT IDEAS

1. Locate a newspaper or magazine article that reports a behavioral science research project.

   a. Determine whether the project is a descriptive, a correlational, or an experimental research design.
   b. What variables are measured in the research?
   c. Is the research applied or basic in orientation?
   d. What are the most important findings of the research?
   e. What do you perceive as potential limitations of the research?

2. Consider whether each of the following research reports seems to describe an applied or a basic research project, and explain why:

   An experimental analysis of the impact of contingent reinforcement on salespersons' performance behavior

   The theory of crystallized and fluid intelligence

   The effect of prison crowding on inmate behavior

   The role of schemata in memory for places

   Neonatal imitation

3. Create predictions about the relationships between behavioral variables that interest you. For each relationship that you develop, indicate how the prediction could be tested using a descriptive, a correlational, and/or an experimental research design. What would be the advantages and disadvantages of studying the relationship using each of the different designs?

CHAPTER TWO
Developing the Research Hypothesis

STUDY QUESTIONS

- How do behavioral scientists get ideas for their research projects?

- What is a literature search? Why is a literature search necessary, and how is it conducted?

- What computer databases contain listings of behavioral research reports?

- How are previous research findings used to develop ideas for further research?

- What role do laws and theories play in scientific research?

- What are research hypotheses, and what is their purpose?

As we have seen in Chapter 1, this book concerns the scientific study of behavior. In this chapter, we will begin our investigation of the research process by considering the initial stages in conducting scientific research, including how scientists get their ideas for research and how they conduct a background literature review to see what research has already been conducted on their topic. We will also consider the principles that are used to organize research—laws, theories, and research hypotheses. Because research hypotheses are the most basic tool of the scientist, we will be spending a major part of this book discussing their development and testing, and this chapter will provide an important background for the chapters to come.

Getting Ideas

As you can well imagine, there are plenty of topics to study and plenty of approaches to studying those topics. For instance, my colleagues within the Psychology Department at the University of Maryland study such diverse topics as:

Anxiety in children

The interpretation of dreams

The effects of caffeine on thinking

How birds recognize each other

How praying mantises hear

How people from different cultures react differently in negotiation

The factors that lead people to engage in terrorism

The point is, there are a lot of things to study!

You may already be developing such ideas for your research projects. As with most things based on creative and original thinking, these ideas will not come to you overnight. For the best scientists, research is always in the back of their minds. Whether they are reading journal articles, teaching classes, driving in the car, or exercising, scientists are continually thinking about ways to use research to study the questions that interest them. Good behavioral scientists are always alert to their experiences and ready to apply those experiences to their research.

Because there are so many things to study, you may think it would be easy to come up with research ideas. On the contrary, informative research ideas are hard to come by. For instance, although you may be interested in studying depression, nurturance, memory, or helping, having an idea of a research interest is only a very preliminary first step in developing a testable research idea. Before you can begin your research project, you must determine what aspects of your topic you wish to focus on and then refine these interests into a specific research design. And for your ideas to result in an accumulation of knowledge, they must be informed by past research. This is going to take time and require a lot of thought on your part.

Scientists develop their ideas about what to study in a number of different ways, and in the next sections we will consider some methods for getting ideas.[1] As you read this section, keep in mind the types of research that we discussed in Chapter 1. You may want to begin your search for ideas by determining whether you are more interested in a basic research project or in a specific applied question. And you will want to think about whether your research question is best tested using a descriptive, a correlational, or an experimental research design.

Solving Important Real-World Problems

Many behavioral scientists develop their research programs around their concerns with human problems. For instance, behavioral scientists have studied how to improve children's reading skills, how to alleviate stress in corporate managers, how to promote volunteering, and how to reduce aggression among gang members. Other scientists have studied methods for reducing risky behavior such as unprotected sex and cigarette smoking. Still others have studied the effectiveness of psychotherapy or how juries make decisions. Thus, one way to get ideas for research is to develop an applied research project that has the goal of producing a better understanding of the causes of, or potential solutions to, everyday problems.

Using Observation and Intuition

Because much behavioral research involves the study of people in their everyday lives, it is often possible to develop research ideas on the basis of intuition or hunches, which are themselves based on observation of everyday behavior. Getting ideas about the relationships among variables by observing specific facts is known as the **inductive method.** In this approach, your own curiosity becomes the source of your ideas. For instance, you may have noticed that several friends of yours have had trouble developing satisfactory romantic relationships. You may have developed a theory about why these particular people have this particular behavioral problem, and you may want to test this idea in a research project. As we have seen in Chapter 1, it is useful to test hunches about behavior because those hunches often "feel" more right to us than they actually turn out to be. Only by subjecting our hunches to systematic investigation can we be sure of their validity.

Some important scientific ideas have been developed through observation. For instance, Sigmund Freud developed his theory of personality by carefully observing the patients in his clinical practice. In a similar way, Jean

---

[1] The social psychologist William McGuire once argued that there were forty-nine different ways of getting research ideas (!), and you may want to look at some of these in his chapter in the *Annual Review of Psychology:* McGuire, W. J. (1997). Creative hypothesis generating in psychology: Some useful heuristics. *Annual Review of Psychology, 48,* 1–30.

Piaget developed his theory of cognitive development in children by watching the development of his own children.

Although using observation and intuition has the potential of producing new ideas and approaches, there is also a possible danger to this approach. Studies that are based on intuition alone but do not relate to existing scientific knowledge may not advance the field very far. Consider a research project designed to test the idea that people learn more in a class taught by left-handed teachers than in a class taught by right-handed teachers. In the long run, such research could make a contribution to science by linking brain symmetry and creativity to teaching effectiveness. But, the results of a single study testing this prediction will probably not make much of a contribution to the larger body of scientific knowledge because there is no existing explanation for why a left-handed instructor should be better than a right-handed instructor other than the hunch of the person who developed the idea.

Although you may use your observations of everyday behavior to generate research ideas, or develop your research around solutions to a practical social problem, you should try to link your research to the findings from other studies investigating the same concepts. A study concerning creative thinking will be more useful if it is related to existing research about creativity, even if the goal of the study is to demonstrate that the existing research has drawn incorrect conclusions or is incomplete. The more links you can draw between your research and existing research, the greater is the likelihood that your research will make an important contribution to the field.

Using Existing Research

The previous discussion has perhaps already suggested to you that I think that the best way to generate research ideas is by reading about and studying existing scientific research and then using this existing knowledge to generate new research ideas and topics. Although basing your research ideas on already existing research may seem to limit the contribution that your project can make, this is not the case. In fact, research that is based on or related to previous research findings tends to advance science more rapidly because it contributes to the accumulation of a unified and integrated body of knowledge. Our substantial knowledge about topics such as the causes of prejudice or the development of reading skills in children exists precisely because of the cumulative work of hundreds of investigators who have conducted research that built on previously conducted research.

Finding Limiting Conditions.   Because every research project is limited in some way or another, the goal of most research is to expand on or improve existing research. One useful strategy for developing research ideas is to consider the potential *limiting conditions* of previous research. For instance, for many years people believed that women were more likely to conform to the opinions of others than men were. Only when scientists began to consider the types of tasks that had been used in conformity research was a basic limiting condition found. Previous research had relied to a large extent on topics (such as football and baseball) in which men were more knowledgeable than women. However, subsequent research demonstrated that the original conclusion was too broad. This research showed that women do conform more than men, but only when the topic is one about which women believe that men have more knowledge than they do (Eagly & Chravala, 1986). If the topic is one in which women believe they are more knowledgeable (for instance, fashion design), then men are found to conform more than women. In this case, research assessing the limiting conditions of existing findings made a significant contribution by developing a new explanation for a phenomenon. A finding that had previously been explained in terms of differences between men and women was now explained in terms of differences in knowledge about the topic.

Explaining Conflicting Findings.   Another strategy for developing research ideas is to attempt to explain conflicting findings in a research area. In many cases, some studies testing a given idea show one pattern of data, whereas other studies do not show that pattern. And some studies may even show the opposite pattern. Research that can account for these discrepancies can be extremely useful. One classic example of this approach occurred in the 1960s when Robert Zajonc (1965) noted that some studies had demonstrated that tasks such as bicycle riding or jogging were performed better in the presence of others, whereas other studies showed that tasks such as solving mathematical problems were usually solved more efficiently when people were alone. There was no known explanation for these differences.

Zajonc proposed that being with others increased psychological arousal and that arousal amplified the "dominant" or most likely response in a given setting. Because the dominant response was usually the correct response on easy or well-learned tasks (such as jogging) but the incorrect response on difficult or poorly learned tasks (such as math problems), the presence of others might either increase or decrease performance depending on task difficulty. This became a very important principle in social psychology, and the findings have been confirmed in many different experiments. Zajonc's research was particularly valuable because it was able to account in a consistent way for what had previously appeared to be inconsistent research findings.

In short, because existing research provides so many ideas for future research, it is very important to be aware of what other research has been done in an area. Indeed, one of the most important qualities of a good scientist is an open mind. Careful and creative analysis of existing research can produce many important ideas for future research projects.

Doing a Literature Search

Because all good research is designed to build on and expand existing knowledge, it would be wasteful for a scientist to begin working on a project without knowing what others working in the area have already done. This is why scientists receive years of training in which they learn both methods of conducting research and the current content of knowledge in their field. It is also why scientists spend a lot of time reading about research in scientific journals and participating at conferences where research is presented. In short, scientists are keenly aware that their research will make a contribution to the field only if it is based on and adds significantly to what is already known.

Once you have begun to develop an idea for your research, you should perform a *literature search* to locate the research articles and books that contain reports of previous research (Reed & Baxter, 1983). Conducting a literature search before beginning a research project is essential because it helps prevent duplication of effort and may help you avoid problems that others have had. The literature search is also a great time-saver because it can provide you with invaluable information about how to measure the variables you are interested in and what research designs will be most useful to you. There is so much literature in behavioral science journals and books that no matter what your research idea is, others will probably have done something relevant to it. This does not mean that your idea is not important—in fact, it suggests that others have also found it to be so.

Locating Sources of Information

There are many sources of research literature relevant to your interest. Probably the most important sources of information are research reports that contain complete descriptions of the collected data and the data analyses. These research reports are known as *primary sources* and usually appear in professional journals. *Secondary sources* are documents that contain only summaries or interpretations of the research reports rather than a complete description of them. Secondary sources include textbooks, books written by a single author, and edited books that contain a collection of chapters on a single topic, each contributed by a different author. Some journals, such as *Psychological Bulletin* and the *Annual Review of Psychology,* also publish primarily secondary-source articles.

In most cases, the sources that you locate can be found online through the databases maintained by university libraries. If the source is not online, you will have to find it on the shelves of your library using the call number of the book or journal. If your library does not subscribe to the journal or have the book on its shelves, you may be able to get it through the interlibrary loan system.

You may also wish to use the Web to get ideas. It is likely that no matter what your topic is, you will find one or more Internet sites that contain data and other relevant information about it. This material might include newsletters, unpublished research papers and reports, and online books and brochures. These sites may be particularly helpful for getting new ideas and for seeing what other people interested in the problem are doing.

One potential problem with web sources, however, is that the information may not be very objective. There are many websites that espouse views of the authors without much fact checking or verifiability. Thus, some web information may be based primarily on intuition rather than on data or facts. It is up to you, as an informed consumer of information, to do the very best you can to determine the validity of the information in the sites that you find. Some sources, such as *www.scholar.google.com* are reputable sources of academic information. And many academic journals can now be found on websites at your university. Other sites may be less valid. As you attempt to determine the validity of the information on the sites you find, keep in mind the distinction between primary and secondary source information, and ask yourself about the likely source, credibility, and currency of the site. Is the information based on scientific research or is it more value-based? Both types of information can be informative, but a good scientist attempts to determine the difference. If you do decide to use information from web-based material, be sure to accurately report the source of this information in the Reference section of the manuscript.

Other valuable sources of information are experts in the field in which you are interested. An instructor may be a good source in this regard or may be able to direct you to an even more knowledgeable expert. Experts can also be useful in directing you to specific journals that are known to contain the best published research in your topic area. Do not be shy about contacting experts. Although they may be busy, scientists are usually happy to put their knowledge to use.

Conducting the Search

Generally, a literature search will be most efficient if it (1) starts at a broad, general level (secondary sources) and then progresses to more specific levels (primary sources) and (2) starts with the newest available information and uses this information to progress backward toward previous research.

One approach to beginning a literature search in an area that you do not know much about is to use one or more introductory textbooks in that field as the most general secondary sources. Choose a chapter in which your topic is discussed, and read the chapter carefully. Although using secondary sources can be a time-saver because they generally provide more information in fewer pages, it is absolutely essential that you also consult primary sources in your literature search. Secondary sources may not adequately summarize the primary-source research. Journal articles are also more complete and objective than secondary sources because (as we will discuss in Appendix A), they have passed a rigorous review process.

After you have begun to focus on a topic area, you will want to move from general information toward more specific treatments of the topic area by reading book chapters and journal articles. As you begin to move deeper into your topic, do not be too inflexible about what you are interested in. It is best to keep an open mind at this point because you may find that your research idea has already been well tested or that another research idea interests you more than the one you began with. Remember that your goal is not only to read about the research but also to use the research to develop and refine ideas for your own research. Being open-minded is important in all stages of the research process, especially because research that originally seemed irrelevant may later turn out to be valuable to you when you have a broader idea of the scope of the topic you are studying. The literature search should be used to help you modify and refine your original ideas.

Investigating Computer Databases.   The most efficient way to find primary sources relevant to your topic is through the use of a computer-aided literature search. Behavioral science databases are provided by most libraries and are available online. The databases contain summaries (called **abstracts**) of thousands of journal articles and book chapters. Reading these abstracts will give you a basic idea of whether the material will provide information you are interested in, and where to locate a journal article or book chapter if you decide to read it.

The most relevant database in psychology is PsycINFO®, which indexes almost 2 million references to psychological literature published from 1887 to the present. Many of these articles will be online in your library. The American Psychological Association website (*www.apa.org*) has more information about this database. Similar databases are found in other fields. For instance, SocialSciIndex® is a sociological database containing abstracts from over 1,600 journals. Medline® indexes journals in the areas of health care, environmental health, and behavioral medicine, and ERIC® is a collection of databases including those related to education and training.

Another useful database is the *Social Science Citation Index* (SSCI). Although the normal search procedure is to use the reference lists of newer journal articles to locate older articles, SSCI allows you to work the other way around. If you have an older article that you have found to be very important to your topic, you can use SSCI to find other, more recent articles that have cited that article in their references.

Using Keywords Effectively.   Before beginning your search in a database, you will need to have a few keywords to use in locating your materials. Most of your keywords will be of subjects, such as *learning, memory, stress,* or *paranoia.* However, you can also use author names or journal titles as keywords. You can develop your own keywords on the basis of your interests, but if you are not sure about what keywords to use, consult the *Thesaurus*—an index of all of the keywords used in the database. Ask your reference librarian for help if you are unsure how to proceed.

Once you have entered a keyword, the computer checks the titles and abstracts of all of the books or articles in the database for the occurrence of that word. One problem is that some keywords are so broad that there are far too many articles using them. For instance, I recently searched PsycINFO® using the keyword *learning* and found over 182,000 journal articles listed! The database thus allows you to combine keywords to make your target more specific. For instance, when I combined the keywords *learning* and *children,* the list was reduced to about 31,735 articles, and a search for *learning* and *children* and *television* produced only 278 articles. Finally, I indicated that I wanted only articles from the years 2000–2002, and this reduced the output to a manageable list of 28 articles. You can also limit your search to include only journal articles, to include only certain authors, and (in case your foreign language skills aren't that good) to include only articles in English.

Figure 2.1 shows the input that I gave to my search. You can see that the database is PsycINFO®, that there are three keywords—*children, learning,* and *television*—and that I have indicated to search only in the years 2000–2002. Figure 2.2 presents the first listing that came out of my search, and you can

FIGURE 2.1 Input to PsycINFO Search

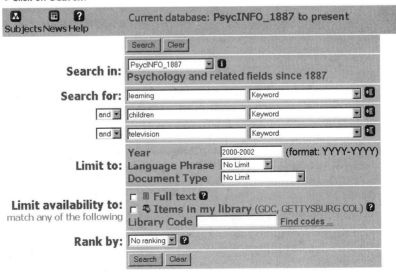

FIGURE 2.2   Output of PsycINFO Search

Author(s): Oates, Caroline ; Blades, Mark ; Gunter, Barrie
               Affiliation: 1. U Sheffield, Management School, Sheffield, England; 2. U
               Sheffield, Dept of Psychology, Sheffield, England; 3. U Sheffield, Dept of
               Journalism Studies, Sheffield, England

Title: **Children and television advertising: When do they understand persuasive intent?**

Source: *Journal of Consumer Behaviour* Vol 1(3), Feb 2002, 238-245.
            Additional Info: United Kingdom : Henry Stewart Publications

Standard No: **ISSN:** 1472-0817 (Print)

Language: English

Abstract: Children's response to television advertising is investigated in this paper.
         Children (aged 4-10 yrs) were tested for their recall, recognition and
         understanding of novel television advertisements and compared to a
         group of 12 adults. Children were able to recognize scenes from the
         advertisements after one exposure but recall of the brand names was
         poor for the younger children, even after three exposures. Recall for the
         advertising content increased by age and number of exposures. None of
         the 6-yr-olds and only a quarter of the 8-yr-olds and a third of the 10-yr-
         olds discussed advertising in terms of persuasion. Therefore, although
         children remember television advertisements, their purpose is not fully
         understood, even by any 10-yr-olds. (PsycINFO Database Record (c)
         2002 APA, all rights reserved):

---

see the type of information it contains. It includes the title and authors of the article, as well as their university affiliations. Also included is information about the journal in which the article is published and the abstract. The listing also allows me to see whether the article is available in my library and whether it is available online. In this case, the full text of the article turned out to be available, and I could go right to reading it.

Using the keyword system will get you started, but it is only the beginning of your literature search. As you read journal articles, you will find that those articles contain other relevant articles in their reference sections. Working backward through the reference lists of the articles you read will allow you to find many new articles that did not appear in the initial keyword search. To adequately prepare a research topic for investigation, you must do an extensive search of the literature, which will take quite a bit of time. Keep in mind that you can often do a large part of the preparation for your research project at this point by taking good notes or making copies of the articles and by thinking about how these references will relate to your final report.

Using Abstracts to Select Important Documents.   Once you have developed a smaller list of articles relevant to your area of interest, you will begin to read their abstracts to determine if the articles may be of interest to you. As you read through journal abstracts, you will probably find that there are certain authors who have published frequently in your topic area. These are the scientists who have made major contributions to the literature, and you may wish to locate their contributions by entering their names as keywords.

Remember that it is important to read at least some of the articles that you have located. It is not sufficient to just read the abstracts, because they are too brief to give you a complete understanding of the research.

Formalizing Ideas Into Research Hypotheses

As you conduct your literature search, you will want to pay close attention to the organizing principles that form the basis of behavioral research. These principles include laws, theories, and research hypotheses. As we will see in the next sections, once you have read a great deal about your topic area, you will begin to develop more specific ideas about what you want to study, and you will be ready to begin formalizing your interests into a specific research hypothesis that you will test.

Laws

Principles that are so general as to apply to all situations are known as **laws.** There are well-known laws in the physical sciences, such as the law of gravity and the laws of thermodynamics, but there currently are very few universally accepted laws within the behavioral sciences. This is partly because behavioral science research has not progressed as far as that in the natural sciences and partly because it is more difficult to specify laws of social behavior. In any case, because laws are such general principles and are considered so only because their validity has already been well established, they are themselves rarely directly subjected to scientific test.

Theories

The next step down from laws in the hierarchy of organizing principles is the **theory.** A theory is an integrated set of principles that explains and predicts many, but not all, observed relationships within a given domain of inquiry. Because theories integrate many observations into a relatively simple whole and yet are not too general to be tested, they form the basic building blocks of science. Existing theories (or ones that you develop) may help provide you with ideas for developing your own research. The process of using a theory to generate specific ideas that can be tested through research is known as the **deductive method.**

The Components of a Good Theory.   Consider, for instance, the stage theory of cognitive development, which states that children pass through a series of cognitive stages and that children cannot perform certain activities until the appropriate cognitive stage has been reached (Piaget, 1952). This is an extremely useful theory in human development because it can be applied to many different content areas and can be tested in many different ways.

The utility of a theory can be judged on the basis of how well it meets some fundamental requirements. First, good theories are **general,** meaning that they summarize many different outcomes. Second, they are **parsimonious,** meaning that they provide the simplest possible account of those outcomes. The stage theory of cognitive development meets both of these requirements. It can account for developmental changes in behavior across a wide variety of domains, and yet it does so parsimoniously—by hypothesizing a simple set of cognitive stages.

Third, good theories provide ideas for future research. For instance, the stage theory suggested many different types of experiments in many different areas that have since been used to study cognitive development. Research has demonstrated, for instance, that children cannot conserve volume or mass until they have reached an appropriate stage of development (Piaget, 1952), that they learn about what it means to be a boy or a girl in stages (Stangor & Ruble, 1987), and that moral reasoning follows a stage sequence (Kohlberg, 1969). Taken together, these different research findings, all predicted by the stage theory, provide overall support for the theory.

Fourth, good theories are **falsifiable** (Popper, 1959), which means that the variables of interest can be adequately measured and the relationships between the variables that are predicted by the theory can be shown through research to be incorrect. The stage theory of cognitive development is falsifiable because the stages of cognitive reasoning can be measured and because if research discovers that children learn new tasks gradually, rather than quickly, as they pass into a new stage, then the theory will be shown to be incorrect. In general, when a theory is falsified, it will be replaced by a new, more accurate theory.

Judgment of a Theory's Utility.

Some theories meet some of the requirements for a good theory but not others. The theory of social reinforcement, for instance, proposes that people will be more likely to subsequently perform a behavior after they have been rewarded for performing it. This is an extremely important theory because it summarizes much of everyday social behavior in a parsimonious manner and also provides ideas for testing it. For instance, the theory would predict that children would more likely share their toys if their mother praises them for doing so.

However, the definitions of "reward" in social behavior involve both external factors, such as money and praise, and internal factors, such as mood improvement and guilt reduction. Because internal factors are difficult to define and measure, a supporter of social learning theory could easily argue that when a behavior occurs, it has been rewarded, and that when a behavior does not occur, it has not been rewarded. For instance, when a person helps a complete stranger escape from a burning building, there is obvious cost to the helper, but the potential reward is not clear. But a supporter of social reinforcement theory would say that the reward was something such as "feeling good about helping" or "avoiding guilt if one didn't help." In this case, the problem is that the theory is not falsifiable because the variable "reward" is defined as "that which increases the occurrence of behavior." Theories in which the variables cannot be measured or in which the variables are vague enough that they cannot provide information to falsify the theory are called **tautological.**

No single theory is able to account for all behavior in all cases. Rather, a theory is inevitably found to be limited in that it makes accurate predictions in some situations or for some people but not in other situations or for other people. As a result, there is a constant interplay between theory and data: existing theories are modified on the basis of collected data, and the new modified theories then make new predictions which are tested by new data, and so forth. In time a theory will either change so much that it becomes a new and different theory or be entirely replaced by another, more accurate theory. A theory survives only to the extent that it is "good enough" and no currently known alternative theory is better. When a better theory is found, it will replace the old one. This is part of the accumulation of scientific knowledge.

The Research Hypothesis

Although good theories are designed to be falsifiable, they are usually framed too broadly to be tested in a single experiment. Therefore, scientists use a more precise statement of the presumed relationship among specific parts of the theory—a *research hypothesis*—as a basis for correlational and experimental research (remember that relationships among variables are never tested in descriptive research). Because research hypotheses are the most basic tool of the scientist, we will be spending a major part of this book discussing their development and testing.

A **research hypothesis** can be defined as a specific and falsifiable prediction regarding the relationship between or among two or more variables. The research hypothesis states the existence of a relationship between the variables of interest and the specific direction of that relationship. For instance:

> Observing violent television shows will cause increased aggressive behavior.

> Participating in psychotherapy will reduce anxiety.

> Smoking marijuana will reduce the ability to learn new information.

As we will discuss more fully in Chapters 10 and 11, in experimental research designs the research hypothesis involves the relationship between an **independent variable** (the experimental manipulation) and a **dependent variable** (the variable that is caused by the independent variable). The independent variable is created by the experimenter through the experimental manipulation, and the research hypothesis is that the manipulated independent variable causes changes in the measured dependent variable. Causal relationships can be depicted graphically using straight arrows that point in one direction:

In correlational research designs, both the independent variable and the dependent variable are measured. Furthermore, because it is not possible to state the causal relationships between variables in correlational designs, the terms *independent variable* and *dependent variable* are sometimes replaced with the terms *predictor variable* and *outcome variable,* respectively. The research hypothesis is that there is a correlation between the variables, and this correlation is shown using a curved line with arrows that point in both directions:

Because the research hypothesis is only a guess and is designed to be falsifiable, its validity must be tested. Moreover, there are many ways to measure the variables of interest and many ways to test the relationship between them. The major focus of this book is on how to develop research designs and test research hypotheses.

SUMMARY

The first stage in a research project is developing an idea. These ideas can come through an interest in solving important social problems, through the use of the inductive method to organize existing facts, and through the exercise of the deductive method to derive predictions from existing theories. The last approach is perhaps the most useful because it ensures that the new research is related to existing research and thus contributes to the accumulation of scientific knowledge.

Before beginning a research project, the scientist conducts a literature search, usually by using computer databases to locate abstracts of relevant articles. The literature search involves locating both secondary- and primary-source material. Being knowledgeable about previous research from other research laboratories is essential to the development of effective research. The literature search frequently leads the scientist to modify and refine his or her original research ideas.

One of the goals of science is to organize relationships into explanatory principles such as laws and theories. Laws are general principles that apply to all situations. Theories are integrated sets of principles that explain and predict many observed events within a given domain. Good theories are both general and parsimonious, they form the basis of future scientific research, and they make predictions that can be tested and falsified.

Theories are tested in the form of research hypotheses—specific and testable predictions regarding the relationship between or among two or more variables. Once a scientist develops a research hypothesis, she or he tests it using either a correlational or an experimental research design.

KEY TERMS

abstracts 32
deductive method 35
dependent variable 37
falsifiable 36
general 36
independent variable 37

inductive method 27
laws 35
parsimonious 36
research hypothesis 37
tautological 37
theory 35

REVIEW AND DISCUSSION QUESTIONS

1. How do scientists get ideas for research? What are the advantages and potential disadvantages of each method for doing so?

2. What guidelines do scientists use to conduct an effective literature search? What specific literature databases are most useful to behavioral scientists?

3. What makes a good theory? Why are theories so important in behavioral research?

4. What makes a theory falsifiable? What makes a theory tautological?

5. What is a research hypothesis? Why are research hypotheses, rather than theories or laws, tested in behavioral research?

RESEARCH PROJECT IDEAS

1. Turn each of the following statements into a research hypothesis and indicate whether the hypothesis is falsifiable:

God answers our prayers.

Birds of a feather flock together.

You can't teach an old dog new tricks.

Elderly individuals don't remember things well.

Practice makes perfect.

Single-parent families produce delinquent children.

Aggression is increasing in our society.

People work harder when they are in a good mood.

Cats can understand English.

2. Consider the following variables. For each one (a) create a research hypothesis in which the variable serves as an independent (or predictor) variable and (b) create a research hypothesis in which the variable serves as a dependent (or outcome) variable.

Helping

Paranoia

Memory

Performance on a mathematics test

Color preference

Life satisfaction

3. Consider how each of the research hypotheses you generated in problems 1 and 2 could (or could not) be tested using a correlational and an experimental research design.

CHAPTER THREE
Ethics in Research

STUDY QUESTIONS

- What are some of the concerns guiding ethical research?

- What are the potential psychological threats to participants in behavioral science research projects?

- What factors may interfere with participants' freedom to choose whether or not to participate in research?

- What is the function of informed consent?

- How might a researcher abuse his or her power in the research relationship?

- When and why is deception used in research?

- What is debriefing, and how is it used?

- What procedures do researchers use to ensure that behavioral research is ethical?

- What procedures do researchers follow to ensure the ethical treatment of animals in behavioral research?

One of the major difficulties involved in studying human beings, and even animals, is that they often behave quite differently when they are being studied than they would otherwise. As a result, behavioral scientists are faced with a basic challenge: to learn what people do when they are not being studied, behavioral scientists must create research designs that measure important everyday phenomena and that allow research participants the freedom and motivation to openly and honestly express their thoughts, feelings, and behavior. And scientists must do this in a way that prevents participants from guessing what is being studied and altering their responses as a result.

To create situations in which behavior can be validly assessed, scientists sometimes engage in practices that may be questioned on ethical grounds. For instance, researchers may lead people to participate in research without telling them that they are participating. Researchers may require introductory psychology students to participate in research projects and then deceive these students, at least temporarily, about the nature of the research. In some cases, researchers may induce stress, anxiety, or negative moods in the participants, expose them to weak electrical shocks, or convince them to behave in ways that violate their moral standards. And researchers may sometimes use animals in their research, potentially harming them in the process.

Of course, behavioral scientists have a basic reason for engaging in these practices. For one, as we will discuss in more detail in the chapters to come, creating such situations is frequently the only way that important behavioral phenomena can be objectively studied. Second, they feel that although there may well be some costs to human research participants when they participate in research, there is also a great benefit to humanity to be gained from the research. This benefit is, of course, the knowledge about human behavior that accrues through the conduct of behavioral research. Furthermore, scientists also believe that there are potential benefits to the research participants in the form of learning about how research is conducted and experiencing the satisfaction of having contributed to the scientific literature. In each case, before beginning to conduct the research, scientists have come to the conclusion that the potential benefits of conducting the research outweigh the potential costs to the research participants.

What Is Ethical Research?

Although the focus of this chapter is the ethical treatment of human and animal participants in behavioral science research, concern about the welfare of research participants is only one aspect of ethics in behavioral research. The ethical concerns of scientists also involve maintaining honesty in conducting and reporting scientific research, giving appropriate credit for ideas and effort, and considering how knowledge gained through research should be used. Determining whether a research project is ethical is a difficult enterprise because there are no clearly "right" or clearly "wrong" answers to ethical questions. By definition, ethics involves values, not facts. Nevertheless, as we will see, there is an agreed-on set of basic ethical principles that must be adhered to by those conducting research.

Ethical concerns are not unique to the behavioral sciences. Rather, they are part of the process of conducting research in any scientific field. Physicists have long debated the ethics of having helped develop the nuclear bomb. Biologists worry about the potential outcomes of creating genetically engineered human babies, and chemists are concerned about the environmental effects of the chemicals they devise. Medical researchers agonize over the ethics of withholding potentially beneficial drugs from control groups in clinical trials in which only some of the participants are given the drugs and of using animals to test potentially dangerous medical treatments. In each of these cases, however, scientists have justified their decision to conduct the research with the belief that in the long run the potential gains of the resulting knowledge will outweigh any potential costs that may be incurred by participants or by society at large.

Some research, such as the forced participation in medical experiments conducted on prisoners by the Nazis during World War II (which gave rise to the Nuremberg code), is perceived as immoral by almost everyone. Other procedures, such as the use of animals in research testing the effectiveness of drugs, or even the practice of asking an individual to complete a questionnaire without first informing him or her what the questionnaire is designed to assess, are more controversial. However, because scientific research is designed to and has provided information that has improved the lives of many people, it is not reasonable to argue that because scientific research has costs, no research should be conducted. This argument fails to consider the fact that there are significant costs to *not* doing research and that these costs may be greater than the potential costs involved in going ahead with the research project (Rosenthal, 1994).

Treating research participants ethically matters not only for the welfare of the individuals themselves but also for the continued effectiveness of behavioral science as a scientific discipline. For one thing, if society begins to question the ethics of behavioral research, this may create a general suspicion about and mistrust of the results of scientific research. Unethical behavior may also lead to government sanctions against the conduct of behavioral research. For instance, the concealed recording of jury sessions by psychologists led to the passing of legislation that entirely banned such studies (Vaughan, 1967). These issues demand that scientists assess the ethical principles of each and every research project and realize that they may have to change or potentially even abandon certain research procedures.

This chapter discusses how scientists make judgments about ethical principles regarding the use of humans and animals as research participants. These decisions rely on the individual values of the scientist, as well as established ethical codes developed by scientific organizations and federal governments. In the United States, the Department of Health and Human Services provides the guidelines for ethical standards in research, and these are available at **www.hhs.gov/ohrp/humansubjects/guidance/45cfr46.htm.** Perhaps the most relevant organization for behavioral scientists is the American Psychological Association (APA); a summary of this organization's guidelines for ethical research with human participants is presented in Table 3.1. The basic goal of the chapter is to inform you about these guidelines and to thoroughly discuss the relevant issues, so that you will be able to use this knowledge to develop your own conclusions and guide your own decisions. We will focus on four basic goals of ethical research (Diener & Crandall, 1978):

- Protecting participants from physical and psychological harm
- Providing freedom of choice about participating in the research
- Maintaining awareness of the power differentials between researcher and participant
- Honestly describing the nature and use of the research to participants

Protecting Research Participants From Physical and Psychological Harm

The most direct ethical concern of the behavioral scientist is the possibility that his or her research will cause harm to the research participants. Fortunately, the danger of physical harm from participation in behavioral science research is very low. Nevertheless, given scientists' interest in studying people's emotions, participation in behavioral research may in some cases produce rather extreme emotional reactions, and these may have long-term negative outcomes.

Types of Threats

Some past research has posed severe threats to the psychological welfare of the participants. One example is the well-known research of Stanley Milgram (1974) investigating obedience to authority. In these studies, participants were induced by an experimenter to administer electric shocks to another person so that Milgram could study the extent to which they would obey the demands of a scientist. Most participants evidenced high levels of stress resulting from the psychological conflict they experienced between engaging in aggressive and dangerous behavior and following the instructions of the experimenter. In another experiment (Bramel, 1962), male college students were told, on the basis of false data, that they had "homosexual tendencies." Although it was later revealed to them that this feedback was not true, the participants may have experienced psychological stress during the course of the experiment and after it was over.

TABLE 3.1 APA Guidelines on Research with Humans

The following are some of the most important ethical principles from the American Psychological Association's guidelines on research with human participants.

General Principles

Psychologists respect and protect civil and human rights and the central importance of freedom of inquiry and expression in research, teaching, and publication.

Psychologists obtain appropriate approval prior to conducting research. They conduct the research in accordance with the approved research protocol.

Informed Consent

Psychologists inform participants about

the purpose of the research, expected duration, and procedures;
their right to decline to participate and to withdraw from the research once participation has begun;
reasonably foreseeable factors that may be expected to influence their willingness to participate;
any prospective research benefits; and
whom to contact for questions about the research and research participants' rights.

Psychologists obtain informed consent from research participants prior to recording their voices or images for data collection unless (1) the research consists solely of naturalistic observations in public places, and it is not anticipated that the recording will be used in a manner that could cause personal identification or harm, or (2) the research design includes deception, and consent for the use of the recording is obtained during debriefing.

Psychologists make reasonable efforts to avoid offering excessive or inappropriate financial or other inducements for research participation when such inducements are likely to coerce participation.

Deception

Psychologists do not conduct a study involving deception unless they have determined that the use of deceptive techniques is justified by the study's significant prospective scientific, educational, or applied value and that effective nondeceptive alternative procedures are not feasible.

Psychologists do not deceive prospective participants about research that is reasonably expected to cause physical pain or severe emotional distress.

Psychologists explain any deception that is an integral feature of the design and conduct of an experiment to participants as early as is feasible, preferably at the conclusion of their participation, but no later than at the conclusion of the data collection, and permit participants to withdraw their data.

Debriefing

Psychologists provide a prompt opportunity for participants to obtain appropriate information about the nature, results, and conclusions of the research, and they take reasonable steps to correct any misconceptions that participants may have of which the psychologists are aware.

If scientific or humane values justify delaying or withholding this information, psychologists take reasonable measures to reduce the risk of harm.

When psychologists become aware that research procedures have harmed a participant, they take reasonable steps to minimize the harm.

Source: American Psychological Association (2002). Ethical principles of psychologists. *American Psychologist, 57,* 1060–1073.

Although studies such as those of Milgram and Bramel would no longer be conducted because the scientific community is now much more sensitized to the potential of such procedures to create emotional discomfort or harm, other studies that present less severe, but potentially real, threats are still conducted. For instance, to study the effects of failure on self-esteem or alcohol consumption, experimenters may convince research participants that they have failed on an important self-relevant task such as a test of social skills or intelligence (Hull & Young, 1983). Or to better understand the effects of depression on learning, researchers may place individuals in negative moods (Bower, 1981).

In other cases, although the research does not directly create stressful situations, it does have the unfortunate outcome of leading the participants to discover something unpleasant about themselves, such as their tendency to stereotype others or to make unwise decisions. Although it might be argued that the participants could make good use of this information and improve their lives from it, having found out the information might nevertheless be stressful to them, and they certainly did not ask to be told about these aspects of their personality. In still other cases, participants are led to perform behaviors that they may later be embarrassed about or ashamed of. For instance, in one experiment investigating the factors that lead college students to cheat (Kahle, 1980), a test was administered to students and the test papers collected. Then the papers were returned to the students for grading, and it was made rather easy for them to change their answers on the exam so as to improve their score. Many students did so. Unknown to the students, however, their original responses had been recorded, so that the experimenters could discover how many students cheated by changing their answers.

The Potential for Lasting Impact

Obviously, procedures that have the potential to create negative moods, stress, self-doubts, and anxiety in research participants involve some potential costs to these individuals. Although the psychological states created in these situations are assumed to be only temporary, there is no guarantee that they will not have longer-lasting consequences. Individuals who have been induced to shock another person or to cheat on an examination may be permanently changed as a result of their participation in the research. Furthermore, these harmful psychological outcomes may not even be immediately apparent to the participant or the experimenter, but occur only later.

Although researchers should always treat the possibility that their research will produce psychological harm seriously, and choose alternative methods of testing their research hypotheses whenever possible, fortunately most evidence suggests that participation in psychological research does not produce long-term psychological damage. For instance, even though the men in Milgram's experiment obviously felt stress during the experiment itself, they did not report any long-term negative outcomes, nor did a team of psychiatrists find any evidence of harmful effects (Milgram, 1974). In fact, the participants in social research usually report that they experienced only minor distur- bances and that they learned much about themselves and about the conduct of social science from their participation. Nevertheless, there is always the possibility that at least some research participants may be psychologically hurt by participating in behavioral research.

Providing Freedom of Choice

The second goal of ethical research is to guarantee that participants have free choice regarding whether they wish to participate in research. In an ideal situ- ation each individual has the opportunity to learn about the research and to choose to participate or not participate without considering any other factors. In reality, freedom of choice is more difficult to attain. An individual who is in financial need of the money being offered for participation by a researcher is less able to decline to participate than one who is not in such need, and a college student who has trekked across campus to a laboratory is likely to choose to participate rather than having to return later for another study.

Conducting Research Outside the Laboratory

Although threats to freedom of choice may occur in experiments con- ducted in scientific laboratories, they are even more common in research conducted in real-world settings, particularly in naturalistic observational studies where the behavior of individuals is observed without their knowl- edge. In lab studies, the individual volunteers to participate and knows that an experiment is occurring. But in observational research, the participant may not even know that research is being conducted. We can ask whether it is ethical to create situations that infringe on passersby, such as research designed to see who helps in a situation created by the researchers (Piliavin, Rodin, & Piliavin, 1969), particularly because the individuals who were the "participants" in the experiment were never informed that the helping situa- tion was staged.

Concerns with free choice also occur in institutional settings, such as schools, psychiatric hospitals, corporations, and prisons, when individuals are required by the institutions to take certain tests, or when employees are as- signed to or asked by their supervisors to participate in research. Such issues are often debated in colleges and universities in which all students enrolled in introductory psychology are required either to participate in research or to perform other potentially less-interesting tasks, such as writing papers about research reports.

University scientists and instructors argue that participation in psychologi- cal research teaches students about the conduct of research and that if there were no research participants, there would be no psychology to study. They also argue that it is more scientifically valid to require students to participate, rather than to have a volunteer system, because volunteer participants react differently from nonvolunteers (Rosenthal & Rosnow, 1975). The students, however, may argue that the time they spend going to these research sessions might be better used studying, that the specific experiments are sometimes not related to the subject matter of their course or are not well explained to them, and thus that the requirement seems more motivated to serve the convenience of researchers.

There are, again, no easy answers to these questions. However, keep in mind that there are potential gains for the participants in the form of knowledge about behavior and the practice of behavioral research. Furthermore, this research can be expected to benefit society at large. However, benefit to the participants occurs only when the researchers fully explain the purposes and expected results of research to participants when the research has ended. It is the duty of the experimenter to do so. Students should make a point to use their participation in research projects to learn something about how and why research is conducted. They should ask questions and attempt to find out what the research is designed to test and how their data will be used.

Securing Informed Consent

The most important tool for providing freedom of choice and reducing psychological stress from participation in behavioral science research is the use of **informed consent.** According to guidelines provided by the U.S. Department of Health and Human Services (2001), informed consent must include

(1) a statement that the study involves research and the expected duration of the participation; a description of the procedures to be followed, and identification of any procedures which are experimental;

(2) a description of any reasonably foreseeable risks or discomforts to the participant;

(3) a description of any benefits to the participant or to others which may reasonably be expected from the research;

(4) a disclosure of appropriate alternative procedures or courses of treatment, if any, that might be advantageous to the participant;

(5) a statement describing the extent, if any, to which confidentiality of records identifying the participant will be maintained;

(6) for research involving more than minimal risk, an explanation as to whether any compensation is to be made and an explanation as to whether any medical treatments are available if injury occurs and, if so, what they consist of, or where further information may be obtained;

(7) an explanation of whom to contact for answers to pertinent questions about the research and research participants' rights, and whom to contact in the event of a research-related injury to the participant; and

(8) a statement that participation is voluntary, refusal to participate will involve no penalty or loss of benefits to which the participant is otherwise entitled, and the participant may discontinue participation at any time without penalty or loss of benefits to which the participant is otherwise entitled.

TABLE 3.2 Sample Informed Consent Form

Consent Form: Interactions

I state that I am eighteen years of age or older and wish to participate in a program of research being conducted by Dr. Charles Stangor at the University of Maryland, College Park, Department of Psychology.

The purpose of the research is to study how individuals get to know each other. In the remainder of the study I will be having a short conversation with another person. This interaction will be videotaped. At the end of the interaction, I will be asked to complete some questionnaires about how I felt during and what I remember about the interaction. The entire experiment will take about forty-five minutes.

I furthermore consent to allow the videotape that has been made of me and my partner to be used in the research. I understand that the videotape will be used for research purposes only, and no one else except the present experimenter and one other person who will help code the tape will ever view it.

I understand that code numbers will be used to identify the videotapes, and that all written material that I contribute will be kept separate from the videos. As a result, it will not be possible to connect my name to my videotape.

I understand that both myself and my partner have the right to withdraw the tape from the study at any point.

I understand that the experiment is not designed to help me personally, but that the researchers hope to learn more about interpersonal interactions.

I understand that I am free to ask questions or to withdraw from participation at any time without penalty.

Dr. Charles Stangor
Department of Psychology
Room 3123
555–5921

Signature of participant _____

Date _____

A sample informed consent form is shown in Table 3.2. Informed consent involves several aspects, each of which is designed to reduce the possibility of ethical problems. First, the potential participant is presented with a sheet of paper on which to record demographic information, including age. This information assures the experimenter that the research participant is old enough to make her or his own decision about whether or not to participate. When children are used in research, the corresponding ethical safeguards are even more rigorous. In this case, a parent or guardian must give approval for the individual to participate in research. The American Psychological Association (APA) and the Society for Research in Child Development (SRCD) have developed guidelines for research with children as well as adults.

Second, the potential participant is given an informed consent form explaining the procedure of the research, who is conducting it, how the results of the research will be used, and what is going to happen during the research session. Third, the potential participant is informed of her or his rights during the research. These rights include the freedom to leave the research project at any point without penalty and the knowledge that the data will be kept confidential. After carefully reading this information, the individual is given the opportunity to ask any questions. At this point, the participant signs the form to indicate that she or he has read and (the researcher hopes) understood the information.

It is rare that an individual declines to participate in or continue a behavioral research project. This is perhaps because of the use of informed consent and the determination by the researcher that the research project is not ethically problematic, but it may also be due to social factors that reduce the likelihood of quitting. Once a participant has arrived at the research session (and even more so when the project has begun), it becomes difficult for him or her to express a desire to leave. As a result, the researcher must continually keep in mind that he or she has great control over the behaviors of the research participant, must continually be on the lookout for signs that the participant is uncomfortable, and must be prepared to stop the research if any problems surface.

Because many students participate in research projects to earn credit in behavioral science courses, one issue that sometimes arises concerns how to treat a student who decides not to participate. When this decision is made before the research begins, it seems reasonable not to give credit because the student can usually find another experiment to participate in with which he or she is more comfortable. However, for a person who has already begun the procedure under the good faith of finishing but later decides to quit, it is usually better to award full credit.

Weighing Informed Consent Versus the Research Goals

Although informed consent has obvious advantages from the point of view of the participant, it has disadvantages from the point of view of the researcher. Consider what might have happened if Milgram had told his research participants that his experiment was about obedience to authority, rather than telling them that he was studying learning. In that case, the participants would probably have carefully monitored their behavior to avoid being seen as "obedient" types, and he would have obtained very different results. However, the participants' behavior in that case would seem to reflect more a reaction to the informed consent form than what might be expected if the participants had not been alerted. In such cases, the preferred strategy is to tell participants as much as possible about the true nature of the study, particularly everything that might be expected to influence their willingness to participate, while still withholding the pieces of information that allow the study to work. Often creative uses of informed consent may allow researchers to provide accurate information to participants and still enable the research to continue. For instance, participants may be told that they may or may not be given alcohol or that their behavior may or may not be videotaped at some point.

In these cases, the individuals are informed of the procedures and potential risks and give their consent to participate in any or all of the procedures they might encounter, but the research is not jeopardized.

Maintaining Awareness of Power Differentials

One of the basic ethical concerns in research with humans involves the inherent power differential between the researcher and the research participant. This differential occurs because the researcher has higher status than the participant and thus is able (and indeed expected) to control the participant's behavior and also how the data contributed are used. The experimenter tells the participant what to do and when to do it and also determines whether the participant receives course credit or payment for participation. Although, as we will discuss in the next section, ethical procedures require that the participant always have the option to choose not to participate in the research and to withdraw his or her data, the high-status researcher may be influential in preventing him or her from doing so.[1]

Avoiding Abuses of Power

The fact that the researcher has power over the participant places the researcher in a position in which there is the possibility for abuse of this power. Such abuse might range from showing up late to the research session without apology, to promising the participant money for participation that is not actually available, or even to hypnotizing the participant and attempting to learn intimate details about his or her life without the participant's knowledge. Any time the research participant is coerced into performing a behavior that he or she later regrets, the power relationship between the researcher and the participant has been misused. The inherent power differential between researcher and participant demands that the former continually and carefully ensure that all research participants have been treated fairly and respectfully.

Respecting Participants' Privacy

One potential source of ethical concern in behavioral research, which stems from the control the researcher has over the use of the participant's data, involves the invasion of the privacy of the research participants or violations of the confidentiality of the data that they contribute. The private lives of research participants may be invaded in field research when, for instance, the researcher searches through the garbage in a neighborhood or observes behavior in a public setting such as in a small town. These issues become

---

[1]This power relationship is explicit in the use of the term *subject* to refer to the research participant. Although it is now more acceptable to use less impersonal terms, such as *participant* or *respondent* (American Psychological Association, 1994), the true power relationship between the experimenter and the research participant has not changed.

particularly problematic when the research results are later published in a manner in which the identities of the individuals might be discovered. As a result, scientists often use fictitious names of persons and places in their research reports.

The privacy of research participants may also be violated in questionnaire and laboratory studies. In many cases, respecting the privacy of participants is not a major problem because the data are not that personally revealing. Exceptions may occur when the questionnaires involve intimate personal information such as sexual behavior or alcohol and drug use. In such cases the data should be kept *anonymous*. The respondent does not put any identifying information onto the questionnaire, and therefore the researcher cannot tell which participant contributed the data. To help ensure that the data are anonymous, individuals can seal their questionnaires in an envelope and place them with other sealed envelopes in a box. (As we will see in later chapters, making the data anonymous may also lead the respondents to answer questions more honestly.)

In other cases, the data cannot be anonymous because the researcher needs to keep track of which respondent contributed the data. This holds true when questionnaires are given to the same people at more than one time point or when participants are selected on the basis of their questionnaires for follow-up research. Here, the solution that respects the privacy of the individual is to keep the data *confidential*. One technique is to have each participant use a unique code number to identify her or his data, such as the last four digits of the social security number. In this way, the researcher can keep track of which person completed which questionnaire, but others will not be able to connect the data with the individual who contributed it. In all cases, collected data that have any identifying information must be kept in locked rooms or storage cabinets to ensure confidentiality, and the researcher must be aware of the potential for abuse of such information. Because many data are now stored on computer disks, the researcher must be especially careful that no copies of these data are in the public domain, such as stored on public-access computer networks.

Honestly Describing the Nature and Use of the Research

Perhaps the most widespread ethical concern to the participants in behavioral research is the extent to which researchers employ deception. **Deception** occurs whenever research participants are not completely and fully informed about the nature of the research project before participating in it. Deception may occur in an active way, such as when the researcher tells the participants that he or she is studying learning when in fact the experiment really concerns obedience to authority. In other cases the deception is more passive, such as when participants are not told about the hypothesis being studied or the potential use of the data being collected. For instance, a researcher studying eyewitness testimony might create a fake crime scene and then later test the participants on their memory of it.

Both active and passive deception can be problematic. For instance, an experiment in which individuals participated in a study about interviewing without first being told that the results of the research were going to be used to develop interrogation procedures for prisoners of war would be highly unethical, even though the deception was passive in nature, because participants might have decided not to participate in the research had they been fully informed.

When Deception Is Necessary

The argument against the use of deception in behavioral research is straightforward. The relationship between the researcher and the participant is based on mutual trust and cooperation. If deception is involved, this trust may be broken. Although some have argued that deception of any sort should never be used in any research (Baumrind, 1985), there are also persuasive arguments supporting its use. Social psychologists defend the use of deception on the grounds that it is needed to get participants to act naturally and to enable the study of social phenomena. They argue that it would be impossible to study such phenomena as altruism, aggression, and stereotyping *without* using deception because if participants were informed ahead of time what the study involved, this knowledge would certainly change their behavior. Furthermore, social psychologists argue that to study some phenomena, such as stress, it is more ethical to deceive the participants into thinking that they are going to participate in a stressful situation than to actually expose them to the stress itself.

One review found that 58 percent of social psychological experiments used some form of deception (Adair, Dushenko, & Lindsay, 1985). The need to employ deception in order to conduct certain types of research has been recognized by scientists, and the code of ethics of the APA allows deception (including concealed observation) when necessary. However, given the potential dangers of deception, the APA code also requires researchers to explicitly consider how their research might be conducted without the use of deception. (Other scientific organizations also have codes of ethics regarding the treatment of research participants.)

Simulation Studies: An Alternative to Deception

One technique for avoiding deception in some cases is the use of simulation studies (Rubin, 1973). In a **simulation study,** participants are fully informed about the nature of the research and asked to behave "as if" they were in a social setting of interest. A situation is set up that is similar to that in the real world in terms of important elements. For instance, people might be asked to imagine that they are a manager of a large corporation and to make decisions the way they think a manager would, or they might be asked to imagine a situation in which they might or might not help another person. Unfortunately, as we have seen in Chapter 1, asking people what they think they would do often does not reflect what they actually do. In fact, the power of much behavioral research is the demonstration that people cannot predict what they, or others, would do in a given setting.

Despite these problems, some simulation studies have been very effective in providing insights into human behavior. One well-known example is the "Stanford Prison Study" (Haney, Banks, & Zimbardo, 1973). In this study, college students were randomly assigned to play the role of either prisoners or prison guards in a mock prison. Those assigned to be prisoners were "arrested," issued prison numbers, and put in cells. The participants who became "guards" were given uniforms and nightsticks. This simulation was so successful in the sense of participants taking it seriously that on the first day the "guards" began to create demeaning experiences for "prisoners" who banded together in a hunger strike. The study had to be canceled after only a few days because of the potential for psychological stress to the "inmates."

The Consequences of Deception

As with any ethical decision, there are differences of opinion about the appropriateness of using deception. Some scientists believe that deception should never be used in any research (Ortmann & Hertwig, 1997), whereas others believe that deception is a normal and useful part of psychological research (Kimmel, 1998). Although it is always preferable, when possible, to avoid the use of deception (and in fact many experiments are entirely "honest"), research investigating the effects of deception on participants in behavioral research suggests that its use does not normally produce any long-lasting psychological harm. In fact, students who have participated in experiments in which they have been deceived report enjoying them more and receiving more educational benefits from them than have those who participated in nondeceptive research (Smith & Richardson, 1983). It is ironic, in fact, that the use of deception may be more harmful to the ability of the researchers to continue their research than it is to the research participants. Because the use of deception is so widespread, participants may arrive at studies expecting to be deceived. As a result, the deception used in the research is not likely to be effective in accomplishing the goals for which it was designed. Thus, the most powerful argument against the use of deception is that its continued use may defeat the goals of behavioral science research itself!

Debriefing

Because behavioral science research has the potential for producing long-term changes in the research participants, these participants should be fully debriefed after their participation. The **debriefing** occurs immediately after the research has ended and is designed to explain the purposes and procedures of the research and remove any harmful aftereffects of participation. Although debriefing is an essential part of all behavioral research, it is particularly important in research that involves deception because it can be used both to assess the effectiveness of the deception and to alleviate its potential impact on research participants. Because this portion of the experiment is so important, sufficient time to do it properly should always be allotted.

Conducting a Postexperimental Interview.   In many cases, the debriefing procedure is rather elaborate and is combined with a **postexperimental interview** in which the participants' reactions to the research are assessed. The participants may first be asked to verbally express or (if they are run in groups) to write down their thoughts about the research. These reactions may often indicate whether the respondents experienced the research as expected, if they were suspicious, and if they have taken the research seriously.

When deception has been used, the researcher may want to determine if it has been effective through the use of a **suspicion check**—questioning the participants to determine whether they believed the experimental manipulation or guessed the research hypothesis. One approach, proposed by Mills (1976), is to tell the participants that "there is more to this experiment than I have told you. I'm curious—do you know what it might be?" The idea is that if the participant is suspicious about the deception, he or she will say so ("I knew that there really wasn't anyone in the other room"), whereas participants who are not suspicious will not know how to answer the question or will answer with something irrelevant.

After this initial part of the debriefing is completed, the researcher next fully explains in detail the purposes of the experiment, including the research hypothesis and how it is being tested. The scientist should explain the goals of the research in an accurate and fair manner, and the importance of the research should not be overstated. Thus, the debriefing also serves an educational function in which the participants learn something about behavioral science research and how it is conducted. Because the educational value of participation in a research project is one of the benefits of behavioral research, the researcher should be sure to design the debriefing to maximize this function.

The last goal of the debriefing is to try to eliminate long-term consequences of having participated in the research. Any deception that has been used is fully explained to the participants, and its necessity is justified. A thorough debriefing procedure has been shown to be an effective method of reducing the harmful effects of deception (Smith & Richardson, 1983).

Finally, the participants are given ample time to ask questions about the research and may be requested not to discuss the research with others until the end of the semester, or whenever the data collection will have finished. The experimenter should be certain to supply his or her name and telephone number to the participants and encourage them to call with any questions or concerns.

Ensuring the Effectiveness of the Debriefing.   Debriefing does not solve all the problems of treating participants with respect, nor does it guarantee that the outcomes of unethical procedures can be "taken back" through follow-up procedures. Ill effects may persist even after debriefing (Ross, Lepper, & Hubbard, 1975), particularly when the participant has been led to engage in embarrassing or stressful behaviors. When this might be the case, the experimenter may conduct a **process debriefing**—an active attempt to undo any changes that might have occurred. For instance, if the experiment has involved the creation of a negative mood state, a positive mood induction procedure

TABLE 3.3 Characteristics of an Ethical Research Project Using Human Participants

Trust and positive rapport are created between the researcher and the participant.

The rights of both the experimenter and participant are considered, and the relationship between them is mutually beneficial.

The experimenter treats the participant with concern and respect and attempts to make the research experience a pleasant and informative one.

Before the research begins, the participant is given all information relevant to his or her decision to participate, including any possibilities of physical danger or psychological stress.

The participant is given a chance to have questions about the procedure answered, thus guaranteeing his or her free choice about participating.

After the experiment is over, any deception that has been used is made public, and the necessity for it is explained.

The experimenter carefully debriefs the participant, explaining the underlying research hypothesis and the purpose of the experimental procedure in detail and answering any questions.

The experimenter provides information about how he or she can be contacted and offers to provide information about the results of the research if the participant is interested in receiving it.

might be given to all participants before they leave. However, despite the use of careful debriefing procedures, it is often almost impossible to entirely undo the effects of experimental manipulations, and a participant who has engaged in behaviors that he or she later regrets may be affected by these behaviors despite a careful debriefing.

In the end, what is most important is that the participants feel that they have been treated fairly in the experiment. Some of the most important characteristics of an ethical research project using human participants are outlined in Table 3.3. The manner in which the debriefing is conducted may have a large impact on the participants' feelings about being deceived and their perceptions of the research. Other experimenter behaviors that can lead to more positive experiences for the participants include showing up on time, acting in a friendly manner, allowing enough time for questions to arise, and offering to send the written results of research projects to participants if they want them (and then actually doing so). Of course, when participants receive course credit for participation, the experimenter is also expected to report their participation in the research to the appropriate people in a timely manner. Because experimenters have higher status than participants, this relationship can easily be abused, and researchers must continually strive to avoid such problems.

Using Animals as Research Participants

To this point in this chapter we have been considering the ethical decisions involved in conducting research with human beings. But because animals make up an important part of the natural world, and because some research cannot be conducted using humans, animals are also participants in behavioral research. Probably to a large extent because of ethical concerns, most research is now conducted with rats, mice, and birds, and the use of other animals in research is declining (Thomas & Blackman, 1992). As with ethical decisions regarding human participants, a set of basic principles has been developed that helps researchers make informed decisions about such research.

Because the use of animals in research involves a personal value, people naturally disagree about this practice. Although many people accept the value of such research (Plous, 1996), a minority of people, including animal-rights activists, believe that it is ethically wrong to conduct research on animals. They base this argument on the assumption that because animals are also living creatures, they have the same status as humans and no harm should ever be done to any living thing.

Most scientists, however, reject this view. They argue that such beliefs ignore the potential benefits that have and continue to come from such research. For instance, drugs that can reduce the incidence of cancer or acquired immune deficiency syndrome may first be tested on animals, and surgery that can save human lives may first be practiced on animals. Research on animals has also led to a better understanding of the physiological causes of depression, phobias, and stress, among other illnesses (Miller, 1985).

In contrast to animal-rights activists, then, scientists believe that because there are many benefits that accrue from animal research, such research can and should continue as long as the humane treatment of the animals used in the research is guaranteed. And the animals that are used in scientific research are treated humanely. The scientists who use them in their research are extremely careful to maintain the animals in good health—after all, a healthy animal is the best research participant. Furthermore, they use the fewest animals necessary for the research, and they subject them to the least possible amount of stress. A summary of the American Psychological Association's guidelines regarding the care and use of animals in research is presented in Table 3.4.

Ensuring That Research Is Ethical

Making decisions about the ethics of research involves weighing the costs and benefits of conducting versus not conducting a given research project. We have seen that these costs involve potential harm to the research participants, and to the field, whereas the benefits include knowledge about human behavior and educational gains to the individual participants. Most generally, the ethics of a given research project are determined through a cost-benefit analysis, in which the costs are compared to the benefits. If the potential costs of the research appear to outweigh any potential benefits that might come from it, then the research should not proceed.

Of course, arriving at a cost-benefit ratio is not simple. For one thing, there is no way to know ahead of time what the effects of a given procedure

TABLE 3.4   APA Guidelines on Humane Care and Use of Animals in Research

The following are some of the most important ethical principles from the American Psychological Association's guidelines on research with animals.

Psychologists acquire, care for, use, and dispose of animals in compliance with current federal, state, and local laws and regulations, and with professional standards.

Psychologists trained in research methods and experienced in the care of laboratory animals supervise all procedures involving animals and are responsible for ensuring appropriate consideration of their comfort, health, and humane treatment.

Psychologists ensure that all individuals under their supervision who are using animals have received instruction in research methods and in the care, maintenance, and handling of the species being used, to the extent appropriate to their role. (See also Standard 2.05, Delegation of Work to Others.)

Psychologists make reasonable efforts to minimize the discomfort, infection, illness, and pain of animal subjects.

Psychologists use a procedure subjecting animals to pain, stress, or privation only when an alternative procedure is unavailable and the goal is justified by its prospective scientific, educational, or applied value.

Psychologists perform surgical procedures under appropriate anesthesia and follow techniques to avoid infection and minimize pain during and after surgery.

When it is appropriate that an animal's life be terminated, psychologists proceed rapidly, with an effort to minimize pain and in accordance with accepted procedures.

Source: American Psychological Association (2002). Ethical principles of psychologists. *American Psychologist, 57,* 1060–1073.

will be on every person or animal who participates or what benefit to society the research is likely to produce. In addition, what is ethical is defined by the current state of thinking within society, and thus costs and benefits change over time. Consider, for instance, a classic experiment by Aronson and Mills (1959) investigating the hypothesis that individuals who underwent a severe initiation in order to be admitted to a group would later have greater attraction to the group than to individuals who had not been so initiated.

Female undergraduates were told that they would subsequently be joining a discussion group on the "psychology of sex." In some of the conditions, participants were asked if they would be embarrassed to talk about sex. If they answered no, they were admitted to the group. But in the "severe initiation" condition, participants were told that they had to prove that they could discuss sex frankly, and they were asked to read aloud (to the male experimenter) a list of twelve obscene words and two vivid descriptions of sexual activity from contemporary novels before joining the group.

Because today's standards are different than they were in 1959, such an experiment would probably be perceived by most as a violation of ethical principles. Society no longer considers it appropriate for a powerful male experimenter to require a less powerful female undergraduate to talk about sexual behavior in his presence. Although the women were given the choice of not participating, it was most certainly difficult for them to do so, as they would have lost their experimental credit as well as the time they had spent signing up for and reporting to the experiment.

One interesting tack on determining the cost-benefit ratio is to assess it empirically. One approach (Berscheid, Baron, Dermer, & Libman, 1973) is to describe the research project in its entirety to a separate group of individuals who are similar to potential participants and inquire whether they would participate. Alternatively, the research could be described and people asked to rate the potential costs to participants (Schlenker & Forsyth, 1977). Again, potential participants do not seem to perceive most research as unethical. In fact, students generally rate the potential benefits as greater than the costs and estimate a lower cost-benefit ratio than do the scientists conducting the research!

The Institutional Review Board

The U.S. Department of Health and Human Services regulations require that all universities receiving funds from the department set up an **institutional review board (IRB)** to determine whether proposed research meets department regulations. The IRB consists of at least five members, including, in addition to scientists, at least one individual whose primary interest is in nonscientific domains (for instance, a community member, a religious leader, or a legal specialist) and at least one member who is not affiliated with the institution at which the research is to be conducted. This composition ensures that the group represents a variety of areas of expertise, not just other scientists, who may tend to overrate the importance of scientific research.

All federally funded research, and almost all university research that is not federally funded, must be approved by the IRB. To gain approval, the scientist submits a written application to the IRB requesting permission to conduct research. This proposal must include a description of the experimental procedure and, if the research uses human participants, an explanation of how informed consent will be obtained and how the participants will be debriefed.

In addition, the application must detail any potential risks to the participants, as well as the potential benefits to be gained from the research. The basic goal of the IRB is to determine, on the basis of the research description, the cost-benefit ratio of a study. The IRB may suggest modifications to the procedure or (in rare cases) may inform the scientist that the research violates Department of Health and Human Services guidelines and thus cannot be conducted at the university. A similar committee, the animal care and use committee, makes decisions about animal research and ensures that animals used in research are treated in a humane manner. Board members conduct regular inspections of all of the animal labs at the institution to be certain that the animals are healthy and free from stress and that the research is conducted in accordance with appropriate guidelines.

The Researcher's Own Ethics

Despite the possibility of empirical assessment of ethical questions and the availability of institutional guidelines, because questions of scientific ethics are at heart issues of personal value, each person must draw her or his own conclusions about what is right and what is wrong in scientific research. Thus, the ultimate responsibility lies with the investigator. Unfortunately, there is no single method for anticipating and alleviating all the possible ethical problems that can arise in the conduct of behavioral research. Rather, what is involved is an attempt to find an appropriate balance between the rights and dignity of the research participants and the importance of continuing scientific inquiry.

Overall, when the proper safeguards are followed, the rights and dignity of human participants are generally upheld. Yet, each research project has to be evaluated in terms of potential ethical problems. Sometimes alternative procedures can be used; at other times the study must be canceled. When in doubt, consult with instructors or colleagues and others outside of the field. In many cases, the IRB at your university will be the final judge of the ethics of your research.

Correctly and Honestly Reporting Research Results

Although to this point we have focused on the safety, rights, and dignity of the research participant, ethical behavior in science includes honesty not only in conducting research, but also in reporting it and giving proper credit for ideas. Science is based on truth, and scientists are expected to be truthful in all aspects of their research. In this sense, the rules are simple—report exactly what you did and what you discovered in your research. Do not lie or mislead the reader in any way. The methods of the research should be completely and fully described, and the statistical analyses reported accurately. According to American Psychology Association guidelines, scientists are also obligated to publish corrections to existing publications if they later discover significant errors in them. Furthermore, scientists are obligated to interpret their data as fairly as they can. Remember that it is completely appropriate to use the work of others as a basis for your research—but do not plagiarize. When you have taken ideas from others, be certain to appropriately cite the sources of the work.

Although we can assume that most scientists are honest, they are nevertheless only human, and therefore, some errors will occasionally be made. In some cases, mistakes are made because the scientist is not careful about how he or she collects and analyzes data. For instance, errors may be made in key-punching the data or in the process of conducting the statistical analyses. It is, therefore, extremely important that researchers check their data carefully to be sure that their statistical analyses are correct. Some suggestions for ensuring that data are analyzed correctly can be found in Appendix B of this book.

In rare cases, a scientist may intentionally alter or fabricate data, and in such cases we say that he or she has committed **scientific fraud.** Although scientific fraud does not happen very often, it is a very serious event when it does occur, because it can lead people to adopt unwise social policies on the basis of the fraudulent data, or can lead scientists to spend time conducting follow-up research that is based on invalid knowledge.

Because scientific fraud is so costly, scientists are naturally concerned to prevent its occurrence. The most effective route is for each scientist to take full responsibility for his or her research and to carefully monitor the behavior of his or her co-workers. Fortunately, most scientists do not want to commit fraud, because if they do so they know that their research results will not be able to be replicated by others, and, as we will see in Chapter 12, it is this replication that leads to scientific progress.

SUMMARY

Because research using humans and animals has the potential to both benefit and harm those participants, the ethics of conducting versus not conducting a research project must be carefully evaluated before it is begun. There are no clear-cut right or wrong answers to questions about research ethics, but there are a set of ethical principles, developed by scientific organizations and regulatory agencies, that must be adhered to by those conducting behavioral research.

Conducting ethical research with human participants involves avoiding psychological and physical harm to research participants, providing freedom of choice, treating participants with respect, and honestly describing the nature and use of the research. Behavioral research with animals must be conducted such that the animals are treated humanely at all times.

Decisions about what research is appropriate and ethical are based on careful consideration of the potential costs and benefits to both the participants in the research and the advancement of science. The procedures that are followed to ensure that no harm is done to the participants include the use of informed consent before the experiment begins and a thorough debriefing in which the purposes and procedures of the research are explained in detail to the participants.

In most cases the institutional review board (IRB) at the institution where the research is being conducted will help the scientist determine whether his or her research is ethical.

KEY TERMS

debriefing 54

deception 52

informed consent 48

institutional review board (IRB) 59

postexperimental interview 55

process debriefing 55

scientific fraud 60

simulation study 53

suspicion check 55

REVIEW AND DISCUSSION QUESTIONS

1. Compare the ethical dilemmas faced by behavioral scientists with those faced by scientists in other scientific fields. What are the particular ethical problems that arise in behavioral science research?

2. Explain why deception is used in behavioral research, and then express your personal feelings about the use of deception. Should deception ever be used? If not, why not? If so, what are the allowable limits of deception?

3. Consider the four principles of ethical research with human participants outlined in the chapter. What procedures are used by behavioral scientists to help ensure that their research conforms to these principles?

4. What are *informed consent* and *debriefing*, and what is their purpose in behavioral research? Is it ever ethical to conduct research that does not use informed consent? Is it ever ethical to conduct behavioral research that does not use debriefing?

5. What are the arguments for and against the use of animals in research? What steps are taken to ensure the health and welfare of research animals?

RESEARCH PROJECT IDEAS

1. For each of the following studies, consider whether or not you think the research is ethical, how the research may have violated principles of ethical behavior, and what, if any, alternative research methods for testing the research hypothesis might have been used:

   a. College students were asked to volunteer for an experiment involving betting behavior. Then they were told that they could choose either to receive $3.00 for their participation or they could gamble for the possibility of earning more money. After the experiment was conducted, participants were told that the experimenters did not actually have any money to pay them, but that the deception had been necessary in order to obtain their participation in the research.

   b. A study was done in a small company in which most of the employees knew each other. Detailed reports of the interactions of the workers were published in a book. Although some attempt was made to disguise the names of the individuals, any employee who read the book could identify who was being referred to.

   c. A researcher was studying initial interactions between people. While two students were supposedly waiting for an experiment to begin, the researcher covertly videotaped their actions and conversation. The researcher then told them about the research and gave them the opportunity to have the tape erased.

d. A researcher worked for a time on the production line of a large manu-facturing plant. His status as a researcher was unknown to his co-workers. It was not until he was about to leave that he revealed his purpose and identity to the workers.

e. Students who were interested in attending medical school participated in a study where the researcher gave them false negative feedback about their scores on the Medical College Admission Tests (MCAT). The stu-dents were presented with "sample" MCAT questions that did not have any correct answers. Consequently, the students performed very poorly on the exam, and the researchers studied their anxiety and how they coped with failure.

f. To study what types of people are most likely to give money to a stranger, people on city streets were asked for money by an individual who said he had just lost his wallet. No one was ever told that he or she was part of a research project.

g. To study the effects of alcohol on decision making, a graduate student interviewed college students after they had left a campus bar. With a portable breathalyzer, he registered their blood alcohol content. Al-though some of them were found to be intoxicated beyond the legal state limits, and although many of them were going to be driving home, he did not inform them of their blood alcohol levels.

h. A psychologist teaching a large lecture class conducted an experiment in which the letter grades assigned the students in different sections of the course were deliberately raised or lowered so that the same score on an examination might be an "A" in one section and a "C" in another section. The purpose of the experiment was to determine the effect of this feed-back on achievement on the final examination.

2. Contact the chairperson of the institutional review board at your university. Find out who the current members of the committee are and what types of research they have recently considered for approval.

3. Consider any potential ethical problems for each of the research designs you developed in Research Project Idea 1 in Chapter 2.

PART **TWO**
Measuring and Describing

CHAPTER FOUR
Measures

STUDY QUESTIONS

- What is the difference between conceptual and measured variables?

- What is an operational definition?

- What are the differences among nominal, ordinal, interval, and ratio scale variables?

- What are projective tests, associative lists, and think-aloud protocols? What is each designed to measure?

- What are Likert, semantic differential, and Guttman scales? What is each used to measure?

- What is reactivity, and how can measured variables be designed to avoid it?

- How are behavioral measures used in research?

- What are the advantages and disadvantages of using self-report versus behavioral measures?

We have seen in Chapters 1 and 2 that the basis of science is empirical measurement of relevant variables. Formally, **measurement** refers to the assignment of numbers to objects or events according to specific rules (Coombs, 1964). We assign numbers to events in everyday life, for instance, when we rate a movie as a "nine out of ten" or when a hotel is rated "three star." As in everyday life, measurement is possible in science because we can use numbers to represent the variables we are interested in studying. In this chapter and the next, we will discuss how behavioral scientists decide what to measure, the techniques they use to measure, and how they determine whether these measures are effective.

Fundamentals of Measurement

You will recall from Chapter 2 that the research hypothesis involves a prediction about the relationship between or among two or more variables—for instance, the relationship between self-esteem and college performance or between study time and memory. When stated in an abstract manner, the ideas that form the basis of a research hypothesis are known as **conceptual variables.** Behavioral scientists have been interested in such conceptual variables as self-esteem, parenting style, depression, and cognitive development.

Measurement involves turning conceptual variables into **measured variables,** which consist of numbers that represent the conceptual variables.[1] The measured variables are frequently referred to as **measures** of the conceptual variables. In some cases, the transformation from conceptual to measured variable is direct. For instance, the conceptual variable "study time" is straightforwardly represented as the measured variable "seconds of study." But other conceptual variables can be assessed by many different measures. For instance, the conceptual variable "liking" could be assessed by a person rating, from one to ten, how much he or she likes another person. Alternatively, liking could be measured in terms of how often a person looks at or touches another person or the number of love letters that he or she writes. And liking could also be measured using physiological indicators such as an increase in heart rate when two people are in the vicinity of each other.

Operational Definition

The term **operational definition** refers to a precise statement of how a conceptual variable is turned into a measured variable. Research can only proceed once an adequate operational definition has been defined. In some cases the conceptual variable may be too vague to be operationalized, and in other

---

[1]You will recall that in correlational research all of the variables are measured, whereas in experiments only the dependent variable is measured.

TABLE 4.1 Operational Definitions

Conceptual Variable	Operational Definitions
Employee satisfaction	Number of days per month that the employee shows up to work on time
	Rating of job satisfaction from 1 (not at all satisfied) to 9 (extremely satisfied)
Aggression	Number of presses of a button that administers shock to another student
	Time taken to honk the horn at the car ahead after a stoplight turns green
Attraction	Number of inches that an individual places his or her chair away from another person
	Number of millimeters of pupil dilation when one person looks at another
Depression	Number of negative words used in a creative story
	Number of appointments with a psychotherapist
Decision-making	Number of people correctly solving a group performance task
	Speed at which a task is solved

cases the variable cannot be operationalized because the appropriate technology has not been developed. For instance, recent advances in brain imaging have allowed new operationalizations of some variables that could not have been measured even a few years ago. Table 4.1 lists some potential operational definitions of conceptual variables that have been used in behavioral research. As you read through this list, note that in contrast to the abstract conceptual variables (employee satisfaction, frustration, depression), the measured variables are very specific. This specificity is important for two reasons. First, more specific definitions mean that there is less danger that the collected data will be misunderstood by others. Second, specific definitions will enable future researchers to replicate the research.

Converging Operations

That there are many possible measures for a single conceptual variable might seem a scientific problem. But it is not. In fact, multiple possible measures represent a great advantage to researchers. For one thing, no single operational definition of a given conceptual variable can be considered the best. Different types of measures may be more appropriate in different research contexts. For instance, how close a person sits to another person might serve as a measure of liking in an observational research design, whereas heart rate might be more appropriate in a laboratory study. Furthermore, the ability to use different operationalizations of the same conceptual variable allows the researcher to hone in, or to "triangulate," on the conceptual variable of interest. When the same conceptual variable is measured using different measures, we can get a fuller and better measure of it. Because this principle is so important, we will discuss it more fully in subsequent chapters. This is an example of the use of *converging operations*, as discussed in Chapter 1.

The researcher must choose which operational definition to use in trying to assess the conceptual variables of interest. In general, there is no guarantee that the chosen measured variable will prove to be an adequate measure of the conceptual variable. As we will see in Chapter 5, however, there are ways to assess the effectiveness of the measures once they have been collected.

Conceptual and Measured Variables

The relationship between conceptual and measured variables in a correlational research design is diagrammed in Figure 4.1. The conceptual variables are represented within circles at the top of the figure, and the measured variables are represented within squares at the bottom. The two vertical arrows, which lead from the conceptual variables to the measured variables, represent the operational definitions of the two variables. The arrows indicate the expectation that changes in the conceptual variables (job satisfaction and job performance in this example) will cause changes in the corresponding measured variables. The measured variables are then used to draw inferences about the conceptual variables.

FIGURE 4.1   Conceptual and Measured Variables in a Correlational
Research Design

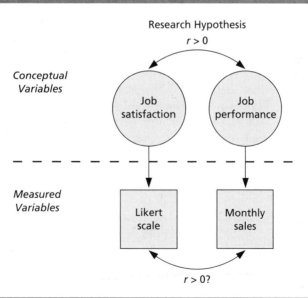

The research depicted here tests the correlational relationship between the conceptual variables of job satisfaction and job performance, using a specific operational definition of each. If the research hypothesis (that job performance is correlated with job satisfaction) is correct, and if the measured variables actually measure the conceptual variables, then a relationship between the two measured variables (the bottom curved arrow) should be observed.

You can see that there are also two curved arrows in Figure 4.1. The top arrow diagrams the research hypothesis—namely, that changes in job satisfaction are related to changes in job performance. The basic assumption involved in testing the research hypothesis is as follows:

- if the research hypothesis (that the two conceptual variables are correlated) is correct, and

- if the measured variables are adequate—that is, if there is a relationship between both of the conceptual and measured variables (the two vertical arrows in the figure)—then

- a relationship between the two measured variables (the bottom arrow in the figure) will be observed (cf. Nunnally, 1978).

The ultimate goal of the research is to learn about the relationship between the conceptual variables. But, the ability to learn about this relationship is dependent on the operational definitions. If the measures do not really measure the conceptual variables, then they cannot be used to draw inferences about the relationship between the conceptual variables. Thus, the adequacy of a test of any research hypothesis is limited by the adequacy of the measurement of the conceptual variables.

Nominal and Quantitative Variables

Measured variables can be divided into two major types: nominal variables and quantitative variables. A **nominal variable** is used to name or identify a particular characteristic. For instance, sex is a nominal variable that identifies whether a person is male or female, and religion is a nominal variable that identifies whether a person is Catholic, Buddhist, Jewish, or some other religion. Nominal variables are also frequently used in behavioral research to indicate the condition that a person has been assigned to in an experimental research design (for instance, whether she or he is in the "experimental condition" or the "control condition").

Nominal variables indicate the fact that people who share a value on the variable (for instance, all men or all the people in the control condition of an experiment) are equivalent in some way, whereas those that do not share the value are different from each other. Numbers are generally used to indicate the values of a nominal variable, such as when we represent the experimental condition of an experiment with the number 1 and the control condition of the experiment with the number 2. However, the numbers used to represent the categories of a nominal variable are arbitrary, and thus we could change which numbers represent which categories, or even label the categories with letters or names instead of numbers, without losing any information.

In contrast to a nominal variable, which names or identifies, a **quantitative variable** uses numbers to indicate the extent to which a person possesses a characteristic of interest. Quantitative variables indicate such things as how attractive a person is, how quickly she or he can complete a task, or how many siblings she or he has. For instance, on a rating of perceived attractiveness, the number 10 might indicate greater attractiveness than the number 5.

Measurement Scales

Specifying the relationship between the numbers on a quantitative measured variable and the values of the conceptual variable is known as **scaling.** In some cases in the natural sciences, the mapping between the measure and the conceptual variable is quite precise. As an example, we are all familiar with the use of the Fahrenheit scale to measure temperature. In the Fahrenheit scale, the relationship between the measured variable (degrees Fahrenheit) and the conceptual variable (temperature) is so precise that we can be certain that changes in the measured variable correspond exactly to changes in the conceptual variable.

In this case, we can be certain that the difference between any two points on the scale (the degrees) refers to equal changes in the conceptual variable across the entire scale. For instance, we can state that the difference in temperature between 10 and 20 degrees Fahrenheit is exactly the same as the difference in temperature between 70 and 80 degrees Fahrenheit. When equal distances between scores on a measure are known to correspond to equal changes in the conceptual variable (such as on the Fahrenheit scale), we call the measure an **interval scale.**

Now consider measures of length, such as feet and inches or the metric scale, which uses millimeters, centimeters, and meters. Such scales have all of the properties of an interval scale because equal changes between the points on the scale (centimeters for instance) correspond to equal changes in the conceptual variable (length). But, measures of length also have a true zero point that represents the complete absence of the conceptual variable—zero length. Interval scales that also have a true zero point are known as **ratio scales** (the Kelvin temperature scale, where zero degrees represents absolute zero, is another example of a ratio scale). In addition to being able to compare intervals, the presence of a zero point on a ratio scale also allows us to multiply and divide scale values. When measuring length, for instance, we can say that a person who is 6 feet tall is twice as tall as a child who is 3 feet tall.

In most behavioral science research, the scaling of the measured variable is not as straightforward as it is in the measurement of temperature or length. Measures in the behavioral sciences normally constitute only ordinal scales. In an **ordinal scale,** the numbers indicate whether there is more or less of the conceptual variable, but they do not indicate the exact interval between the individuals on the conceptual variable. For instance, if you rated the friendliness of five of your friends from 1 (least friendly) to 9 (most friendly), the scores would constitute an ordinal scale. The scores tell us the ordering of the people (that you believe Malik, whom you rated as a 7, is friendlier than Guillermo, whom you rated as a 2), but the measure does not tell us how big the difference between Malik and Guillermo is. Similarly, a hotel that receives a four-star rating is probably not exactly twice as comfortable as a hotel that receives a two-star rating.

Selltiz, Jahoda, Deutsch, and Cook (1966) have suggested that using ordinal scales is a bit like using an elastic tape measure to measure length. Because the tape measure can be stretched, the difference between 1 centimeter and 2 centimeters may be greater or less than the difference between 7 centimeters and 8 centimeters. As a result, a change of 1 centimeter on the measured variable will not exactly correspond to a change of 1 unit of the conceptual variable (length), and the measure is not interval. However, although the stretching may change the length of the intervals, it does not change their order. Because 2 is always greater than 1 and 8 is always greater than 7, the relationship between actual length and measured length on the elastic tape measure is ordinal.

There is some disagreement of opinion about whether measured variables in the behavioral sciences can be considered ratio or interval scales or whether they should be considered only ordinal scales. In most cases, it is safest to assume that the scales are ordinal. For instance, we do not normally know whether the difference between people who score 8 versus 10 on a measure of self-esteem is exactly the same as that between two people who score 4 versus 6 on the same measure. And because there is no true zero point, we cannot say that a person with a self-esteem score of 10 has twice the esteem of a person with a score of 5. Although some measures can, in some cases, be considered interval or even ratio scales, most measured variables in the behavioral sciences are ordinal.

Self-Report Measures

In the next sections, we will consider some of the many types of measured variables used in behavioral research. We begin by considering how we might gain information by directly asking someone about his or her thoughts, feelings, or behavior. To do so involves using **self-report measures,** in which individuals are asked to respond to questions posed by an interviewer or a questionnaire. Then in the following sections we will consider the use of **behavioral measures,** designed to directly measure what people do.

Free-Format Self-Report Measures

Perhaps the most straightforward use of self-report measures involves asking people to freely list their thoughts or feelings as these come to mind. One of the major advantages of such **free-format self-report measures** is that they allow respondents to indicate whatever thoughts or feelings they have about the topic, without any constraints imposed on respondents except the effort it takes to write these thoughts or feelings down or speak them into a tape recorder.

Projective Measures.   A **projective measure** is a measure of personality in which an unstructured image, such as an inkblot, is shown to participants, who are asked to freely list what comes to mind as they view the image. One common use of free-format self-report measures is the assessment of personality variables through the use of projective tests such as the Thematic Apperception Test, or TAT (Morgan & Murray, 1935) or the Rorschach inkblots. The TAT, for instance, consists of a number of sketches of people, either alone or with others, who are engaging in various behaviors, such as gazing out a window or pointing at each other. The sketches are shown to individuals, who are asked to tell a story about what is happening in the picture. The TAT assumes that people may be unwilling or unable to admit their true feelings when asked directly but that these feelings will show up in the stories about the pictures. Trained coders read the stories and use them to develop a personality profile of the respondent.

Associative Lists.   Free-format response formats in the form of associative lists have also been used to study such variables as stereotyping. In one of these studies (Stangor, Sullivan, & Ford, 1991), college students were presented with the names of different social groups (African Americans, Hispanics, Russians) and asked to list whatever thoughts came to mind about the groups. The study was based on the assumption that the thoughts listed in this procedure would be those that the individual viewed as strongest or most central to the group as a whole and would thus provide a good idea of what the person really thought about the groups. One student listed the following thoughts to describe different social groups:

> Whites: "Materialistic and prejudiced."
> Hispanics: "Poor, uneducated, and traditional. Willing to work hard."
> Russians: "Unable to leave their country, even though they want to."

Think-Aloud Protocols.   Another common type of free-format response formats is a **think-aloud protocol** (Ericsson & Simon, 1980). In this procedure, individuals are asked to verbalize into a tape recorder the thoughts that they are having as they complete a task. For instance, the following protocol was generated by a college student in a social psychology experiment who was trying to form an impression of another person who was characterized by conflicting information (Fiske, Neuberg, Beattie, & Milberg, 1987): "Professor. Strong, close-minded, rowdy, red-necked, loud. Hmmmm. I've never met a professor like this. I tend to make a stereotype of a beer-guzzling bigot.... I can sort of picture him sitting in a smoky, white bar, somewhere in, off in the suburbs of Maryland." The researchers used the think-aloud protocols, along with other data, to understand how people formed impressions about others.

The Difficulties of Coding Free-Format Data.   Despite the fact that free-format self-report measures produce a rich set of data regarding the thoughts and feelings of the people being studied, they also have some disadvantages.

Most important, it is very difficult and time-consuming to turn the generated thoughts into a set of measured variables that can be used in data analysis. Because each individual is likely to have used a unique set of thoughts, it is hard to compare individuals. One solution is to simply describe the responses verbally (such as the description of the college professor on this page) and to treat the measures as qualitative data. However, because correlational and experimental research designs require the use of quantitative data (measured variables that can be subjected to statistical analysis), it is frequently useful to convert the free responses into one or more measured variables. For instance, the coders can read the answers given on projective tests and tabulate the extent to which different themes are expressed, or the responses given on associative lists can be tallied into different categories. However, the process of fitting the free responses into a structured coding system tends to reduce the basic advantage of the approach—the freedom of the individual to give unique responses. The process of coding free-response data is known as *content analysis,* and we will discuss it in more detail in Chapter 7.

Fixed-Format Self-Report Measures

Partly because of the difficulty of coding free-format responses, most research using self-report measures relies on **fixed-format self-report measures.** On these measures, the individual is presented with a set of questions (the questions are called **items**), and the responses that can be given are more structured than in free-format measures.

In some cases, the information that we wish to obtain is unambiguous, and only one item is necessary to get it. For instance:

Enter your ethnic identification (please check one):

_____   American Indian or Alaska Native

_____   Asian

_____   Black or African American

_____   Native Hawaiian or Other Pacific Islander

_____   White

_____   Some Other Race

In other cases—for instance, the measurement of personality variables such as self-esteem, anxiety, intelligence, or mood—the conceptual variable is more difficult to assess. In these cases, fixed-format self-report measures containing a number of items may be used. Fixed-format self-report measures that contain more than one item (such as an intelligence test or a measure of self-esteem) are known as **scales.** The many items, each designed to measure the same conceptual variable, are combined together by summing or averaging, and the result becomes the person's score on the measured variable.

One advantage of fixed-format scales is that there is a well-developed set of response formats already available for use, as well as a set of statistical procedures designed to evaluate the effectiveness of the scales as measures of underlying conceptual variables. As we will see in the next chapter, using more than one item is very advantageous because it provides a better measure of the conceptual variable than would any single item.

The Likert Scale. The most popular type of fixed-format scale is the Likert scale (Likert, 1932). A **Likert scale** consists of a series of items that indicate agreement or disagreement with the issue that is to be measured, each with a set of responses on which the respondents indicate their opinions. One example of a Likert scale, the Rosenberg self-esteem scale, is shown in Table 4.2. This scale contains ten items, each of which is responded to on a four-point response format ranging from "strongly disagree" to "strongly agree." Each of the possible responses is assigned a number, and the measured variable is the sum or average of the responses across all of the items.

You will notice that five of the ten items on the Rosenberg scale are written such that marking "strongly agree" means that the person has high self-esteem, whereas for the other half of the items marking "strongly agree" indicates that

TABLE 4.2 The Rosenberg Self-Esteem Scale

Please rate yourself on the following items by writing a number in the blank before each statement, where

4 = Strongly agree

3 = Agree

2 = Disagree

1 = Strongly disagree

___3___ (1) I feel that I'm a person of worth, at least on an equal base with others.

___4___ (2) I feel that I have a number of good qualities.

___2___ (3) All in all, I am inclined to think that I am a failure. (R)

___3___ (4) I am able to do things as well as other people.

___2___ (5) I feel I do not have much to be proud of. (R)

___4___ (6) I take a positive attitude toward myself.

___3___ (7) On the whole, I am satisfied with myself.

___2___ (8) I wish I could have more respect for myself. (R)

___1___ (9) I certainly feel useless at times. (R)

___1___ (10) At times I think I am no good at all. (R)

(R) denotes an item that should be reverse-scored before the total is calculated. The measured variable is the sum or average score across the ten items. For this person, the sum score is 34, and the mean is 3.40.
Source: Rosenberg (1965).

the individual does *not* have high self-esteem. This variation avoids a potential problem on fixed-format scales known as **acquiescent responding** (frequently called a yeah-saying bias). If all the items on a Likert scale are phrased in the same direction, it is not possible to tell if the respondent is simply a "yeah-sayer" (that is, a person who tends to agree with everything) or if he or she really agrees with the content of the item.

To reduce the impact of acquiescent responding on the measured variable, the wording of about one-half of the items is reversed such that agreement with these items means that the person does *not* have the characteristic being measured. Of course, the responses to the reversed items must themselves be *reverse-scored,* so that the direction is the same for every item, before the sum or average is taken. On the Rosenberg scale, the reversed items are changed so that 1 becomes 4, 2 becomes 3, 3 becomes 2, and 4 becomes 1.

Although the Likert scale shown in Table 4.2 is a typical one, the format can vary to some degree. Although "strongly agree" and "strongly disagree" are probably the most common endpoints, others are also possible:

I am late for appointments:

Never   1   2   3   4   5   6   7   Always

It is also possible to label the midpoint of the scale (for instance, "neither agree nor disagree") as well as the endpoints, or to provide a label for each of the choices:

I enjoy parties:

1   Strongly disagree
2   Moderately disagree
3   Slightly disagree
4   Slightly agree
5   Moderately agree
6   Strongly agree

In still other cases, for instance, in the study of children, the response scale has to be simplified:

When an even number of response choices is used, the respondent cannot choose a neutral point, whereas the provision of an odd number of choices allows a neutral response. Depending on the purposes of the research and the type of question, this may or may not be appropriate or desirable. One response format that can be useful when a researcher does not want to restrict the range of input to a number of response options is to simply present a line of known length (for instance 100 mm) and ask the respondents to mark their opinion on the line. For instance:

I enjoy making decisions on my own:

Agree _____ Disagree

The distance of the mark from the end of the line is then measured with a ruler, and this becomes the measured variable. This approach is particularly effective when data are collected on computers because individuals can use the mouse to indicate on the computer screen the exact point on the line that represents their opinion and the computer can precisely measure and record the response.

The Semantic Differential.   Although Likert scales are particularly useful for measuring opinions and beliefs, people's feelings about topics under study can often be better assessed using a type of scale known as a semantic differential (Osgood, Suci, & Tannenbaum, 1957). Table 4.3 presents a semantic differential designed to assess feelings about a university. In a **semantic differential,** the topic being evaluated is presented once at the top of the page, and the items consist of pairs of adjectives located at the two endpoints of a standard response format. The respondent expresses his or her feelings toward the topic by marking one point on the dimension. To quantify the scale, a number is assigned to each possible response, for instance, from −3 (most negative) to +3 (most positive). Each respondent's score is computed by averaging across his or her responses to each of the items after the items in which the negative response has the higher number have been reverse-scored. Although semantic differentials can sometimes be used to assess other dimensions, they are most often restricted to measuring people's evaluations about a topic—that is, whether they feel positively or negatively about it.

TABLE 4.3   A Semantic Differential Scale Assessing Attitudes Toward a University

My university is:

Beautiful	_____	_____	_____	_____	_____	_____	_____	Ugly
Bad	_____	_____	_____	_____	_____	_____	_____	Good
Pleasant	_____	_____	_____	_____	_____	_____	_____	Unpleasant
Dirty	_____	_____	_____	_____	_____	_____	_____	Clean
Smart	_____	_____	_____	_____	_____	_____	_____	Stupid

Respondents are told to check the middle category if neither adjective describes the object better than the other and to check along the scale in either direction if they feel the object is described better by either of the two adjectives. These ratings are usually scored from −3 to +3 (with appropriate reversals). Scores are averaged or summed to provide a single score for each individual.

The Guttman Scale.   There is one more type of fixed-format self-report scale, known as a Guttman scale (Guttman, 1944), that is sometimes used in behavioral research, although it is not as common as the Likert or semantic differential scale. The goal of a Guttman scale is to indicate the extent to which an individual possesses the conceptual variable of interest. But in contrast to Likert and semantic differential scales, which measure differences in the extent to which the participants agree with the items, the Guttman scale involves the creation of differences in the items themselves. The items are created ahead of time to be cumulative in the sense that they represent the degree of the conceptual variable of interest. The expectation is that an individual who endorses any given item will also endorse every item that is less extreme. Thus, the **Guttman scale** can be defined as a fixed-format self-report scale in which the items are arranged in a cumulative order such that it is assumed that if a respondent endorses or answers correctly any one item, he or she will also endorse or correctly answer all of the previous scale items.

Consider, for instance, the gender constancy scale shown in Table 4.4 (Slaby & Frey, 1975). This Guttman scale is designed to indicate the extent

TABLE 4.4   The Gender Constancy Scale

1.   Are you a boy or a girl?
2.   (Show picture of a girl) Is this a boy or a girl?
3.   (Show picture of a boy) Is this a boy or a girl?
4.   (Show picture of a man) Is this a man or a woman?
5.   (Show picture of a woman) Is this a man or a woman?
6.   When you were a baby, were you a girl or a boy?
7.   When you grow up, will you be a man or a woman?
8.   This grownup is a woman (show picture of woman). When this grownup was little, was this grownup a boy like this child (show picture of boy) or a girl like this child (show picture of girl)?
9.   This child is a boy (show picture of boy). When this child grows up, will this child be a woman like this grownup (show picture of woman) or a man like this grownup (show picture of man)?
10. If you wore clothes like this (show picture of a boy who is wearing girls' clothing), would you still be a boy, or would you be a girl?
11. If this child wore clothes like these (show picture of a girl who is wearing boys' clothing), would this child still be a girl, or would she be a boy?
12. If you played games that girls play, would you then be a girl, or would you be a boy?
13. (Show picture of man) If this grownup did the work that women usually do, would this grownup then be a woman, or would this grownup then be a man?
14. (Show picture of woman) If this grownup did the work that men usually do, would this grownup then be a man, or would the grownup then be a woman?

The gender constancy scale (Slaby & Frey, 1975) is a Guttman scale designed to measure the extent to which children have internalized the idea that sex cannot change. The questions are designed to reflect increasing difficulty. Children up to six years old frequently get some of the questions wrong. The version here is one that would be given to a boy. The sex of the actors in questions 8 through 12 would be reversed if the child being tested was a girl.

to which a young child has confidently learned that his or her sex will not change over time. A series of questions, which are ordered in terms of increasing difficulty, are posed to the child, who answers each one. The assumption is that if the child is able to answer a given question correctly, then he or she should also be able to answer all of the questions that come earlier on the scale correctly because those items are selected to be easier. Slaby and Frey (1975) found that although the pattern of responses was not perfect (some children did answer a later item correctly and an earlier item incorrectly), the gender constancy scale did, by and large, conform to the expected cumulative pattern. They also found that older children answered more items correctly than did younger children.

Reactivity as a Limitation in Self-Report Measures

Taken together, self-report measures are the most commonly used type of measured variable within the behavioral sciences. They are relatively easy to construct and administer and allow the researcher to ask many questions in a short period of time. There is great flexibility, particularly with Likert scales, in the types of questions that can be posed to respondents. And, as we will see in Chapter 5, because a fixed-format scale has many items, each relating to the same thought or feeling, they can be combined together to produce a very useful measured variable.

However, there are also some potential disadvantages to the use of self-report. For one thing, with the exception of some indirect free-format measures such as the TAT, self-report measures assume that people are able and willing to accurately answer direct questions about their own thoughts, feelings, or behaviors. Yet, as we have seen in Chapter 1, people may not always be able to accurately self-report on the causes of their behaviors. And even if they are accurately aware, respondents may not answer questions on self-report measures as they would have if they thought their responses were not being recorded. Changes in responding that occur when individuals know they are being measured are known as **reactivity.** Reactivity can change responses in many different ways and must always be taken into consideration in the development of measured variables (Weber & Cook, 1972).

The most common type of reactivity is **social desirability**—the natural tendency for research participants to present themselves in a positive or socially acceptable way to the researcher. One common type of reactivity, known as **self-promotion,** occurs when research participants respond in ways that they think will make them look good. For instance, most people will overestimate their positive qualities and underestimate their negative qualities and are usually unwilling to express negative thoughts or feelings about others. These responses occur because people naturally prefer to answer questions in a way that makes them look intelligent, knowledgeable, caring, healthy, and nonprejudiced.

Research participants may respond not only to make themselves look good but also to make the experimenter happy, even though they would probably not respond this way if they were not being studied. For instance, in one well-known study, Orne (1962) found that participants would perform tedious math problems for hours on end to please the experimenter, even though they had also been told to tear up all of their work as soon as they completed it, which made it impossible for the experimenter to check what they had done in any way.

The desire to please the experimenter can cause problems on self-report measures; for instance, respondents may indicate a choice on a response scale even though they may not understand the question or feel strongly about their answer but want to appear knowledgeable or please the experimenter. In such cases, the researcher may interpret the response as meaning more than it really does. Cooperative responding is particularly problematic if the participants are able to guess the researcher's hypothesis—for instance, if they can figure out what the self-report measure is designed to assess. Of course, not all participants have cooperative attitudes. Those who are required to participate in the research may not pay much attention or may even develop an uncooperative attitude and attempt to sabotage the study.

There are several methods of countering reactivity on self-report measures. One is to administer other self-report scales that measure the tendency to lie or to self-promote, which are then used to correct for reactivity (see, for instance, Crowne and Marlow's [1964] social-desirability scale). To lessen the possibility of respondents guessing the hypothesis, the researcher may disguise the items on the self-report scale or include unrelated filler or distracter items to throw the participants off the track. Another strategy is to use a cover story—telling the respondents that one thing is being measured when the scale is really designed to measure something else. And the researcher may also be able to elicit more honest responses from the participant by explaining that the research is not designed to evaluate him or her personally and that its success depends upon honest answers to the questions (all of which is usually true). However, given people's potential to distort their responses on self-report measures, and given that there is usually no check on whether any corrections have been successful, it is useful to consider other ways to measure the conceptual variables of interest that are less likely to be influenced by reactivity.

Behavioral Measures

One alternative to self-report is to measure behavior. Although the measures shown in Table 4.1 are rather straightforward, social scientists have used a surprising variety of behavioral measures to help them assess the conceptual variables of interest. Table 4.5 represents some that you might find interesting that were sent to me by my social psychology colleagues. Indeed, the types of behaviors that can be measured are limited only by the creativity of the researchers. Some of the types of behavioral variables that form the basis of measured variables in behavioral science include those based on:

Frequency (for instance, frequency of stuttering as a measure of anxiety in interpersonal relations)

Duration (for instance, the number of minutes working at a task as a measure of task interest)

TABLE 4.5 Some Conceptual Variables and the Behavioral Measure That Has Been Used to Operationalize Them

Conceptual Variable	Behavioral Measure
Personality style	Observation of the objects in and the state of people's bedrooms (with their permission, of course!) (Gosling, Ko, Mannarelli, & Morris, 2002)
Aggression	Amount of hot sauce that a research participant puts on other participants' food in a taste test (Lieberman, Solomon, Greenberg, & McGregor, 1999)
Desire for uniqueness	Extent to which people choose an unusual, rather than a common, color for a gift pen (Kim and Markus, 1999)
Honesty	Whether children, observed through a one-way mirror, followed the rule to "take only one candy" when they were trick-or-treating (Diener, Fraser, Beaman, & Kelem, 1976)
Dieting	Number of snacks taken from a snack bowl during a conversation between a man and a woman (Mori, Chaiken, & Pliner, 1987)
Cold severity	Change in the weight of a tissue before and after a research participant blew his or her nose with it (Cohen, Tyrrell, & Smith, 1993)
Interest in a task	Number of extra balls played on a pinball machine in free time (Harackiewicz, Manderlink, & Sansone, 1984)
Environmental behavior	How long participants let the water run during a shower in the locker room after swimming (Dickerson, Thibodeau, Aronson, & Miller, 1992)
Friendliness	How close together a person puts two chairs in preparation for an upcoming conversation (Fazio, Effrein, & Falender, 1981)
Racial prejudice	How far away a person sits from a member of another social category (Macrae, Bodenhausen, Milne, & Jetten, 1994)

Intensity (for instance, how hard a person claps his or her hands as a measure of effort)

Latency (for instance, the number of days before a person begins to work on a project as a measure of procrastination)

Speed (for instance, how long it takes a mouse to complete a maze as a measure of learning)

Although some behaviors, such as how close a person sits to another person, are relatively easy to measure, many behavioral measures are difficult to operationally define and effectively code. For instance, you can imagine that it would be no easy task to develop a behavioral measure of "aggressive play" in children. In terms of the operational definition, decisions would have to be made about whether to include verbal aggression, whether some types of physical aggression (throwing stones) should be weighted more heavily than other types of physical aggression (pushing), and so forth. Then the behaviors would have to be coded. In most cases, complete coding systems are worked out in advance, and more than one experimenter makes ratings of the behaviors, thereby allowing agreement between the raters to be assessed. In some cases, videotapes may be made so that the behaviors can be coded at a later time. We will discuss techniques of coding behavioral measures more fully in Chapter 7.

Nonreactive Measures

Behavioral measures have a potential advantage over self-report measures—because they do not involve direct questioning of people, they are frequently less reactive. This is particularly true when the research participant (1) is not aware that the measurement is occurring, (2) does not realize what the measure is designed to assess, or (3) cannot change his or her responses, even if he or she desires to.

Nonreactive Behavioral Measures. are frequently used to assess attitudes that are unlikely to be directly expressed on self-report measures, such as racial prejudice. For instance, Word, Zanna, and Cooper (1974) coded the nonverbal behavior of White male participants as they conducted an interview with another person, who was either Black or White. The researchers found that the interviewers sat farther away from the Black interviewees than from the White interviewees, made more speech errors when talking to the Blacks, and terminated the interviews with the Blacks sooner than with the Whites. This experiment provided insights into the operation of prejudice that could not have been obtained directly because, until the participants were debriefed, they did not know that their behavior was being measured or what the experiment was about.

Some behavioral measures reduce reactivity because they are so indirect that the participants do not know what the measure is designed to assess. For instance, some researchers studying the development of impressions of others will provide participants with a list of behaviors describing another person and then later ask them to remember this information or to make decisions about it. Although the participants think that they are engaging in a memory test, what they remember about the behaviors and the speed with which they make decisions about the person can be used to draw inferences about whether the participants like or dislike the other person and whether they use stereotypes in processing the information. The use of **nonreactive behavioral measures** is discussed in more detail in a book by Webb, Campbell, Schwartz, Sechrest, and Grove (1981).

Psychophysiological Measures

In still other cases, behavioral measures reduce reactivity because the individual cannot directly control his or her response. One example is the use of **psychophysiological measures,** which are designed to assess the physiological functioning of the body's nervous and endocrine systems (Cacioppo, Tassinary, & Berntson, 2000).

Some psychophysiological measures are designed to assess brain activity, with the goal of determining which parts of the brain are involved in which types of information processing and motor activities. These brain measures include the electroencephalogram (EEG), magnetic resonance imaging (MRI), positron-emission tomography (PET), and computerized axial tomography (CAT). In one study using these techniques, Harmon-Jones and Sigelman (2001) used an EEG measure to assess brain activity after research participants had been insulted by another person. Supporting their hypotheses, they found that electrical brain responses to the insult were stronger on the left side of the brain than on the right side of the brain, indicating that anger involves not only negative feelings about the other person but also a motivational desire to address the insult.

Other psychophysiological measures, including heart rate, blood pressure, respiration speed, skin temperature, and skin conductance, assess the activity of the sympathetic and parasympathetic nervous systems. The electromyograph (EMG) assesses muscle responses in the face. For instance, Bartholow and his colleagues (2001) found that EMG responses were stronger when people read information that was unexpected or unusual than when they read more expected material, and that the responses were particularly strong in response to negative events. Still other physiological measures, such as amount of *cortisol,* involve determining what chemicals are in the bloodstream—for instance, to evaluate biochemical reactions to stress.

Although collecting psychophysiological measures can be difficult because doing so often requires sophisticated equipment and expertise and the interpretation of these measures may yield ambiguous results (For instance, does an increase in heart rate mean that the person is angry or afraid?), these measures do reduce reactivity to a large extent and are increasingly being used in behavioral research.

Choosing a Measure

As we have seen in this chapter, most conceptual variables of interest to behavioral scientists can be operationalized in any number of ways. For instance, the conceptual variable of aggression has been operationalized using such diverse measures as shocking others, fighting on a playground, verbal abuse, violent crimes, horn-honking in traffic, and putting hot sauce on people's food. The possibility of multiple operationalizations represents a great advantage to researchers because there are specific advantages and disadvantages to each type of measure. For instance, as we have seen, self-report measures have the advantage of allowing researchers to get a broad array of information in a short period of time, but the disadvantage of reactivity. On the other hand, behavioral measures may often reduce reactivity, but they may be difficult to operationalize and code, and the meaning of some behaviors may be difficult to interpret.

When designing a research project, think carefully about which measures to use. Your decision will be based on traditional approaches in the area you are studying and on the availability of resources, such as equipment and expertise. In many cases, you will want to use more than one operationaliza-tion of a measure, such as self-report and behavioral measures, in the same research project. In every case, however, you must be absolutely certain that you do a complete literature review before you begin your project, to be sure that you have uncovered measures that have been used in prior research. There is so much research that has measured so many constructs, that it is almost certain that someone else has already measured the conceptual vari-able in which you are interested. Do not be afraid to make use of measures that have already been developed by others. It is entirely appropriate to do so, as long as you properly cite the source of the measure. As we will see in the next chapter, it takes a great amount of effort to develop a good measured variable. As a result, except when you are assessing a new variable or when existing measures are not appropriate for your research design, it is generally advisable to make use of the work that others have already done rather than try to develop your own measure.

Current Research in the Behavioral Sciences: Using Multiple Measured Variables to Assess the Conceptual Variable of Panic Symptoms

Bethany Teachman, Shannan Smith-Janik, and Jena Saporito are clinical psy-chologists who study psychological disorders. In one of their recent research projects (Teachman, Smith-Janik, & Saporito, 2007), they were interested in testing the extent to which a variety of direct and indirect measured variables could be used to help define the underlying conceptual variable of the panic symptoms that are frequently experienced by people with anxiety disorders. They operationalized six different measured variables to assess the single con-ceptual variable.

Their research used a sample of 43 research participants who had been diag-nosed with panic disorder. Each of the participants completed a variety of mea-sures designed to assess their psychological states, both directly and indirectly. In terms of direct, self-report Likert-scale measures, the participants completed the *Anxiety Sensitivity Index* (Reiss, Peterson, Gursky, & McNally, 1986), which is a 16-item questionnaire assessing concern over the symptoms associated with anxiety; the *Fear Questionnaire-Agoraphobia* scale (Marks & Mathews, 1979), which measures level of phobic avoidance toward common situations; and the *Panic Disorder Severity Scale* (Shear et al., 1997), which is a measure of severity score of frequency, distress and impairment associated with panic attacks.

Another direct measure used a different response format. In the *Brief Body Sensations Interpretation Questionnaire* (Clark et al., 1997), participants are presented with ambiguous events and then asked to rank order three al-ternative explanations for why the event might have occurred. For instance, the participants are told, "You notice that your heart is beating quickly and pounding," and had to choose one of three answers among "because you have been physically active," "because there is something wrong with your heart," or "because you are feeling excited."

The researchers also used two indirect measures of panic symptoms, the *Implicit Association Test* (Greenwald et al., 1998), and a version of the *Stroop Color and Word Test*. Participants took these tests on a computer. In the *Implicit Associations Test*, the participants were asked to classify items as either "self" or "other" and as "panicked" or "calm." The measured variable was the difference in the speed of classifying the self and panicked and the self and calm words. The idea is that if the individual has automatic associations with the self and panic symptoms, he or she will be able to classify the stimuli more quickly.

The Stroop Color and Word Test is a reaction time task that measures how fast the participant can name the color in which a word is presented. It is based on the assumption that words related to panic will be named more slowly because of interference caused by their semantic content. The difference in response time for naming the ink color across panic-related and control words was used as the measured variable.

As you can see in Figure 4.2, each of the six measured variables correlated positively with an overall measure of panic symptoms that was derived by statistically combining all of the measures together. You can see that, in this case, the direct measures correlated more highly with the composite than did the indirect measures.

FIGURE 4.2   Measuring Panic Symptoms Using Direct and Indirect Measures

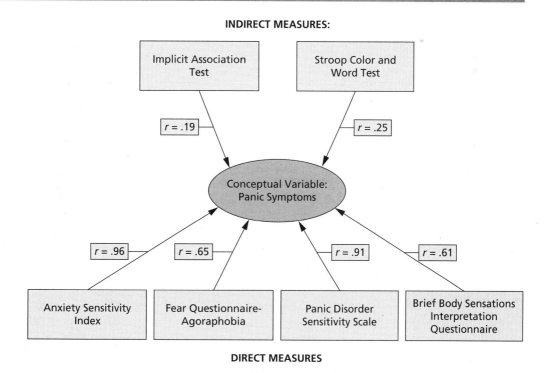

Source: Teachman, Smith-Janik, and Saporito (2007) assessed how three direct and three indirect measured variables correlated with the underlying conceptual variable of panic symptoms. The overall conceptual measure of panic symptoms was derived by statistically combining all of the measures together.

SUMMARY

Before any research hypothesis can be tested, the conceptual variables must be turned into measured variables through the use of operational definitions. This process is known as *measurement*.

The relationship between the conceptual variables and their measures forms the basis of the testing of research hypotheses because the conceptual variables can be understood only through their operationalizations. Measured variables can be nominal or quantitative. The mapping, or scaling, of quantitative measured variables onto conceptual variables in the behavioral sciences is generally achieved through the use of ordinal, rather than interval or ratio, scales.

Self-report measures are those in which the person indicates his or her thoughts or feelings verbally in answer to posed questions. In free-format measures, the participant can express whatever thoughts or feelings come to mind, whereas in fixed-format measures the participant responds to specific preselected questions. Fixed-format measures such as Likert, semantic differential, and Guttman scales contain a number of items, each using the same response format, designed to assess the conceptual variable of interest.

In contrast to self-report measures, behavioral measures can be more unobtrusive and thus are often less influenced by reactivity, such as acquiescent responding and self-promotion. Examples of such nonreactive behavioral measures are those designed to assess physiological responding. However, behavioral measures may be difficult to operationalize and code, and the meaning of some behaviors may be difficult to interpret.

KEY TERMS

acquiescent responding 76
behavioral measures 72
conceptual variables 67
fixed-format self-report measures 74
free-format self-report measures 72
Guttman scale 78
interval scale 71
items 74
Likert scale 75
measured variables 67
measurement 67
measures 67
nominal variable 70
nonreactive behavioral measures 82

operational definition 67
ordinal scale 71
projective measure 73
psychophysiological measures 82
quantitative variable 70
ratio scales 71
reactivity 79
scales 74
scaling 71
self-promotion 79
self-report measures 72
semantic differential 77
social desirability 79
think-aloud protocol 73

REVIEW AND DISCUSSION QUESTIONS

1. Describe in your own words the meaning of Figure 4.1. Why is measurement so important in the testing of research hypotheses?

2. Indicate the relationships between nominal, ordinal, interval, and ratio scales and the conceptual variables they are designed to assess.

3. Generate three examples of nominal variables and three examples of quantitative variables that were not mentioned in the chapter.

4. On a piece of paper make two columns. In one column list all of the advantages of free-format (versus fixed-format) self-report measures. In the other column list all of the advantages of fixed-format (versus free-format) self-report measures. Given these comparisons, what factors might lead a researcher to choose one approach over the other?

5. Behavioral measures frequently have the advantage of reducing participant reactivity. Since they can capture the behavior of individuals more honestly, why are they so infrequently used in behavioral research?

6. Consider some examples of psychophysiological measures that are used in behavioral research.

RESEARCH PROJECT IDEAS

1. Develop at least three behavioral measures of each of the following conceptual variables. Consider measures that are based on frequency, speed, duration, latency, and intensity. Consider the extent to which each of the measures you develop is nonreactive.

   a. Conformity
   b. Enjoyment of reading
   c. Leadership
   d. Paranoia
   e. Independence

2. Develop a ten-item Likert scale to measure one of the conceptual variables in problem 1.

3. Develop a free-format self-report measure for each of the conceptual variables listed in problem 1.

CHAPTER FIVE
Reliability and Validity

STUDY QUESTIONS

- What are random error and systematic error, and how do they influence measurement?

- What is reliability? Why must a measure be reliable?

- How are test-retest and equivalent-forms reliability measured?

- How are split-half reliability and coefficient alpha used to assess the internal consistency of a measured variable?

- What is interrater reliability?

- What are face validity and content validity?

- How are convergent and discriminant validity used to assess the construct validity of a measured variable?

- What is criterion validity?

- What methods can be used to increase the reliability and validity of a self-report measure?

- How are reliability and construct validity similar? How are they different?

We have seen in Chapter 4 that there are a wide variety of self-report and behavioral measured variables that scientists can use to assess conceptual variables. And we have seen that because changes in conceptual variables are assumed to cause changes in measured variables, the measured variables are used to make inferences about the conceptual variables. But how do we know whether the measures that we have chosen actually assess the conceptual variables they are designed to measure? This chapter discusses techniques for evaluating the relationship between measured and conceptual variables.

In some cases, demonstrating the adequacy of a measure is rather straightforward because there is a clear way to check whether it is measuring what it is supposed to. For instance, when a physiological psychologist investigates perceptions of the brightness or color of a light source, she or he can compare the participants' judgments with objective measurements of light intensity and wavelength. Similarly, when we ask people to indicate their sex or their current college grade-point average, we can check up on whether their reports are correct.

In many cases within behavioral science, however, assessing the effectiveness of a measured variable is more difficult. For instance, a researcher who has created a new Likert scale designed to measure "anxiety" assumes that an individual's score on this scale will reflect, at least to some extent, his or her actual level of anxiety. But because the researcher does not know how to measure anxiety in any better way, there is no obvious way to "check" the responses of the individual against any type of factual standard.

Random and Systematic Error

The basic difficulty in determining the effectiveness of a measured variable is that the measure will in all likelihood be influenced by other factors besides the conceptual variable of interest. For one thing, the measured variable will certainly contain some chance fluctuations in measurement, known as **random error.** Sources of random error include misreading or misunderstanding of the questions, and measurement of the individuals on different days or in different places. Random error can also occur if the experimenter misprints the questions or misrecords the answers or if the individual marks the answers incorrectly.

Although random error influences scores on the measured variable, it does so in a way that is self-canceling. That is, although the experimenter may make some recording errors or the individuals may mark their answers incorrectly, these errors will increase the scores of some people and decrease the scores of other people. The increases and decreases will balance each other and thus cancel each other out.

In contrast to random error, which is self-canceling, the measured variable may also be influenced by other conceptual variables that are not part of the conceptual variable of interest. These other potential influences constitute

systematic error because, whereas random errors tend to cancel out over time, these variables systematically increase or decrease the scores on the measured variable. For instance, individuals with higher self-esteem may score systematically lower on the anxiety measure than those with low self-esteem, and more optimistic individuals may score consistently higher. Also, as we have discussed in Chapter 4, the tendency to self-promote may lead some respondents to answer the items in ways that make them appear less anxious than they really are in order to please the experimenter or to feel better about themselves. In these cases, the measured variable will assess self-esteem, optimism, or the tendency to self-promote in addition to the conceptual variable of interest (anxiety).

Figure 5.1 summarizes the impact of random and systematic error on a measured variable. Although there is no foolproof way to determine whether measured variables are free from random and systematic error, there are techniques that allow us to get an idea about how well our measured variables

FIGURE 5.1   Random and Systematic Error

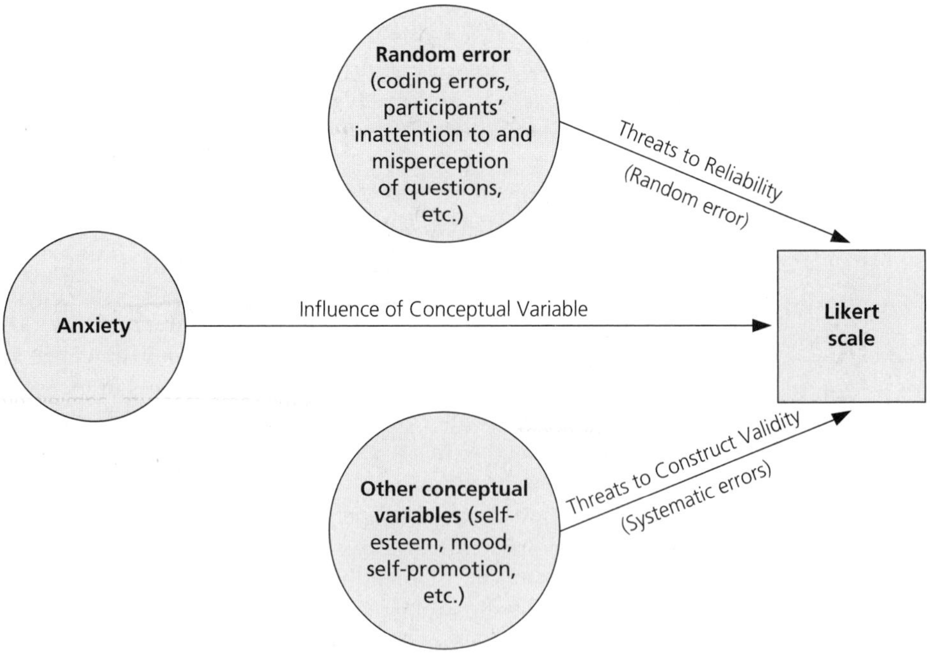

Scores on a measured variable, such as a Likert scale measure of anxiety, will be caused not only by the conceptual variable of interest (anxiety), but also by random measurement error as well as other conceptual variables that are unrelated to anxiety. Reliability is increased to the extent that random error has been eliminated as a cause of the measured variable. Construct validity is increased to the extent that the influence of systematic error has been eliminated.

"capture" the conceptual variables they are designed to assess rather than being influenced by random and systematic error. As we will see, this is accomplished through examination of the correlations among a set of measured variables.[1]

Reliability

The **reliability** of a measure refers to the extent to which it is free from random error. One direct way to determine the reliability of a measured variable is to measure it more than once. For instance, you can test the reliability of a bathroom scale by weighing yourself on it twice in a row. If the scale gives the same weight both times (we'll assume your actual weight hasn't changed in between), you would say that it is reliable. But if the scale gives different weights each time, you would say that it is unreliable. Just as a bathroom scale is not useful if it is not consistent over time, an unreliable measured variable will not be useful in research.

The next section reviews the different approaches to assessing a measure's reliability; these are summarized in Table 5.1.

Test-Retest Reliability

Test-retest reliability refers to the extent to which scores on the same measured variable correlate with each other on two different measurements given at two different times. If the test is perfectly reliable, and if the scores on the conceptual variable do not change over the time period, the individuals

TABLE 5.1 Summary of Approaches to Assessing Reliability

Approach	Description
Test-retest reliability	The extent to which scores on the same measure, administered at two different times, correlate with each other
Equivalent-forms reliability	The extent to which scores on similar, but not identical, measures, administered at two different times, correlate with each other
Internal consistency	The extent to which the scores on the items of a scale correlate with each other. Usually assessed using coefficient alpha.
Interrater reliability	The extent to which the ratings of one or more judges correlate with each other

Reliability refers to the extent to which a measured variable is free from random error. As shown in this table, reliability is assessed by computing the extent to which measured variables correlate with each other.

[1] Be sure to review Appendix B in this book if you are uncertain about the Pearson correlation coefficient.

should receive the exact same score each time, and the correlation between the scores will be $r = 1.00$. However, if the measured variable contains random error, the two scores will not be as highly correlated. Higher positive correlations between the scores at the two times indicate higher test-retest reliability.

Although the test-retest procedure is a direct way to measure reliability, it does have some limits. For one thing, when the procedure is used to assess the reliability of a self-report measure, it can produce reactivity. As you will recall from Chapter 4, reactivity refers to the influence of measurement on the variables being measured. In this case, reactivity is a potential problem because when the same or similar measures are given twice, responses on the second administration may be influenced by the measure having been taken the first time. These problems are known as **retesting effects.**

Retesting problems may occur, for instance, if people remember how they answered the questions the first time. Some people may believe that the experimenter wants them to express *different* opinions on the second occasion (or else why are the questions being given twice?). This would obviously reduce the test-retest correlation and thus give an overly low reliability assessment. Or respondents may try to duplicate their previous answers exactly to avoid appearing inconsistent, which would unnaturally increase the reliability estimate. Participants may also get bored answering the same questions twice. Although some of these problems can be avoided through the use of a long testing interval (say, over one month) and through the use of appropriate instructions (for instance, instructions to be honest and to answer exactly how one is feeling right now), retesting poses a general problem for the computation of test-retest reliability.

To help avoid some of these problems, researchers sometimes employ a more sophisticated type of test-retest reliability known as **equivalent-forms reliability.** In this approach two different but equivalent versions of the same measure are given at different times, and the correlation between the scores on the two versions is assessed. Such an approach is particularly useful when there are correct answers to the test that individuals might learn by taking the first test or be able to find out during the time period between the tests. Because students might remember the questions and learn the answers to aptitude tests such as the Graduate Record Exam (GRE) or the Scholastic Aptitude Test (SAT), these tests employ equivalent forms.

Reliability as Internal Consistency

In addition to the problems that can occur when people complete the same measure more than once, another problem with test-retest reliability is that some conceptual variables are not expected to be stable over time within an individual. Clearly, if optimism has a meaning as a conceptual variable, then people who are optimists on Tuesday should also be optimists on Friday of next week. Conceptual variables such as intelligence, friendliness, assertiveness, and optimism are known as **traits,** which are personality variables that are not expected to vary (or at most to vary only slowly) within people over time.

Other conceptual variables, such as level of stress, moods, or even preference for classical over rock music, are known as **states.** States are personality variables that are expected to change within the same person over short
periods of time. Because a person's score on a mood measure administered
on Tuesday is not necessarily expected to be related to the same measure administered next Friday, the test-retest approach will not provide an adequate
assessment of the reliability of a state variable such as mood. Because of the
problems associated with test-retest and equivalent-forms reliability, another
measure of reliability, known as internal consistency, has become the most
popular and most accurate way of assessing reliability for both trait and state
measures. Internal consistency is assessed using the scores on a single administration of the measure.

You will recall from our discussion in Chapter 4 that most self-report measures contain a number of items. If you think about measurement in terms of
reliability, the reason for this practice will become clear. You can imagine that
a measure that had only one item might be unreliable because that specific
item might have a lot of random error. For instance, respondents might not
understand the question the way you expected them to, or they might read it
incorrectly. In short, any single item is not likely to be very reliable.

True Score and Random Error.   One of the basic principles of reliability is
that the more measured variables are combined together, the more reliable
the test will be. This is so because, although each measured variable will be
influenced in part by random error, some part of each item will also measure the **true score,** or the part of the scale score that is not random error,
of the individual on the measure. Furthermore, because random error is self-
canceling, the random error components of each measured variable will not
be correlated with each other, whereas the parts of the measured variables
that represent the true score will be correlated. As a result, when they are
combined together by summing or averaging, the use of many measured
variables will produce a more reliable estimate of the conceptual variable
than will any of the individual measured variables themselves.

The role of true score and random error can be expressed in the form of
two equations that are the basis of reliability. First, an individual's score on a
measure will consist of both true score and random error:

$$\text{Actual score} = \text{True score} + \text{Random error}$$

and reliability is the proportion of the actual score that reflects true score (and
not random error).

$$\text{Relibility} = \frac{\text{True score}}{\text{Actual score}}$$

To take a more specific example, consider for a moment the Rosenberg
self-esteem scale that we examined in Table 4.2. This scale has ten items, each
designed to assess the conceptual variable of self-esteem in a slightly different way. Although each of the items will have random error, each should also

measure the true score of the individual. Thus if we average all ten of the items together to form a single measure, this overall scale score will be a more reliable measure than will any one of the individual questions.

Internal consistency refers to the extent to which the scores on the items correlate with each other and thus are all measuring the true score rather than random error. In terms of the Rosenberg scale, a person who answers above average on question 1, indicating she or he has high self-esteem, should also respond above the average on all of the other questions. Of course, this pattern will not be perfect because each item has some error. However, to the extent that all of the items are measuring true score, rather than random error the average correlation among the items will approach $r = 1.00$. To the extent that the correlation among the items is less than $r = 1.00$, it tells us either that there is random error or that the items are not measuring the same thing.

Coefficient Alpha.   One way to calculate the internal consistency of a scale is to correlate a person's score on one half of the items (for instance, the even-numbered items) with her or his score on the other half of the items (the odd-numbered items). This procedure is known as **split-half reliability.** If the scale is reliable, then the correlation between the two halves will approach $r = 1.00$, indicating that both halves measure the same thing. However, because split-half reliability uses only some of the available correlations among the items, it is preferable to have a measure that indexes the average correlation among all of the items on the scale. The most common, and the best, index of internal consistency is known as **Cronbach's coefficient alpha,** symbolized as α. This measure is an estimate of the average correlation among all of the items on the scale and is numerically equivalent to the average of all possible split-half reliabilities.

Coefficient alpha, because it reflects the underlying correlational structure of the scale, ranges from $\alpha = 0.00$ (indicating that the measure is entirely error) to $\alpha = +1.00$ (indicating that the measure has no error). In most cases, statistical computer programs are used to calculate coefficient alpha, but alpha can also be computed by hand according to the formula presented in Appendix D.

Item-to-Total Correlations.   When a new scale is being developed, its initial reliability may be low. This is because, although the researcher has selected those items that he or she believes will be reliable, some items will turn out to contain random error for reasons that could not be predicted in advance. Thus, one strategy commonly used in the initial development of a scale is to calculate the correlations between the score on each of the individual items and the total scale score excluding the item itself (these correlations are known as the *item-to-total correlations*). The items that do not correlate highly with the total score can then be deleted from the scale. Because this procedure deletes the items that do not measure the same thing that the scale as a whole does, the result is a shorter scale, but one with higher reliability. However, the approach of throwing out the items that do not correlate highly with the total is used only in the scale development process. Once the final version of the scale is in place, this version should be given again to another sample of participants, and the reliability computed without dropping any items.

Interrater Reliability

To this point we have discussed reliability primarily in terms of self-report scales. However, reliability is just as important for behavioral measures. It is common practice for a number of judges to rate the same observed behaviors and then to combine their ratings to create a single measured variable. This computation requires the internal consistency approach—just as any single item on a scale is expected to have error, so the ratings of any one judge are more likely to contain error than is the averaged rating across a group of judges. The errors of judges can be caused by many things, including inattention to some of the behaviors, misunderstanding of instructions, or even personal preferences. When the internal consistency of a group of judges is calculated, the resulting reliability is known as **interrater reliability.**

If the ratings of the judges that are being combined are quantitative variables (for instance, if the coders have each determined the aggressiveness of a group of children on a scale from 1 to 10), then coefficient alpha can be used to evaluate reliability. However, in some cases the variables of interest may be nominal. This would occur, for instance, if the judges have indicated for each child whether he or she was playing "alone," "cooperatively," "competitively," or "aggressively." In such cases, a statistic known as **kappa (κ)** is used as the measure of agreement among the judges. Like coefficient alpha, kappa ranges from $\kappa = 0$ (indicating that the judges' ratings are entirely random error) to $\kappa = +1.00$ (indicating that the ratings have no error). The formula for computing kappa is presented in Appendix C.

Construct Validity

Although reliability indicates the extent to which a measure is free from random error, it does not indicate what the measure actually measures. For instance, if we were to measure the speed with which a group of research participants could tie their shoes, we might find that this is a very reliable measure in the sense that it shows a substantial test-retest correlation. However, if the researcher then claimed that this reliable measure was assessing the conceptual variable of intelligence, you would probably not agree.

Therefore, in addition to being reliable, useful measured variables must also be construct valid. **Construct validity** refers to the extent to which a measured variable actually measures the conceptual variable (that is, the construct) that it is designed to assess. A measure only has construct validity if it measures what we want it to. There are a number of ways to assess construct validity; these are summarized in Table 5.2.

TABLE 5.2 Construct and Criterion Validity

Type of Validity	Description
Construct validity	The extent to which a measured variable actually measures the conceptual variable that it is designed to measure
Face validity	The extent to which the measured variable appears to be an adequate measure of the conceptual variable
Content validity	The extent to which the measured variable appears to have adequately covered the full domain of the conceptual variable
Convergent validity	The extent to which a measured variable is found to be related to other measured variables designed to measure the same conceptual variable
Discriminant validity	The extent to which a measured variable is found to be unrelated to other measured variables designed to measure other conceptual variables
Criterion validity	The extent to which a self-report measure correlates with a behavioral measured variable
Predictive validity	The extent to which a self-report measure correlates with (predicts) a future behavior
Concurrent validity	The extent to which a self-report measure correlates with a behavior measured at the same time

Face Validity

In some cases we can obtain an initial indication of the likely construct validity of a measured variable by examining it subjectively. **Face validity** refers to the extent to which the measured variable appears to be an adequate measure of the conceptual variable. For example, the Rosenberg self-esteem scale in Table 4.2 has face validity because the items ("I feel that I have a number of good qualities;" "I am able to do things as well as other people") appear to assess what we intuitively mean when we speak of self-esteem. However, if I carefully timed how long it took you and ten other people to tie your shoelaces, and then told you that you had above-average self-esteem because you tied your laces faster than the average of the others did, it would be clear that, although my test might be highly reliable, it did not really measure self-esteem. In this case, the measure is said to lack face validity.

Even though in some cases face validity can be a useful measure of whether a test actually assesses what it is supposed to, face validity is not always necessary or even desirable in a test. For instance, consider how White college students might answer the following measures of racial prejudice:

I do not like African Americans:

Strongly disagree 1 2 3 4 5 6 7 Strongly agree

African Americans are inferior to Whites:

Strongly agree 1 2 3 4 5 6 7 Strongly disagree

These items have high face validity (they appear to measure racial prejudice), but they are unlikely to be valid measures because people are unlikely to answer them honestly. Even those who are actually racists might not indicate agreement with these items (particularly if they thought the experimenter could check up on them) because they realize that it is not socially appropriate to do so.

In cases where the test is likely to produce reactivity, it can sometimes be the case that tests with *low* face validity may actually be more valid because the respondents will not know what is being measured and thus will be more likely to answer honestly. In short, not all measures that appear face valid are actually found to have construct validity.

Content Validity

One type of validity that is particularly appropriate to ability tests is known as **content validity.** Content validity concerns the degree to which the measured variable appears to have adequately sampled from the potential domain of questions that might relate to the conceptual variable of interest. For instance, an intelligence test that contained only geometry questions would lack content validity because there are other types of questions that measure intelligence (those concerning verbal skills and knowledge about current affairs, for instance) that were not included. However, this test might nevertheless have content validity as a geometry test because it sampled from many different types of geometry problems.

Convergent and Discriminant Validity

Although face and content validity can and should be used in the initial stages of test development, they are relatively subjective, and thus limited, methods for evaluating the construct validity of measured variables. Ultimately, the determination of the validity of a measure must be made not on the basis of subjective judgments, but on the basis of relevant data. The basic logic of empirically testing the construct validity of a measure is based on the idea that there are multiple operationalizations of the variable:

> If a given measured variable "*x*" is really measuring conceptual variable "*X*," then it should correlate with other measured variables designed to assess "*X*," and it should not correlate with other measured variables designed to assess other conceptually unrelated variables.

According to this logic, construct validity has two separate components. **Convergent validity** refers to the extent to which a measured variable is found to be related to other measured variables designed to measure the same conceptual variable. **Discriminant validity** refers to the extent to which a measured variable is found to be unrelated to other measured variables designed to assess different conceptual variables.

Assessment of Construct Validity.   Let's take an example of the use of how convergent and discriminant validity were used to demonstrate the construct validity of a new personality variable known as self-monitoring. *Self-monitoring* refers to the tendency to pay attention to the events that are occurring around you and to adjust your behavior to "fit in" with the specific situation you are in. High self-monitors are those who habitually make these adjustments, whereas low self-monitors tend to behave the same way in all situations, essentially ignoring the demands of the social setting.

Social psychologist Mark Snyder (1974) began his development of a self-monitoring scale by constructing forty-one items that he thought would tap into the conceptual variable self-monitoring. These included items designed to directly assess self-monitoring:

> "I guess I put on a show to impress or entertain people."
>
> "I would probably make a good actor."

and items that were to be reverse-scored:

> "I rarely need the advice of my friends to choose movies, books, or music."
>
> "I have trouble changing my behavior to suit different people and different situations."

On the basis of the responses of an initial group of college students, Snyder deleted the sixteen items that had the lowest item-to-total correlations. He was left with a twenty-five-item self-monitoring scale that had a test-retest reliability of .83.

Once he had demonstrated that his scale was reliable, Snyder began to assess its construct validity. First, he demonstrated discriminant validity by showing that the scale did *not* correlate highly with other existing personality scales that might have been measuring similar conceptual variables. For instance, the self-monitoring scale did not correlate highly with a measure of extraversion ($r = +.19$), with a measure of responding in a socially acceptable manner ($r = -.19$), or with an existing measure of achievement anxiety ($r = +.14$).

Satisfied that the self-monitoring scale was not the same as existing scales, and thus showed discriminant validity, Snyder then began to assess the test's convergent validity. Snyder found, for instance, that high self-monitors were more able to accurately communicate an emotional expression when asked to do so ($r = .60$). And he found that professional actors (who should be very sensitive to social cues) scored higher on the scale and that hospitalized psychiatric patients (who are likely to be unaware of social cues) scored lower on the scale, both in comparison to college students. Taken together, Snyder concluded that the self-monitoring scale was reliable and also possessed both convergent and discriminant validity.

One of the important aspects of Snyder's findings is that the convergent validity correlations were not all $r = +1.00$ and the discriminant validity correlations were not all $r = 0.00$. Convergent validity and discriminant validity are never all-or-nothing constructs, and thus it is never possible to definitively "prove" the construct validity of a measured variable. In reality, even measured variables that are designed to measure different conceptual variables will often be at least moderately correlated with each other. For instance, self-monitoring relates, at least to some extent, to extraversion because they are related constructs. Yet the fact that the correlation coefficient is relatively low ($r = .19$) indicates that self-monitoring and extraversion are not identical. Similarly, even measures that assess the same conceptual variable will not, because of random error, be perfectly correlated with each other.

The Nomological Net.   Although convergent reality and discriminant validity are frequently assessed through correlation of the scores on one self-report measure (for instance, one Likert scale of anxiety) with scores on another self-report measure (a different anxiety scale), construct validity can also be evaluated using other types of measured variables. For example, when testing a self-report measure of anxiety, a researcher might compare the scores to ratings of anxiety made by trained psychotherapists or to physiological variables such as blood pressure or skin conductance.

The relationships among the many different measured variables, both self-report and otherwise, form a complicated pattern, called a **nomological net.** Only when we look across many studies, using many different measures of the various conceptual variables and relating those measures to other variables, does a complete picture of the construct validity of the measure begin to emerge—the greater the number of predicted relationships tested and confirmed, the greater the support for the construct validity of the measure.

Criterion Validity

You will have noticed that when Snyder investigated the construct validity of his self-monitoring scale, he assessed its relationship not only to other self-report measures, but also to behavioral measures such as the individual's current occupation (for instance, whether he or she was an actor). There are some particular advantages to testing validity through correlation of a scale with behavioral measures rather than with other self-report measures. For one thing, as we have discussed in Chapter 4, behavioral measures may be less subject to reactivity than are self-report measures. When validity is assessed through correlation of a self-report measure with a behavioral measured variable, the behavioral variable is called a **criterion variable,** and the correlation is an assessment of the self-report measure's **criterion validity.**

Criterion validity is known as **predictive validity** when it involves attempts to foretell the future. This would occur, for instance, when an industrial psychologist uses a measure of job aptitude to predict how well a prospective employee will perform on a job or when an educational psychologist predicts school performance from SAT or GRE scores. Criterion validity is known as **concurrent validity** when it involves assessment of the relationship between a self-report and a behavioral measure that are assessed at the same time. In some cases, criterion validity may even involve use of the self-report measure to predict behaviors that have occurred prior to completion of the scale.

Although the practice of correlating a self-report measure with a behavioral criterion variable can be used to learn about the construct validity of the measured variables, in some applied research settings it is only the ability of the test to predict a specific behavior that is of interest. For instance, an employer who wants to predict whether a person will be an effective manager will be happy to use any self-report measure that is effective in doing so and may not care about what conceptual variable the test measures (for example, does it measure intelligence, social skills, diligence, all three, or something else entirely?). In this case criterion validity involves only the correlation between the variables rather than the use of the variables to make inferences about construct validity.

Improving the Reliability and Validity of Measured Variables

Now that we have considered some of the threats to the validity of measured variables, we can ask how our awareness of these potential threats can help us improve our measures. Most basically, the goal is to be aware of the potential difficulties and to keep them in mind as we design our measures. Because the research process is a social interaction between researcher and participant, we must carefully consider how the participant perceives the research and consider how she or he may react to it. The following are some useful tips for creating valid measures:

1. Conduct a pilot test. **Pilot testing** involves trying out a questionnaire or other research on a small group of individuals to get an idea of how they react to it before the final version of the project is created. After collecting the data from the pilot test, you can modify the measures before actually using the scale in research. Pilot testing can help ensure that participants understand the questions as you expect them to and that they cannot guess the purpose of the questionnaire. You can also use pilot testing to create self-report measures. You ask participants in the pilot study to generate thoughts about the conceptual variables of interest. Then you use these thoughts to generate ideas about the types of items that should be asked on a fixed-format scale.

2. Use multiple measures. As we have seen, the more types of measures are used to assess a conceptual variable, the more information about the variable is gained. For instance, the more items a test has, the more reliable it will be. However, be careful not to make your scale so long that your participants lose interest in taking it! As a general guideline, twenty items are usually sufficient to produce a highly reliable measure.

3. Ensure variability within your measures. If 95 percent of your participants answer an item with the response 7 (strongly agree) or the response 1 (strongly disagree), the item won't be worth including because it won't differentiate the respondents. One way to guarantee variability is to be

sure that the *average* response of your respondents is near the middle of the scale. This means that although most people fall in the middle, some people will fall above and some below the average. Pilot testing enables you to create measures that have variability.

4. Write good items. Make sure that your questions are understandable and not ambiguous. This means the questions shouldn't be too long or too short. Try to avoid ambiguous words. For instance, "Do you regularly feel stress?" is not as good as "How many times per week do you feel stress?" because the term *regular* is ambiguous. Also watch for "double-barreled" questions such as "Are you happy most of the time, or do you find there to be no reason to be happy?" A person who is happy but does not find any real reason for it would not know how to answer this question. Keep your questions as simple as possible, and be specific. For instance, the question "Do you like your parents?" is vaguer than "Do you like your mother?" and "Do you like your father?"

5. Attempt to get your respondents to take your questions seriously. In the instructions you give to them, stress that the accuracy of their responses is important and that their responses are critical to the success of the research project. Otherwise carelessness may result.

6. Attempt to make your items nonreactive. For instance, asking people to indicate whether they agree with the item "I dislike all Japanese people" is unlikely to produce honest answers, whereas a statement such as "The Japanese are using their economic power to hurt the United States" may elicit a more honest answer because the item is more indirect. Of course, the latter item may not assess exactly what you are hoping to measure, but in some cases tradeoffs may be required. In some cases you may wish to embed items that measure something entirely irrelevant (they are called *distracter items*) in your scale to disguise what you are really assessing.

7. Be certain to consider face and content validity by choosing items that seem "reasonable" and that represent a broad range of questions concerning the topic of interest. If the scale is not content valid, you may be evaluating only a small piece of the total picture you are interested in.

8. When possible, use existing measures, rather than creating your own, because the reliability and validity of these measures will already be established.

Comparing Reliability and Validity

We have seen that reliability and construct validity are similar in that they are both assessed through examination of the correlations among measured variables. However, they are different in the sense that reliability refers to correlations among different variables that the researcher is planning to combine into the *same* measure of a single conceptual variable, whereas construct validity refers to correlations of a measure with *different* measures of other conceptual variables. In this sense, it is appropriate to say that reliability comes before validity because reliability is concerned with creating a measure that is then tested in relationship to other measures. If a measure is not reliable, then its construct validity cannot be determined. Tables 5.1 and 5.2 summarize the various types of reliability and validity that researchers must consider.

One important question that we have not yet considered is "How reliable and valid must a scale be in order to be useful?" Researchers do not always agree about the answer, except for the obvious fact that the higher the reliability and the construct validity, the better. One criterion that seems reasonable is that the reliability of a commonly used scale should be at least $\alpha = .70$. However, many tests have reliabilities well above $\alpha = .80$.

In general, it is easier to demonstrate the reliability of a measured variable than it is to demonstrate a variable's construct validity. This is so in part because demonstrating reliability involves only showing that the measured variables correlate with each other, whereas validity involves showing both convergent and discriminant validity. Also, because the items on a scale are all answered using the same response format and are presented sequentially, and because items that do not correlate highly with the total scale score can be deleted, high reliabilities are usually not difficult to achieve.

However, the relationships among different measures of the same conceptual variable that serve as the basis for demonstrating convergent validity are generally very low. For instance, the correlations observed by Snyder were only in the range of .40, and such correlations are not unusual. Although correlations of such size may seem low, they are still taken as evidence for convergent validity.

One of the greatest difficulties in developing a new scale is to demonstrate its discriminant validity. Although almost any new scale that you can imagine will be at least moderately correlated with at least some other existing scales, to be useful, the new scale must be demonstrably different from existing scales in at least some critical respects. Demonstrating this uniqueness is difficult and will generally require that a number of different studies be conducted.

Because there are many existing scales in common use within the behavioral sciences, carefully consider whether you really need to develop a new scale for your research project. Before you begin scale development, be sure to determine if a scale assessing the conceptual variable you are interested in, or at least a similar conceptual variable, might already exist. A good source for information about existing scales, in addition to PsycINFO®, is Robinson, Shaver, and Wrightsman (1991). Remember that it is always advantageous to use an existing measure rather than to develop your own—the reliability and validity of such measures are already established, saving you a lot of work.

Current Research in the Behavioral Sciences: The Hillyer-Joynes Kinematics Scale of Locomotion in Rats With Spinal Injuries

Jessica Hillyer and Robin L. Joynes conduct research on animals with injuries to their spinal cords, with the goal of helping learn how organisms, including humans, may be able to improve their physical movements (locomotion) after injury. One difficulty that they noted in their research with rats was that the existing measure of locomotion (the *BBB Locomotor Rating Scale, (BBB)*, Basso, Beattie, & Bresnahan, 1995) was not sophisticated enough to provide a clear measure of locomotion skills. They therefore decided to create their own, new, measure, which they called the *Hillyer-Joynes Kinematics Scale of Locomotion (HiJK)*. Their measure was designed to assess the locomotion abilities of rats walking on treadmills.

The researchers began by videotaping 137 rats with various degrees of spinal cord injuries as they walked on treadmills. Then three different coders viewed each of the videotapes on a subset of twenty of the rats. For each of these 20 rats, the coders rated the walking skills of the rats on eight different dimensions: *Extension* of the *Hip, Knee,* and *Ankle* joints, *Fluidity* of the joint movement, *Alternation* of the legs during movement, *Placement* of the feet, *Weight support* of the movement and *Consistency* of walking.

Once the raters had completed their ratings, the researchers tested for interrater reliability, to see if the three raters agreed on their coding of each of the five categories that they had rated. Overall, they found high interrater reliability, generally with *r*'s over .9. For instance, for the ratings of foot placement, the correlations among the three coders were as follows:

	Rater 1	Rater 2
Rater 2	.95	
Rater 3	.95	.99

The researchers then had one of the three raters rate all 137 of the rats on the 8 subscales. On the basis of this rater's judgments, they computed the overall reliability of the new measure, using each of the eight rated dimensions as an item in the scale. The Cronbach's alpha for the composite scale, based on 8 items and 137 rats was $\alpha = .86$, denoting acceptable reliability.

Having determined that their new measure was reliable, the researchers next turned to study the validity of the scale. The researchers found that the new measure correlated significantly with scores on the existing measure of locomotion, the *BBB Locomotor Rating Scale*, suggesting that it was measuring the locomotion of the rats in a similar way that it did.

Finally, the researchers tested for predictive validity, by correlating both the *BBB* and the *HiJK* with a physiological assessment of the magnitude of each of the rat's spinal cord injuries. The researchers found that the *HiJK* was better able to predict the nature of the rats' injuries than was the *BBB*, suggesting that the new measure may be a better measure than the old one.

SUMMARY

Assessing the effectiveness of a measured variable involves determining the extent to which the measure is free of both random error and systematic error. These determinations are made through examination of correlations among measures of the same and different conceptual variables.

Reliability refers to the extent to which a measure is free from random error. In some cases, reliability can be assessed through administration of the same or similar tests more than one time (test-retest and equivalent-forms reliability). However, because such procedures can assess only the reliability of traits, and not states, and because they involve two different testing sessions, reliability is more often assessed in terms of the internal consistency of the items on a single scale using split-half reliability or Cronbach's coefficient alpha (α). *Interrater reliability* refers to the reliability of a set of judges or coders.

Construct validity is the extent to which a measure is free from systematic error and thus measures what it is intended to measure. *Face validity* and *content validity* refer to the extent to which a measured variable appears to measure the conceptual variable of interest and to which it samples from a broad domain of items, respectively. *Convergent validity* refers to the extent to which a measured variable correlates with other measured variables designed to measure the same conceptual variable, whereas *discriminant validity* refers to the extent to which a measured variable does not correlate with other measured variables designed to assess other conceptual variables. In some cases, the goal of a research project is to test whether a measure given at one time can predict behavioral measures assessed either at the same time (concurrent validity) or in the future (predictive validity).

KEY TERMS

concurrent validity 99
construct validity 95
content validity 97
convergent validity 97
criterion validity 99
criterion variable 99
Cronbach's coefficient alpha (α) 94
discriminant validity 97
equivalent-forms reliability 92
face validity 96
internal consistency 94
interrater reliability 95
kappa (κ) 95

nomological net 99
pilot testing 100
predictive validity 99
random error 89
reliability 91
retesting effects 92
split-half reliability 94
states 93
systematic error 90
test-retest reliability 91
traits 92
true score 93

REVIEW AND DISCUSSION QUESTIONS

1. Why do self-report scales use many different items that assess the same conceptual variable?

2. Consider a measure that shows high internal consistency but low test-retest reliability. What can be concluded about the measure?

3. What is the relationship between reliability and validity? Why is it possible to have a reliable measure that is not valid but impossible to have a valid measure that is not reliable?

4. Compare the assessment of face, content, and construct validity. Which of the three approaches is most objective, and why? Is it possible to have a measure that is construct valid but not face valid?

5. What is the importance of predictive validity? In what ways does predictive validity differ from construct validity?

6. Discuss the methods that researchers use to improve the reliability and validity of their measures.

RESEARCH PROJECT IDEAS

1. Choose a conceptual variable that can be considered to be a trait of interest to you, and (after conducting a literature review) create a 20-item Likert scale to assess it. Administer the scale to at least 20 people. Compute the scale's reliability, and then, using a statistical software program, delete items until the scale's reliability reaches at least .75 or stops increasing. Consider what sources of random and systematic error might be found in the scale.

2. Develop a behavioral or a free-format self-report measure of the conceptual variable you assessed in problem 1, and collect the relevant data from the same people. Find a partner to help you code the responses, and compute the interrater reliability of the coding. Compute the Pearson correlation coefficient between the new measure and the score on the Likert scale. Does the correlation demonstrate construct validity?

CHAPTER SIX
Surveys and Sampling

STUDY QUESTIONS

- When and why are surveys used in behavioral research?

- What are the advantages and disadvantages of using interviews versus questionnaires in survey research?

- How is probability sampling used to ensure that a sample is representative of the population?

- What is sampling bias, and how does it undermine a researcher's ability to draw conclusions about surveys?

- What statistical procedures are used to report and display data from surveys?

- What is the margin of error of a sample?

Now that we have reviewed the basic types of measured variables and considered how to evaluate their effectiveness at assessing the conceptual variables of interest, it is time to more fully discuss the use of these measures in descriptive research. In this chapter, we will discuss the use of self-report measures, and in Chapter 7, we will discuss the use of behavioral measures. Although these measures are frequently used in a qualitative sense—to draw a complete and complex picture in the form of a narrative—they can also be used quantitatively, as measured variables. As you read these chapters, keep in mind that the goal of descriptive research is to describe the current state of affairs but that it does not by itself provide direct methods for testing research hypotheses. However, both surveys (discussed in this chapter) and naturalistic methods (discussed in Chapter 7) are frequently used not only as descriptive data but also as the measured variables in correlational and experimental tests of research hypotheses. We will discuss these uses in later chapters.

Surveys

A **survey** is a series of self-report measures administered either through an interview or a written questionnaire. Surveys are the most widely used method of collecting descriptive information about a group of people. You may have received a phone call (it usually arrives in the middle of the dinner hour when most people are home) from a survey research group asking you about your taste in music, your shopping habits, or your political preferences.

The goal of a survey, as with all descriptive research, is to produce a "snapshot" of the opinions, attitudes, or behaviors of a group of people at a given time. Because surveys can be used to gather information about a wide variety of information in a relatively short time, they are used extensively by businesspeople, advertisers, and politicians to help them learn what people think, feel, or do.

Interviews

Surveys are usually administered in the form of an **interview,** in which questions are read to the respondent in person or over the telephone. One advantage of in-person interviews is that they may allow the researcher to develop a close rapport and sense of trust with the respondent. This may motivate the respondent to continue with the interview and may lead to more honest and open responding. However, face-to-face interviews are extremely expensive to conduct, and consequently telephone surveys are now more common. In a telephone interview all of the interviewers are located in one place, the telephone numbers are generated automatically, and the questions are read from computer terminals in front of the researchers. This procedure provides such efficiency and coordination among the interviewers that many surveys can be conducted in one day.

Unstructured Interviews. Interviews may use either free-format or fixed-format self-report measures. In an **unstructured interview** the interviewer talks freely with the person being interviewed about many topics. Although a general list of the topics of interest is prepared beforehand, the actual interview focuses in on those topics that the respondent is most interested in or most knowledgeable about. Because the questions asked in an unstructured interview differ from respondent to respondent, the interviewer must be trained to ask questions in a way that gets the most information from the respondent and allows the respondent to express his or her true feelings. One type of a face-to-face unstructured interview in which a number of people are interviewed at the same time and share ideas both with the interviewer and with each other is called a **focus group.**

Unstructured interviews may provide in-depth information about the particular concerns of an individual or a group of people, and thus, may produce ideas for future research projects or for policy decisions. It is, however, very difficult to adequately train interviewers to ask questions in an unbiased manner and to be sure that they have actually done so. And, as we have seen in Chapter 4, because the topics of conversation and the types of answers given in free-response formats vary across participants, the data are difficult to objectively quantify and analyze, and are therefore frequently treated qualitatively.

Structured Interviews. Because researchers usually want more objective data, the **structured interview,** which uses quantitative fixed-format items, is most common. The questions are prepared ahead of time, and the interviewer reads the questions to the respondent. The structured interview has the advantage over an unstructured interview of allowing better comparisons of the responses across different individuals because the questions, time frame, and response format are controlled to be the same for each respondent.

Questionnaires

A **questionnaire** is a set of fixed-format, self-report items that is completed by respondents at their own pace, often without supervision. Questionnaires are generally cheaper than interviews because a researcher can mail the questionnaires to many people or have them complete the questionnaires in large groups. Questionnaires may also produce more honest responses than interviews, particularly when the questions involve sensitive issues such as sexual activity or annual income, because respondents are more likely to perceive their responses as being anonymous than they are in interviews. In comparison to interviews, questionnaires are also likely to be less influenced by the characteristics of the experimenter. For instance, if the topic concerns race-related attitudes, how the respondent answers might depend on the race of the interviewer and how the respondent thinks the interviewer wants him or her to respond. Because the experimenter is not present when a questionnaire is completed, or at least is not directly asking the questions, such problems are less likely.

The Response Rate. Questionnaires are free of some problems that may occur in interviews, but they do have their own set of difficulties. Although
people may be likely to return surveys that have direct relevance to them (for
instance, a survey of college students conducted by their own university),
when mailings are sent to the general population, the **response rate** (that
is, the percentage of people who actually complete the questionnaire and
return it to the investigator) may not be very high. This may lead to incorrect
conclusions because the people who return the questionnaire may respond
differently than those who don't return it would have. Investigators can sometimes increase response rates by providing gifts or monetary payments for
completing the survey, by making the questionnaire appear brief and interesting, by ensuring the confidentiality of all of the data, and by emphasizing
the importance of the individual in the research (Dillman, 1978). Follow-up
mailings can also be used to remind people that they have not completed the
questionnaire, with the hope that they will then do so.

Question Order. Another potential problem with questionnaires that does
not occur with interviews is that people may not answer the questions in the
order they are written, and the researcher does not know whether or not they
have. To take one example, consider these two questions:

1. "How satisfied are you with your relationships with your family?"
2. "How satisfied are you with your relationship with your spouse?"

If the questions are answered in the order that they are presented here, then
most respondents interpret the word *family* in question 1 to include their
spouse. If question 2 is answered before question 1, however, the term *family*
in question 1 is interpreted to mean the rest of the family except the spouse.
Such variability can create measurement error (Schuman & Presser, 1981;
Schwarz & Strack, 1991).

Use of Existing Survey Data

Because it is very expensive to conduct surveys, scientists often work
together on them. For instance, a researcher may have a small number of
questions relevant to his or her research included within a larger survey. Or
researchers can access public-domain data sets that contain data from previous surveys. The U.S. Census is probably the largest such data set, containing
information on family size, fertility, occupation, and income for the entire U.S.
population, as well as a more extensive interview data set of a smaller group
of citizens. The General Social Survey is a collection of over 1,000 items given
to a sample of U.S. citizens (Davis, Smith, & Marsden, 2000). Because the same
questions are asked each year the survey is given, comparisons can be made
over time. Sometimes these data sets are given in comparable forms to citizens
of different countries, allowing cross-cultural comparisons. One such data set is
the Human Area Relations Files. Indexes of some of the most important social
science databases can be found in Clubb, Austin, Geda, and Traugott (1985).

Sampling and Generalization

We have seen that surveys are conducted with the goal of creating an accurate picture of the current attitudes, beliefs, or behaviors of a large group of people. In some rare cases it is possible to conduct a **census**—that is, to measure each person about whom we wish to know. In most cases, however, the group of people that we want to learn about is so large that measuring each person is not practical. Thus, the researcher must test some subset of the entire group of people who could have participated in the research. **Sampling** refers to the selection of people to participate in a research project, usually with the goal of being able to use these people to make inferences about a larger group of individuals. The entire group of people that the researcher desires to learn about is known as the **population,** and the smaller group of people who actually participate in the research is known as the **sample.**

Definition of the Population

The population of interest to the researcher must be defined precisely. For instance, some populations of interest to a survey researcher might be "all citizens of voting age in the United States who plan to vote in the next election," "all students currently enrolled full time at the University of Chicago," or "all Hispanic Americans over forty years of age who live within the Baltimore city limits." In most cases the scientist does not particularly care about the characteristics of the specific people chosen to be in the sample. Rather, the scientist uses the sample to draw inferences about the population as a whole (just as a medical researcher analyzes a sample to make inferences about blood that was not sampled).

Whenever samples are used to make inferences about populations, the researcher faces a basic dilemma—he or she will never be able to know *exactly* what the true characteristics of the population are because all of the members of the population cannot be contacted. However, this is not really as big a problem as it might seem if the sample can be assumed to be representative of the population. A **representative sample** is one that is approximately the same as the population in every important respect. For instance, a representative sample of the population of students at a college or university would contain about the same proportion of men, sophomores, and engineering majors as are in the college itself, as well as being roughly equivalent to the population on every other conceivable characteristic.

Probability Sampling

To make the sample representative of the population, any of several probability sampling techniques may be employed. In **probability sampling,** procedures are used to ensure that each person in the population has a known chance of being selected to be part of the sample. As a result, the likelihood that the sample is representative of the population is increased, as is the ability to use the sample to draw inferences about the population.

Simple Random Sampling.   The most basic probability sample is drawn using **simple random sampling.** In this case, the goal is to ensure that each person in the population has an *equal* chance of being selected to be in the sample. To draw a simple random sample, an investigator must first have a complete list (known as a **sampling frame**) of all of the people in the population. For instance, voting registration lists may be used as a sampling frame, or telephone numbers of all of the households in a given geographic location may be used. The latter list will basically represent the population that lives in that area because almost all U.S. households now have a telephone. Recent advances in survey methodology allow researchers to include cell phone numbers in their sampling frame as well.

Then the investigator randomly selects from the frame a sample of a given number of people. Let's say you are interested in studying volunteering behavior of the students at your college or university, and you want to collect a random sample of 100 students. You would begin by finding a list of all of the students currently enrolled at the college. Assume that there are 7,000 names on this list, numbered sequentially from 1 to 7,000. Then, as shown in the instructions for using Statistical Table A (in Appendix E), you could use a random number table (or a random number generator on a computer) to produce 100 numbers that fall between 1 and 7,000 and select those 100 students to be in your sample.

Systematic Random Sampling.   If the list of names on the sampling frame is itself known to be in a random sequence, then a probability sampling procedure known as **systematic random sampling** can be used. In your case, because you wish to draw a sample of 100 students from a population of 7,000 students, you will want to sample 1 out of every 70 students ($100/7,000 = 1/70$). To create the systematic sample, you first draw a random number between 1 and 70 and then sample the person on the list with that number. You create the rest of the sample by taking every seventieth person on the list after the initial person. For instance, if the first person sampled was number 32, you would then sample number 102, 172, and so on. You can see that it is easier to use systematic sampling than simple random sampling because only one initial number has to be chosen at random.

Stratified Sampling.   Because in most cases sampling frames include such information about the population as sex, age, ethnicity, and region of residence, and because the variables being measured are frequently expected to differ across these subgroups, it is often useful to draw separate samples from each of these subgroups rather than to sample from the population as a whole. The subgroups are called **strata,** and the sampling procedure is known as **stratified sampling.**

To collect a *proportionate stratified sample,* frames of all of the people within each strata are first located, and random samples are drawn from within each of the strata. For example, if you expected that volunteering rates would be different for students from different majors, you could first make separate lists of the students in each of the majors at your school and then randomly sample from each list. One outcome of this procedure is that the different majors are guaranteed to be represented in the sample in the same proportion that they are represented in the population, a result that might not occur if you had used random sampling. Furthermore, it can be shown mathematically that if volunteering behavior does indeed differ among the strata, a stratified sample will provide a more precise estimate of the population characteristics than will a simple random sample (Kish, 1965).

Disproportionate stratified sampling is frequently used when the strata differ in size and the researcher is interested in comparing the characteristics of the strata. For instance, in a class of 7,000 students, only 10 or so might be French majors. If a random sample of 100 students was drawn, there might not be any French majors in the sample, or at least there would be too few to allow a researcher to draw meaningful conclusions about them. In this case, the researcher draws a sample that includes a larger proportion of some strata than they are actually represented in the population. This procedure is called **oversampling** and is used to provide large enough samples of the strata of interest to allow analysis. Mathematical formulas are used to determine the optimum size for each of the strata.

Cluster Sampling.   Although simple and stratified sampling can be used to create representative samples when there is a complete sampling frame for the population, in some cases there is no such list. For instance, there is no single list of all of the currently matriculated college students in the United States. In these cases an alternative approach known as **cluster sampling** can be used. The technique is to break the population into a set of smaller groups (called *clusters*) for which there are sampling frames and then to randomly choose some of the clusters for inclusion in the sample. At this point, every person in the cluster may be sampled, or a random sample of the cluster may be drawn.

Often the clustering is done in stages. For instance, we might first divide the United States into regions (for instance, East, Midwest, South, Southwest, and West). Then we would randomly select states from each region, counties from each state, and colleges or universities from each county. Because there is a sampling frame of the matriculated students at each of the selected colleges, we could draw a random sample from these lists. In addition to allowing a representative sample to be drawn when there is no sampling frame, cluster sampling is convenient. Once we have selected the clusters, we need only contact the students at the selected colleges rather than having to sample from all of the colleges and universities in the United States. In cluster sampling, the selected clusters are used to draw inferences about the nonselected ones. Although this practice loses some precision, cluster sampling is frequently used because of convenience.

Sampling Bias and Nonprobability Sampling

The advantage of probability sampling methods is that their samples will be representative and thus can be used to draw inferences about the characteristics of the population. Although these procedures sound good in theory, in practice it is difficult to be certain that the sample is truly representative. Representativeness requires that two conditions be met. First, there must be one or more sampling frames that list the entire population of interest, and second, all of the selected individuals must actually be sampled. When either of these conditions is not met, there is the potential for **sampling bias.** This occurs when the sample is not actually representative of the population because the probability with which members of the population have been selected for participation is not known.

Sampling bias can arise when an accurate sampling frame for the population of interest cannot be obtained. In some cases there is an available sampling frame, but there is no guarantee that it is accurate. The sampling frame may be inaccurate because some members of the population are missing or because it includes some names that are not actually in the population. College student directories, for instance, frequently do not include new students or those who requested that their name not be listed, and these directories may also include students who have transferred or dropped out.

In other cases there simply is no sampling frame. Imagine attempting to obtain a frame that included all of the homeless people in New York City or all of the women in the United States who are currently pregnant with their first child. In cases where probability sampling is impossible because there is no available sampling frame, *nonprobability samples* must be used. To obtain a sample of homeless individuals, for instance, the researcher will interview individuals on the street or at a homeless shelter. One type of nonprobability sample that can be used when the population of interest is rare or difficult to reach is called **snowball sampling.** In this procedure one or more individuals from the population are contacted, and these individuals are used to lead the researcher to other population members. Such a technique might be used to locate homeless individuals. Of course, in such cases the potential for sampling bias is high because the people in the sample may be different from the people in the population. Snowball sampling at homeless shelters, for instance, may include a greater proportion of people who stay in shelters and a smaller proportion of people who do not stay in shelters than are in the population. This is a limitation of nonprobability sampling, but one that the researcher must live with because there is no possible probability sampling method that can be used.

Even if a complete sampling frame is available, sampling bias can occur if all members of the random sample cannot be contacted or cannot be convinced to participate in the survey. For instance, people may be on vacation, they may have moved to a different address, or they may not be willing to complete the questionnaire or interview. When a questionnaire is mailed, the response rate may be low. In each of these cases the potential for sampling bias exists because the people who completed the survey may have responded differently than would those who could not be contacted.

Nonprobability samples are also frequently found when college students are used in experimental research. Such samples are called **convenience samples** because the researcher has sampled whatever individuals were readily available without any attempt to make the sample representative of a population. Although such samples can be used to test research hypotheses, they may not be used to draw inferences about populations. We will discuss the use of convenience samples in experimental research designs more fully in Chapter 13.

Whenever you read a research report, make sure to determine what sampling procedures have been used to select the research participants. In some cases, researchers make statements about populations on the basis of nonprobability samples, which are not likely to be representative of the population they are interested in. For instance, polls in which people are asked to call a 900 number or log on to a website to express their opinions on a given topic may contain sampling bias because people who are in favor of (or opposed to) the issue may have more time or more motivation to do so. Whenever the respondents, rather than the researchers, choose whether to be part of the sample, sampling bias is possible. The important thing is to remain aware of what sampling techniques have been used and to draw your own conclusions accordingly.

Summarizing the Sample Data

You can well imagine that once a survey has been completed, the collected data (known as the **raw data**) must be transformed in a way that will allow them to be meaningfully interpreted. The raw data are, by themselves, not very useful for gaining the desired snapshot because they contain too many numbers. For example, if we interview 500 people and ask each of them forty questions, there will be 20,000 responses to examine. In this section we will consider some of the statistical methods used to summarize sample data. Procedures for using computer software programs to conduct statistical analyses are reviewed in Appendix B, and you may want to read this material at this point.

Frequency Distributions

Table 6.1 presents some hypothetical raw data from twenty-five participants on five variables collected in a sort of "minisurvey." You can see that the table is arranged such that the variables (sex, ethnic background, age, life satisfaction, family income) are in the columns and the participants form the rows. For nominal variables such as sex or ethnicity, the data can be summarized through the use of a frequency distribution. A **frequency distribution** is a table that indicates how many, and in most cases what percentage, of individuals in the sample fall into each of a set of categories. A frequency distribution of the ethnicity variable from Table 6.1 is shown in Figure 6.1(a). The frequency distribution can be displayed visually in a **bar chart,** as shown for the ethnic background variable in Figure 6.1(b). The characteristics of the sample are easily seen when summarized through a frequency distribution or a bar chart.

TABLE 6.1 Raw Data from a Sample of Twenty-Five Individuals

ID	Sex	Ethnic Background	Age	Life Satisfaction	Family Income
1	Male	White	31	70	$28,000
2	Female	White	19	68	37,000
3	Male	Asian	34	78	43,000
4	Female	White	45	90	87,000
5	Female	African American	57	80	90,000
6	Male	Asian	26	75	43,000
7	Female	Hispanic	19	95	26,000
8	Female	White	33	91	64,000
9	Male	Hispanic	18	74	18,000
10	Female	Asian	20	10	29,000
11	Male	African American	47	90	53,000
12	Female	White	45	82	2,800,000
13	Female	Asian	63	98	87,000
14	Female	Hispanic	37	95	44,000
15	Female	Asian	38	85	47,000
16	Male	White	24	80	31,000
17	Male	White	18	60	28,000
18	Male	Asian	40	33	43,000
19	Female	White	29	96	87,000
20	Female	African American	31	80	90,000
21	Female	Hispanic	25	95	26,000
22	Female	White	32	99	64,000
23	Male	Hispanic	33	34	53,000
24	Male	Asian	22	55	43,000
25	Female	White	52	41	37,000

This table represents the raw data from twenty-five individuals who have completed a hypothetical survey. The individuals are given an identification number, indicated in column 1. The data represent the sex, ethnicity, age, and rated life satisfaction of the respondents, as well as their family income. The life satisfaction measure is a Likert scale that ranges from 0 = "not at all satisifed" to 100 = "extremely satisfied."

One approach to summarizing a quantitative variable is to combine adjacent values into a set of categories and then to examine the frequencies of each of the categories. The resulting distribution is known as a **grouped frequency distribution.** A grouped frequency distribution of the age variable from Table 6.1 is shown in Figure 6.2(a). In this case, the ages have been grouped into five categories (less than 21, 21–30, 31–40, 41–50, and greater than 50).

FIGURE 6.1 Frequency Distribution and Bar Chart

(a) *Frequency Distribution*

Ethnic Background	Frequency Distribution	Percent
African American	3	12
Asian	7	28*
Hispanic	5*	20
White	10	40
Total	25	100

*Twenty-eight percent of the sample are Asians, and there are five Hispanics in the sample.

(b) *Bar Chart*

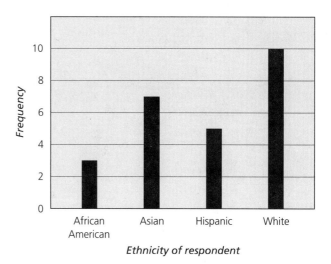

The above figure presents a frequency distribution and a bar chart of the ethnicity variable from Table 6.1.

The grouped frequency distribution may be displayed visually in the form of a histogram, as shown in Figure 6.2(b). A **histogram** is slightly different from a bar chart because the bars are drawn so that they touch each other. This indicates that the original variable is quantitative. If the frequencies of the groups are indicated with a line, rather than bars, as shown in Figure 6.2(c), the display is called a **frequency curve.**

One limitation of grouped frequency distributions is that grouping the values together into categories results in the loss of some information. For instance, it is not possible to tell from the grouped frequency distribution in Figure 6.2(a) exactly how many people in the sample are twenty-three years old. A **stem and leaf plot** is a method of graphically summarizing the raw

FIGURE 6.2 Grouped Frequency Distribution, Histogram, and Frequency Curve

(a) *Grouped Frequency Distribution*

Age	Frequency Distribution	Percent
Less than 21	5	20[*]
21–30	5	20
31–40	9	36
41–50	3[*]	12
Greater than 50	3	12
Total	25	100

[*]Twenty percent of the sample have not reached their twenty-first birthday, and three people in the sample are 41, 42, 43, 44, 45, 46, 47, 48, 49, or 50 years old.

(b) *Histogram*

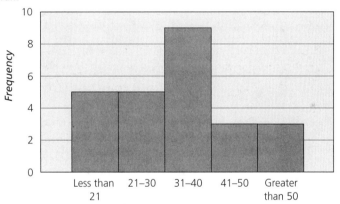

(c) *Frequency Curve*

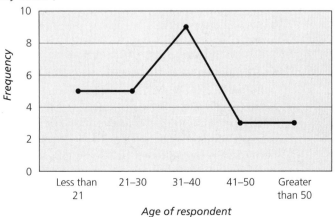

The above presents a grouped frequency distribution, a histogram, and a frequency curve of the age variable from Table 6.1.

FIGURE 6.3   Stem and Leaf Plot

Age

Stem	Leaves
10	8899
20	024569
30	11233478
40	0557
50	27
60	3

This is a stem and leaf plot of the age variable from Table 6.1. The stems on the left represent the 10s place, and the leaves on the right represent the units place. You can see from the plot that there are twenty-five individuals in the sampling, ranging from two who are eighteen years old to one who is sixty-three years old.

data such that the original data values can still be seen. A stem and leaf plot of the age variable from Table 6.1 is shown in Figure 6.3.

Descriptive Statistics

Descriptive statistics are numbers that summarize the pattern of scores observed on a measured variable. This pattern is called the *distribution* of the variable. Most basically, the distribution can be described in terms of its **central tendency**—that is, the point in the distribution around which the data are centered—and its **dispersion,** or spread. As we will see, central tendency is summarized through the use of descriptive statistics such as the *mean,* the *median,* and the *mode,* and dispersion is summarized through the use of the *variance* and the *standard deviation.* Figure 6.4 shows a printout from the IBM Statistical Package for the Social Sciences (IBM SPSS) software of the descriptive statistics for the quantitative variables in Table 6.1.

Measures of Central Tendency.   The arithmetic average, or **arithmetic mean,** is the most commonly used measure of central tendency. It is computed by summing all of the scores on the variable and dividing this sum by the number of participants in the distribution (denoted by the letter N). The sample mean is sometimes denoted with the symbol $\bar{x}$, read as "X-Bar," and may also be indicated by the letter M. As you can see in Figure 6.4, in our sample, the mean age of the twenty-five students is 33.52. In this case, the mean provides an accurate index of the central tendency of the age variable because if you look at the stem and leaf plot in Figure 6.3, you can see that most of the ages are centered at about thirty-three.

FIGURE 6.4   IBM SPSS Printout of Descriptive Statistics

Descriptive Statistics

	N	Minimum	Maximum	Mean	Std. Deviation
Number	25	1.00	25.00	13.0000	7.35980
Age	25	18.00	63.00	33.5200	12.51040
Statis	25	10.00	99.00	74.1600	23.44618
Income	25	18000.00	28000.00	159920.0	550480.16313
Valid N (listwise)	25				

The pattern of scores observed on a measured variable is known as the variable's **distribution.** It turns out that most quantitative variables have distributions similar to that shown in Figure 6.5(a). Most of the data are located near the center of the distribution, and the distribution is symmetrical and bell-shaped. Data distributions that are shaped like a bell are known as **normal distributions.**

In some cases, however, the data distribution is not symmetrical. This occurs when there are one or more extreme scores (known as **outliers**) at one end of the distribution. For instance, because there is an outlier in the family income variable in Table 6.1 (a value of $2,800,000), a frequency curve of this variable would look more like that shown in Figure 6.5(b) than that shown in Figure 6.5(a). Distributions that are not symmetrical are said to be **skewed.** As shown in Figure 6.5(b) and (c), distributions are said to be either *positively* skewed or *negatively* skewed, depending on where the outliers fall.

Because the mean is highly influenced by the presence of outliers, it is not a good measure of central tendency when the distribution is highly skewed. For instance, although it appears from Table 6.1 that the central tendency of the family income variable should be around $40,000, the mean family income is actually $159,920. The single very extreme income has a disproportionate impact on the mean, resulting in a value that does not well represent the central tendency.

The median is used as an alternative measure of central tendency when distributions are skewed. The **median** is the score in the center of the distribution, meaning that 50 percent of the scores are greater than the median and 50 percent of the scores are lower than the median. Methods for calculating the median are presented in Appendix B. In our case, the median household income ($43,000) is a much better indication of central tendency than is the mean household income ($159,920).

A final measure of central tendency, known as the **mode,** represents the value that occurs most frequently in the distribution. You can see from Table 6.1 that the modal value for the income variable is $43,000 (it occurs four times). In some cases there can be more than one mode. For instance, the age variable has modes at 18, 19, 31, 33, and 45. Although the mode does

FIGURE 6.5   Shapes of Distributions

(a) *Normal Distribution*

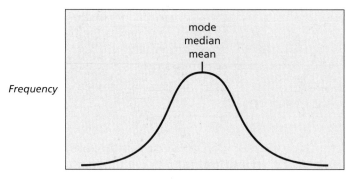

(b) *Positive Skew*

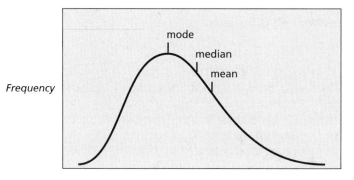

(c) *Negative Skew*

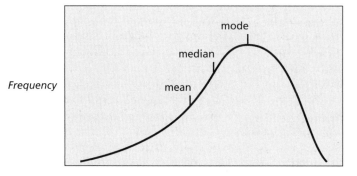

The mean, the median, and the mode are three measures of central tendency. In a normal distribution (a), all three measures fall at the same point on the distribution. When outliers are present, however, the distribution is no longer symmetrical, but becomes skewed. If the outliers are on the right side of the distribution (b), the distribution is considered positively skewed. If the outliers are on the left side of the distribution (c), the distribution is considered negatively skewed. Because the mean is more influenced by the presence of outliers, it falls nearer the outliers in a skewed distribution than does the median. The mode always falls at the most frequently occurring value (the top of the frequency curve.)

represent central tendency, it is not frequently used in scientific research. The relationships among the mean, the median, and the mode are described in Figure 6.5.

Measures of Dispersion.   In addition to summarizing the central tendency of a distribution, descriptive statistics convey information about how the scores on the variable are spread around the central tendency. *Dispersion* refers to the extent to which the scores are all tightly clustered around the central tendency, like this:

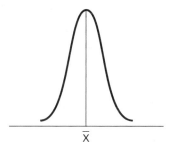

or are more spread out away from it, like this:

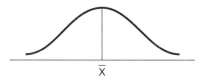

One simple measure of dispersion is to find the largest (the maximum) and the smallest (the minimum) observed values of the variable and to compute the **range** of the variable as the maximum observed score minus the minimum observed score. You can check that the range of the age variable is $63 - 18 = 45$.

The standard deviation, symbolized as s, is the most commonly used measure of dispersion. As discussed in more detail in Appendix B, computation of the standard deviation begins with the calculation of a mean deviation score for each individual. The **mean deviation** is the score on the variable minus the mean of the variable. Individuals who score above the mean have positive deviation scores, whereas those who score below the mean have negative deviation scores. The mean deviations are squared and summed to produce a statistic called the sum of squared deviations, or **sum of squares.** The sum of squares is divided by the sample size (N) to produce a statistic known as the **variance,** symbolized as s^2. The square root of the variance is the **standard deviation, s.** Distributions with a larger standard deviation have more spread. As you can see from Figure 6.4, the standard deviation of the age variable in Table 6.1 is 12.51.

Sample Size and the Margin of Error

To this point, we have discussed the use of descriptive statistics to summarize the raw data in the sample. But recall that the goal of descriptive research is normally to use the sample to provide estimates about characteristics of the population from which it has been selected. We have seen that the ability to use the sample to accurately estimate the population requires that the sample be representative of the population and that this is ensured through the use of probability sampling techniques. But the extent to which the sample provides an accurate estimate of the population of interest is also determined by the size of the sample (N). Increasing the size of a sample makes it more likely that the sample will be representative of the population and thus provides more precise estimates of population characteristics.

Because of random error, the sample characteristics will most likely not be exactly the same as the population characteristics that we wish to estimate. It is, however, possible to use statistical theory to create a **confidence interval** within which we can say with some certainty that a population value is likely to fall. The procedures for creating and interpreting confidence intervals are discussed in detail in Appendix B. The confidence interval is frequently known as the **margin of error** of the sample. For instance, in Table 1.1 you can see that the margin of error of the survey is listed as "plus or minus three percentage points." In this case, the margin of error is interpreted as indicating that the true value of the population will fall between the listed value minus three points and the listed value plus three points 95 percent of the time.

One very surprising fact about sampling is that, although larger samples provide more precise estimates of the population, the size of the population being estimated does not matter very much. In fact, a probability sample of 1,000 people can provide just as good an estimate for the population of the United States as can a sample of 1,000 from a small town of 20,000 people. If you are not familiar with sampling methods, you may believe that small samples cannot tell us anything about larger populations. For instance, you might think that a sample of 1,000 people cannot possibly provide a good estimate of the attitudes of the 250 million people in the United States because it represents only a very small proportion (about four one-thousandths of one percent) of the population. In fact, a carefully collected probability sample of 1,000 people can provide an extremely precise estimate of the attitudes of the U.S. population, and such small samples are routinely used to predict the outcome of national elections. Of course, probability samples are subject to many of the same problems that affect measurement more generally, including random error, reactivity, and construct invalidity. Furthermore, the results of a survey show only what people think today—they may change their minds tomorrow. Thus, although probability sampling methods are highly accurate overall, they do not guarantee accurate results.

Current Research in the Behavioral Sciences: Assessing Americans' Attitudes Toward Health Care

Because so many opinion polls are now conducted, and many of their results are quickly put online, it is now possible to view the estimated opinions of large populations in almost real time. For instance, as I write these words in July, 2009, I can visit the CBS news website and see the results of a number of recent polls regarding the opinions of U.S. citizens about a variety of national issues.

One poll, reported at http://www.cbsnews.com/htdocs/pdf/jul09b_ health_care-AM.pdf used a random sample of 1,050 adults nationwide in the United States, who were interviewed by telephone on July 24–28, 2009. The phone numbers were dialed from random digit dial samples of both standard landline and cell phones. The error due to sampling for results based on the entire sample is plus or minus three percentage points, although the error for subgroups is higher.

The polls provide a snapshot of the current state of thinking in U.S. citizens about health care reform. Here are some findings:

In response to the question "Will health care reform happen in 2009?" most Americans see health care reform as likely, although just 16 percent call it "very" likely. Four in 10 think it is not likely this year.

Very likely	16%
Somewhat likely	43%
Not likely	40%

However, many Americans don't see how they would personally benefit from the health care proposals being considered. In response to the question, "Would the current congressional reform proposals help you? 59 percent say those proposals—as they understand them—would not help them directly. Just under a third says current plans would.

Yes	31%
No	59%

By a 2 to 1 margin, Americans feel President Obama has better ideas for reforming health care than Congressional Republicans. Views on this are partisan, but independents side with the President.

The question asked was "Who has better ideas for health care reform?" Here are the results overall, as well as separately for Democrats, Republicans, and Independents:

	Overall	Democrats	Republicans	Independents
President Obama	55%	81%	27%	48%
Republicans	26%	10%	52%	26%

But, as you can see in the responses to the following question, Mr. Obama's approval rating on handling the overall issue remains under 50 percent, and many still don't have a view yet:

"Do you approve or disapprove of President Obama's health care plans?"

Approve	46%
Disapprove	38%
Don't know	16%

SUMMARY

Surveys are self-report descriptive research designs that attempt to capture the current opinions, attitudes, or behaviors of a group of people. Surveys can use either unstructured or structured formats and can be administered in the form of in-person or telephone interviews or as written questionnaires.

Surveys are designed to draw conclusions about a population of individuals, but because it is not possible to measure each person in the population, data are collected from a smaller sample of people drawn from the population. This procedure is known as sampling.

Probability sampling techniques, including simple random sampling, systematic random sampling, stratified sampling, and cluster sampling, are used to ensure that the sample is representative of the population, thus allowing the researcher to use the sample to draw conclusions about the population.

When nonprobability sampling techniques are used, either because they are convenient or because probability methods are not feasible, they are subject to sampling bias, and they cannot be used to generalize from the sample to the population.

The raw data from a survey are summarized through frequency distributions and descriptive statistics. The distribution of a variable is summarized in terms of its central tendency using the mean, the mode, or the median, as well as its dispersion, summarized in terms of the variance and standard deviation.

The extent to which the sample provides an accurate picture of the population depends to a great extent on the sample size (N). In general, larger samples will produce a more accurate picture and thus have a lower margin of error.

KEY TERMS

arithmetic mean 118	central tendency 118
bar chart 114	cluster sampling 112
census 110	confidence interval 122

REVIEW AND DISCUSSION QUESTIONS

1. Compare the advantages and disadvantages of using interviews versus questionnaires in survey research.

2. Compare a sample and a population. Under what circumstances can a sample be used to draw conclusions about a population?

3. Compare and contrast the different types of probability sampling techniques.

4. When and why would nonprobability sampling methods be used?

5. Under what conditions is sampling bias likely to occur, what are its effects on generalization, and how can it be avoided?

6. Indicate the similarities and differences among the mean, the median, and the mode.

7. What is the standard deviation, and what does it represent?

RESEARCH PROJECT IDEAS

1. Develop a topic of interest to you, and prepare both a structured and an unstructured interview. Collect data from your classmates, and develop a method for coding the findings.

2. Create a sampling frame, and collect a random or stratified random sample of the male and female students in your class.

3. A poll conducted by the *New York Times* shows candidate A leading candidate B by 33 to 31 percent. A poll conducted by the *Washington Post* shows candidate B leading candidate A by 34 to 32 percent. If the margin of error of each poll is plus or minus 3 percent, what should be concluded about the polls and about the public's preferences for the two candidates?

CHAPTER SEVEN
Naturalistic Methods

STUDY QUESTIONS

- What is naturalistic research, and why is it important?

- What is ecological validity, and why do naturalistic research designs have it?

- What are the advantages and disadvantages of being an acknowledged or unacknowledged participant or observer in observational research?

- What are case studies? What are their benefits and drawbacks?

- How are behaviors systematically coded to assess their reliability and validity?

- What is archival research, and what types of questions can it be used to answer?

As we have seen in Chapter 6, self-report measures have the advantage of allowing the researcher to collect a large amount of information from the respondents quickly and easily. On the other hand, they also have the potential of being inaccurate if the respondent does not have access to, or is unwilling to express, his or her true beliefs. And we have seen in Chapter 4 that behavioral measures have the advantage of being more natural and thus less influenced by reactivity. In this chapter, we discuss descriptive research that uses behavioral measures. As we have seen in Chapter 1, descriptive research may be conducted either *qualitatively*—in which case the goal is to describe the observations in detail and to use those descriptions as the results, or *quantitatively*—in which the data is collected using systematic methods and the data are analyzed using statistical techniques. Keep in mind as you read the chapter that, as with most descriptive research, the goal is not only to test research hypotheses, but also to develop ideas for topics that can be studied later using other types of research designs. However, as with survey research, naturalistic methods can also be used to create measured variables for use in correlational and experimental tests of research hypotheses.

Naturalistic Research

Naturalistic research is designed to describe and measure the behavior of people or animals as it occurs in their everyday lives. The behavior may be measured as it occurs, or it could already have been recorded by others, or it may be recorded on videotape to be coded at a later time. In any case, however, because it involves the observation of everyday behavior, a basic difficulty results—the rich and complex data that are observed must be organized into meaningful measured variables that can be analyzed. One of the goals of this chapter is to review methods for turning observed everyday behavior into measured variables.

Naturalistic research approaches are used by researchers in a variety of disciplines, and the data that form the basis of naturalistic research methods can be gathered from many different sources in many different ways. These range from a clinical psychologist's informal observations of his or her clients, to another scientist's more formal observations of the behaviors of animals in the wild, to an analysis of politicians' speeches, to a videotaping of children playing with their parents in a laboratory setting. Although these approaches frequently involve qualitative data, there are also techniques for turning observations into quantitative data, and we will discuss both types in this chapter.

In many cases, naturalistic research is the only possible approach to collecting data. For instance, whereas researchers may not be able to study the impact of earthquakes, floods, or cult membership using experimental research designs, they may be able to use naturalistic research designs to collect a wide variety of data that can be useful in understanding such phenomena.

One particular advantage of naturalistic research is that it has **ecological validity.** *Ecological validity* refers to the extent to which the research is conducted in situations that are similar to the everyday life experiences of the participants (Aronson & Carlsmith, 1968). In naturalistic research the people whose behavior is being measured are doing the things they do every day, and in some cases they may not even know that their behavior is being recorded. In these cases, reactivity is minimized and the construct validity of the measures should therefore be increased.

Observational Research

Observational research involves making observations of behavior and recording those observations in an objective manner. The observational approach is the oldest method of conducting research and is used routinely in psychology, anthropology, sociology, and many other fields.

Let's consider an observational study. To observe the behavior of individuals at work, industrial psychologist Roy (1959–1960) took a job in a factory where raincoats were made. The job entailed boring, repetitive movements (punching holes in plastic sheets using large stamping machines) and went on eight hours a day, five days a week. There was nothing at all interesting about the job, and Roy was uncertain how the employees, some of whom had been there for many years, could stand the monotony.

In his first few days on the job Roy did not notice anything particularly unusual. However, as he carefully observed the activities of the other employees over time, he began to discover that they had a series of "pranks" that they played on and with each other. For instance, every time "Sammy" went to the drinking fountain, "Ike" turned off the power on "Sammy's" machine. And whenever "Sammy" returned, he tried to stamp a piece before "discovering" that the power had been turned off. He then acted angrily toward "Ike," who in turn responded with a shrug and a smirk.

In addition to this event, which occurred several times a day, Roy also noted many other games that the workers effectively used to break up the day. At 11:00 "Sammy" would yell, "Banana time!" and steal the banana out of "Ike's" lunch pail, which was sitting on a shelf. Later in the morning "Ike" would open the window in front of "Sammy's" machine, letting in freezing cold air. "Sammy" would protest and close the window. At the end of the day, "Sammy" would quit two minutes early, drawing fire from the employees' boss, who nevertheless let the activity occur day after day.

Although Roy entered the factory expecting to find only a limited set of mundane observations, he actually discovered a whole world of regular, complicated, and, to the employees, satisfying activities that broke up the monotony of their everyday work existence. This represents one of the major advantages of naturalistic research methods. Because the data are rich, they can be an important source of ideas.

In this example, because the researcher was working at a stamping machine and interacting with the other employees, he was himself a *participant* in the setting being observed. When a scientist takes a job in a factory, joins a religious cult (Festinger, Riecken, & Schachter, 1956), or checks into a mental institution (Rosenhan, 1973), he or she becomes part of the setting itself. Other times, the scientist may choose to remain strictly an *observer* of the setting, such as when he or she views children in a classroom from a corner without playing with them, watches employees in a factory from behind a one-way mirror, or observes behavior in a public restroom (Humphreys, 1975).

In addition to deciding whether to be a participant, the researcher must also decide whether to let the people being observed know that the observation is occurring—that is, to be *acknowledged* or *unacknowledged* to the population being studied. Because the decision about whether to be participant or nonparticipant can be independent of the decision to be acknowledged or unacknowledged, there are, as shown in Table 7.1, altogether four possible types of observational research designs. There are advantages and disadvantages to each approach, and the choice of which to use will be based on the goals of the research, the ability to obtain access to the population, and ethical principles.

The Unacknowledged Participant

One approach is that of the unacknowledged participant. When an observer takes a job in a factory, as Roy did, or infiltrates the life of the homeless in a city, without letting the people being observed know about it, the observer has the advantage of concealment. As a result, she or he may be able to get close to the people being observed and may get them to reveal personal or intimate information about themselves and their social situation, such as their true feelings about their employers or their reactions to being on the street. The unacknowledged participant, then, has the best chance of really "getting to know" the people being observed.

Of course, becoming too close to the people being studied may have negative effects as well. For one thing, the researcher may have difficulty remaining objective. The observer who learns people's names, hears intimate accounts of their lives, and becomes a friend may find his or her perception shaped more by their point of view than by a more objective, scientific one. Alternatively, the observer may dislike the people whom he or she is observing, which may create a negative bias in subsequent analysis and reporting of the data.

The use of an unacknowledged participant strategy also poses ethical dilemmas for the researcher. For one thing, the people being observed may never be told that they were part of a research project or may find it out only later. This may not be a great problem when the observation is conducted in a public arena, such as a bar or a city park, but the problem may be greater when the observation is in a setting where people might later be identified, with potential negative consequences to them. For instance, if a researcher takes a job in a factory and then writes a research report concerning the true feelings of the employees about their employers, management may be able to identify the individual workers from these descriptions.

TABLE 7.1   Participation and Acknowledgement in Observational Research

Approach	Example	Advantages and Disadvantages
Unacknowledged participant	Roy's (1959–1960) observations in the raincoat factory	Chance to get intimate information from workers, but researcher may change the situation; poses ethical questions
Acknowledged participant	Whyte's (1993) study of "street corner society"	Ethically appropriate, but might have been biased by friendships; potential for reactivity
Unacknowledged observer	Recording the behaviors of people in a small town	Limits reactivity problems, but poses ethical questions
Acknowledged observer	Pomerantz et al.'s (1995) study of children's social comparison	Researchers able to spend entire session coding behaviors, but potential for reactivity because children knew they were being watched

When conducting naturalistic observation, scientists may be either acknowledged or unacknowledged and may either participate in the ongoing activity or remain passive observers of the activity. The result is four possible approaches to naturalistic research. Which approach is best for a given project must be determined by the costs and benefits of each decision.

Another disadvantage of the unacknowledged participant approach is that the activities of the observer may influence the process being observed. This may happen, for instance, when an unacknowledged participant is asked by the group to contribute to a group decision. Saying nothing would "blow one's cover," but making substantive comments would change the nature of the group itself. Often the participant researcher will want to query the people being observed in order to gain more information about why certain behaviors are occurring. Although these questions can reveal the underlying nature of the social setting, they may also alter the situation itself.

The Acknowledged Participant

In cases where the researcher feels that it is unethical or impossible to hide his or her identity as a scientist, the acknowledged participant approach can be used. Sociologist W. F. Whyte (1993) used this approach in his classic sociological study of "street corner society." Over a period of a year, Whyte got to know the people in, and made extensive observations of, a neighborhood in a New England town. He did not attempt to hide his identity. Rather, he announced freely that he was a scientist and that he would be recording the behavior of the individuals he observed. Sometimes this approach is necessary, for instance, when the behavior the researcher wants to observe is difficult to gain access to. To observe behavior in a corporate boardroom or school classroom, the researcher may have to gain official permission, which may require acknowledging the research to those being observed.

The largest problem of being acknowledged is reactivity. Knowing that the observer is recording information may cause people to change their speech and behavior, limit what they are willing to discuss, or avoid the researcher altogether. Often, however, once the observer has spent some time with the population of interest, people tend to treat him or her as a real member of the group. This happened to Whyte. In such situations, the scientist may let this habituation occur over a period of time before beginning to record observations.

Acknowledged and Unacknowledged Observers

The researcher may use a nonparticipant approach when he or she does not want to or cannot be a participant of the group being studied. In these cases, the researcher observes the behavior of interest without actively participating in the ongoing action. This occurs, for instance, when children are observed in a classroom from behind a one-way mirror or when clinical psychologists videotape group therapy sessions for later analysis. One advantage of not being part of the group is that the researcher may be more objective because he or she does not develop close relationships with the people being observed. Being out of the action also leaves the observer more time to do the job he or she came for—watching other people and recording relevant data. The nonparticipant observer is relieved of the burdensome role of acting like a participant and maintaining a "cover," activities that may take substantial effort.

The nonparticipant observer may be either acknowledged or unacknowledged. Again, there are pros and cons to each, and these generally parallel the issues involved with the participant observer. Being acknowledged can create reactivity, whereas being unacknowledged may be unethical if it violates the confidentiality of the data. These issues must be considered carefully, with the researcher reviewing the pros and cons of each approach before beginning the project.

Case Studies

Whereas observational research generally assesses the behavior of a relatively large group of people, sometimes the data are based on only a small set of individuals, perhaps only one or two. These qualitative research designs are known as **case studies**—descriptive records of one or more individual's experiences and behavior. Sometimes case studies involve normal individuals, as when developmental psychologist Jean Piaget (1952) used observation of his own children to develop a stage theory of cognitive development. More frequently, case studies are conducted on individuals who have unusual or abnormal experiences or characteristics or who are going through particularly difficult or stressful situations. The assumption is that by carefully studying individuals who are socially marginal, who are experiencing a unique situation, or who are going through a difficult phase in their life, we can learn something about human nature.

Sigmund Freud was a master of using the psychological difficulties of individuals to draw conclusions about basic psychological processes. One classic example is Freud's case study and treatment of "Little Hans," a child whose fear of horses the psychoanalyst interpreted in terms of repressed sexual impulses (1959). Freud wrote case studies of some of his most interesting patients and used these careful examinations to develop his important theories of personality.

Scientists also use case studies to investigate the neurological bases of behavior. In animals, scientists can study the functions of a certain section of the brain by removing that part. If removing part of the brain prevents the animal from performing a certain behavior (such as learning to locate a food tray in a maze), then the inference can be drawn that the memory was stored in the removed part of the brain. It is obviously not possible to treat humans in the same manner, but brain damage sometimes occurs in people for other reasons. "Split-brain" patients (Sperry, 1982) are individuals who have had the two hemispheres of their brains surgically separated in an attempt to prevent severe epileptic seizures. Study of the behavior of these unique individuals has provided important information about the functions of the two brain hemispheres in humans. In other individuals, certain brain parts may be destroyed through disease or accident. One well-known case study is Phineas Gage, a man who was extensively studied by cognitive psychologists after he had a railroad spike blasted through his skull in an accident. An interesting example of a case study in clinical psychology is described by Rokeach (1964), who investigated in detail the beliefs and interactions among three schizophrenics, all of whom were convinced they were Jesus Christ.

One problem with case studies is that they are based on the experiences of only a very limited number of normally quite unusual individuals. Although descriptions of individual experiences may be extremely interesting, they cannot usually tell us much about whether the same things would happen to other individuals in similar situations or exactly why these specific reactions to these events occurred. For instance, descriptions of individuals who have been in a stressful situation such as a war or an earthquake can be used to understand how they reacted during such a situation but cannot tell us what particular long-term effects the situation had on them. Because there is no comparison group that did not experience the stressful situation, we cannot know what these individuals would be like if they hadn't had the experience. As a result, case studies provide only weak support for the drawing of scientific conclusions. They may, however, be useful for providing ideas for future, more controlled research.

Systematic Coding Methods

You have probably noticed by now that although observational research and case studies can provide a detailed look at ongoing behavior, because they represent qualitative data, they may often not be as objective as one might like, especially when they are based on recordings by a single scientist.

Because the observer has chosen which people to study, which behaviors to record or ignore, and how to interpret those behaviors, she or he may be more likely to see (or at least to report) those observations that confirm, rather than disconfirm, her or his expectations. Furthermore, the collected data may be relatively sketchy, in the form of "field notes" or brief reports, and thus not amenable to assessment of their reliability or validity. However, in many cases these problems can be overcome by using systematic observation to create quantitative measured variables (Bakeman & Gottman, 1986; Weick, 1985).

Deciding What to Observe

Systematic observation involves specifying ahead of time exactly which observations are to be made on which people and in which times and places. These decisions are made on the basis of theoretical expectation about the types of events that are going to be of interest. Specificity about the behaviors of interest has the advantage of both focusing the observers' attention on these specific behaviors and reducing the masses of data that might be collected if the observers attempted to record everything they saw. Furthermore, in many cases more than one observer can make the observations, and, as we have discussed in Chapter 5, this will increase the reliability of the measures.

Consider, for instance, a research team interested in assessing how and when young children compare their own performance with that of their classmates (Pomerantz et al., 1995). In this study, one or two adult observers sat in chairs adjacent to work areas in the classrooms of elementary school children and recorded in laptop computers the behaviors of the children. Before beginning the project, the researchers had defined a specific set of **behavioral categories** for use by the observers. These categories were based on theoretical predictions of what would occur for these children and defined exactly what behaviors were to be coded, how to determine when those behaviors were occurring, and how to code them into the computer.

Deciding How to Record Observations

Before beginning to code the behaviors, the observers spent three or four days in the classroom learning, practicing, and revising the coding methods and letting the children get used to their presence. Because the coding categories were so well defined, there was good interrater reliability. And to be certain that the judges remained reliable, the experimenters frequently computed a reliability analysis on the codings over the time that the observations were being made. This is particularly important because there are some behaviors that occur infrequently, and it is important to be sure that they are being coded reliably.

Over the course of each observation period, several types of data were collected. For one, the observers coded *event frequencies*—for instance, the number of verbal statements that indicated social comparison. These included both statements about one's own performance ("My picture is the best.") and questions about the performance of others ("How many did you get wrong?"). In addition, the observers also coded *event duration*—for instance, the amount of time that the child was attending to the work of others. Finally, all the children were interviewed after the observation had ended.

Choosing Sampling Strategies

One of the difficulties in coding ongoing behavior is that there is so much of it. Pomerantz et al. (1995), used three basic sampling strategies to reduce the amount of data they needed to record. First, as we have already seen, they used **event sampling**—focusing in on specific behaviors that were theoretically related to social comparison. Second, they employed **individual sampling.** Rather than trying to record the behaviors of all of the children at the same time, the observers randomly selected one child to be the focus child for an observational period. The observers zeroed in on this child, while ignoring the behavior of others during the time period. Over the entire period of the study, however, each child was observed. Finally, Pomerantz and colleagues employed **time sampling.** Each observer focused on a single child for only four minutes before moving on to another child. In this case, the data were coded as they were observed, but in some cases the observer might use the time periods between observations to record the responses. Although sampling only some of the events of interest may lose some information, the events that are attended to can be more precisely recorded.

The data of the observers were then uploaded from laptop computers for analysis. Using these measures, Pomerantz et al. found, among other things, that older children used subtler social comparison strategies and increasingly saw such behavior as boastful or unfair. These data have high ecological validity, and yet their reliability and validity are well established. Another example of a coding scheme for naturalistic research, also using children, is shown in Figure 7.1.

Archival Research

As you will recall, one of the great advantages of naturalistic methods is that there are so many data available to be studied. One approach that takes full advantage of this situation is **archival research,** which is based on an analysis of any type of existing records of public behavior. These records might include newspaper articles, speeches and letters of public figures, television and radio broadcasts, Internet websites, or existing surveys. Because there are so many records that can be examined, the use of archival records is limited only by the researcher's imagination.

Records that have been used in past behavioral research include the trash in a landfill, patterns of graffiti, wear and tear on floors in museums, litter, and dirt on the pages of library books (see Webb et al., 1981, for examples). Archival

FIGURE 7.1   Strange Situation Coding Sheet

Coder name _____Olive_____

| | Coding Categories | | | |
Episode	Proximity	Contact	Resistance	Avoidance
Mother and baby play alone	1	1	1	1
Mother puts baby down	4	1	1	1
Stranger enters room	1	2	3	1
Mother leaves room, stranger plays with baby	1	3	1	1
Mother reenters, greets and may comfort baby, then leaves again	4	2	1	2
Stranger tries to play with baby	1	3	1	1
Mother reenters and picks up baby	6	6	1	2

The coding categories are:

Proximity.   The baby moves toward, grasps, or climbs on the adult.
Maintaining Contact. The baby resists being put down by the adult by crying or trying to climb back up.
Resistance.   The baby pushes, hits, or squirms to be put down from the adult's arms.
Avoidance.   The baby turns away or moves away from the adult.

This figure represents a sample coding sheet from an episode of the "strange situation," in which an infant (usually about 1 year old) is observed playing in a room with two adults—the child's mother and a stranger. Each of the four coding categories is scored by the coder from 1 = The baby makes no effort to engage in the behavior to 7 = The baby makes an extreme effort to engage in the behavior. The coding is usually made from videotapes, and more than one coder rates the behaviors to allow calculating inter-rater reliability. More information about the meaning of the coding can be found in Ainsworth, Blehar, Waters, and Wall (1978).

researchers have found that crimes increase during hotter weather (Anderson, 1989); that earlier-born children live somewhat longer than later-borns (Modin 2002); and that gender and racial stereotypes are prevalent in current television shows (Greenberg, 1980) and in magazines (Sullivan & O'Connor, 1988).

One of the classic archival research projects is the sociological study of the causes of suicide by sociologist Emile Durkheim (1951). Durkheim used records of people who had committed suicide in seven European countries between 1841 and 1872 for his data. These records indicated, for instance, that suicide was more prevalent on weekdays than on weekends, among those who were not married, and in the summer months. From these data, Durkheim drew the conclusion that alienation from others was the primary cause of suicide. Durkheim's resourcefulness in collecting data and his ability to use the data to draw conclusions about the causes of suicide are remarkable.

Because archival records contain a huge amount of information, they must also be systematically coded. This is done through a technique known as **content analysis.** Content analysis is essentially the same as systematic coding of observational data and includes the specification of coding categories and the use of more than one rater. In one interesting example of an archival research project, Simonton (1988) located and analyzed biographies of U.S. presidents. He had seven undergraduate students rate each of the biographies on a number of predefined coding categories, including "was cautious and conservative in action," "was charismatic," and "valued personal loyalty." The interrater reliability of the coders was assessed and found to be adequate.

Simonton then averaged the ratings of the seven coders and used the data to draw conclusions about the personalities and behaviors of the presidents. For instance, he found that "charismatic" presidents were motivated by achievement and power and were more active and accomplished more while in office. Although Simonton used biographies as his source of information, he could, of course, have employed presidential speeches, information on how and where the speeches were delivered, or material on the types of appointments the presidents made, among other records.

Current Research in the Behavioral Sciences: Detecting Psychopathy From Thin Slices of Behavior

Katherine A. Fowler, Scott O. Lilienfeld, and Christopher J. Patrick (2009) used a naturalistic research design to study whether personality could be reliably assessed by raters who were given only very short samples ("thin slices") of behavior. They were particularly interested in assessing *psychopathy*, a syndrome characterized by emotional and interpersonal deficits that often lead a person to antisocial behavior. According to the authors' definition, psychopathic individuals tend to be "glib and superficially charming," giving a surface-level appearance of intelligence, but are also "manipulative and prone to pathological lying" (p. 68). Many lead a socially deviant lifestyle marked by early behavior problems, irresponsibility, poor impulse control, and proneness to boredom.

Because the researchers felt that behavior was likely to be a better indicator of psychopathy than was self-report, they used coders to assess the disorder from videotapes. Forty raters viewed videotapes containing only very brief excerpts (either 5s, 10s, or 20s in duration) selected from longer videotaped interviews with 96 maximum-security inmates at a prison in Florida. Each inmate's video was rated by each rater on a variety of dimensions related to psychopathy including *overall rated psychopathy*, as well as *antisocial, narcissistic* and *avoidant* characteristics. The raters also rated the prisoners on physical attractiveness, as well as estimates of their violence proneness, and intelligence. To help the coders understand what was to be rated, the researchers provided them with very specific descriptions of each of the dimensions to be rated.

Even though the raters were not experts in psychopathy, they tended to agree on their judgments. Interrater reliability was calculated as the agreement among the raters on each item. As you can see in Table 7.2, the reliability of the codings was quite high, suggesting that the raters, even using very thin slices, could adequately assess the conceptual variables of interest.

TABLE 7.2 Interrater Reliability of Thin-Slice Ratings

Rated Item	Interrater Reliability
Overall psychopathy	.95
Antisocial	.86
Narcissistic	.94
Avoidant PD	.89
Violence proneness	.87
Physical attractiveness	.95
Intelligence	.95

Furthermore, the researchers also found that these ratings had predictive validity, because they correlated significantly with other measures of diagnostic and self-report measures that the prisoners had completed as part of a previous study on the emotional and personality functioning of psychopaths.

SUMMARY

Naturalistic research designs involve the study of everyday behavior through the use of both observational and archival data. In many cases, a large amount of information can be collected very quickly using naturalistic approaches, and this information can provide basic knowledge about the phenomena of interest as well as provide ideas for future research.

Naturalistic data have high ecological validity because they involve people in their everyday lives. However, although the data can be rich and colorful, naturalistic research often does not provide much information about why behavior occurs or what would have happened to the same people in different situations.

Observational research can involve either participant or nonparticipant observers, who are either acknowledged or unacknowledged to the individuals being observed. Which approach an observer uses depends on considerations of ethics and practicality. A case study is an investigation of a single individual in which unusual, unexpected, or unexplained behaviors become the focus of the research. Archival research uses existing records of public behavior as data.

Conclusions can be drawn from naturalistic data when they have been systematically collected and coded. In observational research, various sampling techniques are used to focus in on the data of interest. In archival research, the data are coded through content analysis. In systematic observation and content coding, the reliability and validity of the measures are enhanced by having more than one trained researcher make the ratings.

KEY TERMS

archival research 135
behavioral categories 134
case studies 132
content analysis 136
ecological validity 128
event sampling 135

individual sampling 135
naturalistic research 128
observational research 129
systematic observation 134
time sampling 135

REVIEW AND DISCUSSION QUESTIONS

1. Discuss the situations in which a researcher may choose to use a naturalistic research approach and the questions such an approach can and cannot answer.

2. Consider the consequences of a researcher's decisions about observing versus participating and about being acknowledged versus unacknowledged in naturalistic observation.

3. Explain what a case study is. Discuss the limitations of case studies for the study of human behavior.

4. What is systematic observation, and what techniques are used to make observations systematic?

5. What kinds of questions can be answered through archival research, and what kinds of data might be relevant?

RESEARCH PROJECT IDEAS

1. Design an observational study of your own, including the creation of a set of behavioral categories that would be used to code for one or more variables of interest to you. Indicate the decisions that you have made regarding the sampling of behaviors.

2. Make a tape recording of a student meeting. Discuss methods that could be used to meaningfully organize and code the statements made by the students.

3. Design, and conduct if possible, an archival research study. Consider what type of information you will look for, how you will find it, and how it should be content coded.

PART **THREE**
Testing Research Hypotheses

CHAPTER EIGHT
Hypothesis Testing and Inferential Statistics

STUDY QUESTIONS

- What are inferential statistics, and how are they used to test a research hypothesis?

- What is the null hypothesis?

- What is alpha?

- What is the p-value, and how is it used to determine statistical significance?

- Why are two-sided p-values used in most hypothesis tests?

- What are Type 1 and Type 2 errors, and what is the relationship between them?

- What is beta, and how does beta relate to the power of a statistical test?

- What is the effect-size statistic, and how is it used?

We have now completed our discussion of naturalistic and survey research designs, and in the chapters to come we will turn to correlational research and experimental research, which are designed to investigate relationships among one or more variables. Before doing so, however, we must discuss the standardized method scientists use to test whether the data they collect can be interpreted as providing support for their research hypotheses. These procedures are part and parcel of the scientific method and help keep the scientific process objective.

Probability and Inferential Statistics

Imagine for a moment a hypothetical situation in which a friend of yours claims that she has ESP and can read your mind. You find yourself skeptical of the claim, but you realize that if it were true, the two of you could develop a magic show and make a lot of money. You decide to conduct an empirical test. You flip a coin ten times, hiding the results from her each time, and ask her to guess each time whether the coin has come up heads or tails. Your logic is that if she can read your mind, she should be able to guess correctly. Maybe she won't be perfect, but she should be better than chance.

You can imagine that your friend might not get exactly five out of ten guesses right, even though this is what would be expected by chance. She might be right six times and wrong only four, or she might even guess correctly eight times out of ten. But how many would she have to get right to convince you that she really has ESP and can guess correctly more than 50 percent of the time? Would six out of ten correct be enough? How about eight out of ten? And even if she got all ten correct, how would you rule out the possibility that because guessing has some random error, she might have just happened to get lucky?

Consider now a researcher who is testing the effectiveness of a new behavioral therapy by comparing a group of patients who received therapy to another group that did not, or a researcher who is investigating the relationship between children viewing violent television shows and displaying aggressive behavior. The researchers want to know whether the observed data support their research hypotheses—namely, that the new therapy reduces anxiety and that viewing violent behavior increases aggression. However, you can well imagine that because measurement contains random error, it is unlikely that the two groups of patients will show exactly the same levels of anxiety at the end of the therapy or that the correlation between the amount of violent television viewed and the amount of aggressive behavior displayed will be exactly zero. As a result of random error, one group might show somewhat less anxiety than the other, or the correlation coefficient might be somewhat greater than zero, even if the treatment was not effective or there was no relationship between viewing violence and acting aggressively.

Thus, these scientists are in exactly the same position as you would be if you tried to test your friend's claim of having ESP. The basic dilemma is that it is impossible to ever know for sure whether the observed data were caused by random error. Because all data contain random error, *any pattern of data that might have been caused by a true relationship between variables might instead have been caused by chance*. This is part of the reason that research never "proves" a hypothesis or a theory.

The scientific method specifies a set of procedures that scientists use to make educated guesses about whether the data support the research hypothesis. These steps are outlined in Figure 8.1 and are discussed in the following sections.

FIGURE 8.1 Hypothesis-Testing Flow Chart

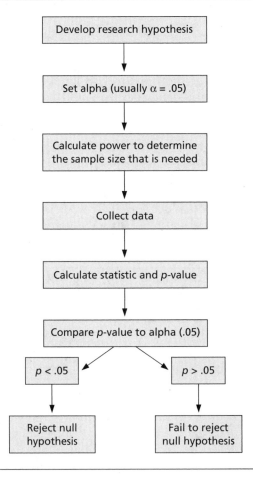

Hypothesis testing begins with the development of the research hypothesis. Once alpha (in most cases it is .05) has been chosen and the needed sample size has been calculated, the data are collected. Significance tests on the observed data may be either statistically significant ($p < .05$) or statistically nonsignificant ($p > .05$). The results of the significance test determine whether the null hypothesis should be accepted or rejected. If results are significant, then an examination of the direction of the observed relationship will indicate whether the research hypothesis has been supported.

These procedures involve the use of probability and statistical analysis to draw inferences on the basis of observed data. Because they use the sample data to draw inferences about the true state of affairs, these statistical procedures are called **inferential statistics.**

Sampling Distributions and Hypothesis Testing

Although directly testing whether a research hypothesis is correct or incorrect seems an achievable goal, it actually is not because it is not possible to specify ahead of time what the observed data would look like if the research hypothesis was true. It is, however, possible to specify in a statistical sense what the observed data would look like if the research hypothesis was *not* true.

Consider, for instance, what we would expect the observed data to look like in our ESP test if your friend did *not* have ESP. Figure 8.2 shows a bar chart of all of the possible outcomes of ten guesses on coin flips calculated under the assumption that the probability of a correct guess (.5) is the same

FIGURE 8.2 The Binomial Distribution

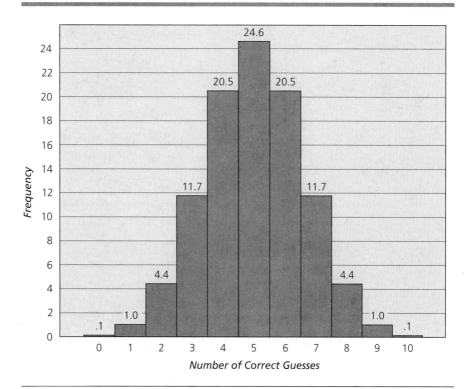

This figure represents all possible outcomes of correct guesses on ten coin flips. More generally, it represents the expected outcomes of any event where $p(a) = p(b)$. This is known as the *binomial distribution*.

as the probability of an incorrect guess (also .5). You can see that some outcomes are more common than others. For instance, the outcome of five correct guesses is expected by chance to occur 24.6 percent of the time, whereas the outcome of ten correct guesses is so unlikely that it will occur by chance only 1/10 of one percent of the time.

The distribution of all of the possible values of a statistic is known as a **sampling distribution.** Each statistic has an associated sampling distribution. For instance, the sampling distribution for events that have two equally likely possibilities, such as the distribution of correct and incorrect guesses shown in Figure 8.2, is known as the **binomial distribution.** There is also a sampling distribution for the mean, a sampling distribution for the standard deviation, a sampling distribution for the correlation coefficient, and so forth.

Although we have to this point made it sound as if each statistic has only one sampling distribution, things are actually more complex than this. For most statistics, there are a series of different sampling distributions, each of which is associated with a different sample size (N). For instance, Figure 8.3 compares the binomial sampling distribution for ten coin flips ($N = 10$) on the left side (this is the same distribution as in Figure 8.2) with the binomial sampling distribution for one hundred coin flips ($N = 100$) on the right side. You can see that the sampling distributions become narrower—squeezed together—as the sample size gets bigger. This change represents the fact that, as sample size increases, extreme values of the statistic are less likely to be observed. The sampling distributions of other statistics, such as for the Pearson correlation coefficient or the F test, look very similar to these distributions, including the change toward becoming more narrow as sample size increases.

The Null Hypothesis

When testing hypotheses, we begin by assuming that the observed data do *not* differ from what would be expected on the basis of chance,

FIGURE 8.3 Two Sampling Distributions

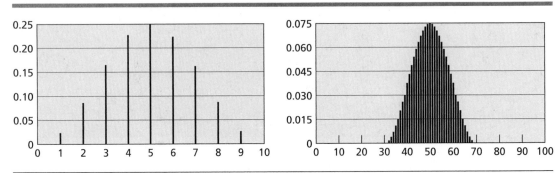

This figure shows the likely outcomes of correct guesses on ten coin flips (left side) and 100 coin flips (right side). You can see that as the sample size gets larger, the sampling distribution (in this case the binomial distribution) gets narrower.

and the sampling distribution of the statistic is used to indicate what is expected to happen by chance. The assumption that the observed data reflect only what would be expected under the sampling distribution is called the **null hypothesis,** symbolized as H_0. As we will see, each test of a research hypothesis begins with a null hypothesis:

> For the coin-guessing experiment, H_0 is that the probability of a correct guess is $= .5$.
>
> For a correlational design, H_0 is that there is no correlation between the two measured variables ($r = 0$).
>
> For an experimental research design, H_0 is that the mean score on the dependent variable is the same in all of the experimental groups (for instance, that the mean of the therapy group equals the mean of the control group).

Because the null hypothesis specifies the least-interesting possible outcome, the researcher hopes to be able to *reject the null hypothesis*—that is, to be able to conclude that the observed data were caused by something other than chance alone.

Testing for Statistical Significance

Setting Alpha.   You may not be surprised to hear that given the conservative nature of science, the observed data must deviate rather substantially from what would be expected under the sampling distribution before we are allowed to reject the null hypothesis. The standard that the observed data must meet is known as the **significance level** or **alpha (α).** By convention, alpha is normally set to $\alpha = .05$.[1] What this means is that we may reject the null hypothesis only if the observed data are so unusual that they would have occurred by chance at most 5 percent of the time. Although this standard may seem stringent, even more stringent significance levels, such as $\alpha = .01$ and $\alpha = .001$, may sometimes be used. The smaller the alpha is, the more stringent the standard is.

Comparing the *p*-value to Alpha.   As shown in Figure 8.1, once the alpha level has been set (we'll discuss how to determine the sample size in a moment), a statistic (such as a correlation coefficient) is computed. Each statistic has an associated **probability value** (usually called a ***p*-value** and indicated with the letter *p*) that shows the likelihood of an observed statistic occurring on the basis of the sampling distribution. Because alpha sets the standard for how extreme the data must be before we can reject the null hypothesis,

---

[1]Although there is some debate within the scientific community about whether it is advisable to test research hypotheses using a preset significant level—see, for instance, Shrout (1997) and the following articles in the journal—this approach is still the most common method of hypothesis testing within the behavioral sciences.

and the p-value indicates how extreme the data are, we simply compare the p-value to alpha:

> If the p-value is less than alpha ($p < .05$), then we reject the null hypothesis, and we say the result is **statistically significant.**
> If the p-value is greater than alpha ($p > .05$), then we fail to reject the null hypothesis, and we say the result is **statistically nonsignificant.**

The p-value for a given outcome is found through examination of the sampling distribution of the statistic, and in our case, the p-value comes from Figure 8.1. For instance, we can calculate that the probability of your friend guessing the coin flips correctly all ten times (given the null hypothesis that she does not have ESP) is 1 in 1,024, or $p = .001$. A p-value of .001 indicates that such an outcome is extremely unlikely to have occurred as a result of chance (in fact, only about once in 1,000 times).

We can also add probabilities together to produce the following probabilities of correct guesses, based on the binomial distribution in Figure 8.2:

> p-value for 9 or 10 correct guesses $= .01 + .001 = .011$
> p-value for 8 or 9 or 10 correct guesses $= .044 + .01 + .001 = .055$
> p-value for 7 or 8 or 9 or 10 correct guesses $= .117 + .044 + .01 + .001 = .172$

In short, the probability of guessing correctly *at least* eight times given no ESP is $p = .055$, and the probability of guessing correctly *at least* seven times given no ESP is $p = .172$.

Using One- and Two-Sided *p*-values.   You can see that these calculations consider the likelihood of your friend guessing better than what would be expected by chance. But for most statistical tests, unusual events can occur in more than one way. For instance, you can imagine that it would be of interest to find that psychotherapy *increased* anxiety, or to find that viewing violent television *decreased* aggression even if the research hypotheses did not predict these relationships. Because the scientific method is designed to keep things objective, the scientist must be prepared to interpret any relationships that he or she finds, even if these relationships were not predicted.

Because data need to be interpreted even if they are in an unexpected direction, scientists generally use **two-sided *p*-values** to test their research hypotheses.[2] Two-sided p-values take into consideration that unusual outcomes may occur in more than one way. Returning to Figure 8.2, we can see that there are indeed two "sides" to the binomial distribution. There is another outcome that is just as extreme as guessing correctly ten times—guessing correctly zero times. And there is another outcome just as extreme as guessing correctly nine times—guessing correctly only once. Because the binomial distribution is

---

[2]Although **one-sided *p*-values** can be used in some special cases, in this book we will use only two-sided p-values.

symmetrical, the two-sided p-value is always twice as big as the one-sided p-value. Although two-sided p-values provide a more conservative statistical test, they allow us to interpret statistically significant relationships even if those differences are not in the direction predicted by the research hypothesis.

Using two-sided p-values, we can construct the following:

p-value for number of guesses as extreme as $10 = .001 \times 2 = .002$
p-value for number of guesses as extreme as $9 = .011 \times 2 = .022$
p-value for number of guesses as extreme as $8 = .055 \times 2 = .11$
p-value for number of guesses as extreme as $7 = .172 \times 2 = .344$

Let us return one last time to our example to finally specify how many correct guesses your friend would have to get before we could reject the null hypothesis that she does not have ESP. If we set $\alpha = .05$, then we could not reject the null hypothesis of no ESP on the basis of eight correct guesses because the two-sided p-value (.11) of an outcome as extreme as eight correct guesses is greater than alpha ($p > .05$). However, the probability of an outcome as extreme as nine correct guesses out of ten given no ESP ($p = .022$) is less than alpha ($p < .05$). Therefore, your friend would have to guess correctly nine times or more before we could reject the null hypothesis of no ESP on the basis of ten coin flips.

We will discuss the specifics of many different statistical tests in the chapters to come, but for now it is sufficient to know that each statistical test produces a p-value and that in each case the p-value is compared to alpha. The research report can notate either the exact p-value (for instance, $p = .022$ or $p = .17$) or the relationship between the p-value and alpha (for instance, $p < .05$ or $p > .05$).

Reduction of Inferential Errors

Because hypothesis testing and inferential statistics are based entirely on probability, we are bound to make errors in drawing conclusions about our data. The hypothesis-testing procedure is designed to keep such errors to a minimum, but it cannot eliminate them entirely. Figure 8.4 provides one way to think about this problem. It indicates that statistical inference can lead to both correct decisions but also, at least in some cases, to errors. Because these errors lead the researcher to draw invalid conclusions, it is important to understand what they are and how we can reduce them. On the left side of Figure 8.4 are the two possible states that we are trying to choose between— the null hypothesis may be true, or the null hypothesis may be false. And across the top of the figure are the two possible decisions that we can make on the basis of the observed data: We may reject the null hypothesis, or we may fail to reject the null hypothesis.

Type 1 Errors

One type of error occurs when we reject the null hypothesis when it is in fact true. This would occur, for instance, when the psychologist draws the conclusion that his or her therapy reduced anxiety when it did not or if you concluded that your friend has ESP even though she doesn't. As shown in the upper left quadrant of Figure 8.4, rejecting the null hypothesis when it is really true is called a **Type 1 error.**

The probability of the researcher making a Type 1 error is equal to alpha. When $\alpha = .05$, we know we will make a Type 1 error not more than five times out of one hundred, and when $\alpha = .01$, we know we will make a Type 1 error not more than one time out of one hundred. However, because of the inherent ambiguity in the hypothesis-testing procedure, the researcher never knows for sure whether she or he has made a Type 1 error. It is always possible that data that are interpreted as rejecting the null hypothesis are caused by random error and that the null hypothesis is really true. But setting $\alpha = .05$ allows us to rest assured that a Type 1 error has most likely not been made.[3]

Type 2 Errors

If you've looked carefully at Figure 8.4, you will have noticed a second type of error that can be made when interpreting research results. Whereas a Type 1 error refers to the mistake of rejecting the null hypothesis when it is actually true, a **Type 2 error** refers to the mistake of failing to reject the null

FIGURE 8.4 Type 1 and Type 2 Errors

		SCIENTIST'S DECISION	
		Reject null hypothesis	Fail to reject null hypothesis
TRUE STATE OF AFFAIRS	*Null hypothesis is true*	Type 1 Error Probability = α	Correct decision Probability = $1 - \alpha$
	Null hypothesis is false	Correct decision Probability = $1 - \beta$	Type 2 Error Probability = β

This figure represents the possible outcomes of statistical inference. In two cases the scientist's decision is correct because it accurately represents the true state of affairs. In two other cases the scientist's decision is incorrect.

---

[3]Alpha indicates the likelihood of making a Type 1 error in a single statistical test. However, when more than one statistical test is made in a research project, the likelihood of a Type 1 error will increase. To help correct this problem, when many statistical tests are being made, a smaller alpha (for instance, $\alpha = .01$) can be used.

hypothesis when the null hypothesis is really false. This would occur when the scientist concludes that the psychotherapy program is not working even though it really is or when you conclude that your friend does not have ESP even though she really can do significantly better than chance.

We have seen that the scientist controls the probability of making a Type 1 error by setting alpha at a small value, such as .05. But what determines **beta,** or β, the probability of the scientist making a Type 2 error? Answering this question requires a discussion of statistical power.

Statistical Power

Type 2 errors occur when the scientist misses a true relationship by failing to reject the null hypothesis even though it should have been rejected. Such errors are not at all uncommon in science. They occur both because of random error in measurement and because the things we are looking for are often pretty small. You can imagine that a biologist might make a Type 2 error when, using a microscope that is not very powerful, he fails to detect a small organism. And the same might occur for an astronomer who misses the discovery of a new planet because Earth's atmosphere creates random error that distorts the telescope's image.

The **power** of a statistical test is the probability that the researcher will, on the basis of the observed data, be able to reject the null hypothesis given that the null hypothesis is actually false and thus should be rejected. Power and beta are redundant concepts because power can be written in terms of beta:

$$\text{Power} = 1 - \beta$$

In short, Type 2 errors are more common when the power of a statistical test is low.

The Effect Size.   Although alpha can be precisely set by the scientist, beta (and thus the power) of a statistical test can only be estimated. This is because power depends in part on how big the relationship being searched for actually is—the bigger the relationship is, the easier it is to detect. The size of a relationship is indicated by a statistic known as the **effect size**. The effect size indicates the magnitude of a relationship: zero indicates that there is no relationship between the variables, and larger (positive) effect sizes indicate stronger relationships.

The problem is that because the researcher can never know ahead of time the exact effect size of the relationship being searched for, he or she cannot exactly calculate the power of the statistical test. In some cases, the researcher may be able to make an educated guess about the likely power of a statistical test by estimating the effect size of the expected relationship on the basis of previous research in the field. When this is not possible, general knowledge about the effect sizes of relationships in behavioral science can be used. The accepted practice is to consider the approximate size of the expected relationship to be "small," "medium," or "large" (Cohen, 1977) and to calculate power on the basis of these estimates. In most cases, a "small" effect size is considered to be .10, a "medium" effect size is .30, and a "large" effect size is .50.

The Influence of Sample Size.   In addition to the actual size of the relationship being assessed, the power of a statistical test is also influenced by the sample size (N) used in the research. As N increases, the likelihood of the researcher finding a statistically significant relationship between the independent and dependent variables, and thus the power of the test, also increases. We will consider this issue in more detail in a later section of this chapter.

The Tradeoff Between Type 1 and Type 2 Errors

Beginning researchers often ask, and professional scientists often still consider, is what alpha is most appropriate? Clearly, if the major goal is to prevent Type 1 errors, then alpha should be set as small as possible. However, in any given research design there is a tradeoff between the likelihood of making a Type 1 and a Type 2 error. For any given sample size, when alpha is set lower, beta will always be higher. This is because alpha represents the standard of evidence required to reject the null hypothesis, and the probability of the observed data meeting this standard is less when alpha is smaller. As a result, setting a small alpha makes it more difficult to find data that are strong enough to allow rejecting the null hypothesis, and makes it more likely that weak relationships will be missed.

You might better understand the basic problem if we return for a moment to our example of testing for the presence of ESP. A person who has some degree of ESP might be able, over a long period of time, to guess the outcome of coin tosses correctly somewhat more than 50 percent of the time. Anyone who could do so would, according to our definition, have ESP, even if he or she was only slightly better than chance. In our test using ten guesses of ten coin flips, we have seen that if $\alpha = .05$, then the individual must guess correctly 90 percent of the time (nine out of ten) for us to reject the null hypothesis. If eight or fewer guesses were correct, we would be forced to accept the null hypothesis that the person does not have ESP. However, this conclusion would represent a Type 2 error if the person was actually able to guess correctly more than 50 percent of the time but less than 90 percent of the time.

Thus, the basic difficulty is that although setting a lower alpha protects us from Type 1 errors, doing so may lead us to miss the presence of weak relationships. This difficulty can be alleviated to some extent, however, by an increase in the power of the research design. As N increases, the likelihood of the scientist detecting relationships with small effect sizes increases, even when alpha remains the same. To return once more to the ESP example, you can see by comparing the two sampling distributions in Figure 8.3 that a relatively lower percentage of correct guesses is needed to reject the null hypothesis as the sample size gets bigger. Remember that when the sample size was 10 (10 flips), your friend had to make nine correct guesses (90 percent correct) before we could reject the null hypothesis. However, if you tested your friend using 100 coin flips ($N = 100$) instead of only 10, you would have a greater chance of detecting "weak" ESP. Keeping alpha equal to .05, you would be able to reject the null hypothesis of no ESP if your friend was able to guess correctly on 61 out of 100 (that is, only 61 percent) of the coin flips. And, if you had your friend guess the outcome of 1,000 coin flips, you would be able to reject the null hypothesis on the basis of only 532 out of 1,000 (that is, only 53 percent) correct guesses.

A decision must be made for each research project about the tradeoff between the likelihood of making Type 1 and Type 2 errors. This tradeoff is particularly acute when sample sizes are small, and this is frequently the case because the collecting of data is often very expensive. In most cases scientists believe that Type 1 errors are more dangerous than Type 2 errors and set alpha at a lower value than beta. However, the choice of an appropriate alpha depends to some extent on the type of research being conducted. There are some situations in applied research where it may be particularly desirable for the scientist to avoid making a Type 2 error. For instance, if the scientist is testing a new type of reading instruction, she or he might want to discover if the program is having even a very small effect on learning, and so the scientist might take a higher than normal chance of making a Type 1 error. In such a case, the scientist might use a larger alpha.

Because Type 1 and Type 2 errors are always a possibility in research, rejection of the null hypothesis does not necessarily mean that the null hypothesis is actually false. Rather, rejecting the null hypothesis simply means that the null hypothesis does not seem to be able to account for the collected data. Similarly, a failure to reject the null hypothesis does not mean that the null hypothesis is necessarily true, only that on the basis of the collected data the scientist cannot reject it.

Statistical Significance and the Effect Size

In this chapter, we have discussed both statistical significance (measured by the relationship between the p-value and alpha) and the effect size as measures of relationships between variables. It is important to remember that the effect size and the p-value are two different statistics and to understand the distinction between them. Each statistical test (for instance, a Pearson correlation coefficient) has both an associated p-value and an effect-size statistic.

The relationship among statistical significance, sample size (N), and effect size is summarized in the following conceptual equation (Rosenthal & Rosnow, 1991):

$$\text{Statistical significance} = \text{Effect size} \times \text{Sample size}$$

This equation makes clear three important principles that guide interpretation of research results:

- First, increasing the sample size (N) will increase the statistical significance of a relationship whenever the effect size is greater than zero. Because observed relationships in small samples are more likely to have been caused by random error, and because the p-value represents the likelihood that the observed relationship was caused by random error, larger samples are more likely to produce statistically significant results.

- Second, because the p-value is influenced by sample size, as a measure of statistical significance the p-value is not itself a good indicator of the size of a relationship. If a large sample size is used, even a very small relationship can be statistically significant. In this sense the term *significance* is somewhat misleading because although a small p-value does imply that the results are unlikely to be due to random error, it does not imply anything about the magnitude or practical importance of the observed relationship. When we determine that a test is statistically significant, we can be confident that there *is* a relationship between the variables, but that relationship may still be quite small.

- Third, we can see that the effect size is an index of the strength of a relationship that is not influenced by sample size. As we will see in the next section, this property of the effect size makes it very useful in research. When interpreting research reports, we must keep in mind the distinction between effect size and statistical significance and the effect of sample size on the latter.

Practical Uses of the Effect-Size Statistic

As we have seen, the advantage of the effect-size statistic is that it indicates the strength of the relationship between the independent and the dependent variables and does so independently of the sample size. Although the relationship between two or more variables is almost always tested for statistical significance, the effect-size statistic provides important practical information that cannot be obtained from the p-value. In some cases, particularly in applied research, the effect size of a relationship may be more important than the statistical significance of the relationship because it provides a better index of a relationship's strength.

The Effect-Size in Applied Research.   Consider, for instance, two researchers who are both studying the effectiveness of programs to reduce drug use in teenagers. The first researcher studies a classroom intervention program in which one hundred high school students are shown a videotape about the dangers of drug use. The second researcher studies the effects of a television advertising campaign by sampling over 20,000 high school students who have seen the ad on TV. Both researchers find that the programs produce statistically significant increases ($p < .05$) in the perceptions of the dangers of drug use in the research participants.

In such a case, the statistical significance of the relationship between the intervention and the outcome variable may not be as important as the effect size. Because the sample size of one researcher is very large, even though the relationship was found to be statistically significant, the effect size might nevertheless be very small. In this case, comparing the effect size of a relationship with the cost of the intervention may help determine whether a program is worth continuing or whether other programs should be used instead (Rossi & Freeman, 1993).

The Proportion of Variance Statistic.   It is sometimes convenient to consider the strength of a relationship in terms of the proportion of the dependent variable that is "explained by" the independent variable or variables, as opposed to being "explained by" random error. The **proportion of explained variability** in the dependent variable is indicated by the square of the effect-size statistic.

In many cases, the proportion of explained variability is quite small. For instance, it is not uncommon in behavioral research to find a "small" effect size—that is, one of about .10. In a correlational design, for instance, this would mean that only 1 percent of the variability in the outcome variable is explained by the predictor variable (.10 $\times$ .10 = .01), whereas the other 99 percent of the variability is explained by other, unknown sources. Even a "large" effect size of .50 means that the predictor variable explains only 25 percent of the total variability in the outcome variable and that the other 75 percent is explained by other sources. Considering that they are usually quite small, it comes as no surprise that the relationships studied in behavioral research are often missed.

Determination of the Necessary Sample Size.   Another use of the effect-size statistic is to compute, during the planning of a research design, the power of a statistical test to determine the sample size that should be used. As shown in Figure 8.1, this is usually done in the early stages of the research process. Although increasing the sample size increases power, it is also expensive because recruiting and running research participants can require both time and money. In most cases, it is not practical to reduce the probability of making a Type 2 error to the same probability as that of making a Type 1 error because too many individuals would have to participate in the research. For instance, to have power = .95 (that is β = .05) to detect a "small" effect-size relationship using a Pearson correlation coefficient, one would need to collect data from over one thousand individuals!

Because of the large number of participants needed to create powerful research designs, a compromise is normally made. Although many research projects are conducted with even less power, it is usually sufficient for the estimated likelihood of a Type 2 error to be about β = .20. This represents power = .80 and thus, an 80 percent chance of rejecting the null hypothesis, given that the null hypothesis is false (see Cohen, 1977).

Statistical Table G in Appendix E presents the number of research participants needed with various statistical tests to obtain power = .80 with α = .05, assuming small, medium, or large estimated effect sizes. The specifics of these statistical tests will be discussed in detail in subsequent chapters, and you can refer to the table as necessary. Although the table can be used to calculate the power of a statistical test with some precision, in most cases, a more basic rule of thumb applies—run as many people in a given research project as is conveniently possible, because when there are more participants, there is also a greater likelihood of detecting the relationship of interest and thus of detecting relationships between variables.

SUMMARY

Hypothesis testing is accomplished through a set of procedures designed to determine whether observed data can be interpreted as providing support for the research hypothesis. These procedures, based on inferential statistics, are specified by the scientific method and are set in place before the scientist begins to collect data. Because it is not possible to directly test the research hypothesis, observed data are compared to what is expected under the null hypothesis, as specified by the sampling distribution of the statistic.

Because all data have random error, scientists can never be certain that the data they have observed actually support their hypotheses. Statistical significance is used to test whether data can be interpreted as supporting the research hypothesis. The probability of incorrectly rejecting the null hypothesis (known as a Type 1 error) is constrained by setting alpha to a known value such as .05 and only rejecting the null hypothesis if the likelihood that the observed data occurred by chance (the p-value) is less than alpha. The probability of incorrectly failing to reject a false null hypothesis (a Type 2 error) can only be estimated. The power of a statistical test refers to the likelihood of correctly rejecting a false null hypothesis.

The effect-size statistic is often used as a measure of the magnitude of a relationship between variables because it is not influenced by the sample size in the research design. The strength of a relationship may also be considered in terms of the proportion of variance in the dependent measure that is explained by the independent variable. The effect size of many relationships in scientific research is small, which makes them difficult to discover.

KEY TERMS

alpha (α) 147
beta (β) 151
binomial distribution 146
effect size 151
inferential statistics 145

null hypothesis (H_0) 147
one-sided p-values 148
power 151
probability value (p-value) 147
proportion of explained variability 155

REVIEW AND DISCUSSION QUESTIONS

1. With reference to the flow chart in Figure 8.1, use your own words to describe the procedures of hypothesis testing. Be sure to use the following terms in your explanation: *alpha, beta, null hypothesis, probability value, statistical significance*, and *Type 1* and *Type 2 errors.*

2. Explain why scientists can never be certain whether their data really support their research hypothesis.

3. Describe in your own words the techniques that scientists use to help them avoid drawing statistically invalid conclusions.

4. What is a statistically significant result? What is the relationship among statistical significance, *N,* and effect size?

5. What are the implications of using a smaller, rather than a larger, alpha in a research design?

6. What is the likelihood of a Type 1 error if the null hypothesis is actually true? What is the likelihood of a Type 1 error if the null hypothesis is actually false?

7. What is meant by the power of a statistical test, and how can it be increased?

8. What are the practical uses of the effect-size statistic?

9. What is the meaning of the proportion of explained variability?

RESEARCH PROJECT IDEAS

1. Flip a set of ten coins one hundred times, and record the number of heads and tails each time. Construct a frequency distribution of the observed data. Check whether the observed frequency distribution appears to match the expected frequency distribution shown in the binomial distribution in Figure 8.2.

2. For each of the following patterns of data,

   • What is the probability of the researcher having made a Type 1 error?

   • What is the probability of the researcher having made a Type 2 error?

   • Should the null hypothesis be rejected?

- What conclusions can be drawn about the possibility of the researcher having drawn a statistically invalid conclusion?

	p-value	*N*	*alpha*	*beta*
a.	.03	100	.05	.05
b.	.13	100	.05	.30
c.	.03	50	.01	.20
d.	.03	25	.01	.20
e.	.06	1,000	.05	.70

3. A friend of yours reports a study that obtains a *p*-value of .02. What can you conclude about the finding? List two other pieces of information that you would need to know to fully interpret the finding.

CHAPTER NINE
Correlational Research Designs

STUDY QUESTIONS

- What are correlational research designs, and why are they used in behavioral research?

- What patterns of association can occur between two quantitative variables?

- What is the Pearson product–moment correlation coefficient? What are its uses and limitations?

- How does the chi-square statistic assess association?

- What is multiple regression, and what are its uses in correlational research designs?

- How can correlational data be used to make inferences about the causal relationships among measured variables? What are the limitations of correlational designs in doing so?

- What are the best uses for correlational designs?

Correlational research designs are used to search for and describe relationships among measured variables. For instance, a researcher might be interested in looking for a relationship between family background and career choice, between diet and disease, or between the physical attractiveness of a person and how much help she or he receives from strangers. There are many patterns of relationships that can occur between two measured variables, and an even greater number of patterns can occur when more than two variables are assessed. It is exactly this complexity, which is also part of everyday life, that correlational research designs attempt to capture.

In this chapter, we will first consider the patterns of association that can be found between one predictor and one outcome variable and the statistical techniques used to summarize these associations. Then we will consider techniques for simultaneously assessing the relationships among more than two measured variables. We will also discuss when and how correlational data can be used to learn about the causal relationships among measured variables.

Associations Among Quantitative Variables

Let's begin our study of patterns of association by looking at the raw data from a sample of twenty college students, presented in Table 9.1. Each person has a score on both a Likert scale measure of optimism (such as the Life Orientation Test; Scheier, Carver, & Bridges, 1994) and a measure that assesses the

TABLE 9.1 Raw Data From a Correlational Study

Participant #	Optimism Scale	Reported Health Behavior
1	6	13
2	7	24
3	2	8
4	5	7
5	2	11
6	3	6
7	7	21
8	9	12
9	8	14
10	9	21
11	6	10
12	1	15
13	9	8
14	2	7
15	4	9
16	2	6
17	6	9
18	2	6
19	6	12
20	3	5

extent to which he or she reports performing healthy behaviors such as going for regular physical examinations and eating low-fat foods. The optimism scale ranges from 1 to 9, where higher numbers indicate a more optimistic personality, and the health scale ranges from 1 to 25, where higher numbers indicate that the individual reports engaging in more healthy activities.

At this point, the goal of the researcher is to assess the strength and direction of the relationship between the variables. It is difficult to do so by looking at the raw data because there are too many scores and they are not organized in any meaningful way. One way of organizing the data is to graph the variables using a scatterplot. As shown in Figure 9.1, a **scatterplot** uses a standard coordinate system in which the horizontal axis indicates the scores on the predictor variable and the vertical axis represents the scores on the outcome variable. A point is plotted for each individual at the intersection of his or her scores on the two variables.

Scatterplots provide a visual image of the relationship between the variables. In this example, you can see that the points fall in a fairly regular pattern in which most of the individuals are located in the lower left corner, in the center, or in the upper right corner of the scatterplot. You can also see that a straight line, known as the **regression line,** has been drawn through the points. The regression line is sometimes called the line of "best fit" because it is the line that minimizes the squared distance of the points from the line. The regression line is discussed in more detail in the appendix on Bivariate Statistics.

FIGURE 9.1 Scatterplot of Optimism by Health Behavior

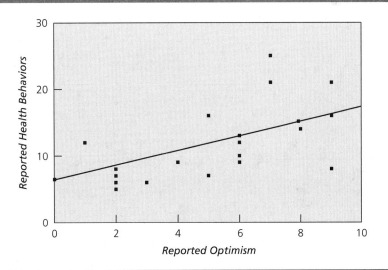

In this scatterplot of the data in Table 9.1, the predictor variable (optimism) is plotted on the horizontal axis and the dependent variable (health behaviors) is plotted on the vertical axis. The regression line, which minimizes the squared distances of the points from the line, is drawn. You can see that the relationship between the variables is positive linear.

Linear Relationships

When the association between the variables on the scatterplot can be easily approximated with a straight line, as in Figure 9.1, the variables are said to have a **linear relationship.** Figure 9.2 shows two examples of scatterplots of linear relationships. When the straight line indicates that individuals who have above-average values on one variable also tend to have above-average values on the other variable, as in Figure 9.2(a), the relationship is said to be *positive linear. Negative linear* relationships, in contrast, occur when above-average values on one variable tend to be associated with below-average values on the other variable, such as in Figure 9.2(b). We have considered examples of these relationships in Chapter 1, and you may wish to review these now.

Nonlinear Relationships

Not all relationships between variables can be well described with a straight line, and those that are not are known as **nonlinear relationships.** Figure 9.2(c) shows a common pattern in which the distribution of the points is essentially random. In this case, there is no relationship at all between the two variables, and they are said to be **independent.** When the two variables are independent, it means that we cannot use one variable to predict the other.

FIGURE 9.2 Patterns of Relationships Between Two Variables

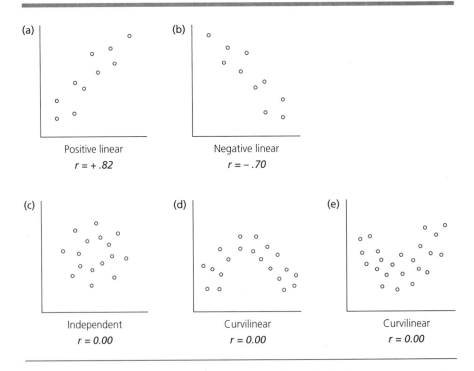

This figure shows five of the many possible patterns of association between two quantitative variables.

Figures 9.2(d) and 9.2(e) show patterns of association in which, although there is an association, the points are not well described by a single straight line. For instance, Figure 9.2(d) shows the type of relationship that frequently occurs between anxiety and performance. Increases in anxiety from low to moderate levels are associated with performance increases, whereas increases in anxiety from moderate to high levels are associated with decreases in performance. Relationships that change in direction and thus are not described by a single straight line are called **curvilinear relationships.**

Statistical Assessment of Relationships

Although the scatterplot gives a pictorial image, the relationship between variables is frequently difficult to detect visually. As a result, descriptive statistics are normally used to provide a numerical index of the relationship between or among two or more variables. The descriptive statistic is in essence shorthand for the graphic image.

The Pearson Correlation Coefficient

As we have seen in Chapter 1, a descriptive statistic known as the Pearson product–moment correlation coefficient is normally used to summarize and communicate the strength and direction of the association between two quantitative variables. The Pearson correlation coefficient, frequently referred to simply as the correlation coefficient, is designated by the letter r. The correlation coefficient is a number that indicates both the direction and the magnitude of association. Values of the correlation coefficient range from $r = -1.00$ to $r = +1.00$.

The direction of the relationship is indicated by the sign of the correlation coefficient. Positive values of r (such as $r = .54$ or $r = .67$) indicate that the relationship is positive linear (that is, that the regression line runs from the lower left to the upper right), whereas negative values of r (such as $r = -.3$ or $r = -.72$) indicate negative linear relationships (that is, that the regression line runs from the upper left to the lower right). The strength or effect size (see Chapter 8) of the linear relationship is indexed by the distance of the correlation coefficient from zero (its absolute value). For instance, $r = .54$ is a stronger relationship than $r = .30$, whereas $r = .72$ is a stronger relationship than $r = .57$.

Interpretation of r. The calculation of the correlation coefficient is described in Appendix C, and you may wish to verify that the correlation between optimism and health behavior in the sample data in Table 9.1 is $r = .52$. This confirms what we have seen in the scatterplot in Figure 9.1—that the relationship is positive linear. The p-value associated with r can be calculated as described in Appendix C, and in this case r is significant at $p < .01$.

A significant r indicates that there is a linear association between the variables and thus that it is possible to use knowledge about a person's score on one variable to predict his or her score on the other variable. For instance, because optimism and health behavior are significantly positively correlated, we can use optimism to predict health behavior. The extent to which we can predict is indexed by the effect size of the correlation, and the effect size for the Pearson correlation coefficient is r, the correlation coefficient itself. As you will recall from our discussion in Chapter 8, each test statistic also has an associated statistic that indicates the proportion of variance accounted for. The proportion of variance measure for r is r^2, which is known as the **coefficient of determination.**

When the correlation coefficient is not statistically significant, this indicates that there is not a positive linear or a negative linear relationship between the variables. However, a nonsignificant r does not necessarily mean that there is no systematic relationship between the variables. As we have seen in Figure 9.2(d) and 9.2(e), the correlation between two variables that have curvilinear relationships is likely to be about zero. What this means is that although one variable can be used to predict the other, the Pearson correlation coefficient does not provide a good estimate of the extent to which this is possible. This represents a limitation of the correlation coefficient because, as we have seen, some important relationships are curvilinear.

Restriction of Range.   The size of the correlation coefficient may be reduced if there is a restriction of range in the variables being correlated. **Restriction of range** occurs when most participants have similar scores on one of the variables being correlated. This may occur, for instance, when the sample under study does not cover the full range of the variable. One example of this problem occurs in the use of the Scholastic Aptitude Test (SAT) as a predictor of college performance. It turns out that the correlation between SAT scores and measures of college performance, such as grade-point average (GPA), is only about $r = .30$. However, the size of the correlation is probably greatly reduced by the fact that only students with relatively high SAT scores are admitted to college, and thus there is restriction of range in the SAT measure among students who also have college GPAs. When there is a smaller than normal range on one or both of the measured variables, the value of the correlation coefficient will be reduced and thus will not represent an accurate picture of the true relationship between the variables. The effect of restriction of range on the correlation coefficient is shown in Figure 9.3.

The Chi-Square Statistic

Although the correlation coefficient is used to assess the relationship between two quantitative variables, an alternative statistic, known as the **chi-square (χ^2) statistic,** must be used to assess the relationship between two nominal variables (the statistical test is technically known as the *chi-square test of independence*). Consider as an example a researcher who is

FIGURE 9.3   Restriction of Range and the Correlation Coefficient

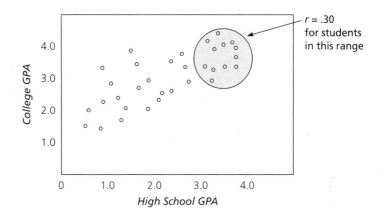

The correlation between high school GPA and college GPA across all students is about
$r = .80$. However, since only the students with high school GPAs above about 2.5 are
admitted to college, data are only available on both variables for the students who fall
within the circled area. The correlation for these students is much lower ($r = .30$). This
phenomenon is know as *restriction of range*.

interested in studying the relationship between a person's ethnicity and his or
her attitude toward a new low-income housing project in the neighborhood.
A random sample of 300 individuals from the neighborhood is asked to express opinions about the housing project.

Calculating the Chi-Square Statistic.   To calculate χ^2, the researcher first constructs a **contingency table**, which displays the number of individuals in each
of the combinations of the two nominal variables. The contingency table in
Table 9.2 shows the number of individuals from each ethnic group who favor or oppose the housing project. The next step is to calculate the number
of people who would be expected to fall into each of the entries in the table
given the number of individuals with each value on the original two variables.
If the number of people actually falling into the entries is substantially different
from the expected values, then there is an association between the variables,
and if this relationship is strong enough, the chi-square test will be statistically
significant and the null hypothesis that the two variables are independent can
be rejected. In our example, χ^2 is equal to 45.78, which is highly significant,
$p < .001$. The associated effect size statistic for χ^2 is discussed in Appendix C.
   Although a statistically significant chi square indicates that there is an association between the two variables, the specific pattern of the association is
usually determined through inspection of the contingency table. In our example, the pattern of relationship is very clear—African Americans and Hispanics are more likely to favor the project, whereas whites and Asians are more
likely to be opposed to it.

TABLE 9.2　Contingency Table and Chi-Square Analysis

	Opinion		
Ethnicity	Favor	Oppose	Total
White	56	104	160
African American	51	11	62
Asian	31	29	60
Hispanic	14	4	18
Total	152	148	300

This contingency table presents the opinions of a sample of 300 community residents about the construction of a new neighborhood center in their area. The numbers in the lighter-shaded cells indicate the number of each ethnic group who favor or oppose the project. The data are analyzed using the chi statistic, which evaluates whether the different ethnic groups differ in terms of their opinions. In this case the test is statistically significant, chi ($N = 300$) = 45.78, $p < .001$, indicating that the null hypothesis of no relationship between the two variables can be rejected.

Reporting Correlations and Chi-Square Statistics.　As we have seen, when the research hypothesis involves the relationship between two quantitative variables, the correlation coefficient is the appropriate statistic. The null hypothesis is that the variables are independent ($r = 0$), and the research hypothesis is that the variables are not independent (either $r > 0$ or $r < 0$). In some cases, the correlation between the variables can be reported in the text of the research report, for instance, "As predicted by the research hypothesis, the variables of optimism and reported health behavior were significantly positively correlated in the sample, $r(20) = .52$, $p < .01$." In this case, the correlation coefficient is .52, 20 refers to the sample size (N), and .01 is the p-value of the observed correlation.

When there are many correlations to be reported at the same time, they can be presented in a **correlation matrix,** which is a table showing the correlations of many variables with each other. An example of a correlation matrix printed out by the statistical software program IBM SPSS® is presented in Table 9.3. The variables that have been correlated are SAT, Social Support, Study Hours, and College GPA, although these names have been abbreviated by IBM SPSS into shorter labels. The printout contains sixteen cells, each indicating the correlation between two of these variables. Within each box are the appropriate correlations (r) on the first line, the p-value on the second line, and the sample size (N) on the third line. Note that IBM SPSS indicates the (two-tailed) p-values as "sig."

Because any variable correlates at $r = 1.00$ with itself, the correlations on the diagonal of a correlation matrix are all 1.00. The correlation matrix is also symmetrical in the sense that each of the correlations above the diagonal is also represented below the diagonal. Because the information on the diagonal is not particularly useful, and the information below the diagonal is redundant with the information above the diagonal, it is general practice to report only the upper triangle of the correlation matrix in the research report. An example of a correlation matrix based on the output in Table 9.3 as reported using APA format is shown in Table 9.4. You can see that only the upper triangle of correlations has been presented, and that rather than reporting the exact *p*-values, they are instead indicated using a legend of asterisks. Because the sample size for each of the correlations is the same, it is only presented once, in a note at the bottom of the table.

When the chi-square statistic has been used, the results are usually reported in the text of the research report. For instance, the analysis shown in Table 9.2 would be reported as χ^2 (3, $N = 300$) = 45.78, $p < .001$, where 300 represents the sample size, 45.78 is the value of the chi-square statistic, and .001 is the *p*-value. The number 3 refers to the *degrees of freedom* of the chi square, a statistic discussed in Appendix C.

TABLE 9.3 A Correlational Matrix as an IBM SPSS Output

		SAT	Support	Hours	GPA
SAT	*Pearson Correlation*	1	−.020	.240**	.250**
	Sig. (2-tailed)	.	.810	.003	.002
	N	155	155	155	155
SUPPORT	*Pearson Correlation*	−.020	1	.020	.140
	Sig. (2-tailed)	.810	.	.806	.084
	N	155	155	155	155
HOURS	*Pearson Correlation*	.240**	.020	1	.240**
	Sig. (2-tailed)	.003	.806	.	.003
	N	155	155	155	155
GPA	*Pearson Correlation*	.250**	.140	.240**	1
	Sig. (2-tailed)	.002	.084	.003	.
	N	155	155	155	155

**Correlation is significant at the 0.01 level (2-tailed).

TABLE 9.4 The Same Correlational Matrix Reported in APA Format

Predictor Variables	1	2	3	4
1. Rated social support	—	−.02	.24*	.25*
2. High school SAT score		—	.02	.14
3. Weekly reported hours of study			—	.24*
4. High school GPA				—

Note: Correlations indicated with an asterisk are significant at $p < .01$. All correlations are based on $N = 155$.

Multiple Regression

Although the goal of correlational research is frequently to study the relationship between two measured variables, it is also possible to study relationships among more than two measures at the same time. Consider, for example, a scientist whose goal is to predict the grade-point averages of a sample of college students. As shown in Figure 9.4, the scientist uses three predictor variables (perceived social support, number of study hours per week, and SAT score) to do so. Such a research design, in which more than one predictor variable is used to predict a single outcome variable, is analyzed through **multiple regression** (Aiken & West, 1991). Multiple regression is a statistical technique based on Pearson correlation coefficients both between each of the predictor variables and the outcome variable and among the predictor variables themselves. In this case, the original correlations that form the input to the regression analysis are shown in the correlation matrix in Table 9.3.[1]

If you look at Table 9.3 carefully, you will see that the correlations between the three predictor variables and the outcome variable range from $r = .14$ (for the correlation between social support and college GPA) to $r = .25$ (for the correlation between SAT and college GPA). These correlations, which serve as the input to a multiple-regression analysis, are known as *zero-order correlations*. The advantage of a multiple-regression approach is that it allows the researcher to consider how all of the predictor variables, taken together, relate to the outcome variable. And if each of the predictor variables has some (perhaps only a very small) correlation with the outcome variable, then the ability to predict the outcome variable will generally be even greater if all of the predictor variables are used to predict at the same time.

Because multiple regression requires an extensive set of calculations, it is always conducted on a computer. The outcome of our researcher's multiple-regression analysis is shown in Figure 9.4. There are two pieces of information. First, the ability of all of the predictor variables together to predict the outcome variable is indicated by a statistic known as the **multiple correlation coefficient,** symbolized by the letter $\boldsymbol{R}$. For the data in Figure 9.4, $R = .34$. The statistical significance of R is tested with a statistic known as F, described in Appendix D. In our case, the R is significant, $p < .05$. Because R is the effect size statistic for a multiple-regression analysis, and R^2 is the proportion of variance measure, R and R^2 can be directly compared to r and r^2, respectively. You can see that, as expected, the ability to predict the outcome measure using all three predictor variables at the same time ($R = .34$) is better than that of any of the zero-order correlations (which ranged from $r = .14$ to $r = .25$).

Second, the regression analysis shows statistics that indicate the relationship between each of the predictor variables and the outcome variable. These statistics are known as the **regression coefficient**s[2] or **beta weights,** and

---

[1]As described more fully in Appendix D, multiple regression can also be used to examine the relationships between nominal predictor variables and a quantitative outcome variable.

[2]As we will see in Appendix D, these are technically standardized regression coefficients.

FIGURE 9.4 Multiple Regression

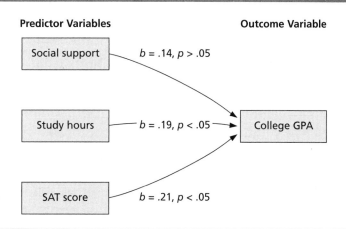

This figure represents the simultaneous impact of three measured independent variables (perceived social support, hours of study per week, and SAT score) as predictors of college GPA based on a hypothetical study of 155 college students. The numbers on the arrows indicate the regression coefficients of each of the predictor variables with the outcome variable. The ability of the three predictor variables to predict the outcome variable is indexed by the multiple correlation, *R*, which in this case equals .34.

their interpretation is very similar to that of *r*. Each regression coefficient can be tested for statistical significance, and both the regression coefficients and their *p*-values are indicated on the arrows connecting the predictor variables and outcome variable in Figure 9.4.

The regression coefficients are not exactly the same as the zero-order correlations because they represent the effects of each of the predictor measures in the regression analysis, holding constant or *controlling for* the effects of the other predictor variables. This control is accomplished statistically. The result is that the regression coefficients can be used to indicate the relative contributions of each of the predictor variables. For instance, the regression coefficient of .19 indicates the relationship between study hours and college GPA, controlling for both social support and SAT. In this case, the regression coefficient is statistically significant, and the relevant conclusion is that estimated study hours predicts GPA even when the influence of social support and SAT is controlled. Furthermore, we can see that SAT (b = .21) is somewhat more predictive of GPA than is social support (b = .14). As we will see in the next section, one of the important uses of multiple regression is to assess the relationship between a predictor and an outcome variable when the influence of other predictor variables on the outcome variable is statistically controlled.

Correlation and Causality

As we have seen in Chapter 1, an important limitation of correlational research designs is that they cannot be used to draw conclusions about the causal relationships among the measured variables. An observed correlation between two variables does not necessarily indicate that either one of the variables caused the other. Thus, even though the research hypothesis may have specified a predictor and an outcome variable, and the researcher may believe that the predictor variable is causing the outcome variable, the correlation between the two variables does not provide support for this hypothesis.

Interpreting Correlations

Consider, for instance, a researcher who has hypothesized that viewing violent behavior will cause increased aggressive play in children. He has collected, from a sample of fourth-grade children, a measure of how many violent TV shows the child views per week, as well as a measure of how aggressively each child plays on the school playground. Furthermore, the researcher has found a significant positive correlation between the two measured variables. Although this positive correlation appears to support the researcher's hypothesis, because there are alternative ways to explain the correlation it *cannot* be taken to indicate that viewing violent television causes aggressive behavior.

Reverse Causation.   One possibility is that the causal direction is exactly opposite from what has been hypothesized. Perhaps children who have behaved aggressively at school develop residual excitement that leads them to want to watch violent TV shows at home:

Although the possibility that aggressive play causes increased viewing of violent television, rather than vice versa, may seem less likely to you, there is no way to rule out the possibility of such **reverse causation** on the basis of this observed correlation. It is also possible that both causal directions are operating and that the two variables cause each other. Such cases are known as **reciprocal causation:**

Common-Causal Variables.   Still another possible explanation for the observed correlation is that it has been produced by the presence of a **common-causal variable** (sometimes known as a *third* variable). Common-causal variables are variables that are not part of the research hypothesis but that cause both the predictor and the outcome variable and thus produce the observed correlation between them. In our example, a potential common-causal variable is the discipline style of the children's parents. For instance, parents who use a harsh and punitive discipline style may produce children who both like to watch violent TV and behave aggressively in comparison to children whose parents use less harsh discipline:

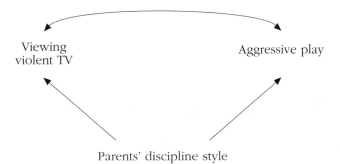

In this case, TV viewing and aggressive play would be positively correlated (as indicated by the curved arrow), even though neither one caused the other but they were both caused by the discipline style of the parents (the straight arrows).

When the predictor and outcome variables are both caused by a common-causal variable, the observed relationship between them is said to be spurious. In a **spurious relationship,** the common-causal variable produces and "explains away" the relationship between the predictor and outcome variables. If effects of the common-causal variable were taken away, or controlled for, the relationship between the predictor and outcome variables would disappear. In our example, the relationship between aggression and TV viewing might be spurious because if we were to control for the effect of the parents' disciplining style, the relationship between TV viewing and aggressive behavior might go away. You can see that if a common-causal variable such as parental discipline was operating, this would lead to a very different interpretation of the data. And the identification of the true cause of the relationship would also lead to a very different plan to reduce aggressive behavior—a focus on parenting style rather than the presence of violent television.

I like to think of common-causal variables in correlational research designs as "mystery" variables because, as they have not been measured, their presence and identity are usually unknown to the researcher. Because it is not possible to measure every variable that could cause both the predictor and outcome variables, the existence of an unknown common-causal variable is always a possibility. For this reason, we are left with the basic limitation of correlational research: "Correlation does not demonstrate causation." And, of course, this is exactly why, when possible, it is desirable to conduct experimental research.

When you read about correlational research projects, keep in mind the possibility of spurious relationships, and be sure to interpret the findings appropriately. Although correlational research is sometimes reported as demonstrating causality without any mention being made of the possibility of reverse causation or common-causal variables, informed consumers of research, like you, are aware of these interpretational problems.

Extraneous Variables.   Although common-causal variables are the most problematic because they can produce spurious relationships, correlational research designs are also likely to have other variables that are not part of the research hypothesis and that cause one or more of the measured variables. For instance, how aggressively a child plays at school is probably caused to some extent by the disciplining style of the child's teacher, but TV watching at home is probably not:

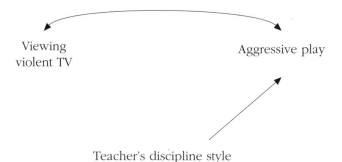

Variables other than the predictor variable that cause the outcome variable *but that do not cause the predictor variable* are called **extraneous variables.** The distinction between extraneous variables and common-causal variables is an important one because they lead to substantially different interpretations of observed correlations. Extraneous variables may reduce the likelihood of finding a significant correlation between the predictor variable and outcome variable because they cause changes in the outcome variable. However, because they do not cause changes in the predictor variable, extraneous variables cannot produce a spurious correlation.

Mediating Variables.   Another type of variable that can appear in a correlational research design and that is relevant for gaining a full understanding of the causal relationships among measured variables is known as a **mediating variable** or **mediator.** In a correlational design, a mediating variable is a variable that is caused by the predictor variable and that in turn causes the outcome variable. For instance, we might expect that the level of arousal of the child might mediate the relationship between viewing violent material and displaying aggressive behavior:

Violent TV $\longrightarrow$ Arousal $\longrightarrow$ Aggressive play

In this case, the expected causal relationship is that violent TV causes arousal and that arousal causes aggressive play. Other examples of mediating variables would include:

Failure on a task $\longrightarrow$ Low self-esteem $\longrightarrow$ Less interest in the task

and

More study time $\longrightarrow$ Greater retention of material in long-term memory $\longrightarrow$ Better task performance

Mediating variables are important because they explain *why* a relationship between two variables occurs. For instance, we can say that viewing violent material increases aggression *because* it increases arousal, and that failure on a task leads to less interest in the task *because* it decreases self-esteem. Of course, there are usually many possible mediating variables in relationships. Viewing violent material might increase aggression because it reduces inhibitions against behaving aggressively:

Violent TV $\longrightarrow$ Fewer inhibitions $\longrightarrow$ Aggressive play

or because it provides new ideas about how to be aggressive:

Violent TV $\longrightarrow$ Violence-related ideas $\longrightarrow$ Aggressive play

rather than (or in addition to) its effects on arousal. Mediating variables are often measured in correlational research as well as in experimental research to help the researcher better understand why variables are related to each other.

Using Correlational Data to Test Causal Models

Although correlational research designs are limited in their ability to demonstrate causality, they can in some cases provide at least some information about the likely causal relationships among measured variables. This evidence is greater to the extent that the data allow the researcher to rule out the possibility of reverse causation and to control for common-causal variables.

Conducting Longitudinal Research. One approach to ruling out reverse causation is to use a longitudinal research design. **Longitudinal research designs** are those in which the same individuals are measured more than one time and the time period between the measurements is long enough that changes in the variables of interest could occur. Consider, for instance, research conducted by Eron, Huesman, Lefkowitz, and Walder (1972). They measured both violent television viewing and aggressive play behavior in a group of children who were eight years old, but they also waited and measured these two variables again when the children were eighteen years old. The resulting data were a set of correlation coefficients among the two variables, each measured at each time period.

Correlational data from longitudinal research designs are often analyzed through a form of multiple regression that assesses the relationships among a number of measured variables, known as a **path analysis.** The results of the path analysis can be displayed visually in the form of a **path diagram,** which represents the associations among a set of variables, as shown for the data from the Eron et al. study in Figure 9.5. As in multiple regression, in a path diagram the paths between the variables represent the regression coefficients, and each regression coefficient again has an associated significance test.

Recall that Eron and his colleagues wished to test the hypothesis that viewing violent television causes aggressive behavior, while ruling out the possibility of reverse causation—namely, that aggression causes increased television viewing. To do so, they compared the regression coefficient linking television viewing at age eight with aggression at age eighteen ($b = .31$) with the regression coefficient linking aggression at age eight with television viewing at age eighteen ($b = .01$). Because the former turns out to be significantly greater than the latter, the data are more consistent with the hypothesis that viewing violent television causes aggressive behavior than the reverse. However, although this

FIGURE 9.5 Path Diagram

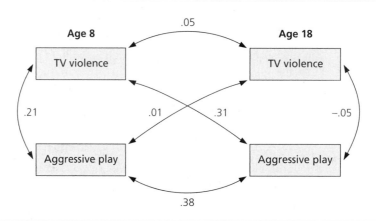

Source: From L. D. Eron, L. R. Huesman, M. M. Lefkowitz, and D. O. Walder, "Does Television Watching Cause Aggression?" *American Psychologist,* 1972, Vol. 27, 254–263. Copyright © 1972 by the American Psychological Association. Adapted with permission.

This figure presents data from a longitudinal study in which children's viewing of violent television and their displayed aggressive behavior at school were measured at two separate occasions spaced ten years apart. Each path shows the regression coefficient between two variables. The relevant finding is that the regression coefficient between TV viewing at time 1 and aggressive behavior at time 2 ($b = .31$) is significantly greater than the regression coefficient between aggressive behavior at time 1 and television viewing at time 2 ($b = .01$). The data are thus more supportive of the hypothesis that television viewing causes aggressive behavior than vice versa.

longitudinal research helps rule out reverse causation, it does not rule out the possibility that the observed relationship is spurious.[3]

As you can imagine, one limitation of longitudinal research designs is that they take a long time to conduct. Eron and his colleagues, for instance, had to wait ten years before they could draw their conclusions about the effect of violent TV viewing on aggression! Despite this difficulty, longitudinal designs are essential for providing knowledge about causal relationships. The problem is that research designs that measure people from different age groups at the same time—they are known as **cross-sectional research designs**—are very limited in their ability to rule out reverse causation. For instance, if we found that older children were more aggressive than younger children in a cross-sectional study, we could effectively rule out reverse causation because the age of the child could not logically be caused by the child's aggressive play. We could not, however, use a cross-sectional design to draw conclusions about what other variables caused these changes. A longitudinal design in which both the predictor and the outcome variables are measured repeatedly over time can be informative about these questions.

Controlling for Common-Causal Variables.   In addition to helping rule out the possibility of reverse causation, correlational data can in some cases be used to rule out, at least to some extent, the influence of common-causal variables. Consider again our researcher who is interested in testing the hypothesis that viewing violent television causes aggressive behavior in elementary school children. And imagine that she or he has measured not only television viewing and aggressive behavior in the sample of children but also the discipline style of the children's parents. Because the researcher has measured this potential common-causal variable, she or he can attempt to control for its effects statistically using multiple regression.

The idea is to use both the predictor variable (viewing violent TV) and the potential common-causal variable (parental discipline) to predict the outcome variable (aggressive play):

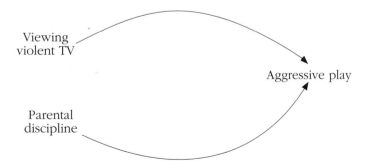

---

[3] The procedures for conducting a path analysis, including the significance test that compares the regression coefficients, can be found in Kenny (1979, p. 239).

If the predictor variable still significantly relates to the outcome variable when the common-causal variable is controlled (that is, if the regression coefficient between violent TV and aggressive play is significant), we have more confidence that parental discipline is not causing a spurious relationship. However, this conclusion assumes that the measured common-causal variable really measures parental discipline (that is, that the measure has construct validity), and it does not rule out the possibility of reverse causation. Furthermore, there are still other potential common-causal variables that have not been measured and that could produce a spurious relationship between the predictor and the outcome variables.

Assessing the Role of Mediating Variables.   Multiple-regression techniques can also be used to test whether hypotheses about proposed mediators are likely to be valid. As we have seen, mediational relationships can be expressed in the form of a path diagram:

Viewing
violent $\longrightarrow$ Arousal $\longrightarrow$ Aggressive play
TV

If arousal is actually a mediator of the relationship, then the effects of viewing violent material on aggression are expected to occur because they influence arousal, and not directly. On the other hand, if arousal is *not* a mediator, then violent TV should have a direct effect on aggressive play, which is not mediated through arousal:

Viewing violent TV   Arousal   Aggressive play

To test whether arousal is a likely mediator, we again enter both the predictor variable (in this case, viewing violent TV) as well as the proposed mediating variable (in this case, arousal) as predictors of the outcome variable in a regression equation. If arousal is a mediator, then when its effects are controlled in the analysis, the predictor variable (viewing violent TV) should no longer correlate with the outcome variable (that is, the regression coefficient for viewing violent TV should no longer be significant). If this is the case, then we have at least some support for the proposed mediational variable.

Structural Equation Analysis.   Over the past decades, new statistical procedures have been developed that allow researchers to draw even more conclusions about the likely causal relationships among measured variables using correlational data. One of these techniques is known as structural equation analysis. A **structural equation analysis** is a statistical procedure that tests whether the observed relationships among a set of variables conform to a theoretical prediction about how those variables should be causally related.

One advantage of structural equation analysis over other techniques is that it is designed to represent both the conceptual variables as well as the measured variables in the statistical analysis. Normally, each conceptual variable is assessed using more than one measured variable, which allows the analysis to also calculate the reliability of the measures. When conducting a structural equation analysis, the scientist enters the variables that have been used to assess each of the conceptual variables. The conceptual variables are usually called **latent variables** in a structural equation analysis, and the analysis is designed to assess both the relationships between the measured and the conceptual variables and the relationships among the conceptual variables. The conceptual variables can include both independent and dependent variables.

Consider as an example an industrial psychologist who has conducted a correlational study designed to predict the conceptual variable of "job performance" from three conceptual variables of "supervisor satisfaction," "coworker satisfaction," and "job interest." As shown in Figure 9.6, the researcher has used three measured variables (represented as squares) to assess each of the four conceptual variables (supervisor satisfaction, coworker satisfaction, job interest, and job performance), represented as circles. Rather than computing a separate reliability analysis on the three independent variables and the dependent variable, combining each set of three scores together, and then using a regression analysis with three independent variables and one dependent variable, the scientist could use a structural equation analysis to test the entire set of relationships at the same time. In the structural equation analysis, all of the relationships among the variables—some of which involve the relationship between the measured variables and the conceptual variables and others of which involve the relationships among the conceptual variables themselves—are simultaneously tested. More information about the use of structural equation analyses can be found in Appendix D.

When Correlational Designs Are Appropriate

We have seen in this chapter that correlational research designs have both strengths and limitations. Their greatest strength may be that they can be used when experimental research is not possible because the predictor variables cannot be manipulated. For instance, it would be impossible to test, except through a correlational design, the research hypothesis that people who go to church regularly are more helpful than people who do not go to church. An experimental design is not possible because we cannot randomly assign some people to go to church and others to stay at home. Correlational designs also have the advantage of allowing the researcher to study behavior as it occurs in everyday life.

Scientists also frequently use correlational research designs in applied research when they want to predict scores on an outcome variable from knowledge about a predictor variable but do not need to know exactly what causal

FIGURE 9.6 Structural Equation Model

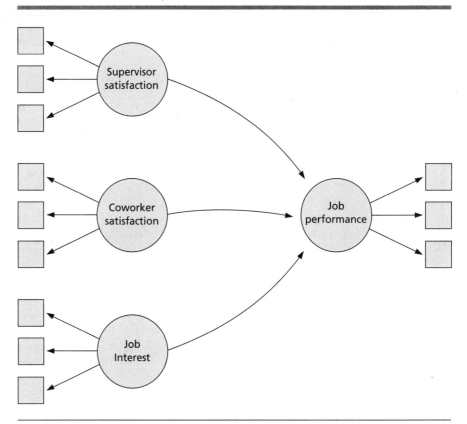

This hypothetical structural equation analysis uses nine measures of job satisfaction, which are combined into three latent variables, to predict a single latent variable of job performance, as measured by three dependent variables. The value of the overall fit of the model to the collected data can be estimated. The structural equation analysis tests both the measurement of the latent variables and the relationships among them.

relationships are involved. For instance, a researcher may use a personality test to determine which employees will do well on a job but may not care whether the relation is produced by the personality variable or another common-causal variable.

However, although sometimes used to provide at least some information about which patterns of causal relationships are most likely, correlational studies cannot provide conclusive information about causal relationships among variables. Only experimental research designs in which the independent variable is manipulated by the experimenter can do this. And it is to such designs that we now turn.

Current Research in the Behavioral Sciences: Moral Conviction, Religiosity, and Trust in Authority

Daniel Wisneski, Brad Lytle, and Linda Skitka (2009) conducted a correlational study to investigate how people's moral convictions and their religious convictions would predict their trust in authority figures such as the U.S. Supreme Court to make the "right" decisions. They predicted that people with stronger moral convictions would have less trust in authorities, whereas people with strongly religious convictions would have greater trust in authorities.

The researchers tested these hypotheses using a survey of a nationally representative sample of 727 Americans. The survey assessed measures of morality (for instance, "Do your feelings about physician-assisted suicide represent your core moral values and convictions?") and religiosity ("My religious faith is extremely important to me"), as well as a measure of the degree to which people trusted the U.S. Supreme Court to rule on the legal status of physician-assisted suicide ("I trust the Supreme Court to make the right decision about whether physician-assisted suicide should be allowed").

To test their hypothesis, the researchers entered both morality and religiosity, as well as other variables that they thought might be important (including age, education, gender, income, and attitude position and attitude toward physician-assisted suicide) into a simultaneous multiple-regression analysis with trust in the Supreme Court as the dependent variable.

As you can see in Table 9.5, the overall multiple-regression analysis was significant, $R^2 = .27$, $p < 0.01$, indicating that, overall, the predictor variables predicted the dependent variable. Furthermore, even with the control variables

TABLE 9.5 Morality and Religiosity as Predictors of Trust in the Supreme Court

Predictor	beta	t-value	p-value
Hypothesized Relationships			
Moral conviction	−.10	−2.51	<.01*
Religiosity	.11	2.97	<.001*
Control Variables			
Age	−.07	−1.91	.06
Education	.03	0.71	.47
Gender	−.04	−1.11	.27
Income	.00	−0.10	.92
Attitude position	.04	1.14	.25
Attitude extremity	−.14	−3.72	<.001*
$R^2 = .27$, $p < 0.01$			

This table presents the results of the multiple-regression analysis used by Wisnseski et al. (2009) to study how moral conviction predicted attitudes toward trust in the U.S. Supreme Court.

in the equation, the researchers hypotheses were supported. People with stronger moral convictions about physician-assisted suicide had significantly greater distrust in the Supreme Court to make a decision about this issue, $b = -.10$, $t(704) = 2.51, p < .01$, whereas people with higher religiosity trusted the Supreme Court more to make this decision than those low in religiosity, $b = .11$, $t(704) = 2.97, p < .01$.

SUMMARY

Correlational research is designed to test research hypotheses in cases where it is not possible or desirable to experimentally manipulate the independent variable of interest. It is also desirable because it allows the investigation of behavior in naturally occurring situations. Correlational methods range from analysis of correlations between a predictor and an outcome variable to multiple-regression and path analyses assessing the patterns of relationships among many measured variables.

Two quantitative variables can be found to be related in either linear or nonlinear patterns. The type of relationship can be ascertained graphically with a scatterplot. If the relationships are linear, they can be statistically measured with the Pearson correlation coefficient (r). Associations between two nominal variables are assessed with the χ^2 test of independence.

Multiple regression uses more than one predictor variable to predict a single outcome variable. The analysis includes a test of the statistical significance between the predictor and outcome variables collectively (the multiple R) and individually (the regression coefficients).

Correlational research can in some cases be used to make at least some inferences about the likely causal relationships among variables if reverse causation and the presence of common-causal variables can be ruled out. In general, the approach is to examine the pattern of correlations among the variables using either multiple regression or structural equation analysis. Correlational data can also be used to assess whether hypotheses about proposed mediating variables are likely to be valid. However, because even the most sophisticated path analyses cannot be used to make definitive statements about causal relations, researchers often rely, at least in part, on experimental research designs.

KEY TERMS

beta weights 168
chi-square (χ^2) statistic 164
coefficient of determination (r^2) 164
common-causal variable 170

contingency table 165
correlation matrix 166
cross-sectional research designs 175
curvilinear relationships 163

REVIEW AND DISCUSSION QUESTIONS

1. When are correlational research designs used in behavioral research? What are their advantages and disadvantages?

2. What are a linear relationship and a curvilinear relationship? What does it mean if two variables are independent?

3. Interpret the meanings of, and differentiate between, the two Pearson correlation coefficients $r = .85$ and $r = -.85$.

4. What is multiple regression, and how is it used in behavioral science research?

5. What is a spurious relationship?

6. What is the difference between a common-causal variable, an extraneous variable, and a mediating variable?

7. In what ways can correlational data provide information about the likely causal relationships among variables?

RESEARCH PROJECT IDEAS

1. List an example of each of the following:

   a. Two quantitative variables that are likely to have a positive linear relationship
   b. Two quantitative variables that are likely to have a negative linear relationship
   c. Two quantitative variables that are likely to be independent
   d. Two quantitative variables that are likely to have a curvilinear relationship
   e. Two nominal variables that are likely to be associated
   f. Two nominal variables that are likely to be independent

2. Find two variables that you think should be either positively or negatively correlated. Measure these two variables in a sample of participants (for instance, your classmates). Calculate the Pearson correlation coefficient between the variables. Was your hypothesis about the nature of the correlation supported?

3. Consider potential common-causal variables that might make each of the following correlational relationships spurious:

   a. Height and intelligence in children
   b. Handgun ownership and violent crime in a city
   c. The number of firefighters at a fire and the damage done by the fire
   d. The number of ice cream cones sold and the number of drownings

CHAPTER TEN
Experimental Research: One-Way Designs

STUDY QUESTIONS

- What types of evidence allow us to conclude that one variable causes another variable?

- How do experimental research designs allow us to demonstrate causal relationships between independent and dependent variables?

- How is equivalence among the levels of the independent variable created in experiments?

- How does the Analysis of Variance test hypotheses about differences between the experimental conditions?

- What are repeated-measures experimental designs?

- How are the results of experimental research designs presented in the research report?

- What are the advantages and disadvantages of experimental designs versus correlational research?

Because most scientists are particularly interested in answering questions about how and when changes in independent variables cause changes in dependent variables, they frequently employ experimental research designs. In contrast to correlational research in which the independent and dependent variables are measured, in an experiment, the investigator manipulates the independent variable or variables by arranging different experiences for the research participants and then assesses the impact of these different experiences on one or more measured dependent variables.[1]

As we will see in this chapter and in Chapter 11, there are many different varieties of experimental designs. Furthermore, as we will see in Chapter 12, to be used to make inferences about causality, experiments must be conducted very carefully and with great attention to how the research participants are treated and how they are responding to the experimental situation. However, when experiments are conducted properly, the fact that the independent variable is manipulated rather than measured allows us to be more confident that any observed changes on the dependent measure were caused by the independent variable.

Demonstration of Causality

How can we tell when one event causes another event to occur? For instance, how would we determine whether watching violent cartoons on TV causes aggressive play in children or whether participating in a program of psychotherapy causes a reduction in anxiety? To answer such questions—that is, to make inferences of causality—we must consider three factors: association, temporal priority, and control of common-causal variables. These form the basis of experimental research (Mill, 1930).

Association

Before we can infer that the former causes the latter, there must first be an association, or correlation, between an independent and a dependent variable. If viewing violent television programs causes aggressive behavior, for instance, there must be a positive correlation between television viewing and aggression. Of course, the correlation between the two variables will not be perfect. That is, we cannot expect that every time the independent variable (viewing a violent TV show) occurs, the dependent variable (acting aggressively) will also occur or that acting aggressively will occur only after viewing violent TV.

Rather than being perfect, the causal relationships between variables in behavioral science, as well as in many other fields, are *probabilistic*. To

---

[1]Although the word *experiment* is often used in everyday language to refer to any type of scientific study, the term should really only be used for research designs in which the independent variable is manipulated.

take another well-known example, consider the statement "Cigarette smoking causes lung cancer." Because there are lots of other causes of cancer, and because precise specification of these causes is not currently possible, this causal statement is also probabilistic. Thus, although we can state that when smoking occurs, lung cancer is more likely to occur than if no smoking had occurred, we cannot say exactly when or for whom smoking will cause cancer. The same holds true for causal statements in the behavioral sciences.

Temporal Priority

A second factor that allows us to draw inferences about causality is the temporal relation between the two associated variables. If event A occurs before event B, then A could be causing B. However, if event A occurs after event B, it cannot be causing that event. For instance, if children view a violent television show before they act aggressively, the viewing may have caused the behavior. But the viewing cannot have been the causal variable if it occurred only after the aggressive behavior. The difficulty in determining the temporal ordering of events in everyday life makes the use of correlational research to draw causal inferences problematic.

Control of Common-Causal Variables

Although association and temporal priority are required for making inferences about causality, they are not sufficient. As we have seen in Chapter 9, to make causal statements also requires the ability to rule out the influence of common-causal variables that may have produced spurious relationships between the independent and dependent variables. As we will see in the following sections, one of the major strengths of experimental designs is that through the use of **experimental manipulations,** the researcher can rule out the possibility that the relationship between the independent and dependent variables is spurious.

One-Way Experimental Designs

Let us consider the experimental research design diagrammed in Figure 10.1. The experiment is known as a **one-way experimental design** because it has one independent variable. In the experiment, twenty fourth-grade boys and girls watched a sequence of five cartoons that had been selected by a panel of experts to be extremely violent, and another twenty children watched a series of nonviolent cartoons. After viewing the cartoons, the children were taken to a play area where they were allowed to play with toys, while a team of observers (who did not know which cartoons the children had seen) coded the aggressiveness of the children's play. The research hypothesis was that the children who had viewed the violent cartoons would play more aggressively than those who had viewed the nonviolent cartoons.

FIGURE 10.1   One-Way Between-Participants Experimental Design Using Random Assignment to Conditions

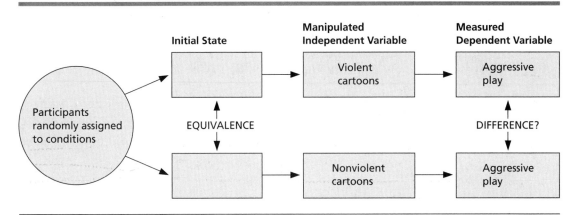

This is a one-way experimental design with two levels of the independent variable. Equivalence has been created through random assignment to conditions. The research hypothesis is that there will be a significant difference in aggressive play between the two experimental conditions such that children who have viewed the violent cartoons will play more aggressively than children who have viewed the nonviolent cartoons.

The Experimental Manipulation

To guarantee that the independent variable occurs prior to the dependent variable, in experimental designs the independent variable or variables are created or, in experimental terms, **manipulated.** In an experiment the manipulation becomes the independent variable, and it is given a name that reflects the different situations that have been created. In this experiment, the independent variable refers to the type of cartoons that the children have viewed. The independent variable is called *cartoon type* to indicate that the manipulation involved children viewing either violent or nonviolent cartoons. The term **levels** refers to the specific situations that are created within the manipulation. In our example, the manipulated independent variable (cartoon type) has two levels: "violent cartoons" and "nonviolent cartoons." In one-way designs the levels of the independent variable are frequently called the experimental **conditions.**

Equivalence and Control.   In addition to guaranteeing that the independent variable occurs prior to measurement of the dependent variable, an experimental manipulation also allows the researcher to rule out the possibility of common-causal variables—variables that cause both the independent and the dependent variable. In experimental designs, the influence of common-causal variables is eliminated (or *controlled*) through creation of equivalence among the participants in each of the experimental conditions before the manipulation occurs. As we will see in the sections to come, equivalence can be created either through using different but equivalent participants in each level of the experiment (**between-participants designs**) or through using the same people in each of the experimental conditions (**repeated-measures designs**).

Random Assignment to Conditions.   In a between-participants experimental design such as that shown in Figure 10.1, the researcher compares the scores on the dependent variable between different groups of participants. However, the participants in the groups are equated before the manipulation occurs. The most common method of creating equivalence among the experimental conditions is through **random assignment to conditions**.[2] Random assignment involves the researcher determining separately for each participant which level of the independent variable she or he will experience; the researcher does this through a random process such as flipping a coin, drawing numbers out of an envelope, or using a random number table. In essence, random assignment involves the researcher drawing separate simple random samples of participants to be in each of the levels of the independent variable. And because the samples are drawn from the same population, we can be confident that before the manipulation occurs, the participants in the different levels of the independent variable are, on average, equivalent in every respect except for differences that are due to chance.

In our case, because the children have been randomly assigned to conditions, those who are going to view the violent cartoons will, on average, be equivalent to those who are going to view the nonviolent cartoons in terms of every possible variable, including variables that are expected to be related to aggression, such as hormones and parental discipline. This does not, of course, mean that the children do not differ on the variables. There are some children who are more aggressive than others, who are in better moods than others, and who have stricter parents. These variables are (as we have discussed in Chapter 9) extraneous variables. However, random assignment to conditions ensures that the average score on all of these variables will be the same for the participants in each of the conditions. Although random assignment does not guarantee that the participants in the different conditions are *exactly* equivalent before the experiment begins, it does greatly reduce the likelihood of differences. And the likelihood of chance differences between or among the conditions is reduced even further as the sample size in each condition increases.

Selection of the Dependent Variable

Experiments have one or more measured dependent variables designed to assess the state of the participants after the experimental manipulation has occurred. In our example, the dependent variable is a behavioral measure of

---

[2]Be careful not to confuse *random assignment,* which involves assignment of participants to levels of an independent variable, with *random sampling,* which (as described in Chapter 6) is used to draw a representative sample from a population.

aggressive play, but any of the many types of measures discussed in Chapter 4 could serve as a dependent variable. It is necessary, as in all research, to ensure that the dependent measures are reliable and valid indicators of the conceptual variable of interest (see Chapter 5).

The research hypothesis in an experimental design is that *after* the manipulation occurs, the mean scores on the dependent variable will be significantly different between the participants in the different levels of the independent variable. And if the experimenter does observe significant differences between the conditions, then he or she can conclude that the manipulation, rather than any other variable, caused these differences. Because equivalence was created before the manipulation occurred, common-causal variables could not have produced the differences. In short, except for random error, the *only* difference between the participants in the different conditions is that they experienced different levels of the experimental manipulation.

Variety and Number of Levels

Experiments differ in both the number of levels of the independent variable and the type of manipulation used. In the simplest experimental design there are only two levels. In many cases, one of the two levels involves the presence of a certain situation (for instance, viewing violent cartoons), whereas the other level involves the absence of that situation (for instance, viewing nonviolent cartoons). In such a case, the level in which the situation of interest was created is often called the **experimental condition,** and the level in which the situation was not created is called the **control condition.**

Adding Control Conditions.   There are many different types of control conditions, and the experimenter must think carefully about which one to use. As we will discuss more fully in Chapter 12, the control condition is normally designed to be the same as the experimental condition except for the experimental manipulation; thus, the control condition provides a comparison for the experimental condition. For instance, in our example the children in the control condition watched nonviolent, rather than violent, cartoons. Not all experiments have or need control conditions. In some cases, the manipulation might involve changes in the level of intensity of the independent variable. For instance, an experiment could be conducted in which some children viewed ten violent cartoons and other children viewed only five violent cartoons. Differences between the conditions would still be predicted, but neither condition would be considered a control condition.

Adding More Levels.   While satisfactory for testing some hypotheses, experimental designs with only two levels have some limitations. One is that it can sometimes be difficult to tell which of the two levels is causing a change in the dependent measure. For instance, if our research showed that children behaved more aggressively after viewing the violent cartoons than they did after viewing the nonviolent cartoons, we could conclude that the nonviolent cartoons *decreased* aggression rather than that the violent cartoons increased aggression. Perhaps the children who watched the nonviolent cartoons got bored and were just too tired to play aggressively. One possibility in such a case would be to include a control condition in which no cartoons are viewed at all. In this case, we could compare aggressive behavior in the two cartoon conditions with that in the no-cartoon control condition to determine which cartoon has made a difference.

Detecting Nonlinear Relationships. Another limitation of experiments with only two levels is that in cases where the manipulation varies the strength of the independent variable, it is difficult to draw conclusions about the pattern of the relationship between the independent and dependent variables. The problem is that some relationships are *curvilinear* such that increases in the independent variable cause increases in the dependent variable at some points but cause decreases at other points. As we have seen in Chapter 9, one such example involves the expected relationship between anxiety and performance. As anxiety rises from low to moderate levels, task performance tends to increase. However, once the level of anxiety gets too high, further increases in anxiety cause performance decreases. Thus, the relationship between anxiety and performance is curvilinear.

As shown in Figure 10.2, a two-level experiment could conclude that anxiety improved performance, that it decreased performance, or that it did not change performance at all, *depending on what specific levels of anxiety were induced by the manipulation.* But an experiment with only two levels would never be able to demonstrate the true, curvilinear relationship between the

FIGURE 10.2 Detecting Curvilinear Relationships

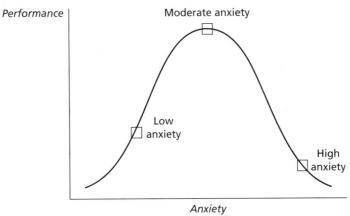

The relationship between anxiety and performance is curvilinear. An experimental design that used only two levels of anxiety could conclude that anxiety either increased, decreased, or had no effect on performance, depending on whether the levels of anxiety that were created were low and medium, medium and high, or low and high. However, only a three-level experiment that included all three levels of anxiety (low, medium, and high) could determine that the true relationship between anxiety and performance is curvilinear.

variables. However, an experiment that used three or more levels of the independent variable would be able to demonstrate that the relationship between anxiety and performance was curvilinear. Although experiments with more than two levels may provide a more complete picture of the relationship between the independent and dependent variables, they also require more participants. Therefore, they should be used only when they are likely to provide specific information that would not be available in a two-level experiment.

Analysis of Variance

We have now seen that experimental designs help us determine causality by ensuring that the independent variable occurs prior to the dependent variable and by creating equivalence among the levels of the independent variable before the manipulation occurs. But how do we determine if there is an association between the independent and the dependent variable—that is, whether there are differences on the dependent measure across the levels? This question is answered through the use of a statistical procedure, known as the **Analysis of Variance (ANOVA),** that is specifically designed to compare the means of the dependent variable across the levels of an experimental research design. The ANOVA can be used for one-way research designs and, as we will see in Chapter 11, for research designs with more than one independent variable.[3]

Hypothesis Testing in Experimental Designs

Recall from our discussion in Chapter 8 that hypothesis testing always begins with a null hypothesis. In experimental designs the null hypothesis is that the mean score on the dependent variable is the same at all levels of the independent variable except for differences due to chance and thus that the manipulation has had no effect on the dependent variable. In our example, the null hypothesis is

$$\text{Mean}_{\text{Violent cartoons}} = \text{Mean}_{\text{Nonviolent cartoons}}$$

The research hypothesis states that there is a difference among the conditions and normally states the specific direction of those differences. For instance, in our example the research hypothesis is that the children in the violent-cartoon condition will show more aggression than the children in the nonviolent-cartoon condition:

$$\text{Mean}_{\text{Violent cartoons}} > \text{Mean}_{\text{Nonviolent cartoons}}$$

---

[3]Just as the correlation coefficient (r) tests the association between two quantitative variables and the chi-square test for independence tests the association between two nominal variables, the one-way ANOVA tests the relationship between one nominal (independent) variable and one quantitative (dependent) variable.

Although the goal of the ANOVA is to compare the means on the dependent variable across the different levels of the independent variable, it actually accomplishes this by analyzing the variability of the dependent variable. The ANOVA treats the null hypothesis in terms of the absence of variability among the condition means. That is, if all of the means are equivalent, then there should be no differences among them except those due to chance. But, if the experimental manipulation has influenced the dependent variable, then the condition means should not all be the same, and thus there will be significantly more variability (that is, more differences) among them than would be expected by chance.

Between-Groups and Within-Groups Variance Estimates

As described in Chapter 7, the variance (s^2) is a measure of the dispersion of the scores on a variable. The ANOVA compares the variance of the means of the dependent variable *between* the different levels to the variance of individuals on the dependent variable *within* each of the conditions. The variance among the condition means is known as the **between-groups variance,** and the variance within the conditions is known as the **within-groups variance.** If the between-groups variance is significantly greater than the within-groups variance, then we conclude that the manipulation has influenced the dependent measure because the influence of the manipulation across the levels is greater than the random fluctuation among individuals within the levels. A statistic called *F* is calculated as the ratio of the two variances:

$$F = \frac{\text{Between-groups variance}}{\text{Within-groups variance}}$$

As the condition means differ more among each other in comparison to the variance within the conditions, *F* increases. *F* has an associated *p*-value, which is compared to alpha. If the *p*-value is less than alpha, then the null hypothesis (that all the condition means are the same) is rejected. The effect size measure for *F* is known as **eta (η),** and the proportion of variance in the dependent variable accounted for by the experimental manipulation is η^2. The formula for computing a one-way Analysis of Variance is presented in Appendix B.

The ANOVA Summary Table

The ANOVA calculations are summarized in an **ANOVA summary table,** as shown in Figure 10.3. The summary table includes the between-groups and the within-groups variances (usually labeled the "mean squares"), as well as *F* and the *p*-value ("Sig."). In our case the *F* (10.98) is statistically significant ($p = .01$). The summary table also indicates the number of levels of the independent variable as well as the number of research participants in the entire study. This information is presented in the form of statistics known as **degrees of freedom (*df*).** The between-groups degrees of freedom are equal to the

FIGURE 10.3 ANOVA Summary Table

ANOVA

		Sum of Squares	df	Mean Square	F	Sig.
DV	Between groups	14.40	1*	14.400	10.980	.010
	Within groups	49.78	38[†]	1.310		
	Total	64.18	39			

$*df_{between\ groups}$ = number of conditions (2) minus 1.
$^†df_{within\ groups}$ = number of participants (N) minus number of conditions, $40 - 2 = 38$.
$\bar{X}_{violent\ cartoons} = 2.89$. $\bar{X}_{nonviolent\ cartoons} = 1.52$.

number of levels in the independent variable minus 1, and the within-groups degrees of freedom are equal to the number of participants minus the number of conditions. In the case of Figure 10.3, the degrees of freedom indicate that there are two levels of the independent variable and forty participants.

The first step in interpreting the results of an experiment is to inspect the ANOVA summary table to determine whether the condition means are significantly different from each other. If the F is statistically significant, and thus the null hypothesis of no differences among the levels can be rejected, the next step is to look at the means of the dependent variable in the different conditions. The results in the summary table are only meaningful in conjunction with an inspection of the condition means. The means for our example experiment are presented at the bottom of Figure 10.3.

In a one-way experiment with only two levels, a statistically significant F tells us that the means in the two conditions are significantly different.[4] However, the significant F only means that the null hypothesis can be rejected. To determine if the research hypothesis is supported, the experimenter must then examine the particular pattern of the condition means to see if it supports the research hypothesis. For instance, although the means in Figure 10.3 show that the research hypothesis was supported, a significant F could also have occurred if aggression had been found to be significantly *lower* in the violent-cartoons condition.

When there are more than two levels of the independent variable, interpretation of a significant F is more complicated. The significant F again indicates that there are differences on the dependent variable among the levels and thus that the null hypothesis (that all of the means are the same) can be rejected.

---

[4]A statistic known as the **t test** may be used to compare two group means using either a between-participants design (an *independent samples t test*) or a repeated-measures design (a *paired-samples t test*). However, the *t* test is a special case of the F test that is used only for comparison of two means. Because the F test is more general, allowing the comparison of differences among any number of means, it is more useful.

But a significant *F* does not tell us which means differ from each other. For instance, if our study had included three levels, including a condition in which no cartoons were viewed at all, we would need to make further statistical tests to determine whether aggression was greater in the violent-cartoons condition than in either of the other two conditions. We will look at how to statistically compare the means of experimental conditions in Chapter 11.

Repeated-Measures Designs

As you read about between-participant designs, you might have wondered why random assignment to conditions is necessary. You might have realized that there is no better way to ensure that participants are the same in each experimental condition than to actually have the *same* people participate in each condition! When equivalence is created in this manner, the design is known as a **within-participants (within-subjects) design** because the differences across the different levels are assessed within the same participants. Within-participants designs are also called repeated-measures designs because the dependent measure is assessed more than one time for each person.

In most cases, the same research hypothesis can be tested with a between-participants or a repeated-measures research design. Consider, for instance, that the repeated-measures experimental design shown in Figure 10.4

FIGURE 10.4 One-Way Repeated-Measures Experimental Design

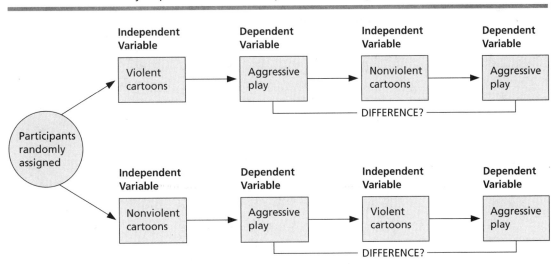

This is a one-way experimental design where equivalence has been created through use of the same participants in both levels of the independent variable. It tests the same hypothesis as the between-subjects design shown in Figure 10.1. The experiment is counterbalanced, such that one half of the participants view the violent cartoons first and the other half view the nonviolent cartoons first.

within participants

tests exactly the same hypothesis as the between-participants design shown in Figure 10.1. The difference is that in the repeated-measures design each child views both the violent cartoons and the nonviolent cartoons and aggression is measured two times, once after the child has viewed each set of cartoons. Repeated-measures designs are also evaluated through Analysis of Variance, and the ANOVA summary table in a repeated-measures design is very similar to that in a between-participants design except for changes in the degrees of freedom. The interpretation of the effect size statistic, η, is also the same.

Advantages of Repeated-Measures Designs

Repeated-measures designs have advantages in comparison to between-participants designs using random assignment to conditions.

Increased Statistical Power. One major advantage of repeated-measures designs is that they have greater statistical power than between-participants designs. Consider, for instance, a child in our experiment who happens to be in a particularly bad mood on the day of the experiment, and assume that this negative mood state increases his or her aggressive play. Because the child would have been assigned to either the violent-cartoon condition or the nonviolent-cartoon condition in a between-participants design, the mean aggression in whichever group the child had been assigned to would have been increased. The researcher, however, would have no way of knowing that the child's mood state influenced his or her aggressive play.

In a repeated-measures design, however, the child's aggressive play after viewing the violent cartoons is compared to his or her aggressive play after viewing the nonviolent cartoons. In this case, although the bad mood might increase aggressive play, it would be expected to increase it on both aggression measures equally. In short, because the responses of an individual in one condition (for instance, after seeing nonviolent cartoons) can be directly compared to the same person's responses in another condition (after seeing violent cartoons), the statistical power of a repeated-measures design is greater than the power of a between-participants design in which different people are being compared across conditions.

Economy of Participants. A related advantage of repeated-measures designs is that they are more efficient because they require fewer participants. For instance, to have twenty participants in each of the two levels of a one-way design, forty participants are required in a between-participants design. Only twenty participants are needed in a repeated-measures design, however, because each participant is measured in both of the levels.

Disadvantages of Repeated-Measures Designs

Despite the advantages of power and economy, repeated-measures designs also have some major disadvantages that may in some cases make them inappropriate. These difficulties arise because the same individuals participate in more than one condition of the experiment and the dependent measure is assessed more than once.

Carryover   One problem is that it is sometimes difficult to ensure that each measure of the dependent variable is being influenced only by the level it is designed to assess. For instance, consider the diagram at the top half of Figure 10.4 in which the children are first shown violent cartoons and then shown nonviolent cartoons. If the effects of viewing the violent cartoons last for a period of time, they may still be present when the children are measured after viewing the nonviolent cartoons. Thus, the second measure of aggression may be influenced by both the nonviolent cartoons and the violent cartoons seen earlier. When effects of one level of the manipulation are still present when the dependent measure is assessed for another level of the manipulation, we say that **carryover** has occurred.

Practice and Fatigue.   In addition to carryover, the fact that participants must be measured more than once may also be problematic. For instance, if the dependent measure involved the assessment of physical skills such as typing into a computer, an individual might improve on the task over time through practice, or she or he might become fatigued and perform more poorly over time. In this case, the scores on the dependent variable would change over time for reasons unrelated to the experimental manipulation. One solution to carryover, practice, and fatigue effects is to increase the time period between the measurement of the dependent measures. For instance, the children might view the violent cartoons on one day and be observed and then be brought back a week later to view the nonviolent cartoons and be observed again. Although separation of the measures may reduce carryover, practice, and fatigue effects, it also has the disadvantage of increasing the cost of the experiment (the participants have to come on two different days), and the children themselves may change over time, reducing equivalence.

Counterbalancing.   One approach to problematic carryover, practice, or fatigue effects is **counterbalancing**. Counterbalancing involves arranging the order in which the conditions of a repeated-measures design are experienced so that each condition occurs equally often in each position. For instance, as shown in Figure 10.4, in our experiment the conditions would be arranged such that one half of the children viewed the violent cartoons first and the other half viewed the nonviolent cartoons first, with the order of viewing determined randomly. This would ensure that carryover from the nonviolent cartoons occurred just as often as did carryover from the violent cartoons. Although counterbalancing does not reduce carryover, it does allow the researcher to estimate its effects by comparing the scores on the dependent variable for the participants who were in the two different orders.

In repeated-measures designs with more than two levels, there are several possible approaches to counterbalancing. The best approach, when possible, is to use each possible order of conditions. Although this technique works well when there are two or three conditions, it becomes problematic as the number of conditions increases. Consider, for instance, a researcher who is interested in testing the ability of workers to type on a computer keyboard under six different lighting conditions: blue light, green light, orange light, red light, yellow light, and white light. Because of the possibility of practice or fatigue effects on the typing task, counterbalancing the conditions is desirable.

Latin Square Designs. The problem in this case is that when there are six conditions, there are 720 possible orders of conditions! Because each order should be used an equal number of times, at least 720 participants would be needed. An alternative approach is to use a subset of all of the possible orders, but to ensure that each condition appears in each order. A **Latin square design** is a method of counterbalancing the order of conditions so that each condition appears in each order but also follows equally often after each of the other conditions.

The Latin square is made as follows: First, label each of the conditions with a letter (ABC for three conditions, ABCDEF for six conditions, and so forth) and then use the following ordering to create the first row of the square (A, B, L, C, L-1, D, L-2, E ...) where L is the letter of the last condition. In other words, the order for the first row when there are four conditions will be ABDC and the order for the first row when there are six conditions will be ABFCED.

At this point, the rest of the rows in the Latin square are constructed by increasing by one each letter in the row above. The last letter (in our case F) cannot be increased, of course, so it is changed to the letter A. If there are an odd number of conditions, you must make an additional Latin square that is a reversal of the first one, such that in each row the first condition becomes the last condition, the second condition is next to last, and so on. In this case, you will use both Latin squares equally often in your research design (that is, you will have twice as many orders as experimental conditions). Once the Latin square or squares are made, each participant is assigned to one of the rows. In the case with six conditions, the Latin square is:

ABFCED

BCADFE

CDBEAF

DECFBA

EFDACB

FAEBDC

When to Use a Repeated-Measures Design

Although carryover, practice, and fatigue effects pose problems for repeated-measures designs, they can be alleviated to a great extent through counterbalancing. There are, however, some cases in which a repeated-measures design is simply out of the question—for example, when the participants, because they are in each of the experimental conditions, are able to guess the research hypothesis and change their responses according to what they think the researcher is studying. You can imagine that children who are first shown a violent film, observed, and then shown a control film and observed again might become suspicious that the experiment is studying their reactions to the cartoons. In such cases, repeated-measures designs are not possible.

In other cases, counterbalancing cannot be done effectively because something that occurs in one level of the independent variable will always influence behavior in any conditions that follow it. For instance, in an experiment testing whether creation of a mental image of an event will help people remember it, the individuals given this memory strategy will probably continue using it in a later control condition.

Nevertheless, the problems caused by a repeated-measures strategy do not occur equally in all research. With unobtrusive behavioral measures, for instance, the problem of guessing the hypothesis might not be severe. And some measures may be more likely than others to produce practice or fatigue effects. It is up to the researcher to determine the likelihood of a given problem occurring before deciding whether to use a repeated-measures design. In short, repeated-measures research designs represent a useful alternative to standard between-participants designs in cases where carryover effects are likely to be minimal and where repeated administration of the dependent measure does not seem problematic.

Presentation of Experiment Results

Once the experiment has been conducted and the results analyzed, it will be necessary to report the findings in the research report. Although the F and the p-value will be presented, the discussion of the results will be focused on the interpretation of the pattern of the condition means. Because the condition means are so important, they must be presented in a format that is easy for the reader to see and to understand. The means may be reported in a table, in a figure, or in the research report itself, but each mean should be reported using only one of these methods. Figure 10.5 presents the means from our hypothetical experiment, reported first as they would be in a table and then as they would be in a bar chart. You can see that one advantage to using a table format is that it is easy to report the standard deviations and the sample size of each of the experimental conditions. On the other hand, the use of a figure makes the pattern of the data easily visible.

In addition to the condition means, the research report must also present F and the p-value. Generally, a reporting of the entire ANOVA summary table is not necessary. Rather, the information is reported in the text, as in the following example:

There were significant differences on rated aggression across the levels of the cartoon condition, $F(1, 38) = 10.98$, $p < .01$. Children who viewed the violent cartoons ($M = 2.89$) were rated as playing more aggressively than children who had viewed the nonviolent cartoons ($M = 1.52$).

FIGURE 10.5 Presenting Means in Experimental Designs

(a) Table format

Aggressive play as a function of cartoons viewed

Cartoons viewed	$\bar{x}$	s	N
Violent	2.89	1.61	20
Nonviolent	1.52	.91	20

(b) Figure format (bar chart)

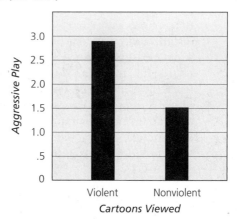

The results of experiments include both the ANOVA summary table and the condition means. This figure shows how the condition means from a one-way experimental design would be reported in a table (a) or in the form of a bar chart in figure (b).

In addition to the F value (10.98) and the p-value (< .01), the within-groups (1) and between-groups (38) degrees of freedom are also reported. When the variable means are presented in the text, they are labeled with an "*M*." If the condition means are reported in the text, as they are in the preceding paragraph, they should not also be reported in a table or a figure.

When Experiments Are Appropriate

In comparison to correlational research designs, experiments have both advantages and disadvantages. Their most important advantage is that they maximize the experimenter's ability to draw conclusions about the causal relationship between the independent and dependent variables. This is the result of the use of an experimental manipulation and the creation of equivalence. In experiments, we can be more confident that the relationship between the independent and dependent variables is not spurious than we can in correlational designs because equivalence has made it unlikely that there are differences among the participants in the different conditions except for the effects of the manipulation itself.

A first disadvantage to experimental research is that many of the most interesting behavioral variables cannot be experimentally manipulated. We cannot manipulate a person's sex, race, intelligence, family background, or religious practice, and such variables must be studied through correlational research designs.[5] A second disadvantage is that because experiments are usually conducted in a laboratory situation, and because the experimental manipulation never provides a perfect match to what would occur in everyday life, we can be virtually certain that participants who participate in experiments will not behave exactly as they would behave if observed outside of the lab. Although experiments may be designed to test real-world phenomena, such as the effects of viewing violent behavior on displaying aggression, they always do so under relatively controlled and artificial conditions.

A third potential disadvantage of experiments is that they necessarily oversimplify things. Because the creation of equivalence is designed to reduce the influence of variables other than the independent variable, it is not possible to ascertain whether these variables would have influenced the dependent variable if their impact had not been controlled. Of course, in everyday life many of these variables probably do influence the dependent variable, which is why they must be controlled in experiments. Thus, although the goal of a one-way experimental research design is to demonstrate that a given independent variable can cause a change in the measured dependent variable, we can never assume that it is the only causal variable. We learn about causation by eliminating common-causal variables, but this also necessarily oversimplifies reality. However, not all experiments are limited to testing the effects of a single independent variable, and it is to experimental designs that involve more than one independent variable that we now turn.

Current Research in the Behavioral Sciences: Does Social Exclusion "Hurt"?

Naomi Eisenberger and her colleagues (Eisenberger, Lieberman, & Williams, 2003) tested the hypothesis that people who were excluded by others would report emotional distress and that images of their brain would show that they experienced pain in the same part of the brain where physical pain is normally experienced. In their experiment, 13 participants were each placed into an functional magnetic resonance imaging (fMRI) brain imaging machine. The participants were told that they would be playing a computer "Cyberball" game

---

[5]This does not mean that such questions cannot be studied, however; we will discuss methods of doing so in Chapter 14.

with two other players who were also in fMRI machines (the other two players did not actually exist), and their responses were controlled by the computer.

The research used a within-participants design in which each of the 12 participants was measured under three different conditions. In the first part of the experiment, the participants were told that as a result of technical difficulties the link to the other two scanners could not yet be made and thus, at first, they would be able to watch but not play with the other two players. This allowed the researchers to take a *baseline* fMRI reading (the first scan). Then, during a second (*inclusion*) scan the participants played the game, supposedly with the two other players. In the third (*exclusion*) scan, participants received seven throws and were then excluded when the two players stopped throwing participants the ball for the remainder of the scan (45 throws).

To test their hypothesis, Eisenberger et al. conducted a within-participants ANOVA comparing fMRI activity during the inclusion scan with activity during the exclusion scan. As predicted, this analysis indicated that activity in both the anterior cingulate cortex $F(1, 12) = 20.16$, $p < .01$ and the right ventral prefrontal cortex $F(1, 12) = 24.60$, $p < .01$ were significantly greater during the exclusion scan than during the inclusion scan. Because these brain regions are known from prior research to be active for individuals who are experiencing physical pain, the authors conclude that these results show that the physiological brain responses associated with being excluded are similar to the pain experienced upon physical injury.

SUMMARY

Experimental research designs enable the researcher to draw conclusions about the causal relationship between the independent variable and the dependent variable. The researcher accomplishes this by manipulating, rather than measuring, the independent variable. The manipulation guarantees that the independent variable occurs prior to the dependent variable.

The creation of equivalence among the conditions in experiments rules out the possibility of a spurious relationship. In between-participants research designs, equivalence is created through random assignment to conditions, whereas in repeated-measures designs, equivalence is created through the presence of the same participants in each of the experimental conditions. In experiments, we can be more confident that the relationship between the independent and dependent variables is not due to common-causal variables than we can in correlational designs because equivalence makes it unlikely that there are any differences among the participants in the different conditions before the experimental manipulation occurred.

Repeated-measures designs have the advantages of increased statistical power and economy of participants, but these designs can be influenced by carryover, practice, and fatigue. These difficulties can, however, be eliminated to some extent through counterbalancing. When there are many conditions to be counterbalanced, a Latin square design may be used. The Analysis of Variance tests whether the mean scores on the dependent variable are different in the different levels of the independent variable, and the results of the ANOVA are presented in the ANOVA summary table.

Although experiments do allow researchers to make inferences about causality, they also have limitations. Perhaps the most important of these is that many of the most interesting behavioral variables cannot, for ethical or practical reasons, be experimentally manipulated.

KEY TERMS

Analysis of Variance (ANOVA) 190
ANOVA summary table 191
between-groups variance 191
between-participants designs 186
carryover 195
conditions 186
control condition 188
counterbalancing 195
degrees of freedom (*df*) 191
eta (η) 191
experimental condition 188
experimental manipulations 185

F 191
Latin square design 196
levels 186
manipulated 186
one-way experimental design 185
random assignment to conditions 187
repeated-measures designs 187
t test 192
within-groups variance 191
within-participants (within-subjects) design 193

REVIEW AND DISCUSSION QUESTIONS

1. In what ways are experimental research designs preferable to correlational or descriptive designs? What are the limitations of experimental designs?

2. What is the purpose of random assignment to conditions?

3. Describe how the ANOVA tests for differences among condition means.

4. Consider the circumstances under which a repeated-measures experimental research design, rather than a between-participants experimental design, might be more or less appropriate.

5. Explain what *counterbalancing* refers to and which potential problems it can and cannot solve.

6. Why is it important in experimental designs to examine both the condition means and the ANOVA summary table?

7. What are the advantages and disadvantages of using (a) figures, (b) tables, and (c) text to report the results of experiments in the research report?

8. Differentiate between random sampling and random assignment. Which is the most important in survey research, and why? Which is the most important in experimental research, and why?

RESEARCH PROJECT IDEAS

1. Read and study the following experimental research designs. For each:

   a. Identify and provide a label for the independent and dependent variables.
   b. Indicate the number of levels in the independent variable, and provide a label for each level.
   c. Indicate whether the research used a between-participants or a within-participants research design.

   • The researchers are interested in the effectiveness of a particular treatment for insomnia. Fifty adult insomnia sufferers are contacted from a newspaper ad, and each is given a pill with instructions to take it before going to sleep that night. The pill actually contains milk powder (a placebo). The participants are randomly assigned to receive one of two instructions about the pill: One half are told that the pill will make them feel "sleepy," and the other half are told that the pill will make them feel "awake and alert." The next day the patients return to the lab and are asked to indicate how long it took them to fall asleep the previous night after taking the pill. The individuals who were told the pill would make them feel alert report having fallen asleep significantly faster than the patients who were told the pill would make them feel sleepy.

   • An experimenter wishes to examine the effects of massed versus distributed practice on the learning of nonsense syllables. He uses three randomly assigned conditions of college students. Group 1 practices a twenty nonsense-syllable list for ninety minutes on one day. Group 2 practices the same list for forty-five minutes per day for two successive days. Group 3 practices the same list for thirty minutes per day for three successive days. The experimenter assesses each condition's performance with a free recall test after each condition completes the designated number of sessions. The mean recall of the twenty syllables for condition 1 is 5.2; for condition 2, 10.0; and for condition 3, 14.6. These means are significantly different from one another, and the experimenter concludes that distributed practice is superior to massed practice.

   • Saywitz and Snyder (1996) studied whether practice would help second-through sixth-grade children recall more accurately events that happened to them. During one of their art classes, a person entered the classroom and accused the teacher of stealing the markers that the children were using. The intruder and the teacher argued at first, but then developed a plan to share the markers. Two weeks after the incident, the children were asked to recall as much as they could about the event. Before they did so, the children were separated into three groups. One was given instructions, such as noting who were the people involved and what each said and did, to help recall what happened. The second group was given both instructions and practice in recalling the event, while the third group was given no specific instructions at all. The results showed that the instructions-plus-practice group was able to recall significantly more information about the original incident than either of the other groups.

- Ratcliff and McKoon (1996) studied how having previously seen an image of an object may influence one's ability to name it again when it reappears later. Participants were first shown pictures of common objects—a purse, a loaf of bread, etc.—on a computer screen. The participants then left and returned one week later. At this time, they were shown some of the original pictures they had seen in the first session, some similar but not identical images, and some entirely new ones, and then were asked to name the objects as quickly as possible. The researchers found that the original objects were named significantly faster than the new objects, but that the similar objects were named more slowly than the new ones.

2. Design a one-way experiment to test each of the following research hypotheses:

   a. The more a person tries *not* to think of something, the more he or she will actually end up thinking about it.
   b. People are more helpful when they are in a good mood than when they are in a bad mood.
   c. Consumption of caffeine makes people better at solving mathematics problems.
   d. People learn faster before they eat a big meal than after they eat a big meal.

3. Perform the following test to determine the effectiveness of random assignment to conditions. Use random assignment to divide your class into two halves. Then calculate the mean of the two halves on (a) the following three variables and (b) three other variables of your own choice.

   Number of sporting events attended last year

   Number of different restaurants eaten at in the past month

   Number of hours of study per week

   Compare the means of the two halves using a one-way ANOVA. Was random assignment to conditions successful in creating equivalence?

PART **FOUR**

Designing and Interpreting Research

CHAPTER ELEVEN
Experimental Research: Factorial Designs

STUDY QUESTIONS

- What are factorial experimental designs, and what advantages do they have over one-way experiments?

- What is meant by crossing the factors in a factorial design?

- What are main effects, interactions, and simple effects?

- What are some of the possible patterns that interactions can take?

- How are the data from a factorial design presented in the research report?

- What is a mixed factorial design?

- What is the purpose of means comparisons, and what statistical techniques are used to compare means?

Although one-way experiments are used to assess the causal relationship between a single independent and a dependent variable, in everyday life behavior is simultaneously influenced by many different independent variables. For instance, aggressive behavior is probably influenced by the amount of violent behavior that a child has recently watched, the disciplining style of the child's parents, his or her current mood state, and so forth. Similarly, the ability to memorize new information is probably influenced by both the type of material to be learned and the study method used to learn it. To try capturing some of this complexity, most experimental research designs include more than one independent variable, and it is these designs that are the topic of this chapter.

Factorial Experimental Designs

Experimental designs with more than one independent (manipulated) variable are known as **factorial experimental designs.** The term **factor** refers to each of the manipulated independent variables. Just as experiments using one independent variable are frequently called one-way designs, so experiments with two independent variables are called two-way designs, those with three factors are called three-way designs, and so forth.

Factorial research designs are described with a notational system that concisely indicates both how many factors there are in the design and how many levels there are in each factor. This is accomplished through a listing of the number of levels of each factor, separated by "×" signs. Thus, a two-way design with two levels of each factor is described as a 2 × 2 (read as "2 by 2") design. This notation indicates that because there are two numerals, there are two factors, and that each factor has two levels. A 2 × 3 design also has two factors, one with two levels and one with three levels, whereas a 2 × 2 × 2 design has three factors, each with two levels. The total number of conditions (the conditions in factorial designs are sometimes known as the **cells**) can always be found through multiplication of the number of levels in each factor. In the case of a 2 × 2 design, there are four conditions, in a 3 × 3 design there are nine conditions, and in a 2 × 4 × 2 design there are sixteen conditions.[1]

As we will see, the use of more than one independent variable in a single experiment increases the amount of information that can be gained from the experimental design. And it is also always cheaper in terms of the number of research participants needed to include two or more factors within a single experiment rather than running separate one-way experiments. This is because the factorial design provides all of the information that would be gained from two separate one-way designs, as well as other information that would not have been available if the experiments had been run separately.

---

[1]Whereas in a one-way ANOVA the number of levels is the same as the number of conditions (and thus either term can be used to describe them), in a factorial design there is a difference. *Levels* refer to the number of groups in each of the factors, whereas *conditions* refer to the total number of groups in the experiment.

Because factorial designs also begin with the creation of initial equivalence among the participants in the different conditions (see Chapter 10), these designs (like one-way designs) also help researchers draw conclusions about the causal effects of the independent variables on the dependent variable.

The Two-Way Design

In many cases, factorial designs involve the addition of new independent variables to one-way experiments, often with the goal of finding out whether the original results will hold up in new situations. Consider, for instance, a one-way experiment that has demonstrated that children who have viewed violent cartoons subsequently play more aggressively than those who have viewed nonviolent cartoons. And consider a possible extension of this research design that has as its goal a test of the conditions under which this previously demonstrated relationship might or might not be observed. In this case, the researcher is interested in testing whether the relationship between the viewing of violent cartoons and aggression will hold up in all situations or whether the pattern might be different for children who have previously been frustrated.

As shown in Figure 11.1, a researcher could accomplish such a test using a two-way factorial experimental design by manipulating two factors in the same experiment. The first factor is the same as that in the one-way experiment—the type of cartoons viewed (violent versus nonviolent). In addition, the researcher also manipulates a second variable—the state of the children before viewing the cartoons (frustrated versus nonfrustrated). In the experiment, all of the children are allowed to play with some relatively uninteresting toys in a play session before they view the cartoons. However, for

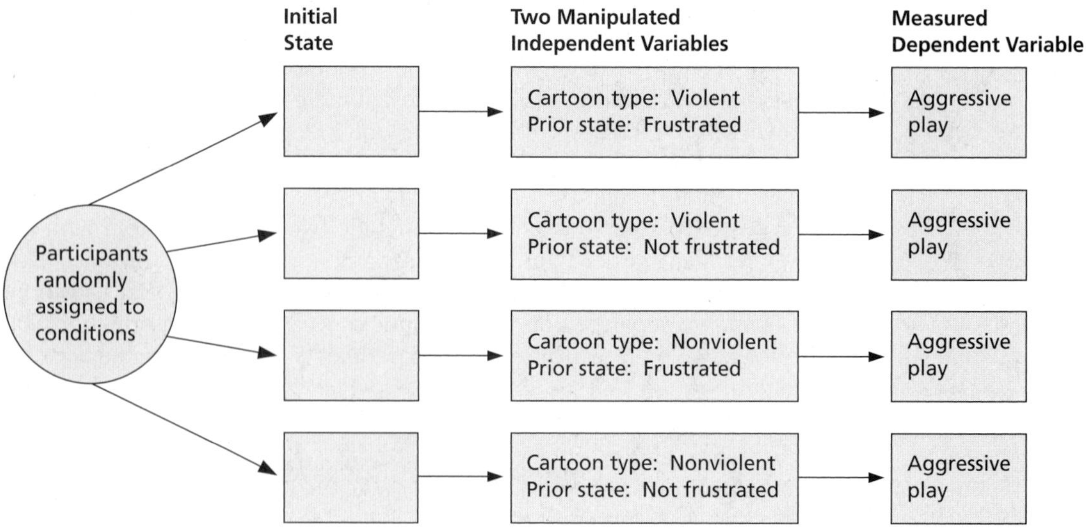

FIGURE 11.1   Two-Way Factorial Design: Assignment to Conditions

half of the children (the frustration condition) the experimenter places some really fun toys in the room but does not allow the children to play with them. The other half of the children (the no-frustration condition) are not shown the fun toys. Then the children view the cartoons before their behavior is observed in a subsequent play session.

In factorial designs, the conditions are arranged such that each level of each independent variable occurs with each level of the other independent variables. This is known as *crossing* the factors. It is important in factorial designs that the conditions be equated before the manipulations occur. This is usually accomplished through random assignment of participants to one of the conditions, although, as we will see later, it is also possible to use repeated-measure factors. Figure 11.1 shows the process of assigning participants to our between-participants factorial design and the four resulting conditions. You can see that crossing two factors, each with two levels, results in four different conditions, each specified by one level of the cartoon factor and one level of the prior state factor. Specifically, the four conditions are "violent cartoons—frustrated," "violent cartoons—not frustrated," "nonviolent cartoons—frustrated," and "nonviolent cartoons—not frustrated." In the research report, the design of the experiment would be described (using both the names and the levels of the factors) as a "2 (cartoon type: violent, nonviolent) × 2 (prior state: frustrated, not frustrated) design."

The research hypothesis in a factorial design normally makes a very specific prediction about the pattern of means that is expected to be observed on the dependent measure. In this case, the researcher has predicted that the effect of viewing violent cartoons would be reversed for the frustrated children because for these children the act of viewing the violent cartoons would release their frustration and thus *reduce* subsequent aggressive behavior. The research hypothesis is: "For nonfrustrated children, those who view the violent cartoons will behave more aggressively than those who view the nonviolent cartoons. However, for frustrated children, those who view the violent cartoons will behave less aggressively than those who view the nonviolent cartoons."

Figure 11.2 presents a *schematic diagram* of the factorial design in which the specific predictions of the research hypothesis are notated. In the schematic diagram, greater than (>) and less than (<) signs are used to show the expected relative values of the means.

Main Effects

Let us now pretend for a moment that the 2 × 2 experiment we have been discussing has now been conducted, and let us consider for a moment one possible outcome of the research. You can see that in Figure 11.3 the schematic diagram of the experiment has now been filled in with the observed means on the aggression dependent variable in each of the four conditions.

Pretend for a moment that the prior state variable (frustration versus no frustration) had not been included in the design, and consider the means of the dependent variable in the two levels of the cartoon condition. These means

FIGURE 11.2   Two-Way Factorial Design: Predictions

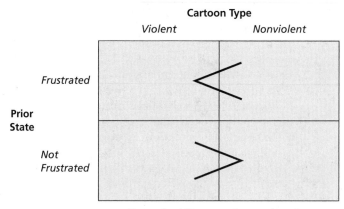

Dependent Measure: Aggressive play

are shown at the bottom of Figure 11.3. The mean of 4.15 is the average aggression score for all of the children (both frustrated and nonfrustrated) who viewed the violent cartoons, and the mean of 2.71 is the mean of all of the children (both frustrated and nonfrustrated) who viewed the nonviolent cartoons.

When means are combined across the levels of another factor in this way, they are said to *control for* or to *collapse across* the effects of the other factor and are called **marginal means.** Differences on the dependent measure across the levels of any one factor, controlling for all other factors in the experiment, are known as the **main effect** of that factor. As we will see, in this experiment the difference between the two marginal means at the bottom

FIGURE 11.3   Observed Condition Means from a Two-Way Factorial Design

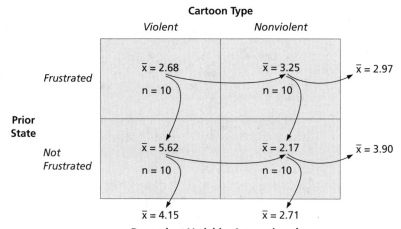

Dependent Variable: Aggressive play

of the figure is statistically significant—the children who viewed the violent cartoons behaved significantly more aggressively ($M = 4.15$) than did those who viewed the nonviolent cartoons ($M = 2.71$).

The main effect of the prior state factor can also be tested, this time controlling for the conditions of the cartoon variable. The two marginal means on the right side of Figure 11.3, which control for the influence of cartoon, provide a test of the main effect of prior state. You can see that the children who had been frustrated ($M = 2.97$) behaved somewhat less aggressively than children who had not been frustrated ($M = 3.90$), although, as we will see, this difference is not statistically significant.

Interactions and Simple Effects

The two main effects in this experiment give the researcher all of the information that would have been provided if she or he had conducted two different one-way experiments, one of which manipulated the cartoon variable and one of which manipulated the prior state variable. The two main effects test the influence of each of the independent variables, controlling for the influence of the other variable. However, the purpose of factorial designs is not only to assess main effects. It is also to make predictions about interactions between or among the factors. An **interaction** is a pattern of means that may occur in a factorial experimental design when the influence of one independent variable on the dependent variable is different at different levels of another independent variable or variables.

You will recall that in our experiment the researcher's hypothesis was in the form of an interaction. The hypothesis predicted that the effect on children of viewing violent cartoons would be different for those children who had previously been frustrated than it would be for those children who had not already been frustrated. The effect of one factor within a level of another factor (for instance, the effect of viewing violent versus nonviolent cartoons for frustrated children) is known as a **simple effect** of the first factor.

The observed means for the four conditions in our experiment, as shown in Figure 11.3, demonstrate that there is indeed an interaction between the cartoon variable and the frustration variable because the simple effect of cartoon type is different in each level of the prior state variable. For the children who had not been frustrated, the simple effect of a cartoon viewed is such that those who viewed the violent cartoons showed *more* aggression ($M = 5.62$) than those who viewed the nonviolent cartoons ($M = 2.17$). But the simple effect was reversed for the children who had been frustrated. For the frustrated children, those who had viewed the violent cartoons actually behaved somewhat *less* aggressively ($M = 2.68$) than those who had viewed the nonviolent cartoons ($M = 3.25$).

The ANOVA Summary Table

Factorial designs are very popular in behavioral research because they provide so much information. Although two separate experiments manipulating the cartoon variable and the frustration variable, respectively, would have provided information about the main effects of each variable, because the two variables were crossed in a single experiment, the interaction between them can also be tested statistically. In a factorial design, the statistical tests for the main effects and the significance test of the interaction may each be significant or nonsignificant. For instance, in a 2×2 design there may or may not be a significant main effect of the first factor, there may or may not be a significant main effect of the second factor, and there may or may not be a significant interaction between the first and second factor.

As in one-way experimental designs, the F values and significance tests in factorial designs are presented in an ANOVA summary table. The ANOVA summary table for the data shown in Figure 11.3 is presented in Figure 11.4, along

---

FIGURE 11.4 ANOVA Summary Table

(a) Factorial Design

		Sum of Squares	df	Mean Square	F	Sig.
Dependent	Cartoon viewed	23.56	1	23.56	4.56	.04*
variable:	Prior state	11.33	1	11.33	2.00	.17
Aggressive	Cartoon viewed by prior state	29.45	1	29.45	5.87	.03†
play						
	Residual	41.33	36	5.17		
	Total	94.67	39	59.51		

*Main effect of cartoon viewed is significant.
† Interaction between cartoon viewed and prior state is significant.

(b) Bar Chart of Means

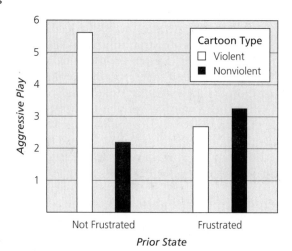

with a bar chart showing the means. As you can see, this table is very similar to that in a one-way design except that there are F values for each of the main effects and interactions and the within-groups sum of squares, degrees of freedom, and mean squares are labeled as "residual" rather than "within-groups."

In factorial designs, each main effect and each interaction has its own F test, as well as its own associated degrees of freedom and p-value. The first df (numerator) for the F test is always printed on the same line as the name of the variable, whereas the second df (denominator) is on the line labeled "residual." Thus, in this table, the main effect of cartoons viewed is significant, $F(1, 36) = 4.56$, $p < .05$, whereas the main effect of prior state is not, $F(1, 36) = 2.00$, $p > .05$. The interaction is also significant, $F(1, 36) = 3.76$, $p < .05$. It is also possible to compute, for each main effect and interaction, an associated effect size statistic, η. This statistic indicates the size of the relationship between the manipulated independent variable (or the interaction) and the dependent variable.

The presentation of the results of factorial designs in the research report is similar to that of one-way designs except that more means and F tests need to be reported. We first inspect the ANOVA summary table to determine which F tests are significant, and we then study the condition means to see if they are in the direction predicted by the research hypothesis. Because of the large number of condition means in factorial designs, it is usually better to report them in a chart (for instance, in the form of a bar chart, as shown in Figure 11.4), or in a table. However, each mean should be reported only once using only one of these methods.

Understanding Interactions

Because there are many conditions in factorial research designs, it is often useful to visualize the relationships among the variables using a line chart. In a two-way design, the levels of one of the factors are indicated on the horizontal axis at the bottom of the chart, and the dependent variable is represented and labeled on the vertical axis. Points are drawn to represent the value of the observed mean on the dependent variable in each of the experimental conditions. To make clear which point is which, lines are connected between the points that indicate each level of the second independent variable.

Patterns of Observed Means

Figure 11.5 presents some of the many possible patterns of main effects and interactions that might have been observed in our sample experiment. In these line charts, the main effects and interactions are interpreted as follows:

- A main effect of the cartoon variable is present when the average height of the two points above the violent cartoon condition is greater than

FIGURE 11.5   Hypothetical Outcomes of a Two-Way Factorial Design

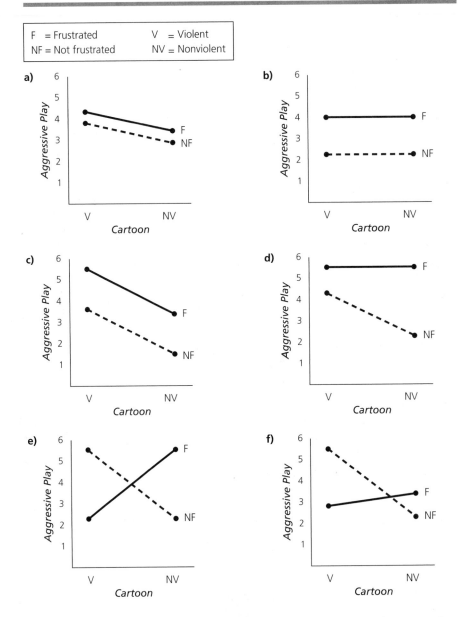

or less than the average height of the two points above the nonviolent cartoon condition.

- A main effect of the prior state variable is present when the average height of the line representing the frustration condition (the solid line) is greater than or less than the average height of the line representing the no-frustration condition (the dashed line).

• An interaction is present when the two lines are not parallel. The fact that they are not parallel demonstrates that the simple effect of cartoons (across the bottom) is different in the frustration condition (the solid line) than it is in the no-frustration condition (the dashed line).

Patterns with Main Effects Only.   In Figure 11.5(a) there is only a main effect of the cartoon variable, but no interaction. In this case, the proposed research hypothesis in our sample experiment is clearly incorrect—the children showed more aggression after viewing violent (versus nonviolent) cartoons regardless of whether they were frustrated. Figure 11.5(b) shows another possible (but unexpected) pattern—a main effect of the prior state variable only, demonstrating that frustrated children were more aggressive than nonfrustrated children. Figure 11.5(c) shows two main effects, but no interaction. In this case, both violent cartoons and frustration increased aggression.

Patterns With Main Effects and Interactions.   You can see in Figure 11.5(d) that the lines are not parallel, indicating that there is an interaction. But if you look closely, you will see that the interaction is not exactly in the form predicted by the research hypothesis. Part of the hypothesis seems to have been supported because the viewing of violent (versus nonviolent) cartoons increased aggression for children in the nonfrustrated condition. However, the type of cartoon made no difference for the children who were frustrated. In this case the main effect of prior state is also significant—the solid line is higher than the dashed line.

Figure 11.5(e) shows the pattern of means originally predicted by the research hypothesis. In a case such as this, when the interaction is such that the simple effect in one level of the second variable is *opposite,* rather than just *different,* from the simple effect in the other level of the second variable, the interaction is called a **crossover interaction.** Finally, Figure 11.5(f) shows the actual pattern found (these means correspond exactly to those presented in Figure 11.3). Here, the research hypothesis is supported because the predicted crossover interaction is observed, but there is also an unanticipated main effect of the cartoon factor (the mean in the violent cartoon condition is greater than the mean in the nonviolent cartoon condition).

Interpretation of Main Effects When Interactions Are Present

As you design or interpret a factorial experiment, keep in mind that the predictions are always stated in the form of expected main effects and interactions. Furthermore, once the data are collected, it is the exact pattern of condition means that provides support (or lack of support) for the research hypothesis. There is rarely a perfect correspondence between the pattern of means that is predicted by the research hypothesis and the actual pattern of observed means. For instance, in our example, the predictions (shown in Figure 11.2) do not exactly match the observed results of the experiment (shown in Figure 11.3), even though there is a significant interaction and thus the research hypothesis is supported. Nevertheless, even a significant interaction will not provide support for the research hypothesis if the means are not in the predicted pattern.

Although each of the three statistical tests in a two-way factorial design may or may not be significant, whether the interaction test is significant will influence how the main effects are interpreted. When there is a statistically significant interaction between the two factors, the main effects of each factor must be interpreted with caution. This is true precisely because the presence of an interaction indicates that the influence of each of the two independent variables cannot be understood alone. Rather, the main effects of each of the two factors are said to be *qualified* by the presence of the other factor. To return to Figure 11.3, because there is an interaction, it would be inappropriate to conclude on the basis of this experiment that the viewing of violent cartoons increases aggressive behavior, even though the main effect of the cartoon variable is significant, because the interaction demonstrates that this pattern is true only for nonfrustrated children. For the frustrated children, viewing violent cartoons tended to decrease aggression.

More Factorial Designs

The factorial design is the most common of all experimental designs, and the 2 × 2 design represents the simplest form of the factorial experiment. However, the factorial design can come in many forms, and in this section we will discuss some of these possibilities.

The Three-Way Design

Although many factorial designs involve two independent variables, it is not uncommon for experimental designs to have even more. Consider, for instance, the 2 × 2 experimental design we have been discussing. Because the research used both boys and girls as participants, you can imagine that the researcher might be interested in knowing if there were any differences in how boys and girls reacted to the cartoons and to frustration. Because both boys and girls participated in each of the original four conditions, we can treat the sex of the child as a third factor and conduct a three-way ANOVA.[2] The experimental design now has three independent variables, each of which has two levels. The design is a 2 (cartoon viewed: violent, nonviolent) × 2 (prior state: frustrated, not frustrated) × 2 (sex of child: male, female) design. The ANOVA summary table is shown in Table 11.1, along with the condition means.

---

[2]Because the sex of the child was not, of course, manipulated by the experimenters, it is technically a *participant variable*. We will discuss such variables more fully in Chapter 14.

TABLE 11.1   Observed Condition Means and ANOVA Summary Table From a Three-Way Factorial Design

(a) Means

Aggressive Play as a Function of Cartoon Viewed and Prior State

	Boys	**Girls**
Violent cartoon		
Frustrated	2.91	2.45
Nonfrustrated	6.69	4.55
Nonviolent cartoon		
Frustrated	4.39	2.11
Nonfrustrated	1.68	2.66

(b) ANOVA Summary Table

Source	Sum of Squares	df	Mean Square	F	Sig.
Main effects					
Cartoon	23.56	1	23.56	4.56	.05
Prior state	11.33	1	11.33	2.00	.34
Sex of child	28.55	1	28.55	5.52	.05
2-way interactions					
Cartoon **x** prior state	17.32	1	17.32	3.35	.01
Cartoon **x** sex of child	5.25	1	5.25	1.02	.93
Sex of child **x** prior state	7.73	1	7.73	1.50	.52
3-way interaction					
Cartoon **x** prior state **x** sex of child	32.11	1	32.11	6.21	.01
Residual	41.33	32	5.17		
Total	94.67	39			

The ANOVA Summary Table.   In addition to a greater number of means (there are now eight), the number of main effects and interactions has also increased in the three-way design. There is now a significance test of the main effect for each of the three factors. You can see in Table 11.1 that both the main effect of the cartoon factor and the main effect of the sex of child factor are statistically significant. Interpreting the main effects requires collapsing over the other two factors in the design. If you average the top four means and the bottom four means in Table 11.1(a), you will find that the appropriate interpretation of the cartoon viewed main effect is that more aggression was observed after violent than after nonviolent cartoons. You can collapse the means across cartoon viewed and prior state to discover the direction of the main effect of sex of child.

There are also three *two-way interactions* (that is, interactions that involve the relationship between two variables, controlling for the third variable). The two-way interaction between cartoon and prior state tests the same hypothesis as it did in the original 2 × 2 analysis because it collapses over sex of child. You can see that this interaction is still statistically significant even though the exact *F* value has changed slightly from the two-way interaction shown in Figure 11.4. This change reflects the fact that the residual variance estimate has changed because the addition of sex of child as a factor results in eight, rather than four, conditions.

The sex of child by cartoon type interaction tests whether boys and girls were differentially affected by the cartoon viewed (controlling for prior state), and the sex of child by prior state interaction considers whether boys and girls were differentially affected by prior state (controlling for cartoon viewed). Neither of these interactions is significant.

The Three-Way Interaction.   The three-way interaction tests whether all three variables simultaneously influence the dependent measure. In a three-way interaction, the null hypothesis is that the two-way interactions are the same at the different levels of the third variable. In this case, the three-way interaction *F* test is significant, which demonstrates that the interaction between cartoon and prior state is different for boys than it is for girls. If you look at the means carefully (you may wish to create line charts), you will see that the original crossover interaction pattern is found much more strongly for boys than it is for girls.

When a three-way interaction is found, the two-way interactions and the main effects must be interpreted with caution. We saw in the two-way analysis that it would be inappropriate to conclude that viewing violent material always increases aggression because this was true only for nonfrustrated children. The three-way analysis shows that even this conclusion is incorrect because the crossover interaction between cartoon and prior state is found only for boys.

You can see that interpretation of a three-way interaction is complicated. Thus, although the addition of factors to a research design is likely to be informative about the relationships among the variables, it is also costly. As the number of conditions increases, so does the number of research participants needed, and it also becomes more difficult to interpret the patterns of the means. There is thus a practical limit to the number of factors that can profitably be used. Generally, ANOVA designs will have two or three factors.

Factorial Designs Using Repeated Measures

Although the most common way to create equivalence in factorial research designs is through random assignment to conditions, it is also possible to use repeated-measures designs in which individuals participate in more than one condition of the experiment. Any or all of the factors may involve repeated measures. Thus, factorial designs may be entirely between participants (random assignment is used on all of the factors), may be entirely repeated measures (the same individuals participate in all of the conditions), or may be some of each. Designs in which some factors are between participants and some are repeated measures are known as **mixed factorial designs.** Figure 11.6 shows how the same research hypothesis could be tested with both a repeated-measures design and a mixed design. As we discussed in Chapter 10, the use of repeated-measures designs has both advantages and disadvantages, and the researcher needs to weigh these before making a decision about whether to use these designs.

Comparison of the Condition Means in Experimental Designs

One of the complexities in interpreting the results of the ANOVA is that when more than two groups are being compared, a significant F does not indicate which groups are significantly different from each other. For instance, although the significant interaction test shown in Figure 11.4 for the means in Figure 11.3 tells us that the effect of viewing violent cartoons is significantly different for frustrated than for nonfrustrated children, it does not tell us which means are significantly different from each other. To fully understand the results, we may want more specific information about the significance of the simple effects. That is, we may want to know whether viewing violent cartoons caused significantly more aggression for children who were not frustrated and whether viewing the violent cartoons significantly decreased aggression for children in the frustration condition.

Because a significant F value does not provide answers to these specific questions, further statistical tests known as **means comparisons** are normally conducted to discover which group means are significantly different from each other. These comparisons are used both in one-way designs with more than two levels and in factorial designs.

Pairwise Comparisons

The most common type of means comparison is a **pairwise comparison** in which any one condition mean is compared with any other condition mean. One problem with pairwise comparisons is that there can be a lot of them. For instance, in a 2×2 factorial design, there are six possible pairwise comparisons:

Violent cartoons–frustrated with violent cartoons–not frustrated

Violent cartoons–frustrated with nonviolent cartoons–frustrated

Violent cartoons–frustrated with nonviolent cartoons–not frustrated

Violent cartoons–not frustrated with nonviolent cartoons–frustrated

Violent cartoons–not frustrated with nonviolent cartoons–not frustrated

Nonviolent cartoons–frustrated with nonviolent cartoons–not frustrated

FIGURE 11.6 Repeated-Measures and Mixed Factorial Designs

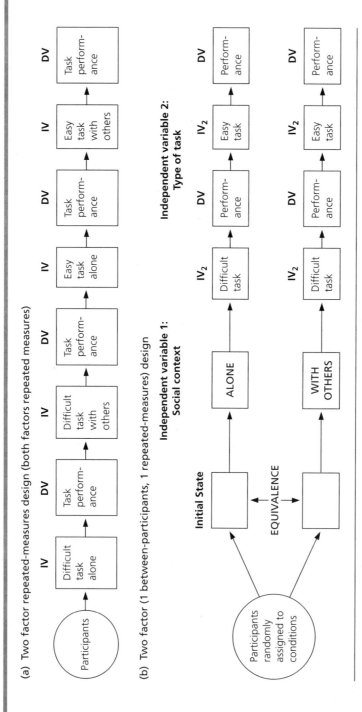

This figure shows two methods of conducting a 2 × 2 factorial experiment including type of task (easy versus difficult) as the first factor and social context (alone versus with others) as the second factor. In Figure (a) both factors are repeated measures and the participant is in all four of the conditions. In this design the order that the participants experience each of the four conditions would be counterbalanced. Figure (b) shows a mixed factorial design in which the social context factor is between participants and the task factor is repeated measures.

In the three-way factorial design shown in Table 11.1 there are twenty-eight possible pairwise comparisons!

Because there are so many possible pairwise comparisons, it is normally not appropriate to conduct a statistical test on each pair of condition means because each possible comparison involves a statistical test and each test has a probability of a Type 1 error equivalent to alpha (normally .05). As each comparison is made, the likelihood of a Type 1 error increases by alpha. As a result, the **experimentwise alpha**—that is, the probability of the experimenter having made a Type 1 error in at least one of the comparisons—also increases. When six comparisons are made, the experimentwise alpha is .30 (.05 × 6), whereas when twenty comparisons are made, the experimentwise alpha is 1.00, indicating that one significant comparison would be expected by chance alone.

Planned Comparisons.   There are three ways to reduce the experimentwise alpha in means comparison tests. The first approach is to compare only the means in which specific differences were predicted by the research hypothesis. Such tests are called **planned comparisons** or **a priori comparisons**. For instance, because in our experiment we explicitly predicted ahead of time that the viewing of violent cartoons would cause more aggression than the viewing of nonviolent cartoons for the nonfrustrated children, we could use a planned comparison to test this simple effect. However, because we had not explicitly predicted a difference, we would not compare the level of aggression for the children who saw the violent cartoons between the frustration and the no-frustration conditions. In this case, the planned comparison test (as described in Appendix D) indicates that for the nonfrustrated children aggression was significantly greater in the violent-cartoon condition ($M = 5.62$) than in the nonviolent cartoon condition ($M = 2.17$), $F(1, 36) = 4.21, p < .05$.

Post Hoc Comparisons.   When specific comparisons have not been planned ahead of time, increases in experimentwise alpha can be reduced through the use of a second approach: **post hoc comparisons.** These are means comparisons that, by taking into consideration that many comparisons are being made and that these comparisons were not planned ahead of time, help control for increases in the experimentwise alpha. One way that post hoc tests are able to prevent increases in experimentwise alpha is that in some cases they only allow the researchers to conduct them if the F test is significant. Examples of popular post hoc tests include the *Least Significant Difference (LSD) Test*, the *Tukey Honestly Significant Difference (HSD) Test*, and the *Scheffé Test*. These tests are discussed in more detail in Appendix D.

Complex Comparisons

The third approach to dealing with increases in experimentwise alpha is to conduct **complex comparisons** in which more than two means are compared at the same time. For instance, we could use a complex comparison to compare aggression in the violent cartoon–frustration condition to the average aggression in the two no-frustration conditions. Or we could use a complex comparison to study the four means that produce the interaction between cartoon viewed and prior state for boys only in Table 11.1(a), while ignoring the data from the girls. Complex comparisons are usually conducted with **contrast tests;** this procedure is discussed in Appendix D.

Current Research in the Behavioral Sciences: Using Feelings in the Ultimatum Game

Andrew T. Stephen and Michel Tuan Pham (2007) conducted research on how people use their emotions when making decisions in games that involve negotiations with others. They used a version of the *ultimatum game*, in which one person (the proposer) makes an offer to another person that the other person may either accept or reject.

The researchers predicted that people who were focusing on their emotions would be more likely to attend to the game itself and the potential money that they might get and less likely to consider the possibility that the other person might reject the offer. Thus, they expected that the people focused on emotions would make less generous offers.

In one of their studies, 60 college students participated as proposers in the ultimatum game, in exchange for a $5 payment, plus whatever they earned in the game (which ranged between $0 and $12 in this study). The momentary trust that participants had in their feelings (higher or lower) was manipulated between participants by having the participants list times in which they had relied on their feelings in the past. Participants in the *higher-trust-in-feelings condition* were asked to list two instances in which they "relied on their feelings to make decisions in the past and it was the right thing to do," whereas participants in the *lower-trust-in-feelings condition* were asked to list ten such instances. Participants asked to identify two such situations found it easy to do so, which increased their trust in their feelings and therefore their reliance on feelings; conversely, participants asked to identify ten such situations found it difficult to do so, which decreased their trust in their feelings and therefore their reliance on feelings (Avnet & Pham, 2007).

To test the effectiveness of the experimental manipulation, the researchers had a separate group of 36 students experience the experimental manipulation and then complete a manipulation check. After listing either two or ten instances, these students were asked to imagine that they were making a proposal to another person and indicate how they would decide on an offer by using 7-point scales to rate their agreement with three items (e.g., "I would trust my feelings"). This manipulation check demonstrated that the experimental manipulation was successful: Participants in the higher-trust-in-feelings condition were significantly more likely to report trusting their feelings ($M = 5.20$,

$SD = 0.91$), than were participants in the lower-trust-in-feelings condition ($M = 4.33$, $SD = 1.37$), $F(1, 34) = 5.15$, $p = .03$.

At the experiment itself, the participants were first randomly assigned to complete one of the two trust-in-feelings conditions, and then were taken to what they thought was a separate study where they played the ultimatum game using a computer interface.

Participants were led to believe that on each round they would be connected via the Internet with a different person at another university and that they would be playing against that person in real time (in fact, the responder was computer simulated). All participants were assigned the role of the proposer, but were told that the roles were assigned randomly in each round. In each round, participants were told the amount of money to be allocated (either $5 or $15) and made their offer to the other player.

As you can see in Figure 11.7, the researchers found that, regardless of the amount of money to be allocated, proposers in the higher-trust-in-feelings condition made less generous offers ($M = 42.3\%$, $SD = 8.83$) than proposers in the lower-trust-in-feelings condition ($M = 48.0\%$, $SD = 9.25$), $F(1, 58) = 5.97$, $p = .05$. This result is consistent with the idea that proposers

FIGURE 11.7   Percentage of Money Offered by Proposer in the Two Trust in Feelings Conditions (from Stephen and Pham, 2007)

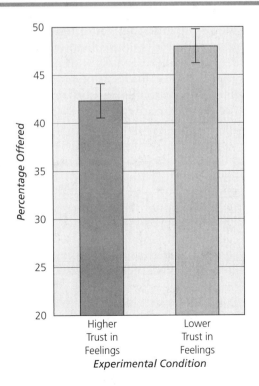

in the higher-trust-in-feelings condition focused on how they felt toward the possible offers, paying less attention to the responder's possible responses.

SUMMARY

In most cases, one-way experimental designs are too limited because they do not capture much of the complexity of real-world behavior. Factorial experimental designs are usually preferable because they assess the simultaneous impact of more than one manipulated independent variable on the dependent variable of interest. Each of the factors in a factorial experimental design may be either between participants or repeated measures. Mixed experimental designs are those that contain both between-participants and repeated-measures factors.

In factorial experimental designs, the independent variables are usually crossed with each other such that each level of each variable occurs with each level of each other independent variable. This is economical because it allows tests, conducted with the Analysis of Variance, of the influence of each of the independent variables separately (main effects), as well as tests of the interaction between or among the independent variables.

All of the main effect and interaction significance tests are completely independent of each other, and an accurate interpretation of the observed pattern of means must consider all the tests together. It is useful to create a schematic diagram of the condition means to help in this regard. In many cases, it is desirable to use means comparisons to compare specific sets of condition means with each other within the experimental design. These comparisons can be either planned before the experiment is conducted (a priori comparisons) or chosen after the data are collected (post hoc comparisons).

KEY TERMS

a priori comparisons 221
cells 207
complex comparisons 221
contrast tests 222
crossover interaction 215
experimentwise alpha 221
factor 207
factorial experimental designs 207
interaction 211

main effect 210
marginal means 210
means comparisons 219
mixed factorial designs 219
pairwise comparisons 219
planned comparisons 221
post hoc comparisons 221
simple effect 211

REVIEW AND DISCUSSION QUESTIONS

1. What are three advantages of factorial experimental designs over one-way experimental designs?

2. What are main effects, simple effects, and interactions? How should significant main effects be interpreted when one or more of the interactions are significant?

3. For each of the following research designs, indicate the number of factors, the number of levels within each factor, the number of main effects, the number of interactions, and the number of conditions:

   a. $2 \times 3 \times 2$
   b. 3×4
   c. $3 \times 5 \times 7$
   d. 2×5

4. How are the results of factorial experimental designs reported in the research report?

5. What is the purpose of means comparisons, and what different types of means comparisons are there? What do they tell the researcher that the significance test for F cannot?

RESEARCH PROJECT IDEAS

1. Read and study the following experimental designs. For each:

   a. Identify the number of factors and the number of levels within each of the factors. Identify whether each of the factors is between participants or repeated measures.
   b. Indicate the format of the research design. How many conditions are in the design?
   c. Identify the dependent variable.
   d. Draw a schematic diagram of the experiment. Indicate the name of each of the factors, the levels of each of the factors, and the dependent variable.
   e. State the research hypothesis or hypotheses in everyday language, and diagram the hypothesis using correlational operators ($<$, $>$, $=$) in the schematic diagram.

   • The principle of social facilitation states that people perform well-learned tasks faster when they work with others but perform difficult tasks better when they work alone. To test this idea, Markus (1978) brought 144 participants to a lab. Some of them were randomly assigned to work in a room by themselves. Others were randomly assigned to work in a room with other people. Each person performed two tasks: taking off his or her shoes and socks (an easy task) and putting on a lab coat that ties in the back (a difficult task). Results show that people working alone performed the difficult task *faster* than people working with others but performed the easy task *slower* than people working with others. The results thus support the social facilitation model.

- A study explores the hypothesis that attitude change will be more likely to occur on the basis of salient but actually very uninformative characteristics of the communicator when individuals listening to the message are distracted from carefully processing it. College students are randomly assigned to hear a persuasive message given either by an attractive or an unattractive person and to hear this message either when there is a lot of construction noise in the next room or when conditions are quiet. Results show that students who were exposed to the attractive communicator showed significantly more attitude change than the participants who saw the unattractive communicator, but that this difference occurred only in the distraction conditions.

- Kassin and Kiechel (1996) researched whether presenting false incriminating evidence leads people to accept guilt for a crime they did not commit. Participants began the experiment by typing letters on a computer keyboard while another person dictated. The letters were read at either a slow pace (43 letters per minute) or a fast pace (67 letters per minute). Before they began, the participants were warned not to press the "ALT" key positioned near the space bar, because doing so would cause the computer program to crash and data would be lost. After one minute of typing, the computer supposedly crashed, and the experimenter then accused the participant of having touched the "ALT" key. All of the participants were in fact innocent and initially denied the charge. The person who had been reading the letters (a confederate of the experimenter) then said that either he or she hadn't seen anything or that he or she had seen the participant hit the "ALT" key. The participant was then asked to sign a false confession stating: "I hit the 'ALT' key and caused the program to crash. Data were lost." The predictions for the experiment were that more participants would sign the confession when they had been accused by a witness, and particularly when the letters had been read at a fast pace, leading the participant to believe the validity of the (false) accusation. You may want to look up the surprising results of this experiment!

2. Locate a research report that uses a factorial design. Identify the independent and dependent variables and the levels of each of the factors, and indicate whether each factor is between participants or repeated measures.

3. Make predictions about what patterns of main effects and interactions you would expect to observe in each of the following factorial designs:

a. The influence of study time and sleep time on exam performance

b. The effects of exposure time and word difficulty on memory

CHAPTER TWELVE
Experimental Control and Internal Validity

STUDY QUESTIONS

- What are the potential threats to the validity of research?

- What is experimental control?

- What effects do extraneous variables have on the validity of research?

- What is meant by confounding? Why does confounding reduce an experiment's internal validity?

- What are some methods of controlling for extraneous variables in experimental research designs?

- What are some methods for increasing the validity of experimental manipulations?

- What are manipulation checks and confound checks, and what can they tell us?

- What are some common artifacts in experimental research, and how can they produce confounding?

We have now completed our discussion of the goals and the logic of descriptive, correlational, and experimental research designs. And we have seen that each of these three research approaches is useful for answering some types of research questions. Understanding the basics of research designs is the first step in becoming a proficient consumer and practitioner of research in the behavioral sciences. But research that looks good on the surface may sometimes, when scrutinized carefully, be found to have serious flaws. We will consider potential threats to the validity of research in this chapter, as well as in Chapters 13 and 14. These chapters are perhaps the most important in the entire book, for it is here that you will learn how to evaluate the quality of research that you read about and how to design experiments that are able to fully answer your research questions.

Threats to the Validity of Research

Good research is *valid* research. By *valid,* we mean that the conclusions drawn by the researcher are legitimate. For instance, if a researcher concludes that a new drug reduces headaches, or that people prefer Coca-Cola over Pepsi, the research is valid only if the new drug really works or if people really do prefer Coke. Unfortunately, there are many threats to the validity of research, and these threats may sometimes lead to unwarranted conclusions. Of course, researchers do not attempt to conduct invalid research—that is, they do not attempt to draw inaccurate conclusions about their data. Yet often, despite researchers' best intentions, some of the research reported in newspapers, magazines, and even scientific journals is invalid. Validity is not an all-or-none phenomenon, and yet some research is better than other research in the sense that it is more valid. Only by understanding the potential threats to validity will you be able to make knowledgeable decisions about the conclusions that can or cannot be drawn from a research project.

As shown in Table 12.1, there are four major types of threats to the validity of research. The first is one that should be familiar to you, as we have already discussed it in Chapter 5. A threat to *construct validity* occurs when the measured variables used in the research are invalid because they do not adequately assess the conceptual variables they were designed to measure. In this chapter, we will see that in experimental research, in addition to being certain that the dependent measure is construct valid, the experimenter must also be certain that the manipulation of the independent variable is construct valid in the sense that it appropriately creates the conceptual variable of interest.

TABLE 12.1 Four Threats to the Validity of Research

1. **Threats to construct validity.** Although it is claimed that the measured variables or the experimental manipulations relate to the conceptual variables of interest, they actually may not. (Chapters 5 and 12)
2. **Threats to statistical conclusion validity.** Conclusions regarding the research may be incorrect because a Type 1 or Type 2 error was made. (Chapter 8)
3. **Threats to internal validity.** Although it is claimed that the independent variable caused the dependent variable, the dependent variable may have actually been caused by a confounding variable. (Chapter 12)
4. **Threats to external validity.** Although it is claimed that the results are more general, the observed effects may actually only be found under limited conditions or for specific groups of people. (Chapter 13)

These four threats to the validity of research are discussed in the indicated chapters of this book.

In Chapter 8, we considered a second type of potential threat, which can be referred to as a threat to the *statistical conclusion validity* of the research. This type of invalidity occurs when the conclusions that the researcher draws about the research hypothesis are incorrect because either a Type 1 error or a Type 2 error has occurred. A Type 1 error occurs when the researcher mistakenly rejects the null hypothesis, and a Type 2 error occurs when the researcher mistakenly fails to reject the null hypothesis. We have already discussed the use of alpha as a method for reducing Type 1 errors and have considered statistical power as a measure of the likelihood of avoiding Type 2 errors. In this chapter, we will more fully discuss ways to increase the power of research designs and thus reduce the likelihood of the researcher making Type 2 errors.

In addition to threats to construct validity and statistical conclusion validity, there are two other major threats to the validity of research. These threats are present even when the research is statistically valid and the construct validity of the manipulations and measures is ensured. Behavioral scientists refer to these two potential problems as threats to the *internal validity* and to the *external validity* of the research design (Campbell & Stanley, 1963). As we will see, *internal validity* refers to the extent to which we can trust the conclusions that have been drawn about the causal relationship between the independent and dependent variable, whereas *external validity* refers to the extent to which the results of a research design can be generalized beyond the specific settings and participants used in the experiment to other places, people, and times.

Experimental Control

One of the important aspects of a good experiment is that it has **experimental control,** which occurs to the extent that the experimenter is able to eliminate effects on the dependent variable other than the effects of the independent variable. The greater the experimental control is, the more confident we can be that it is the independent variable, rather than something else, that caused changes in the dependent variable. We have already discussed in Chapter 10 how experimental control is created in part through the establishment of initial equivalence across the experimental conditions. In this chapter, we will expand our discussion of experimental control by considering how control is reduced through the introduction into the research of *extraneous variables* and *confounding variables*. Then, we will turn to ways to reduce the influence of these variables.

Extraneous Variables

One of the greatest disappointments for a researcher occurs when the statistical test of his or her research hypothesis proves to be nonsignificant. Unfortunately, the probabilistic nature of hypothesis testing makes it impossible to determine exactly why the results were not significant. Although the research hypothesis may have been incorrect and thus the null hypothesis should not have been rejected, it is also possible that a Type 2 error was made. In the latter case, the research hypothesis was correct and the null hypothesis should have been rejected, but the researcher was not able to appropriately do so.

One cause of Type 2 errors is the presence of extraneous variables in the research. As we have seen in Chapter 9, extraneous variables are variables other than the independent variable that cause changes in the dependent variable. In experiments, extraneous variables include both initial differences among the research participants in such things as ability, mood, and motivation, and differences in how the experimenter treats the participants or how they react to the experimental setting. Because these variables are not normally measured by the experimenter, their presence increases the within-groups variability in an experimental research design, thus making it more difficult to find differences among the experimental conditions on the dependent measure. Because extraneous variables constitute random error or noise, they reduce power and increase the likelihood of a Type 2 error.

Confounding Variables

In contrast to extraneous variables, which constitute random error, **confounding variables** are variables other than the independent variable on which the participants in one experimental condition differ *systematically* or on average from those in other conditions. As we have seen in Chapter 10, although random assignment to conditions is designed to prevent such systematic differences among the participants in the different conditions before the experiment begins, confounding variables are those that are created during the experiment itself and that are unintentionally created by the experimental manipulations.

Consider, for instance, a researcher who uses an experimental research design to determine whether working in groups, rather than alone, causes people to perform better on mathematics problems. Because lab space is at a premium, the experimenter has the participants working alone complete the problems in a small room with no windows in the basement of the building, whereas the groups complete the task in a large classroom with big windows on the top floor of the building. You can see that even if the groups did perform better than the individuals, it would not be possible to tell what caused them to do so. Because the two conditions differ in terms of the presence or absence of windows as well as in terms of the presence or absence of other people, it is not possible to tell whether it was the windows or the other people who changed performance.

Confounding and Internal Validity.   When another variable in addition to the independent variable of interest differs systematically across the experimental conditions, we say that the other variable is confounded with the independent variable. **Confounding** means that the other variable is mixed up with the independent variable, making it impossible to determine which of the variables has produced changes in the dependent variable. The extent to which changes in the dependent variable can confidently be attributed to the effect of the independent variable, rather than to the potential effects of confounding variables, is known as the **internal validity** of the experiment. Internal validity is ensured only when there are no confounding variables.

Alternative Explanations.   The presence of a confounding variable does not necessarily mean that the independent variable did not cause the changes in the dependent variable. Perhaps the effects on task performance in our experiment really were due to group size, and the windows did not influence performance. The problem is that the confounding variable always produces potential **alternative explanations** for the results. The alternative explanation is that differences in the confounding variable (the windows), rather than the independent variable of interest (group size), caused changes on the dependent measure. To the extent that there are one or more confounding variables, and to the extent that these confounding variables provide plausible alternative explanations for the results, the confidence with which we can be sure that the experimental manipulation really produced the differences in the dependent measure, and thus the internal validity of the experiment, is reduced.

Control of Extraneous Variables

Now that we have seen the difference between extraneous and confounding variables, we will turn to a consideration of how they can be recognized and controlled in research designs. Keep in mind that both types of variables are problematic in research and that good experiments will attempt to control each.

Control of extraneous variables →

Limited-Population Designs

We have seen that one type of extraneous variable involves initial differences among the research participants within the experimental conditions. To the extent that these differences produce changes in the dependent variable, they constitute random error, and because they undermine the power of the research, they should be reduced as much as possible. One approach to controlling variability among participants is to select them from a limited, and therefore relatively homogeneous, population. One type of limited population that behavioral scientists frequently use is college students. Although this practice is used partially because of convenience (there are many college students available to researchers on college campuses), there is another advantage that comes from the relative homogeneity of college students in comparison to human beings at large.

Consider a psychologist who is interested in studying the performance of mice in mazes. Rather than capturing mice at the local landfill, he or she is more likely to purchase white mice that have been bred to be highly similar to each other in terms of genetic makeup. The psychologist does this to reduce variability among the mice on such things as intelligence and physical strength, which would constitute random error in the research. For similar reasons, behavioral scientists may prefer to use college students in research because students are, on average, more homogeneous than a group of people that included both college students and other types of people. College students are of approximately the same age, live in similar environments, have relatively similar socioeconomic status, and have similar educational background. This does not mean that there is no variability among college students, but it does mean that many sources of random error are controlled. Of course, using only college students has a potential disadvantage—there is no way to know whether the findings are specific to college students or would also hold up for other groups of people (see Sears, 1986). We will discuss this problem more fully in Chapter 13 when we consider the external validity of research designs.

Before-After Designs

A second approach to controlling for differences among the participants is the use of **before-after research designs.** Imagine an experiment in which the research hypothesis is that participants who are given instructions to learn a list of words by creating a sentence using each one will remember more of the words on a subsequent memory test than will participants who are not given any specific method for how to learn the words. To test this hypothesis, an experimental design is used in which college students are given a list of words to remember. One half of the students are randomly assigned to a condition in which they construct sentences using each of the words, and the other half are just told to remember the words the best they can. After a brief delay all participants are asked to remember the words.

FIGURE 12.1   Controlling Extraneous Variables: Multiple-Group Before-After Design

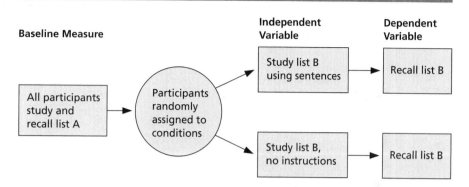

You can well imagine that there are many differences, even without the manipulation, in the ability of the students to remember the words on the memory test. These differences would include IQ and verbal skills, current mood, and motivation to take the experiment seriously. As shown in Figure 12.1, in a before-after design the dependent measure (in this case, memory) is assessed both before and after the experimental manipulation. In this design, the students memorize and are tested on one set of words (list A). Then they are randomly assigned to one of the two memory instructions before learning the second set of words (list B) and being tested again. The first memory test is known as a **baseline measure,** and the second memory test is the dependent variable.

Advantages.   The logic of the before-after design is that any differences among the participants will influence both the baseline memory measure and the memory measure that serves as the dependent variable. For instance, a student with a particularly good memory would score better than average on both list A and list B. Thus we can compare each individual's memory performance on list A to his or her performance on list B.[1]

You may have noticed that before-after research designs share some similarities with repeated-measures designs in the sense that the dependent variable (in this case, memory) is measured more than one time. And both repeated-measures and before-after designs increase the power of an experiment by controlling for variability among the research participants. The difference is that in repeated-measures designs each individual is in more than one condition of the experiment. In our before-after design, each person is in only one condition, but the dependent variable is measured more than one time, with the first measurement serving as a baseline measure.

[1]This comparison can be made either through statistical control of performance on the baseline memory measure (that is, by including it, along with a variable indicating the participant's experimental condition, as a predictor variable in a multiple regression analysis) or through treatment of the two memory measures as two levels of a repeated-measures factor in a mixed-model ANOVA.

Disadvantages. Although completion of the dependent measure more than once in a before-after design helps reduce random error, as you will recall from Chapter 4, doing so also creates the possibility of retesting effects. For instance, fatigue may occur, or the participants who are given an initial memory test may begin to develop their own memory strategies for doing better on the second test, and these strategies may conflict with the strategies being experimentally manipulated. In addition, having participants complete the same or similar measures more than one time increases the likelihood that they will be able to guess the research hypothesis.

Matched-Group Designs

In cases where retesting seems a potential problem, one approach is not to control for differences by measuring the dependent measure more than once, but to collect, either before or after the experiment, a different measure that is expected to influence the dependent measure. For instance, in a memory experiment if there is concern about similar memory measures being taken twice, we might measure participants' intelligence on the basis of an IQ test, with the assumption that IQ is correlated with memory skills and that controlling for IQ will reduce between-person variability.

A researcher who wanted to conduct such a design might administer the intelligence test before the experimental session and select participants on the basis of their scores. As shown in Figure 12.2, in a **matched-group research design,** participants are measured on the variable of interest (for instance, IQ) before the experiment begins and then are assigned to conditions on the basis of their scores on that variable. For instance, during assignment of participants to conditions in the memory experiment, the two individuals with the two highest IQs would be randomly assigned to the sentence-creation

FIGURE 12.2 Controlling Extraneous Variables: Matched-Group Design

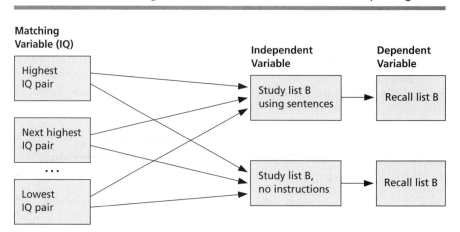

condition and the no-instructions conditions, respectively. Then the two participants with the next highest IQs would be randomly assigned to the two conditions, and so on. Because this procedure reduces differences between the conditions on the matching variable, it increases the power of the statistical tests. Participants can also be matched through the use of more than one variable, although it is difficult to find participants who are similar on all of the measured characteristics.

In some cases, it is only possible to obtain the participants' scores on the matching variable after the experiment has been completed. For instance, if the participants cannot be selected on the basis of their IQ, they might nevertheless be asked to complete a short IQ test at the end of the memory experiment. In such cases, it is obviously not possible to assign participants to conditions based on their scores. Rather, differences among people on the matching variable are controlled statistically through multiple regression analysis. As long as the matching variable (for instance, IQ) actually correlates with the dependent measure (memory), the use of a matched-group design will reduce random error and increase the statistical power of the research design.

It should be kept in mind that the use of matched-group designs is not normally necessary in experimental research. Random assignment is sufficient to ensure that there are no differences *between* the experimental conditions—matching is used only if one feels that it is necessary to attempt to reduce variability among participants *within* the experimental conditions. Matching is most useful when there are measures that are known to be correlated with the dependent measure that can be used to match the participants, when there are expected to be large differences among the participants on the measure, and when sample sizes are small and thus reducing within-conditions variability is critical.

Standardization of Conditions

In addition to minimizing extraneous variables that come from differences among the experimental participants, an experimenter should also try to minimize any differences that might occur within the experiment itself. **Standardization of conditions** is accomplished when, as much as is possible, all participants in all levels of the independent variable are treated in exactly the same way, with the single exception of the manipulation itself. The idea is to hold constant every other possible variable that could potentially influence the dependent measure.

To help ensure standardization, a researcher contacts all participants in all of the experimental conditions in the same manner, provides the exact same consent form and instructions, ensures interaction with the same experimenters in the same room, and, if possible, runs the experiment at the same time of day. Furthermore, as the experiment proceeds, the activities of the groups are kept the same. In an ideal experiment, all participants take the same amount of time, interact with the same people, learn the same amount of information, and complete the same activities except for the changes in the experimental manipulation.

The Experimental Script. The most useful tool for ensuring standardization of conditions is the **experimental script** or **protocol**. The script is just like a script in a stage play—it contains all the information about what the experimenter says and does during the experiment, beginning with the greeting of the participants and ending with the debriefing.

Automated Experiments. One potential method of producing standardization is to use automated devices, such as tape recorders or computers, to run the experiment. The machine presents all of the instructions and in the case of the computer may also record responses to questions, reaction times, or physiological responses. In some cases all the experimenter has to do is turn on the machine—the rest of the experiment is completely standardized. Although automated techniques ensure standardization because exactly the same instructions are given to each and every participant, they also have some disadvantages. If the participant is daydreaming or coughing and thus misses an important part of the instructions, there is no way to know about or correct this omission. These techniques also do not allow the participants to ask questions and thus may reduce the impact of the experimental manipulation in comparison to interaction with a human experimenter. It is often better, therefore, when using computers, for the experimenter to be present for one or more initial practice trials to enable the participant to ask questions and ensure that he or she understands the procedure. The experimenter then leaves the room once the experimental trials begin.

Creation of Valid Manipulations

You may recall from our discussion in Chapter 5 that *construct validity* refers to the extent to which the operational definition of a measured variable proves to be an adequate measure of the conceptual variable it is designed to assess. But construct validity can also refer to the effectiveness of an experimental manipulation. The manipulation has construct validity to the extent that it produces the hoped-for changes in the conceptual variable it is designed to manipulate, but at the same time does not create confounding by simultaneously changing other conceptual variables.

Impact and Experimental Realism

The manipulations used in experimental designs must be strong enough to cause changes in the dependent variable despite the presence of extraneous variables. When the manipulation creates the hoped-for changes in the conceptual variable, we say that it has had **impact.** Because the types of manipulations used in behavioral science research are highly varied, what is meant by an "impactful" manipulation also varies from experiment to experiment. In some cases, the manipulation is rather straightforward, such as when participants are asked to memorize a list of words that appear at either a fast or a slow pace. In this case the trick is to vary the speed of presentation enough to make a difference.

In other cases, the effectiveness of the manipulation requires that the experimenter get the participants to believe that the experiment is important and to attend to, believe in, and take seriously the manipulation. For instance, in research designed to assess how changes in the type of arguments used by a speaker influence persuasion, the research participants must be given a reason to pay attention to the speaker's message and must actually do so, or these changes will not have impact. To create this interest, researchers frequently use topics that are relevant to students, such as proposed changes in the curriculum requirements or increases in tuition at their college or university (Cacioppo, Petty, & Morris, 1983). And if participants are told that they have failed at a task, the feedback must be given in such a way that the participants actually believe it.

The extent to which the experimental manipulation involves the participants in the research is known as **experimental realism.** This is increased when the participants take the experiment seriously and thus are likely to be influenced by the manipulations. For instance, in a well-known experiment on obedience by Milgram (1974), male participants were induced to punish another person by administering heavy doses of what they thought was electrical shock. The reactions of the participants clearly showed that they were experiencing a large amount of stress. These reactions raise questions about the ethics of conducting such an experiment but leave no doubt that the manipulation had experimental realism and impact.

In general we can say that, particularly when you are first creating a new experimental manipulation, it is best to make the manipulation as strong as you possibly can, subject to constraints on ethics and practicality. For instance, if you are studying variation in speed of exposure to words, then make the slow condition very slow, and the fast condition very fast. Similarly, if your manipulation involves changes in exposure to violent versus nonviolent material, then choose material that is extremely violent to use as the stimuli in the violence condition. Using strong manipulations as well as attempting to involve the participants in the research by increasing experimental realism will increase the likelihood of your manipulation being successful.

Manipulation Checks

Experimenters often rely on the face validity of an experimental manipulation to determine its construct validity—that is, does the manipulation appear to create the conceptual variable of interest? But it is also possible to directly measure whether the manipulation is having the hoped-for impact on the participants. **Manipulation checks** are measures used to determine whether the experimental manipulation has had the intended impact on the conceptual variable of interest (Sigall & Mills, 1998).

Designing and Interpreting Manipulation Checks.   Manipulation checks are sometimes used simply to ensure that the participants notice the manipulation. For instance, in an experiment designed to measure whether people respond differently to requests for help from older versus younger people, the participants might be asked when the experiment was over to estimate the age of the person who had asked them for help. The manipulation could be considered successful if the participants who received help from older individuals estimated a higher age than those who received help from younger individuals. Although in this case it might seem unlikely that they would not have noticed the age of the person, participants are likely to be distracted by many other things during the experiment, and thus it is easier than you might think for them to entirely miss or ignore experimental manipulations.

In most cases, however, manipulation checks are designed not to assess whether the participants noticed the manipulation but to see if the manipulation had the expected impact on them. For instance, in an experiment designed to manipulate mood state, the participants might be asked to indicate their current mood using a couple of Likert scales.

Manipulation checks are usually given after the dependent variables have been collected because if given earlier, these checks may influence responses on the dependent measures. For instance, if the goal of an experiment was to assess the effects of mood state on decision making, but people were asked to report on their mood before they completed the decision-making task, they might realize that the experiment concerned the influence of mood on decision making. Of course, there is also a potential difficulty if the manipulation checks are given at the end of the experiment because by then the impact of the manipulation (in this case, the mood induction) may have worn off. Giving the manipulation check at the end of the experiment may thus underestimate the true impact of the experimental manipulation.

Manipulation checks turn out to be particularly important when no significant relationship is found between the independent and dependent variables. Without manipulation checks, the experimenter is left in the awkward position of not knowing whether the participants did not notice the manipulation; whether they noticed the manipulation, but it did not have the expected impact; or whether the manipulation actually had the hoped-for impact but nevertheless did not have the expected effect on the dependent variable. Because it is usually very easy to include one or more manipulation checks, they should almost always be used. Inspecting the scores on the manipulation checks can help the experimenter determine exactly what impact the experimental manipulation had on the participants.

Internal Analyses.   One other potential advantage of a manipulation check is that it can be used to make alternative tests of the research hypothesis in cases where the experimental manipulation does not have the expected effect on the dependent measure. Consider, for instance, an experiment in which the independent variable (a manipulation of a positive versus a neutral mood state) did not have the expected effect on the dependent variable (helping behavior). However, on the basis of a manipulation check, it is also clear that the manipulation did not have the expected impact. That is, the positive mood manipulation did not produce positive mood for all of the participants in the positive-mood condition and some of the participants in the neutral-mood condition reported being in very positive moods anyway.

Although one option at this point would be to conduct an analysis including only those participants in the positive-mood condition who reported being in a positive mood, and only those in the control condition who did not report being in a positive mood, this procedure would require deleting many participants from the analysis and would result in a loss in statistical power. An alternative approach is to conduct an **internal analysis,** which involves computing a correlation of the scores on the manipulation check measure with the scores on the dependent variable as an alternative test of the research hypothesis. In our case, we would correlate reported mood state with helping, and we would predict that participants who were in more positive moods (regardless of their experimental condition) would help more frequently. However, because an internal analysis negates much of the advantage of experimental research by turning an experimental design into a correlational study, this procedure is used only when no significant relationship between the experimental manipulation and the dependent variable is initially found.

Confound Checks

In addition to having impact by causing differences on the independent variable of interest, the manipulation must avoid changing other, confounding conceptual variables. Consider, for instance, an experiment designed to test the hypothesis that people will make fewer errors in detecting misspellings in an interesting text than in a boring one. The researcher manipulates interest in the experiment by having one half of the participants look for errors in a text on molecular biology (a boring task), while the other half searches for errors in the script of a popular movie (an interesting task).

You can see that even if the participants who read the biology text did detect fewer spelling errors, it would be difficult to conclude that these differences were caused by differences in the interest value of the task. There is a threat to the internal validity of the research because, in addition to being less interesting, the biology text might also have been more difficult to spell-check. If so, task difficulty would have been confounded with task interest, making it impossible to determine whether performance differences were caused by task interest or task difficulty.

In such a case, we might use a manipulation check (asking the participants how interesting they found the proofreading task) to confirm that those who read the movie script, rather than the passage from the biology text, would report having found it more interesting. But we might also want to use one or more confound checks to see if the manipulation also had any unintended effects. **Confound checks** are measures used to determine whether the manipulation has unwittingly caused differences on confounding variables. In this study, as a confound check the participants might also be asked to indicate how difficult they had found the proofreading task, with the hope that the rated difficulty would *not* have differed between the biology and the movie texts.

How to Turn Confounding Variables Into Factors

Although one of the goals of valid experiments is to be certain that everything stays the same for all participants except the experimental manipulation, this may not always be possible. For example, it may not be possible to use the same experimenter for each participant or to run all of the participants in the same room. This is not usually a great problem as long as these differences occur such that they are *crossed with,* rather than *confounded with,* the levels of the manipulation. That is, the experiment should be designed such that rather than having the different experimenters each run different conditions, each experimenter runs an equal number of participants in each of the conditions. And rather than running all of one condition in one room and all of the other condition in another room, the experimenter should run each condition the same number of times in each of the rooms. Furthermore, if a record is kept of which experimenter and which room were used, it is even possible for the researcher to determine if these variables actually influenced the dependent variable by including them as factors in the data analysis.

Although confounding variables are sometimes nuisance variables such as room size and experimenter, in other cases the potential confounds are more meaningful conceptual variables. Consider again the experiment described previously in which the interest value and the difficulty of a text passage could have been confounded. Perhaps the best solution to this potential problem would be to conduct the experiment as a 2 × 2 factorial design in which task difficulty and task interest were separately manipulated. In short, participants would proofread a difficult but interesting text, a difficult but boring text, an easy but interesting text, or an easy but boring text. This design would allow the researcher to separate out the effects of interest value and task difficulty on the dependent measure.

Pilot Testing

It takes practice to create an experimental manipulation that produces at the same time an impactful manipulation and a lack of confounding variables. Such difficulties are particularly likely in cases where it is not certain that the participants will believe the manipulation or where they might be able to guess the research hypothesis.

One strategy that can be useful when you are not sure that a manipulation is going to be successful is to conduct a **pilot test** of the manipulation on a few participants before you begin the experiment itself. Participants are brought to the lab, administered the manipulation, and then given the manipulation checks and perhaps some confound checks. A post-experimental interview (see Chapter 3) can also be used to help determine how the participants interpreted the experimental manipulation and whether they were suspicious of the manipulations or able to guess the hypothesis.

Pilot testing before the experiment helps to ensure that the manipulation checks and confound checks administered in the experiment will show the expected patterns. For example, the experimenters in our proofreading experiment could pilot test the passages on participants who were not going to participate in the experiment until they had found two passages rated equally difficult, but varying in the degree of interest. This would help eliminate the potential confound of task difficulty before the experiment was to begin.

Sometimes pilot testing can take quite a bit of time. For instance, in some of the research that I and my colleagues recently conducted, we were interested in getting our research participants to believe that they were either very good at a task or that their skills were more average (Stangor & Carr, 2002). We had to pilot test for a whole semester before we were able to find a task that the participants did not already think that they were very good at, so that the half of them who received feedback suggesting that they were only average would believe it. Pilot testing can also be useful for helping determine the effectiveness of your dependent variable or variables. It will help you ensure that there is variability in the measure (that the memory test is not too easy or too hard, for instance), and you can do a preliminary check on the reliability of the measure using the data from the pilot study. If necessary, the dependent measures can be altered before the experiment is run.

Although pilot testing takes time and uses up participants, it may be worthwhile if it allows you to determine whether the manipulation is working as you hope it will. Careful reading about other experiments in the area may also give you ideas of what types of manipulations and dependent variables have been successful in the past, and in many cases it is better to use these previously tested variables than try to develop new ones of your own.

Threats to Internal Validity

Although there are many potential threats to the internal validity of an experimental design, some are common enough that they deserve to be investigated here.[2] In this section, we will consider how to recognize and avoid three common threats to internal validity in behavioral research: placebo effects, demand characteristics, and experimenter bias. We will also consider how to

---

[2]Many of these threats are summarized in important books by Campbell and Stanley (1963) and Cook and Campbell (1979). Because some of the threats to internal validity discussed by these authors are more likely to occur in quasi-experimental, rather than in experimental, research, they will be discussed in Chapter 14.

most effectively assign participants to conditions to avoid confounding. These threats to internal validity are sometimes known as **artifacts**—aspects of the research methodology that may go unnoticed and that may inadvertently produce confounding.

Placebo Effects

Consider an experimental design in which a researcher tests the hypothesis that drinking alcohol makes members of the opposite sex look more attractive. Participants over the age of twenty-one are randomly assigned either to drink orange juice mixed with vodka or to drink orange juice alone. However, to reduce deception, the participants are told whether their drink contains vodka. After enough time has passed for the alcohol to take effect, the participants are asked to rate the attractiveness of a set of pictures of members of the opposite sex. The results of the experiment show that, as predicted, the participants who have had vodka rate the photos as significantly more attractive.

If you think about this experiment for a minute, it may occur to you that although the researcher wants to draw the conclusion that alcohol is causing the differences in perceived attractiveness, the expectation of having consumed alcohol is confounded with the presence of alcohol. That is, the people who drank alcohol also knew they drank alcohol, and those who did not drink alcohol knew they did not. Just knowing that they were drinking alcohol, rather than the alcohol itself, may have caused the differences. Whenever participants' expectations about what effect an experimental manipulation is supposed to have influences the dependent measure independently of the actual effect of the manipulation, we call the change in the dependent measure a **placebo effect.**

Placebo effects are particularly problematic in medical research, where it is commonly found that patients who receive placebos (that is, medications that have no actual physiological effect) can frequently experience a large reduction in symptoms (Price, 1984). Thus the researcher cannot give some patients a medication and other patients no medication because the first group's knowledge of having taken the medication would then be confounded with its potential effect. The solution in medical research is to give a medication to all of the patients in the research, but to arrange it so that a randomly selected half of the participants gets the true medication, whereas the other half gets a drug that has no real effect (a placebo). The participants do not know which they have received. This procedure does not prevent placebo effects, but it controls for them by making sure that, because all of the participants now think they have received a medication, the effects occur equally in each condition.

Similar procedures can be used in behavioral research. For instance, because it turns out that it is very difficult to tell whether vodka has been mixed with orange juice, our experimenter might tell both groups that they are drinking orange juice and vodka but really give alcohol to only half of the participants. If differences in perceived attractiveness were found, the experimenter could then confidently attribute them to the alcohol rather than to a placebo effect. Notice that this use of an appropriate control group is one example of standardization of conditions—making sure that everything (in this case, including expectations about having consumed alcohol) is the same in all conditions except for the changes in the independent variable of interest. These techniques are frequently used in research studying the effects of alcohol (see, for instance, Knight, Barbaree, & Boland, 1986).

Demand Characteristics

Another common threat to internal validity in behavioral research occurs when the research participant is able to guess the research hypothesis. The ability to do so is increased by the presence of **demand characteristics**—aspects of the research that allow participants to guess the research hypothesis. For instance, in an experiment designed to study the effects of mood states on helping behavior, participants might be shown either a comedy film or a control, nonhumorous film before being given an opportunity to help, such as by volunteering to participate in another experiment without compensation. It might not be too difficult in such a situation for an observant participant in the comedy film condition to guess that the experiment is testing the effects of mood on helping and that the research hypothesis is that people will be more helpful when they are in a positive mood.

Demand characteristics are potentially problematic because, as we have seen in Chapter 4, participants who have been able to guess the research hypothesis may frequently behave cooperatively, attempting to act in ways that they think will help confirm the hypothesis. Thus, when demand characteristics are present, the internal validity of the study is threatened because changes in the dependent measure might be due to the participants' desire to please the experimenter and confirm the hypothesis rather than to any actual impact of the experimental manipulation. In the following sections we will consider some of the most common approaches to reducing the likelihood of demand characteristics.

Cover Stories.   In some cases a cover story can be used to prevent the participants from guessing the research hypothesis. The **cover story** is a false or misleading statement about what is being studied. For instance, in experiments designed to study the effects of mood states on helping, participants might view either a comedy film or a control film. The cover story might be that the goal of the research is to learn about what specific aspects of films lead people to like them. This cover story might be enhanced by having the participants complete a questionnaire on which they rate how much they liked each of the actors, whether the dialogue and story line were clear, and so forth. Providing a cover story might help keep the participants from guessing that the real goal of the film was to change mood.

Although the use of a cover story means that the participants are not told until the debriefing what the researcher is really studying, the cover story does not have to be completely untrue. For instance, in research in my lab we often tell participants that the research is studying how individuals perform tasks when in groups versus when alone. Although this information is completely true, we do not mention that we are specifically interested in how initial confidence in one's task ability affects this performance (Stangor & Carr, 2002).

The Unrelated-Experiments Technique.   In some cases the cover story involves the use of the **unrelated-experiments technique.** In this technique, participants are told that they will be participating in two separate experiments conducted by two separate experimenters. In reality, the experimental manipulation is presented in the first experiment, and the dependent measure is collected in the second experiment. For instance, in an experiment testing the effects of mood states on decision making, participants might first be asked to participate in an experiment concerning what leads people to enjoy a film. They would then be placed in either a positive or a neutral mood by their viewing one of two films and, as part of the cover story, would make some ratings of the film they had viewed; debriefing would follow. At this point, the participants would be asked to move to another room where another experiment on decision making was being run. They would meet a new experimenter who has them sign a new consent form before they work on a decision-making task that serves as the dependent measure. You can see that this technique will reduce the likelihood of the participants being able to guess the hypothesis because they will think that the two experiments are unrelated.

Because cover stories involve deception, they should be used only when necessary, and the participants must be fully debriefed at the end of the second experiment. In some cases other approaches to avoidance of demand characteristics are possible, such as simulation studies (see Chapter 3). In cases where demand characteristics are likely to be a problem, suspicion checks (see Chapter 3) should also be used to help determine whether the participants might have guessed the research hypothesis.

Use of Nonreactive Measures.   Another approach to avoiding demand characteristics, and one that can in some cases avoid the deception involved in a cover story, is to use nonreactive dependent measures. As we have discussed in Chapter 4, nonreactive measures are those in which the participants do not realize what is being measured or cannot control responding on them. For instance, in the experiment by Macrae and his colleagues described in Chapter 1, the dependent measure was how far the participants sat from the chair on which the skinhead had supposedly left his belongings. It is unlikely that any of the participants in that study could have guessed the hypothesis that the chair that they sat down on was a nonreactive measure of their attitudes toward the skinhead. As another example, in the study of the effects of mood on helping, the helping task might be presented in the form of a nonreactive behavioral measure, such as having a confederate drop some books and measuring whether the participants helped pick them up (Isen & Levin, 1972).

Although nonreactive measures are frequently used to assess the dependent variable, in some cases the manipulation can itself be nonreactive in the sense that it appears to have occurred by accident or is very subtle. For instance, in studies of the effects of mood on helping and decision making, Isen and her colleagues have used subtle mood manipulations such as finding a coin in a phone booth or receiving a small gift such as a bag of candy (Isen & Levin, 1972; Isen, Nygren, & Ashby, 1988). These manipulations were able to induce a positive mood state as assessed by manipulation checks, and yet they were so unobtrusive that it is unlikely that the participants had any idea what was being studied. Although I have argued earlier that it is generally useful, at least in initial stages of research, to use manipulations that are likely to produce a large impact, when subtle manipulations are found to have an influence on the dependent measures, we can often be sure that the participants were not able to guess the research hypothesis and thus that demand characteristics are not a problem (Prentice & Miller, 1992).

Taken together, there are many approaches to reducing the potential of demand characteristics, and one of the important aspects of experimentation is figuring out how to do so. Also, keep in mind that demand characteristics can influence the results of research, without the experimenter ever being aware of it, if the participants discuss the research with future participants after they leave the experiment. In this case new participants may arrive at the experiment having already learned about the research hypothesis. This is why it is usual to ask participants not to discuss the nature of the research with other people until the experiment is completed (for instance, at the end of the academic semester) and to attempt to determine, using suspicion checks, what participants have already heard about the study.

Experimenter Bias

Experimenter bias is an artifact that is due to the simple fact that the experimenter usually knows the research hypothesis. Although this may seem to be a relatively trivial matter, it can in fact pose a grave danger to the internal validity of research. The danger is that when the experimenter is aware of the research hypothesis, and also knows which condition the participants he or she is running are in, the experimenter may treat the research participants in the different conditions differently, such that an invalid confirmation of the research hypothesis is created.

In a remarkable demonstration of the possibility of experimenter bias, Rosenthal and Fode (1963) sent twelve students to test a research hypothesis concerning maze learning in rats. Although the students were not initially told so, they were actually the participants in an experiment. Six of the students were randomly told that the rats they would be testing had been bred to be highly intelligent, whereas the other six students were led to believe that the rats had been bred to be unintelligent. But there were actually no differences among the rats given to the two groups of students.

When the students returned with their data, a startling result emerged. The rats run by students who expected them to be intelligent showed significantly better maze learning than the rats run by students who expected them to be unintelligent. Somehow the students' expectations influenced their data. They evidently did something different when they tested the rats, perhaps subtly changing how they timed the maze running or how they treated the rats. And this experimenter bias probably occurred entirely out of their awareness.

Naive Experimenters.   Results such as these make it clear that experimenters may themselves influence the performance of their participants if they know the research hypothesis and also know which condition the participants are in. One obvious solution to the problem is to use experimenters who do not know the research hypothesis—we call them **naive experimenters**. Although in some cases this strategy may be possible (for instance, if we were to pay people to conduct the experiment), in most cases the use of naive experimenters is not practical. The person who developed the research hypothesis will often also need to run the experiment, and it is important to fully inform those working on a project about the predictions of the research so that they can answer questions and fully debrief the participants.

Blind Experimenters.   Although it is not usually practical or desirable to use naive experimenters, experimenters may be kept blind to condition. In this case the experimenter may be fully aware of the research hypothesis, but his or her behavior cannot influence the results because he or she does not know what condition each of the research participants is in. In terms of Rosenthal's experiments, the students, even though they might have known that the study involved intelligent versus unintelligent rats, could have remained blind to condition if they had not been told ahead of time which rats were expected to have which characteristic.

One way of keeping experimenters blind to condition is to use automated experiments or tape recordings. In an automated experiment the computer can randomly determine which condition the participant is in without the experimenter being aware of this. Or the experimenter might create two tape recordings, one containing the instructions for one condition and another containing instructions for the other condition. Then these two tapes (which look identical) are marked by a person who is not involved in running the experiment with the letter "A" and the letter "B," respectively, but without the experimenter running the experiment being told which tape is which. The experimenter starts the tape for each participant but leaves the room before the critical part of the tape that differs between conditions is played. Then the experimenter reenters, collects the dependent measures, and records which tape was played. Only later, after all the participants have been run, does the experimenter learn which tape was which.

Another method of keeping experimenters blind to condition is to use two experimenters. In this procedure, one experimenter creates the levels of the independent variable, whereas the other experimenter collects the dependent variable. The behavior of the second experimenter cannot influence the results because he or she is blind to the condition created by the first experimenter. In still other cases it is not feasible to keep the experimenter blind to condition, but it is possible to wait until the last minute to effect the manipulation. For instance, the experimenter might pick up a card that indicates which condition the participant is to be in only at the last minute before the manipulation occurs. This ensures that the experimenter cannot differentially influence the participants before that time.

Random Assignment Artifacts

Before leaving the discussion of confounding, we must consider one more potential artifact that can cause internal invalidity. Although random assignment to conditions is used to ensure equivalence across the experimental conditions, it must be done correctly, or it may itself result in confounds. To understand how this might occur, imagine that we had a 2 × 2 between-participants experimental design, that we desired during the course of a semester to run fifteen students in each condition, and that the conditions were labeled as "A," "B," "C," and "D." The question is, "How do we determine which participants are assigned to which of the four conditions?"

One approach would be to place sixty pieces of paper in a jar, fifteen labeled with each of the four letters, and to draw one of the letters at random for each arriving participant. There is, however, a potential problem with this approach because it does not guarantee which conditions will be run at which time of the semester. It could happen by chance that the letter A was drawn more frequently than the letter D in the beginning of the semester and that the letter D was drawn more often near the end of the semester. The problem if this were to happen is that because condition A has been run, on average, earlier in the semester than condition D, there is now a confound between condition and time of the semester. The students in the different conditions might no longer have been equivalent before the experimental manipulation occurred if, for instance, the students who participated earlier in the semester were more intelligent or more motivated than the students who participated later, or if those who participated near the end of the semester were more knowledgeable about the material or more suspicious.

When considering this problem, you might decide to take another approach, which is simply to run the conditions sequentially, beginning with condition A and continuing through condition D and then beginning again with condition A. Although this reduces the problem somewhat, it also has the unwanted outcome of guaranteeing that condition A will be run, on average, earlier in the semester than condition D.

The preferred method of assigning participants to conditions, known as **blocked random assignment,** has the advantages of each of the two previous approaches. An example of this approach is shown in Table 12.2. Four letters are put into a jar and then randomly selected until all four

TABLE 12.2 Blocked Random Assignment

Blocks	Participants	Order of Conditions
1	1, 2, 3, 4	A, C, D, B
2	5, 6, 7, 8	B, A, D, C
3	9, 10, 11, 12	D, A, C, B
4	13, 14, 15, 16	A, B, C, D
5	17, 18, 19, 20	B, C, A, D
6	21, 22, 23, 24	D, A, C, B
7	25, 26, 27, 28	C, A, D, B
8	29, 30, 31, 32	A, C, D, B
9	33, 34, 35, 36	B, C, D, A
10	37, 38, 39, 40	A, B, D, C

In an experimental design, it is important to avoid confounding by being very careful about the order in which participants are run. The blocked random design is the best solution. In this case there are four conditions in the experiment, indicated as "A," "B," "C," and "D." Each set of four participants are treated as a block and are assigned to the four conditions randomly within the block. Because it is desired to have forty participants in total, ten blocks are used.

conditions have been used. Then all four letters are replaced in the jar, and the process is repeated fifteen times. This creates a series of blocks of four letters, each block containing all four conditions, but the order of the conditions within each of the blocks is random.

A randomized block procedure can also be used to help reduce confounding in experiments. Consider a situation in which different experimenters (or experimental rooms or computers) have to be used in the research. In general, it will be desirable to turn these potential confounding variables into extraneous variables by being certain that each experimenter is assigned to each experimental condition an equal number of times. An easy solution to this problem is to assign participants to experimenter by blocks. Ideally, each experimenter will run an equal number of blocks in the end, but this is not absolutely necessary. As long as each experimenter completes running an entire block of participants before beginning a new block, he or she will end up running each condition an equal number of times.

Current Research in the Behavioral Sciences: Testing the "Romantic Red" Hypothesis

Andrew Eliott and Daniela Niesta (2008) conducted a series of studies to test the hypothesis that men would be more attracted to women when the color red is on or around the woman than when other colors were present. The authors argued that this might be due to both social conditioning and biological, evolutionary factors, or the combination of both.

In Study 1, a sample of men viewed, for 5 seconds, a black and white photograph of a woman who had been rated in a pilot study to be average in attractiveness. However, according to random assignment, one half of the men saw the women on a white background whereas the other half saw her on a red background. Then the men rated how sexually attracted they were to her. The researchers found that the men in the red background condition were more attracted to the woman than were those in the white background condition.

Can you see that there are potential alternative explanations for this effect, and thus that the internal validity of the study could be compromised? The problem is that it is difficult to find an appropriate control condition. The researchers wanted to conclude that a red background increased the attractiveness of the woman, but it is also possible that the white background decreased her attractiveness. Furthermore, perhaps the colors varied on other dimensions—maybe the red background was darker than the white background, or maybe red backgrounds are less common than white ones.

In an attempt to rule out these alternative explanations, the researchers then conducted more studies in which they varied the backgrounds in different ways. In Study 2 the same study was run, but men were randomly assigned to either red or gray backgrounds. Gray was chosen for this study because, unlike white, gray can be matched in lightness to red, and doing so allowed the researchers to control this potential confounding variable. Again, significant group differences were found with the red background woman rated as significantly more attractive than the gray background woman. In Study 3 the men were randomly assigned to red or green conditions. Because green is chromatic, the opposite of red on the color spectrum, and also has positive connotations, the authors thought this would be a good comparison color to test the red effect. Again, the men in the red background condition rated themselves as more attracted to the woman than did the men in the green background condition.

You can see that in some cases it is difficult or even impossible to rule out all alternative explanations for a finding. After trying to rule out as many as reasonably possible, however, it is usually safe to assume that the research hypothesis (in this case that red increases sexual attraction) is more likely to be the causing factor than is any other possibility.

SUMMARY

Although experimental research designs are used to maximize the experimenter's ability to draw conclusions about the causal effects of the independent variable on the dependent variable, even experimental research contains threats to validity and thus the possibility of the experimenter drawing invalid conclusions about these relationships.

One potential problem is that the presence of extraneous variables may threaten the statistical conclusion validity of the research because these variables make it more difficult to find associations between the independent and dependent variables. Researchers therefore attempt to reduce extraneous variables within the experimental conditions through the use of such techniques as limited-population, before-after, or matched-group designs, as well as through standardization of conditions.

Although extraneous variables may lead to Type 2 errors, the presence of confounding variables leads to internal invalidity, in which it is no longer possible to be certain whether the independent variable or the other confounding variables produced observed differences in the dependent measure. To avoid internal invalidity, researchers use appropriate control groups, cover stories, and blocked random assignment to conditions.

Some of the most common threats to the internal validity of experiments include placebo effects, demand characteristics, and experimenter bias. Creating valid experiments involves thinking carefully about these potential threats to internal validity and designing experiments that take them into consideration. Blocked random assignment is used to avoid artifacts when assigning participants to conditions in an experiment.

KEY TERMS

alternative explanations 231
artifacts 242
baseline measure 233
before-after research designs 232
blocked random assignment 247
confound checks 240
confounding 231
confounding variables 230
cover story 243
demand characteristics 243
experimental control 229
experimental realism 237
experimental script 236

experimenter bias 245
impact 236
internal analysis 239
internal validity 231
manipulation checks 237
matched-group research design 234
naive experimenters 246
pilot test 240
placebo effect 242
protocol 236
standardization of conditions 235
unrelated-experiments technique 244

REVIEW AND DISCUSSION QUESTIONS

1. Describe four types of invalidity that can be found in experimental research designs.

2. What are extraneous and confounding variables? Which type of variable is most dangerous to the statistical conclusion validity and the internal validity of experimental research, and why?

3. What is confounding, and how does confounding produce alternative explanations?

4. What are the techniques by which experimenters attempt to control extraneous variables within an experimental design?

5. What methods are used to help ensure that experiments are internally valid?

6. How are manipulation checks and confound checks used to help interpret the results of an experiment?

7. What are placebo effects, and how can they be avoided?

8. What are demand characteristics, and how can they be avoided?

9. In what ways may experimenters unwittingly communicate their expectations to research participants, and what techniques can they use to avoid doing so?

RESEARCH PROJECT IDEAS

1. Each of the following research designs has a potential threat to the internal validity of the research. For each, indicate what the confounding variable is and how it might have been eliminated.

   a. The Pepsi-Cola Company conducted the "Pepsi Challenge" by randomly assigning individuals to taste either a Pepsi or a Coke. The researchers labeled the glasses with only an "M" (Pepsi) or a "Q" (Coke) and asked the participants to indicate which they preferred. The research showed that subjects overwhelmingly preferred glass "M" over glass "Q." Why can't the researchers conclude that Pepsi was preferred to Coke?

   b. Researchers gave White college students two résumés in an experiment in which they were asked to play the role of an employment officer. The résumés were designed to have equal qualifications, but one had a photo of an African American applicant attached, and the other had a photo of a White applicant. The researcher found that there were no significant differences between the evaluations of the Black applicant and the White applicant. Why can't the researcher conclude that the student's judgments were not influenced by the race of the applicant?

   c. In a study of helping behavior, Ellsworth and Langer (1976) predicted that when the person who needed help made eye contact with the potential helper, situations in which the need for help was clear and unambiguous would produce more helping than would situations in which the need for help was less clear. To manipulate the ambiguity of the need for help, participants were randomly assigned to discover a person who had lost a contact lens, whereas in the other condition the person in need of help was apparently ill. Even if more help was given in the latter condition than the former, why should the researchers not conclude that it is the ambiguity of the situation that caused the difference?

d. McCann and Holmes (1984) tested the hypothesis that exercise reduces depression. They randomly assigned depressed undergraduate women either to an exercise condition (attending an aerobics class a couple of times a week for ten weeks) or to a relaxation training condition (the individuals relaxed at home by watching a videotape over the same period of time). Although the results showed that the exercise group reported less depression at the end of the ten-week period than did the relaxation group, why can't the researchers conclude that exercise reduces depression?

e. Ekman, Friesen, and Scherer (1976) tested whether lying influenced one's voice quality. Participants were randomly assigned to view either a pleasant film or an unpleasant film, but all of the participants were asked to describe the film they saw as being pleasant. (Thus, the subjects who watched the unpleasant film had to lie about what they saw.) An analysis of voice quality showed that participants used significantly higher voices when they were describing the unpleasant film rather than the pleasant film. Why can't the authors conclude that lying produced the differences in voice quality?

f. A researcher studying the "mere exposure" phenomenon (Zajonc, 1980) wants to show that people like things more if they have seen them more often. He shows a group of participants a list of twenty words at an experimental session. One week later, the participants return for a second session in which they are randomly assigned to view either the same words again or a different set of twenty words, before indicating how much they like the twenty words that everyone had seen during the first session. The results show that the participants who have now seen the words twice like the words better than the group that only saw the words once. Why can't the researcher conclude that people like the words more because they have seen them more often?

g. A researcher wants to show that people with soft voices are more persuasive than people with harsh voices. She has a male actor with a loud voice give an appeal to one set of participants and a woman with a soft voice give the exact same appeal to another set of participants. The researcher finds that the soft voice is indeed more persuasive because people change their attitudes more after hearing the appeal from the female. Why can't the researcher conclude that soft voices are more persuasive?

h. An elementary school teacher wants to show that parents' involvement helps their children learn. She randomly chooses one half of the boys and one half of the girls in her class and sends a note home with them. The note asks the parents to spend more time each day working with the child on his or her math homework. The other half of the children do not receive a note. At the end of the school year, the teacher finds that the children whose parents she sent notes to have significantly better final math grades. Why can't the researcher conclude that parental involvement increased the students' scores?

i. Employees in a large factory are studied to determine the influence of providing incentives on task performance. Two similar assembly rooms are chosen for the study. In one room, the experimenters talk about the research project that is being conducted and explain that the employees will receive a reward for increased performance: Each worker will receive a weekly bonus if he or she increases his or her performance by 10 percent. In the other room, no mention is made of any research. If the reward is found to increase the performance in the first assembly room, why can't the researchers conclude that it was the financial bonus that increased production?

CHAPTER THIRTEEN
External Validity

STUDY QUESTIONS

- What is meant by the external validity of a research design?

- How is research limited in regard to generalization to other groups of people?

- How does ecological validity help increase confidence that an experiment will generalize to other research settings?

- What is the purpose of replication? What are the differences among exact, conceptual, and constructive replications?

- What is a participant replication, and when is it used?

- What is the purpose of review papers and meta-analyses? What are the differences between the two?

In Chapter 12, we considered the internal validity of experiments. In this chapter, we will consider a second major set of potential threats to the validity of research. These threats are known collectively as threats to *external validity* because they concern the extent to which the experiment allows conclusions to be drawn about what might occur outside of or beyond the existing research.

Understanding External Validity

Imagine for a moment that you are reading a research report that describes an experiment that used a sample of children from an elementary school in Bloomington, Indiana. These children were randomly assigned to watch either a series of very violent Bugs Bunny cartoons or a series of less violent cartoons before their aggressive behavior was assessed during a play session. The results showed that children who viewed the violent cartoons displayed significantly more physical aggression in a subsequent free play period than did the children who watched the less violent cartoons. You can find no apparent alternative explanations for the results, and you believe that the researcher has drawn the appropriate conclusion—in this case, the viewing of violent cartoons caused increased aggressive behavior.

What implications do you think that such a study should have on public policy? Should it be interpreted as indicating that violent television shows are likely to increase aggression in children and thus that violent network programming should be removed from the airwaves? If you think about this question a bit, you may well decide that you are not impressed enough by the results of the scientist's experiment to suggest basing a new social policy on it. For one, you might reasonably conclude that since the result has been found only once, it may be statistically invalid, and thus the finding really represents a Type 1 error. You might also note that although the experiment did show the expected relationship, there may have been many other experiments that you do not know about that showed no relationship between viewing violence and displaying aggressive behavior.

Thinking about it further, you could develop even more arguments concerning the research. For one, the results were found in a laboratory setting, where the children were subjected to unusual conditions—they were forced to watch a cartoon that they might not have watched in everyday life. Furthermore, they watched only cartoons and not other types of aggressive TV shows, and only one measure of aggression was used. In short, perhaps there is something unique about the particular experiment conducted by this scientist that produced the observed results, and the same finding would not be found in other experiments, much less in everyday life.

You might also argue that the observed results might not hold up for other children. Bloomington, Indiana, is a small university town where many children are likely to have college professors as parents, and these children may react differently to violent television shows than would other children. You might wonder whether the results would hold up for other children, such as those living in large urban areas.

Arguments of the type just presented relate to the external validity of an experiment. **External validity** refers to the extent to which the results of a research design can be generalized beyond the specific way the original experiment was conducted. For instance, these might include questions about the specific participants, experimenters, methods, and stimuli used in the experiment. The important point here is that any research, even if it has high internal validity, may be externally invalid if its findings cannot be expected to or cannot be shown to hold up in other tests of the research hypothesis.

Generalization

The major issue underlying external validity is that of **generalization.** *Generalization* refers to the extent to which relationships among conceptual variables can be demonstrated in a wide variety of people and a wide variety of manipulated or measured variables. Because any research project is normally conducted in a single laboratory, uses a small number of participants, and employs only a limited number of manipulations or measurements of each conceptual variable, it is inherently limited. Yet the results of research are only truly important to the extent that they can be shown to hold up across a wide variety of people and across a wide variety of operational definitions of the independent and dependent variables. The extent to which this occurs can only be known through further research.

Generalization Across Participants

When conducting experimental research, behavioral scientists are frequently not particularly concerned about the specific characteristics of the sample of people they use to test their research hypotheses. In fact, as we have seen in Chapter 12, experiments in the behavioral sciences frequently use convenience samples of college students as research participants. This is advantageous to researchers, both because it is efficient and because it helps minimize variability within the conditions of the experiment and thus provides more powerful tests of the research hypothesis. But the use of college students also has a potential disadvantage because it may not be possible to generalize the results of a study that included only college students from one university to college students at another university or to people who are not college students. However, although the use of college students poses some limitations, it must be realized that *any* sample of research participants, no matter who they are, will be limited in some sense. Let us consider this problem in more detail.

As we have seen, the goal of experimental research is not to use the sample to provide accurate descriptive statistics about the characteristics of a specific population of people. Rather, the goal of experimental research is to elucidate underlying causal relationships among conceptual variables. And in many cases, these hypothesized relationships are expected to be so encompassing that they will hold for every human being at every time and every place. For instance, the principle of distributed versus massed practice suggests that the same amount of study will produce greater learning if it is done in several shorter time periods (distributed) rather than in one longer time period (massed). And there is much research evidence to support this hypothesis (Baddeley, 1990). Of course, the principle does not state that this should be true only for college students or only for Americans. Rather, the theory predicts that learning will be better for all people under distributed versus massed practice no matter who they are, where they live, and whether they went to college. In fact, we can assume that this theory predicts that people who are already dead would have learned better under distributed versus massed practice, and so will people who are not yet born once they are alive!

Although the assumption of many theories in the behavioral sciences is that they will hold, on average, for all human beings, it is obviously impossible to ever be completely sure about this. Naturally, it is not possible to test every human being. And because the population that the relationship is assumed to apply to consists of every human being, in every place, and every time, it is also impossible to take a representative sample of the population of interest. People who are not yet born, who live in unexplored territories, or who have already died simply cannot be included in the scientist's sample.

Because of the impossibility of the scientist drawing a representative sample of all human beings, true generalization across people is not possible. No researcher will ever be able to know that his or her favorite theory applies to all people, in all cultures and places, and at all times because he or she can never test or even sample from all of those people. For this reason, we frequently make the simplifying assumption that unless there is a specific reason to believe otherwise, relationships between conceptual variables that are observed in one group of people will also generally be observed in other groups of people.

Because the assumed relationships are expected to hold for everyone, behavioral scientists are often content to use college students as research participants. In short, they frequently assume that college students have the same basic characteristics as all other human beings, that college students will interpret the meaning of the experimental conditions the same way as any other group of human beings, and thus that the relationships among conceptual variables that are found for college students will also be found in other groups of people.

Of course, this basic assumption may, at least in some cases, be incorrect. There may be certain characteristics of college students that make them different. For instance, college students may be more impressionable than are older people because they are still developing their attitudes and their self-identity. As a result, college students may be particularly likely to listen to those in positions of authority. College students may also be more cognitively (rather than emotionally) driven than the average person and have a higher need for peer approval than most people (Sears, 1986). And there are some theories that are only expected to hold for certain groups of people—such as young children or those with an anxiety disorder.

In some cases, then, there may be a compelling reason to suspect that a relationship found in college students would not be found in other populations. And whenever there is reason to suspect that a result found for college students (or for any specific sample that has been used in research) would not hold up for other types of people, then research should be conducted with these other populations to test for generalization. However, unless the researcher has a specific reason to believe that generalization will not hold, it is appropriate to assume that a result found in one population (even if that population is college students) *will* generalize to other populations. In short, because the researcher can never demonstrate that his or her results generalize to all populations, it is not expected that he or she will attempt to do so. Rather, the burden of proof rests on those who claim that a result will *not* generalize to demonstrate that this is indeed the case.

Generalization Across Settings

Although most people learning about behavioral research immediately realize the potential dangers of generalizing from college students to "people at large," expert researchers are generally at least, if not more, concerned with the extent to which a research finding will generalize beyond the specific settings and techniques used in the original test of the hypothesis. The problem is that a single experiment usually uses only one or two experimenters and is conducted in a specific place. Furthermore, an experiment uses only one of the many possible manipulations of the independent variable and at most a few of the many possible measured dependent variables. The uniqueness of any one experiment makes it possible that the findings are limited in some way to the specific settings, experimenters, manipulations, or measured variables used in the research.

Although these concerns may seem less real to you than concerns about generalization to other people, they can actually be quite important. For instance, it is sometimes found that different researchers may produce different behaviors in their research participants. Researchers who act in a warm and engaging manner may capture the interest of their participants and thus produce different research findings than do cold researchers to whom people are not attracted. It is also the case that the sex, age, and ethnicity of the experimenter may also influence whether a relationship is or is not found (Ickes, 1984).

Ecological Validity. As we will discuss later in this chapter, repeating the experiment in different places and with different experimenters and different operationalizations of the variables is the best method of demonstrating generalization across settings. But it is also possible to increase the potential generalization of a single experiment by increasing its ecological validity.[1] As we have seen in Chapter 7, the ecological validity of a research design refers to the extent to which the research is conducted in situations that are similar to the everyday life experiences of the participants (Aronson & Carlsmith, 1968). For instance, a research design that deals with how children learn to read will have higher ecological validity if the children read a paragraph taken from one of their textbooks than it would if they read a list of sentences taken from adult magazines.

Field Experiments.   One approach that can be used to increase the ecological validity of experiments in some cases is to actually conduct them in natural situations. **Field experiments** are experimental research designs that are conducted in a natural environment such as a library, a factory, or a school rather than in a research laboratory. Because field experiments are true experiments, they have a manipulation, the creation of equivalence, and a measured dependent variable.

Because field experiments are conducted in the natural environment of the participants, they will generally have higher ecological validity than laboratory experiments. Furthermore, they may also have an advantage in the sense that research participants may act more naturally than they would in a lab setting. However, there are also some potential costs to the use of field experiments. For one, it is not always possible to get permission from the institution to conduct them, and even if access is gained, it may not be feasible to use random assignment. Children often cannot be randomly assigned to specific teaching methods or workers to specific tasks. Furthermore, in field settings there is usually a greater potential for systematic and random error because unexpected events may occur that could have been controlled for in the lab.

In general, we have more confidence that a finding will generalize if it is tested in an experiment that has high ecological validity, such as a field experiment. However, field experiments are not *necessarily* more externally valid than are laboratory experiments. An experiment conducted in one particular factory may not generalize to work in other factories in other places any more than the data collected in one laboratory would be expected to generalize to other laboratories or to everyday life. And lab experiments can frequently provide a very good idea of what will happen in real life (Banaji & Crowder, 1989; Berkowitz & Donnerstein, 1982). Field experiments, just like laboratory experiments, are limited because they involve one sample of people at one place at one particular time. In short, no matter how well an experiment is designed, there will always be threats to its external validity. Just as it is impossible to show generalization across all people, it is equally impossible to ever show that an observed relationship holds up in every possible situation.

---

[1]When referring to experimental designs, ecological validity is sometimes referred to as *mundane realism*.

Replications

Because any single test of a research hypothesis will always be limited in terms of what it can show, important advances in science are never the result of a single research project. Rather, advances occur through the accumulation of knowledge that comes from many different tests of the same theory or research hypothesis, made by different researchers using different research designs, participants, and operationalizations of the independent and dependent variables. The process of repeating previous research, which forms the basis of all scientific inquiry, is known as **replication.** Although replications of previous experiments are conducted for many different purposes, they can be classified into four general types, as discussed in the following sections.

Exact Replications

Not surprisingly, the goal of an **exact replication** is to repeat a previous research design as exactly as possible, keeping almost everything about the experiment the same as it was the first time around. Of course, there really is no such thing as an *exact* replication—when a new experiment replicates an old one, new research participants will have to be used, and the experiment will be conducted at a later date. It is also likely that the research will also occur in a new setting and with new experimenters, and in fact, the most common reason for attempting to conduct an exact replication is to see if an effect that has been found in one laboratory or by one researcher can be found in another lab by another researcher.

Although exact replications may be used in some cases to test whether a finding can be discovered again, they are actually not that common in behavioral science. This is partly due to the fact that even if the exact replication does not reproduce the findings from the original experiment, this does not necessarily mean that the original experiment was invalid. It is always possible that the experimenter who conducted the replication did not create the appropriate conditions or did not measure the dependent variable properly. However, to help others who wish to replicate your research (and it is a great honor if they do because this means they have found it interesting), you must specify in the research report the procedures you followed in enough detail that another researcher would be able to follow your procedures and conduct an exact replication of your study.

Conceptual Replications

In general, other types of replication are more useful than exact replications because in addition to demonstrating that a result can be found again, they provide information about the specific conditions under which the original relationship might or might not be found. In a **conceptual replication** the scientist investigates the relationship between the same conceptual variables that were studied in previous research, but she or he tests the hypothesis using different operational definitions of the independent variable and/or the measured dependent variable. For example, when studying the effects of exposure to violence on aggression, the researcher might use clips from feature films, rather than cartoons, to manipulate the content of the viewed stimuli, and he or she might measure verbal aggression, rather than physical aggression, as a dependent variable.

If the same relationship can be demonstrated again with different manipulations or different dependent measures, the confidence that the observed relationship is not specific to the original measures is increased. And if the conceptual replication does *not* find the relationship that was observed in the original research, it may nevertheless provide information about the situations in and measures for which the effect does or does not occur. For example, if the same results of viewing violent material were found on a measure of verbal aggression (such as shouting or swearing) as had earlier been found on physical aggression (such as hitting or pushing), we would learn that the relationship between exposure to aggressive material generalizes. But if the same results were not found, this might suggest that the original relationship was limited to physical, rather than verbal, aggression.

Although generally more useful than exact replications, conceptual replications are themselves limited in the sense that it is difficult to draw conclusions about exactly what changes between the original experiment and the replication experiment might have produced differences in the observed relationships. For instance, if a conceptual replication fails to replicate the original finding, this suggests that something that has been changed is important, but it does not conclusively demonstrate what that something is.

Constructive Replications

Because it is important to know exactly how changes in the operational definitions of the independent and dependent variables in the research change the observed relationships between them, the most popular form of replication is known as a constructive replication. In a **constructive replication** the researcher tests the same hypothesis as the original experiment (in the form of either an exact or a conceptual replication), but also adds new conditions to the original experiment to assess the specific variables that might change the previously observed relationship. In general, the purpose of a constructive replication is to rule out alternative explanations or to add new information about the variables of interest.

Some Examples.   We have already considered some examples of constructive replications. For one, in Chapter 10 we considered a case in which the constructive replication involved adding a new control condition to a one-way experimental design. In this case, adding a condition in which participants did not view any films at all allowed us to test the possibility that the nonviolent cartoons were reducing aggressive behavior rather than that the violent cartoons were increasing aggressive behavior. In this case, the goal of the constructive replication is to rule out an alternative explanation for the initial experiment.

In Chapter 11, we looked at another type of constructive replication—a study designed to test limitations on the effects of viewing violence on aggressive behavior. The predictions of this experiment are shown in Figure 11.2 in Chapter 11. The goal of the experiment was to replicate the finding that exposure to violent behavior increased aggression in the nonfrustrated condition, but then to show that this relationship reverses if the children have previously been frustrated. Notice that in this constructive replication the original conditions of the experiment have been retained (the no-frustration conditions), but new conditions have been added (the frustration conditions).

Moderator Variables. As in this case, constructive replications are often factorial experimental designs where a new variable (in this case, the prior state of the children) is added to the variable that was manipulated in the original experiment (violent or nonviolent cartoons). One level of the new variable represents an exact or a conceptual replication of the original experiment, whereas the other level represents a condition where it is expected that the original relationship does not hold or reverses. The prediction is that there will be an observed interaction between the original variable and the new variable.

When the interaction in a constructive replication is found to be statistically significant, the new variable is called a moderator variable, and the new variable can be said to *moderate* the initial relationship. A **moderator variable** is a variable that produces an interaction of the relationship between two other variables such that the relationship between them is different at different levels of the moderator variable (Baron & Kenny, 1986).

You might wonder why it is necessary to include the conditions that replicate the previous experiment when it is the new conditions, in which a different relationship is expected, that are of interest. That is, why not just test the children under the frustration condition rather than including the original non-frustration condition as well? The reason is that if the original conditions are not included, there is no guarantee that the new experiment has adequately recreated the original experimental situation. Thus, because constructive replications create both conditions designed to demonstrate that the original pattern of results can be replicated and conditions where the original pattern of results is changed, these replications can provide important information about exactly what changes influence the original relationship.

Participant Replications

Although the previous types of replication have dealt with generalization across settings, in cases where there is reason to believe that an observed relationship found with one set of participants will not generalize to or will be different in another population of people, it may be useful to conduct replications using new types of participants. To be most effective, a **participant**

replication should not simply repeat the original experiment with a new population. As we have previously discussed, such repetition is problematic because if a different relationship between the independent and dependent variables is found, the experimenter cannot know if that difference is due to the use of different participants or to other potentially unknown changes in the experimental setting. Rather, the experiment should be designed as a constructive replication in which both the original population and the new one are used. Again, if the original result generalizes, then only a main effect of the original variable will be observed, but if the result does not generalize, an interaction between the original variable and the participant population will be observed.

One type of participant replication involves testing people from different cultures. For instance, a researcher might test whether the effects on aggression of viewing violent cartoons are the same for Japanese children as they are for U.S. children by showing violent and nonviolent films to a sample of both U.S. and Japanese schoolchildren. Interpreting the results of cross-cultural replications can be difficult, however, because it is hard to know if the manipulation is conceptually equivalent for the new participants. For instance, the cartoons must be translated into Japanese, and although the experimenter may have attempted to adequately translate the materials, children in the new culture may interpret the cartoons differently than the children in the United States did. The same cartoons may have appeared more (or less) aggressive to the Japanese children. Of course, the different interpretations may themselves be of interest, but there is likely to be ambiguity regarding whether differences in aggression are due to cultural differences in the effects of the independent variable on the dependent variable or to different interpretations of the independent variable.

Summarizing and Integrating Research Results

If you have been carefully following the topics in the last two chapters, you will have realized by now that every test of a research hypothesis, regardless of how well it is conducted or how strong its findings, is limited in some sense. For instance, some experiments are conducted in such specific settings that they seem unlikely to generalize to other tests of the research hypothesis. Other experiments are undermined by potential alternative explanations that result from the confounding of other variables with the independent variable of interest. And, of course, every significant result may be invalid because it represents a Type 1 error.

In addition to the potential of invalidity, the drawing of conclusions about research findings is made difficult because the results of individual experiments testing the same or similar research hypotheses are never quite consistent among one another. Some studies find relationships, whereas others do not. Of those that do, some show stronger relationships, some show weaker relationships, and still others may find relationships that are in the opposite direction from what most of the other studies show. Other studies suggest that the observed relationship is stronger or weaker under certain conditions or with the use of certain experimental manipulations or measured variables.

Research Programs

The natural inconsistency among different tests of the same hypothesis and the fact that any one study is potentially invalid make it clear why science is never built on the results of single experiments but rather is cumulative—building on itself over time through replication. Because scientists are aware of the limitations of any one experiment, they frequently conduct collections of experiments, known as **research programs,** in which they systematically study a topic of interest through conceptual and constructive replications over a period of time. The advantage of the research program is that the scientists are able to increase their confidence in the validity and the strength of a relationship, as well as the conditions under which it occurs or does not occur, by testing the hypothesis using different operationalizations of the independent and dependent variables, different research designs, and different participants.

Review Papers

The results of research programs are routinely reviewed and summarized in review papers, which appear in scientific books and journals. A **review paper** is a document that discusses the research in a given area with the goals of summarizing the existing findings, drawing conclusions about the conditions under which relationships may or may not occur, linking the research findings to other areas of research, and making suggestions for further research. In a review paper, a scientist might draw conclusions about which experimental manipulations and dependent variables seem to have been most successful or seem to have been the most valid, attempt to explain contradictory findings in the literature, and perhaps propose new theories to account for observed findings.

Meta-Analysis

Many review papers use a procedure known as meta-analysis to summarize research findings. A **meta-analysis** is a statistical technique that uses the results of existing studies to integrate and draw conclusions about those studies. Because meta-analyses provide so much information, they are very popular ways of summarizing research literatures. Table 13.1 presents examples of some recent meta-analyses in the behavioral sciences.

A meta-analysis provides a relatively objective method of reviewing research findings because it (1) specifies **inclusion criteria** that indicate exactly which studies will or will not be included in the analysis, (2) systematically searches for all studies that meet the inclusion criteria, and (3) uses the effect size statistic to provide an objective measure of the strength of observed relationships. Frequently, the researchers also include—if they can find them—studies that have not been published in journals.

TABLE 13.1   Examples of Meta-Analyses

Meta-Analysis	Findings
Twenge and Nolen-Hoeksema (2002)	Compared levels of depression among children at different ages and of different ethnic groups
Hardy and Hinkin (2002)	Studied the effect of HIV infection on cognition by comparing reaction times of infected and noninfected patients
Gully, Incalcaterra, Joshi, and Beaubien (2002)	Studied the relationship between group inter dependence and task performance in teams
Schmitt (2002)	Found that different social contexts (for instance, mixed- versus single-sex interactions) influenced our perceptions of others' physical attractiveness
Dowden and Brown (2002)	Found that different patterns of drug and alcohol use predicted criminal recidivism
Brierley, Shaw, and David (2002)	Measured the normal size of the amygdala in humans, and studied how it changes with age

This table presents examples of some of the more than 300 meta-analyses published in 2002.

One example of the use of meta-analysis involves the summarizing of the effects of psychotherapy on the mental health of clients. Over the years, hundreds of studies have been conducted addressing this question, but they differ among each other in virtually every imaginable way. These studies include many different types of psychological disorders (for instance, anxiety, depression, and schizophrenia) and different types of therapies (for instance, hypnosis, behavioral therapy, and Freudian therapy). Furthermore, the dependent measures used in the research have varied from self-report measures of mood or anxiety to behavioral measures, such as amount of time before release from psychological institutions. And the research has used both correlational and experimental research designs.

Defining Inclusion Criteria.   Despite what might have appeared to be a virtually impossible task, Smith, Glass, and Miller (1980) summarized these studies and drew important conclusions about the effects of psychotherapy through the use of a meta-analysis. The researchers first set up their inclusion criteria to be studies in which two or more types of psychotherapy were compared or in which one type of psychotherapy was compared against a control group. They further defined psychotherapy to include situations in which the clients had an emotional or behavioral problem, they sought or were referred for treatment, and the person delivering the treatment was identified as a psychotherapist by virtue of training or professional affiliation.

The researchers then systematically searched computer databases and the reference sections of previous research reports to locate every single study that met the inclusion criteria. Over 475 studies were located, and these studies used over 10,000 research participants.

Coding the Studies. At this point, each of these studies was systematically coded and analyzed. As you will recall from our discussion in Chapter 8, the effect size is a statistical measure of the strength of a relationship. In a meta-analysis, one or more effect size statistics are recorded from each of the studies, and it is these effect sizes that are analyzed in the meta-analysis. In some cases, the effect size itself is reported in the research report, and in other cases it must be calculated from other reported statistics.

Analyzing the Effect Size. One of the important uses of meta-analysis is to combine many different types of studies into a single analysis. The meta-analysis can provide an index of the overall strength of a relationship within a research literature. In the case of psychotherapy, for instance, Smith and her colleagues found that the average effect size for the effect of therapy was +.85, indicating that psychotherapy had a relatively large positive effect on recovery (recall from Chapter 8 that in the behavioral sciences a "large" effect size is usually considered to be about .40). In addition to overall statements, the meta-analysis allows the scientist to study whether other coded variables moderate the relationship of interest. For instance, Smith et al. found that the strength of the relationship between therapy and recovery (as indexed by the effect size) was different for different types of therapies and on different types of recovery measures.

Benefits and Limitations of Meta-Analyses. Meta-analyses have both benefits and limitations in comparison to narrative literature reviews. On the positive side, the use of explicit inclusion criteria and an in-depth search for all studies that meet these ensures objectivity in what is and what is not included in the analysis. Readers can be certain that *all* of the relevant studies have been included, rather than just a subset of these, which is likely in a paper that does not use meta-analysis. Second, the use of the effect size statistic provides an objective measure of the strength of observed relationships.

As a result of these features, meta-analyses are therefore more accurate than narrative research reviews. In fact, it has been found that narrative reviews tend to underestimate the magnitude of the true relationships between variables in comparison to meta-analyses (Cooper & Rosenthal, 1980; Mann, 1994). This seems to occur in part because, since research is normally at least in part contradictory, the narrative reviews tend to reach correct, but potentially misleading conclusions such as "some evidence supports the hypothesis, whereas other evidence contradicts it." Meta-analyses, in contrast, frequently tend to show that, although there is of course some contradiction across studies, the underlying tendency is much stronger in one direction than in the other.

However, because meta-analyses are based on archival research, the conclusions that can be drawn will always be limited by the data that have been published. This can be problematic if the published studies have not measured or manipulated all of the important variables or are not representative of all of the studies that have been conducted. For instance, because studies that have significant results are more likely to be published than those that are non-significant, the published studies may overestimate the size of a relationship between variables.

In the end, meta-analyses are really just another type of research project. They can provide a substantial amount of knowledge about the magnitude and generality of relationships. And as with any research, they have both strengths and limitations, and the ability to adequately interpret them involves being aware of these.

Interpretation of Research Literatures

The primary goal of replication is to determine the extent to which an observed relationship generalizes across different tests of the research hypothesis. However, just because a finding does not generalize does not mean it is not interesting or important. Indeed, science proceeds by discovering limiting conditions for previously demonstrated relationships. Few relationships hold in all settings and for all people. Scientific theories are modified over time as more information about their limitations is discovered. As an example, one of the interesting questions in research investigating the effects of exposure to violent material on aggression concerns the fact that although it is well known that the viewing of violence tends to increase aggression on average, this does not happen for all people. So it is extremely important to conduct participant replications to determine which people will, and which will not, be influenced by exposure to violent material.

The cumulative knowledge base of a scientific literature, gained through replication and reported in review papers and meta-analysis, is much more informative and accurate than is any individual test of a research hypothesis. However, the skilled consumer of research must learn to evaluate the results of research programs to get an overall feel for what the data in a given domain are showing. There is usually no clear-cut right or wrong answer to these questions, but the individual reader has to be the judge of the quality of a research result.

Finally, it is worth mentioning that replication also serves to keep the process of scientific inquiry honest. If the results of a scientist's research are important, then other scientists will want to try to replicate them to test for generalizability of the findings. Still other scientists will attempt to apply the research results to make constructive advances. If a scientist has fabricated or altered data, the results will not be replicable, and the research will not contribute to the advancement of science.

Current Research in the Behavioral Sciences: A Meta-Analysis of the Effectiveness of Current Treatment Approaches for Withdrawal From Tranquilizer Addictions

The research reported in a recent issue of the journal *Addiction* (Parr, Kavanagh, Cahill, Young, & Mitchell, 2009) was a meta-analysis designed to determine the effectiveness of different treatments for benzodiazepine discontinuation (tranquilizer withdrawal) in general practice and out-patient settings.

The authors began with a systematic search of three online databases: (PsycLIT, MEDLINE, and EBASE [drugs and pharmacology]) to identify studies that evaluated the effectiveness of treatments for cessation of benzodiazepine use. This search identified 278 papers. An additional 53 papers were identified from journal citations, and a future search conducted in 2007 found a further 16.

Two of the authors were assigned to determine whether the articles included in the meta-analysis met the inclusion criteria. Studies were included if they compared an adjunctive treatment with either routine care or gradual dose reduction (GDR), and participants were out-patients who had used benzodiazepines continuously for three months or longer prior to the commencement of the study. Trials had at least ten participants in each condition at baseline, and reported information had to allow calculation of cessation rates for each condition. Agreement of 100% was achieved for the judgment that a study met inclusion criteria.

A total of 32 studies were include in the meta-analysis. The count of the treatment comparisons was as follows:

3 - Brief intervention vs. routine care (individuals randomized)

2 - Brief intervention vs. routine care (practices randomized)

1 - Gradual dose reduction vs. routine care*

3 - Psychological treatment vs. routine care*

7 - GDR + Psychological interventions vs. GDR*

17 - GDR + Substitutive pharmacotherapy vs. GDR

1 - GDR + Psychological vs. abrupt withdrawal + psychological

The results of the meta-analysis showed that, across the 32 studies, GDR and brief interventions provided superior cessation rates at post-treatment in comparison to routine care. Psychological treatment plus GDR was superior to both routine care and GDR alone. However, substitutive pharmacotherapies did not add to the impact of GDR and abrupt substitution of benzodiazepines by other pharmacotherapy was less effective than GDR alone.

The authors concluded that, based on the current research, providing an intervention is more effective than routine care and that psychological interventions may improve discontinuation above GDR alone. They also concluded that, while some alternative pharmacotherapies may have promise, current evidence is insufficient to support their use.

SUMMARY

External validity refers to the extent to which relationships between independent and dependent variables that are found in a test of a research hypothesis can be expected to be found again when tested with other research designs, other operationalizations of the variables, other participants, other experimenters, or other times and settings.

A research design has high external validity if the results can be expected to generalize to other participants and to other tests of the relationship. External validity can be enhanced by increasing the ecological validity of an experiment by making it similar to what might occur in everyday life or by conducting field experiments.

Science relies primarily on replications to test the external validity of research findings. Sometimes the original research is replicated exactly, but more often conceptual replications with new operationalizations of the independent or dependent variables, or constructive replications with new conditions added to the original design, are employed. Replication allows scientists to test both the generalization and the limitations of research findings.

Because each individual research project is limited in some way, scientists conduct research programs in which many different studies are conducted. These programs are often summarized in review papers. Meta-analysis represents a relatively objective method of summarizing the results of existing research that involves a systematic method of selecting studies for review and coding and analyzing their results.

KEY TERMS

conceptual replication 260
constructive replication 261
exact replication 260
external validity 256
field experiments 259
generalization 256
inclusion criteria 265

meta-analysis 264
moderator variable 262
participant replication 262
replication 260
research programs 264
review paper 264

REVIEW AND DISCUSSION QUESTIONS

1. Define *external validity,* and indicate its importance to scientific progress.

2. Why is it never possible to know whether a research finding will generalize to all populations of individuals? How do behavioral scientists deal with this problem?

3. What are the four different types of replication, and what is the purpose of each?

4. Explain how replication can be conceptualized as a factorial experimental design.

5. Why are research programs more important to the advancement of science than are single experiments?

6. Define a meta-analysis, and explain its strengths and limitations.

RESEARCH PROJECT IDEAS

1. In each of the following cases, the first article presents a study that has a confound and the second article represents a constructive replication designed to eliminate the confound. Report on one or more of the pairs of articles:

   a. Aronson, E., & Mills, J. (1959). The effect of severity of initiation on liking for a group. *Journal of Abnormal and Social Psychology, 59,* 177–181.
   Gerard, H. B., & Matthewson, G. C. (1966). The effects of severity of initiation on liking for a group: A replication. *Journal of Experimental Social Psychology, 2,* 278–287.

   b. Zimbardo, P. G. (1970). The human choice: Individuation, reason, and order versus deindividuation, impulse, and chaos. In W. J. Arnold and D. Levine (Eds.), *Nebraska Symposium on Motivation, 1969.* Lincoln: University of Nebraska Press.
   Johnson, R. D., & Downing, L. L. (1979). Deindividuation and the valence of cues: Effects on prosocial and antisocial behavior. *Journal of Personality and Social Psychology, 37,* 1532–1538.

   c. Pennebaker, J. W., Dyer, M. A., Caulkins, R. S., Litowitz, D. L., Ackerman, P. L., & Anderson, D. B. (1979). Don't the girls get prettier at closing time: A country and western application to psychology. *Personality and Social Psychology Bulletin, 5,* 122–125.
   Madey, S. F., Simo, M., Dillworth, D., & Kemper, D. (1996). They do get more attractive at closing time, but only when you are not in a relationship. *Basic and Applied Social Psychology, 18,* 387–393.

    d. Baron, R. A., & Ransberger, V. M. (1978). Ambient temperature and the occurrence of collective violence: The "long, hot summer" revisited. *Journal of Personality and Social Psychology, 36,* 351–360.

    Carlsmith, J. M., & Anderson, C. A. (1979). Ambient temperature and the occurrence of collective violence: A new analysis. *Journal of Personality and Social Psychology, 37,* 337–344.

2. Locate a research report that contains a replication of previous research. Identify the purpose of the replication and the type of replication that was used. What are the important findings of the research?

3. Develop a research hypothesis, and propose a specific test of it. Then develop a conceptual replication and a constructive replication that investigate the expected boundary conditions for the original relationship.

CHAPTER FOURTEEN
Quasi-Experimental Research Designs

STUDY QUESTIONS

- What is program evaluation research, and when is it used?

- What is a quasi-experimental research design? When are such designs used, and why?

- Why do quasi-experimental designs generally have lower internal validity than true experiments?

- What are the most common quasi-experimental research designs?

- What are the major threats to internal validity in quasi-experimental designs?

- What is regression to the mean, and what problems does it pose in research?

- What is a participant-variable research design?

- What is a single-participant research design?

We have seen in Chapter 10 that the strength of experimental research lies in the ability to maximize internal validity. However, a basic limitation of experimental research is that, for practical or ethical reasons, the independent variables of interest cannot always be experimentally manipulated. In this chapter, we will consider research designs that are frequently used by researchers who want to make comparisons among different groups of individuals but cannot randomly assign the individuals to the groups. These comparisons can be either between participants (for instance, a comparison of the scholastic achievement of autistic versus nonautistic children) or repeated measures (for instance, a comparison of the mental health of individuals before and after they have participated in a program of psychotherapy). These research designs are an essential avenue of investigation in domains such as education, human development, social work, and clinical psychology because they are frequently the only possible approach to studying the variables of interest.

Program Evaluation Research

As we have seen in Chapter 1, one type of applied research that involves the use of existing groups is program evaluation research (Campbell, 1969; Rossi & Freeman, 1993). Program evaluation research is research designed to study intervention programs, such as after-school programs, clinical therapies, or prenatal-care clinics, with the goal of determining whether the programs are effective in helping the people who make use of them.

Consider as an example a researcher who is interested in determining the effects on college students of participation in a study-abroad program. The researcher expects that one outcome of such programs, in which students spend a semester or a year studying in a foreign country, is that the students will develop more positive attitudes toward immigrants to their own country than students who do not participate in exchange programs.

You can see that it is not going to be possible for the researcher to exert much control in the research, and thus there are going to be threats to its internal validity. For one, the students cannot be randomly assigned to the conditions. Some students spend time studying abroad, and others do not, but whether they do or do not is determined by them, not by the experimenter. And there are many variables that may determine whether a student does or does not participate, including his or her interests, financial resources, and cultural background. These variables are potential common-causal variables in the sense that they may cause both the independent variable (participation in the program) and the dependent variable (attitudes toward immigrants). Their presence will thus limit the researcher's ability to make causal statements about the effectiveness of the program.

In addition to the lack of random assignment, because the research uses a longitudinal design in which measurements are taken over a period of time, the researcher will have difficulty controlling what occurs during that time. Other changes are likely to take place, both within the participants and in their environment, and these changes become extraneous or confounding variables within the research design. These variables may threaten the validity of the research.

Quasi-Experimental Designs

Despite such difficulties, with creative planning a researcher may be able to create a research design that is able to rule out at least some of the threats to the internal validity of the research, thus allowing conclusions about the causal effects of the independent variable on the dependent variable to be drawn. Because the independent variable or variables are measured, rather than manipulated, these research designs are correlational, not experimental. Nevertheless, the designs also have some similarity to experimental research because the independent variable involves a grouping and the data are usually analyzed with ANOVA. For these reasons, such studies have been called **quasi-experimental research designs.**[1]

In the following sections, we will consider some of the most important research designs that involve the study of naturally occurring groups of individuals, as well as the particular threats to internal validity that are likely to occur when these designs are used. Figure 14.1 summarizes these designs as they would apply to the exchange program research example, and Table 14.1 summarizes the potential threats to the internal validity of each design.

Single-Group Design

One approach that our scientist might take is to simply locate a group of students who have spent the past year studying abroad and have now returned to their home university, set up an interview with each student, and assess some dependent measures, including students' attitudes toward immigrants in the United States.

Research that uses a single group of participants who are measured after they have had the experience of interest is known as a **single-group design.**[2] You can see, however, that there is a major limitation to this approach—because there is no control group, there is no way to determine what the attitudes of these students would have been if they hadn't studied abroad. As a result, our researcher cannot use the single-group design to draw conclusions about the effect of study abroad on attitudes toward immigrants.

Despite these limitations, single-group research designs are frequently reported in the popular literature, and they may be misinterpreted by those who read them. Examples include books reporting the experiences of people

---

[1]For further information about the research designs discussed in this chapter, as well as about other types of quasi-experimental designs, you may wish to look at books by Campbell and Stanley (1963) and Cook and Campbell (1979).
[2]Campbell and Stanley (1963) called these "one-shot case studies."

FIGURE 14.1   Summary of Quasi-Experimental Research Designs

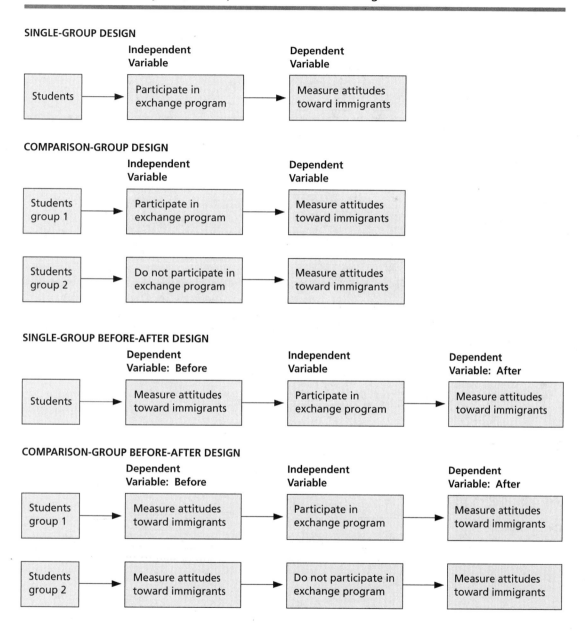

SINGLE-GROUP DESIGN

Students → Independent Variable: Participate in exchange program → Dependent Variable: Measure attitudes toward immigrants

COMPARISON-GROUP DESIGN

Students group 1 → Independent Variable: Participate in exchange program → Dependent Variable: Measure attitudes toward immigrants

Students group 2 → Do not participate in exchange program → Measure attitudes toward immigrants

SINGLE-GROUP BEFORE-AFTER DESIGN

Students → Dependent Variable: Before: Measure attitudes toward immigrants → Independent Variable: Participate in exchange program → Dependent Variable: After: Measure attitudes toward immigrants

COMPARISON-GROUP BEFORE-AFTER DESIGN

Students group 1 → Dependent Variable: Before: Measure attitudes toward immigrants → Independent Variable: Participate in exchange program → Dependent Variable: After: Measure attitudes toward immigrants

Students group 2 → Measure attitudes toward immigrants → Do not participate in exchange program → Measure attitudes toward immigrants

who have survived stressful experiences such as wars or natural disasters or those who have lived through traumatic childhood experiences. If the goal of the research is simply to describe the experiences that individuals have had or their reactions to them (for instance, to document the reactions of the residents of California to an earthquake), the data represent naturalistic

TABLE 14.1   Threats to the Internal Validity of Quasi-Experimental Designs

Research Design	Threat to Validity						Interpretational Difficulties
	Selection	Attrition	Maturation	History	Retesting	Regression	
Single group	✓						No causal interpretation is possible because there is no comparison group.
Comparison group	✓						Comparisons are possible only to the extent that the comparison group is equivalent to the experimental group.
Single group before-after		✓	✓	✓	✓		Selection is not a problem because the same participants are measured both times. Attrition, maturation, history, and retesting cause problems.
Comparison group before-after		✓				✓	Maturation, history, and retesting should be controlled because the comparison group has experienced the same changes. Regression to mean is still problematic, as is the potential for differential attrition.

descriptive research, as we have discussed in Chapter 7. In these cases, we may be able to learn something about the experience itself by studying how the individuals experienced these events and reacted to them.

Single-group studies can never, however, be used to draw conclusions about how an experience has affected the individuals involved. For instance, research showing that children whose parents were alcoholics have certain psychological problems cannot be interpreted to mean that their parents' alcoholism caused these problems. Because there is no control group, we can never know what the individuals would have been like if they had not experienced this stressful situation, and it is quite possible that other variables, rather than their parents' alcoholism, caused these difficulties. As an informed consumer of scientific research, you must be aware that although single-group studies may be informative about the current characteristics of the individuals who have had the experiences, these studies cannot be used to draw conclusions about how the experiences affected them.

Comparison-Group Design

You can see that if our researcher wishes to draw any definitive conclusions about the effects of study abroad on attitudes toward immigrants, he or she will need one or more groups for comparison. A **comparison group** is a group that is expected to be similar but not equivalent to the experimental group (random assignment has not been used). One possibility is to include a second group of students who did not participate in the student exchange program. Ideally, this comparison group would be equivalent to the group that did participate on all characteristics except the participation itself. For instance, we could use as a comparison group students from the same university who had the same major but did not participate in the study-abroad program. Even better would be a group of students who had an alternative study experience, such as spending a year at another university in the United States, but who did not travel abroad. The prediction is that if study abroad changes attitudes toward immigrants, then the students in this group should express more tolerance than the group that did not study abroad. This prediction would be tested with a one-way between-participants ANOVA with two levels of the independent variable.

Although the **comparison-group design** provides more information than a single-group design, you can see that there are still some serious threats to internal validity. These arise because it is possible that any observed differences on the dependent measure were due not to the effects of the study-abroad program, but to differences between the groups that existed before the sojourn began. Threats to internal validity that occur because individuals select themselves into groups, rather than being randomly assigned to groups, are called **selection threats.** In our case, the major selection threat is that students who were interested in studying abroad were more tolerant of immigrants to begin with.

The more similar the two groups are to each other before they participate in the exchange program, the less problematic will be selection threats, and the stronger will be the conclusions drawn about the effects of the independent variable on the dependent variable. But even if the comparison group had been selected to be as equivalent as possible to the study group, it would almost certainly differ to some extent on at least some variables. In some cases potential differences between the groups can be statistically controlled, as we have discussed in Chapter 9.

Single-Group Before-After Design

Because the addition of one or more comparison groups in a comparison-group design involves recruiting another group of students, and because this design does not allow us to know how those groups differed before the experience occurred, you can imagine that it might be preferable in some cases to take a longitudinal approach. In this case, the scientist would measure the attitudes of a group of students before they went abroad and then measure the attitudes again after the students returned home. Comparisons would be made over time, with the expectation that the students would express more tolerance toward immigrants after they returned home than they did before they left. The statistical comparison would be a one-way repeated-measures ANOVA with two levels.

One obvious advantage of the **single-group before-after design** is in terms of equivalence. The individuals who complete the measures after their exchange program are equivalent to those who completed them before they left because they are the same people. However, a before-after approach has its own set of potential threats to internal validity.

Retesting Threats. One such threat involves the danger of retesting. As we have seen in Chapter 5, whenever the dependent measures are assessed more than once, participants may be able to guess the research hypothesis, and this may lead them to respond differently to the second set of measures than they otherwise would have. In our case, an astute and cooperative student might guess that the researcher expected a positive change in attitudes over time and might, therefore, complete the questionnaire in a manner that would support this prediction.

Attrition Threats. Another problem with the before-after approach in this case is that some of the students may drop out of college, transfer to another university, or stay abroad rather than returning home and thus never complete the second measure. This problem, known as **attrition** or **mortality,** poses a threat to internal validity in longitudinal research designs because the students who stay with the program may be different from those who drop out. In our example, for instance, the influence of the exchange program on attitudes may be overestimated if those students who had the most positive attitudes in the beginning are also the most likely to stay in the program.

Maturation and History Threats. The addition of a time delay in a before-after design also introduces other extraneous variables into the research design. While the students were abroad, other things may have happened that were not related to the research hypothesis and yet may have caused changes in the dependent variable. One obvious change is that when the students return home, they are one year older than they were when they left. Because older students may be less prejudiced than younger students, the students might have become more tolerant toward immigrants over the time period even if they hadn't gone abroad. Threats to internal validity that involve potential changes in the research participants over time but that are unrelated to the independent variable are called **maturation threats.**

In addition to changes in the individuals themselves, other events unrelated to the exchange program that occur over the time period might influence the dependent variable. For instance, political events in the United States during the time under study might have caused changes in attitudes toward immigrants in the students. Threats to internal validity that occur due to the potential influence of changes in the social climate during the course of a study are called **history threats.**

Comparison-Group Before-After Design

Because both comparison-group and before-after designs have their unique sets of threats to internal validity, it is often desirable, when possible, to combine them, making use of a **comparison-group before-after design.** In this design, more than one group of individuals is studied, and the dependent measure is assessed for both groups before and after the intervening event. The comparison group either engages in other comparable activities during this time or else does not engage in any activity. If we used a group of students who did not study abroad as a comparison group, for instance, they would also be measured both before and after the study group visited abroad. In this case, the appropriate statistical test would be a two-way ANOVA with one between-participants factor (group) and one repeated-measures factor (time of measurement). The prediction is for an interaction such that the group that studies abroad shows more change over time than does the comparison group.

The use of a comparison group allows the scientist to control for some of the threats to validity that occur in before-after studies that last over a period of time. For one, maturation is less likely to provide a threat to internal validity because the students in the comparison group also mature to the same extent over the time period. This design also controls for history threats when these events influence both groups equally. It is still possible, however, that if the two groups are in different locations, they may be differentially affected by history. For instance, if the U.S. government made important decisions about immigration policy during the time period of the study, this may have had a different impact on students in the United States (who were more likely to know about the decision) than it did for those who were abroad (who may have been more likely not to have known about the decision). This design also controls for attrition, unless the amount of attrition is different in the two groups.

Regression to the Mean as a Threat to Internal Validity

In short, measurement of the dependent variable before the experience in the comparison-group before-after design has the advantage of allowing the researcher to know if and how the groups differed before the differences in the independent variable occurred. Although this knowledge is helpful, whenever participants in different groups differ on the dependent variable before the independent variable occurs, the researcher cannot be certain that it was the independent variable, rather than something else, that caused differences on the measurements made after the independent variable occurred.

One threat to validity that occurs whenever there is not initial equivalence between the groups results from a statistical artifact known as *regression to the mean*. One way to understand why this artifact occurs is to recall that a regression equation can be used to predict a person's score on the outcome variable if the score on the predictor variable is known (see Chapter 9). If variables are first converted to standard (z) scores, the following equation holds:

$$z_y = r \times z_x$$

where r is the Pearson correlation coefficient between the two variables.

You will see from this equation that whenever the correlation between the independent variable (z_x) and the dependent variable (z_y) is less than $r = 1.00$ or greater than $r = -1.00$, a given score on the independent variable will always result in a prediction for the dependent variable that is nearer the mean (that is, less extreme). For instance, if $r = .30$, then a person who received a score of $z_x = 2$ on the independent variable would be expected to receive a score of $z_y = .67$ on the dependent variable, and a person who received a score of $z_x = -2$ on the independent variable would be expected, by chance, to receive a score of $z_y = -.67$.

What this means for the interpretation of quasi experiments is that whenever the same variable is measured more than once, to the extent that the correlation between the two measures is less than $r = 1.00$ or greater than $r = -1.00$, individuals will tend to score more toward the average score of the group on the second measure than they did on the first measure, even if nothing has changed between the two measures. This change is known as **regression to the mean.**

Misinterpreting Results as a Result of Regression to the Mean. When regression to the mean occurs in everyday life, people often attribute a meaning to the change that it does not deserve. For instance, the first recordings produced by a musical group are frequently the best recordings it ever makes. Although people may interpret this pattern to mean that the group got worse, such effects can be easily explained by regression to the mean—extremely good outcomes at one time point tend to be followed by more average ones later. Another example is that athletes who, because of an exceptional athletic performance, are pictured on the cover of *Sports Illustrated* generally do not perform as well afterward as they did before they received the honor. Although it is commonly thought that being featured in the magazine causes the players to do more poorly (perhaps because they then experience more pressure to do well), a more likely explanation is regression to the mean. Just as very intelligent parents tend to have less intelligent children, and very short parents tend to have taller children, most things tend to become more average over time.

Regression to the mean causes interpretational difficulties whenever there is initial nonequivalence between the groups in a quasi-experimental research design. And these difficulties are enhanced under two conditions. First, regression to the mean is more problematic to the extent that the groups have extreme scores on the initial measure because the farther a group is from the mean, the greater the regression to the mean will be. Second, as you will recall from Chapter 5, one reason that scores on the same measured variable might not correlate highly over time is that the measure is unreliable. Thus we can say that unreliable measures are more likely to produce regression to the mean.

Consider as an example a comparison-group before-after design that compares the reading skills of a group of children before and after they complete a reading-skill training program with another group of children who do not participate in the program. However, because the program is offered only to very poor readers, the group that received the training had much lower reading scores to begin with than did the comparison group. Even if the reading skills of the children in the training program increased significantly more than the skills of the comparison group over time, this does not necessarily indicate that the program was effective. Because the poor readers initially scored extremely low on the reading test, they would be expected to show more improvement over time than the comparison group even without the benefit of instruction.

In some cases the effect of regression to the mean is to make it more difficult to demonstrate that programs had the expected effect. To return to our example testing whether study-abroad programs increase tolerance, it would be difficult to know how to interpret a result showing that the students did not develop more positive attitudes over time. Because students who enroll in such programs are likely to initially be very positive toward foreigners, their scores will tend to decrease over time through regression to the mean, and this change will tend to cancel out any positive effects of the program. In fact, some research findings show that students who volunteer for foreign exchange programs often develop *less* favorable attitudes toward foreigners over the course of their experience, but this is probably due, at least in part, to regression to the mean. Because students who participate in study-abroad programs probably have very positive attitudes toward foreigners to begin with, their attitudes may become more neutral over time (cf. Stangor, Jonas, Stroebe, & Hewstone, 1996).

Avoiding Problems Associated with Regression to the Mean. Difficulties such as regression to the mean make it clear why, whenever possible, experimental research designs, rather than quasi-experimental research designs, should be used. For instance, in some cases a treatment program is implemented, but there are not enough places in the program for everyone who wishes to participate. In this case, participants may be put on a waiting list, and participants can be randomly assigned to be allowed into the program. Those who are able to get into the program would then be equivalent to those who did not.

In many cases, however, practical considerations of time, money, and the cooperation of those in charge of the program limit the researcher to a quasi-experimental approach. Of course, the ability to control for threats to internal validity in quasi-experimental research is dependent on the type of research design, and some designs allow at least some of the many threats to internal validity to be ruled out. Furthermore, no research is perfectly valid. As in other research, the evidence for a relationship between variables accumulates over time as more and more studies, each using different research designs, are conducted. Because different research projects have different threats to internal validity, they may, when taken together, allow strong conclusions about the causal relationships among variables to be drawn.

Time-Series Designs

The basic logic of the before-after research design can be taken a step further through the use of longitudinal research designs in which the dependent measure is assessed for one or more groups more than twice, at regular intervals, both before and after the experience of interest occurs. Such research designs are collectively known as **time-series designs,** and they may in some cases be able to rule out more threats to internal validity than can the designs we have investigated to this point.

Consider, for instance, a hypothetical time-series design that uses archival data to investigate the incidence of street robberies in a large U.S. city at regular, one-month intervals over a period of three years. The goal of the research is to investigate the effects on crime of the institution of a "cop on the streets" program in which a substantial number of police officers moved out of their cruisers and began walking street beats.

You can see from the data in Figure 14.2 that there was a consistent trend of increasing street robberies in the years preceding the enactment of the new program, but that this trend leveled off and even began to decrease slightly after the enactment of the program. The advantage of the time-series approach in this case is that it allows us to see trends in the data over time, something that would not have been possible if we had measured the crime rate only twice—once before and once after the program was initiated.

Although the results of this time-series study are consistent with the hypothesis that the police on the streets program reduced the incidence of robberies, something else occurring at the same time as the initiative may have caused

FIGURE 14.2 Hypothetical Results of a Time-Series Study

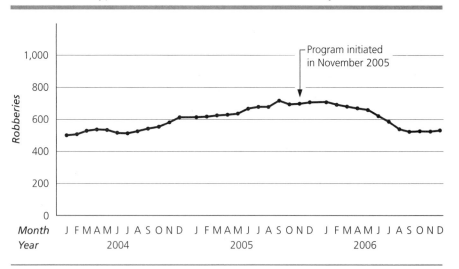

These are the results of a hypothetical study that uses archival data to track the incidence of street robberies in a large U.S. city at regular, one-month intervals over a period of three years, before and after the institution of a "cop on the street" program in which a substantial number of police officers moved out of their cruisers and began walking street beats.

the difference. However, time-series designs can be even more conclusive if the events of interest produce changes in the dependent variable more than once over the series. For instance, in a classic study of the effects of violent crimes on aggression, Berkowitz and Macaulay (1971) found that the number of murders in the United States increased dramatically in the months following the assassination of President John Kennedy in 1963 and also increased after the highly publicized mass murders by Richard Speck in 1966. Because homicides increased after *both* events, it is less likely (but not impossible) that something else unrelated to the crimes might have been the causal variable.

Participant-Variable Designs

Although to this point we have considered comparisons across groups of people who have had different experiences, perhaps the most common type of quasi-experimental research design is one in which one or more of the independent variables is a naturally occurring characteristic of individuals—for instance, a demographic variable such as sex or ethnicity or a personality variable such as parenting style, anxiety, or level of prejudice. When the grouping variable involves preexisting characteristics of the participants, the design is known as a **participant-variable design** and the variable that differs across the participants is known as a **participant variable.**

Demographic Variables

We have already considered in Chapter 11 the use of a participant-variable research design where the participant variable is a demographic characteristic—namely, the sex of the participant. The research described in Table 11.1 found that the relationship between viewing violent cartoons and behaving aggressively was different for boys than it was for girls. Similar comparisons could also be made on the basis of the race or the religion of the children, or on any other demographic variable.

Perhaps the most commonly studied demographic variable within the behavioral sciences is age. The fields of developmental psychology and human development are based to a large extent on participant-variable studies that compare the cognitive and social skills of individuals, particularly children, across different age levels. As we have discussed in Chapter 9, these comparisons can be made either between groups (**cross-sectional designs**) or by observing the children repeatedly over time (longitudinal designs). For instance, to study differences in children's memory skills, we could compare kindergarten, second-grade, and fourth-grade children at one time point (a cross-sectional approach), or we could follow the same children as they progress from kindergarten to fourth grade. Because each type of approach has some advantages, both types of designs are sometimes used together (see Applebaum & McCall, 1983).

Personality Variables

In other cases, the participant variable of interest is a trait rather than a demographic characteristic. For instance, a clinical psychologist might compare the social skills of a group of highly anxious individuals (as determined by an anxiety test) with those of a group of less anxious individuals, or a health psychologist might compare the health behaviors of individuals with optimistic personalities with those who have less optimistic personalities.

In some cases, the researcher may be able to select, from a large pool of individuals who have completed the personality test, two groups who have scored high and low. In other cases, when it is not possible to select people ahead of time, the personality measure may be given at the experimental session, and the participants may be divided into those who are above and below the median score on the measure to represent two levels of the personality variable. In other cases, rather than creating groups of individuals, the original quantitative personality variable can be used to predict the dependent variable using a regression analysis (Bissonnette, Ickes, Bernstein, & Knowles, 1990).

Interpretational Difficulties

Because the participant variable is measured, rather than manipulated, causal conclusions about the effect of the participant variable on the dependent variable are difficult to draw. For instance, if participants in a research project are selected on the basis of their scores on an anxiety measure, they are likely to differ as well on many other characteristics. One of these other characteristics, rather than anxiety, may have caused the differences on the dependent measure.

Single-Participant Designs

We have seen that participant-variable studies are used to compare groups of people, whereas time-series designs are used to study behavior over a period of time. However, the ability to track the behavior of individuals over time makes it possible in some cases to draw conclusions about the changes in behavior of a single person. Such studies are called **single-participant research designs.** Consider, for instance, a study designed to assess the effectiveness of a reinforcement therapy program on the speech behavior of an autistic child. As shown in Figure 14.3, the number of speech vocalizations that the child displayed in school was recorded by the child's teachers over a period of three months, both before and after the therapy program was instituted.

Although the goal of this study was to determine the impact of the reinforcement therapy program, the program was not immediately initiated when the study began. Rather, the behavior of the child was tracked for one month to observe the baseline level of vocalization. As you can see, the number of

FIGURE 14.3 Results From a Single-Participant Design

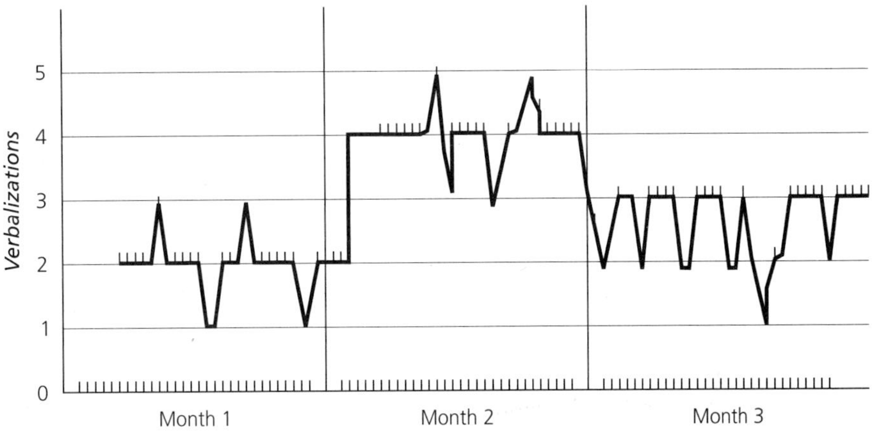

These are the results of a hypothetical study designed to assess the effectiveness of a reinforcement therapy program on the verbal behavior of an autistic child. The data report the number of verbalizations that the child displays in school, as recorded by the child's teacher over a period of three months, both before and after a reinforcement therapy program was instituted.

vocalizations during the baseline period is highly stable—the child had almost an equal number of vocalizations every day. The reinforcement therapy intervention, begun in the second month, caused a very large increase in vocalization in comparison to the variability before the experience. Furthermore, when the reinforcement was removed at the end of the second month, the child's vocalizations again decreased dramatically, although they remained at a somewhat higher level than before the intervention.

You can see that this study is a type of repeated-measures experimental design where behavior is initially measured during a baseline period, measured again after the intervention of interest begins, and then measured once more after the intervention is removed. Such a design is frequently called an **A-B-A design** or a **reversal design** because the condition of interest is first created and then reversed or taken away. It was possible, in this case, to use the A-B-A design to study only one child because behavior during the baseline period was very stable over time and because the therapy intervention had a relatively large effect. Furthermore, despite the fact that only one participant was used because the experimenter was able to control the occurrence of the intervention, the internal validity of the study was high. It was clearly the introduction of the reinforcement therapy that caused the changes in the child's behavior.

Although single-participant designs are useful when the researcher wants to investigate the effects of a particular intervention on a specific individual, they are not common in the behavioral sciences. For one, they can be used only where the effect size of the intervention is relatively large and there is a stable baseline period. But, in most cases, in the behavioral sciences the effect size is relatively small in comparison to the amount of random error. Furthermore, there are no statistical tests for assessing the effectiveness of the intervention in a single-participant design. In some cases, the effects of the intervention are so large that no statistical analysis is necessary and the results can be seen visually. For example, it is clear that the reinforcement therapy increased verbalizations in our example. In other cases, however, the effects are not so clear. For instance, it is difficult to tell whether the rate of verbalizations for our child was meaningfully higher in the third month, after the therapy was over, than it had been in the first month baseline period. Finally, single-participant designs also suffer from threats to external validity because there is little guarantee that the results found for one individual will generalize to others.

Current Research in the Behavioral Sciences: Damage to the Hippocampus Abolishes the Cortisol Response to Psychosocial Stress in Humans

Tony W. Buchanan, Daniel Tranel, and Clemens Kirschbaum (2009) studied the role of the brain region known as the hippocampus in behaviors related to stress and anxiety. They used a comparison-group before-after design in which they compared the responses of participants with damage to their hippocampus to control individuals who had similar brain damage to other regions of the brain as well as to a group of normal individuals, both before and after they experienced a stressful situation. This approach allowed the researchers to view the responses to stress over time, and also to control for brain damage more generally (the brain damage comparison group). And the authors also increased their control by matching the groups on other variables that might have been important, including age and sex. The dependent measures were reaction to stress, operationalized in terms of salivary cortisol, heart rate, and self-reported affective responses.

The participants in the study included 7 participants with bilateral hippocampus lesions, 12 participants with brain damage outside of the hippocampus, and 28 healthy, normal comparison participants who were matched to the hippocampus participants on age and sex. During the laboratory experiment, the participants all completed the Trier Social Stress Test (Kirschbaum, Pirke, & Hellhammer, 1993) in which they delivered a speech in front of two experimenters. Saliva samples were obtained at three time points: 15 minutes after arrival in the laboratory, and at 10 minutes and 30 minutes after the speech. Salivary cortisol was measured with a commercial immunoassay kit. The participants also completed two self-report measures of affect, and their heart rate was measured.

Although the three groups of participants did not significantly differ on the self-report measure or on heart rate, their measured cortisol levels

FIGURE 14.4   Responses to Stress Across Groups With and Without Brain Lesions

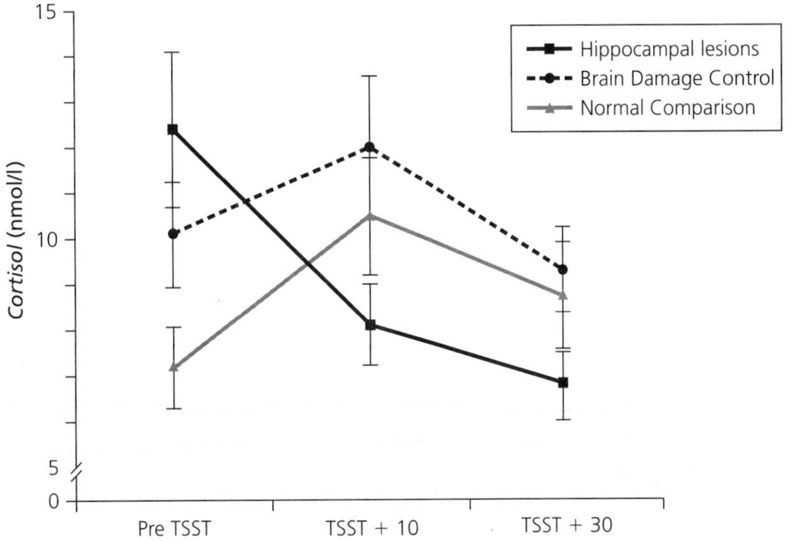

This chart shows mean measured salivary cortisol levels before, 10 min, and 30 min after the Trier Social Stress Test (TSST) in the hippocampal group (HC), the brain damage comparison group (BDC), and the normal comparison group (NC). Data are from Buchanan, T. W., Tranel, D., & Kirschbaum, C. (2009). Hippocampal damage abolishes the cortisol response to psychosocial stress in humans. *Hormones and Behavior, 56*(1), 44–50.

were significantly different across the three time periods. As you can seen in Figure 14.4, within-participant analyses of each of the three groups showed that both control groups showed highest levels of cortisol at 10 minutes after the end of the stress test, whereas the group with the hippocampus lesions did not show any increases at all (in fact, their cortisol levels decreased over time). The authors concluded that damage to the hippocampus (but not other types of brain lesion) abolishes the cortisol response to stress.

SUMMARY

Quasi-experimental research designs are used when it is not possible to randomly assign individuals to groups. Such studies are common in program evaluation research, which involves assessing the effects of training and therapy programs. In other cases the research involves comparisons among individuals who differ on demographic or personality variables.

There are several common quasi-experimental research designs, including the single-group design, the comparison-group design, the before-after design, and the comparison-group before-after design. In general, because participants have not been randomly assigned to the groups, quasi-experimental research has more threats to internal validity than do true experiments. Because the participants select whether to participate in a given treatment, the individuals in the different groups are not equivalent before the differences in the independent variable occur. Furthermore, the participants may decide to drop out of the research before it is over. Other threats result from the presence of extraneous variables, such as changes in the individuals (maturation) or in the experimental setting (history) that occur over time and that influence the dependent measure.

Time-series designs involve the measurement of behavior more than twice over a period of time. Such designs allow the researcher to get a good idea about what changes occur over the time period being studied. When the initial rate of a behavior is very stable, it is sometimes possible to draw inferences about the behavior of a single participant by observing him or her over time.

KEY TERMS

A-B-A design 285
attrition 278
comparison group 276
comparison-group before-after
    design 279
comparison-group design 277
cross-sectional designs 283
history threats 278
maturation threats 278
mortality 278
participant variable 283

participant-variable design 283
quasi-experimental research
    designs 274
regression to the mean 280
reversal design 285
selection threats 277
single-group before-after design 278
single-group design 274
single-participant research
    designs 284
time-series designs 282

REVIEW AND DISCUSSION QUESTIONS

1. What are quasi-experimental research designs, and when are they used in behavioral research? What advantages and disadvantages do they have in comparison to experimental research?

2. What are the most important threats to validity that occur in quasi-experimental research designs when individuals are not randomly assigned to groups? What techniques can be used to minimize these potential interpretive problems?

3. What are the most important threats to validity that occur in quasi-experimental research designs when the research is conducted over a period of time? What techniques can be used to minimize these potential interpretive problems?

4. What is regression to the mean, and why is it a threat to the validity of research designs in which random assignment has not been used?

5. What are time-series research designs, and how are they used to learn about changes in behavior over time?

6. What types of independent variables can be used in participant-variable research designs, and what conclusions can and cannot be drawn from their use?

7. What are single-participant research designs? When are they used, and what are their limitations?

RESEARCH PROJECT IDEAS

1. A researcher has developed the hypothesis that teenagers are better able to learn about and remember technological information than are older adults, whereas older adults are better able to remember information about historical events than are teenagers. Develop a 2 × 2 factorial design that could test this research hypothesis. What type of design is the research? What pattern of data is expected, and what conclusions could be drawn if the data come out as expected?

2. Make up an example, other than those used in the text, of an everyday phenomenon that might be explained in terms of regression to the mean but that people might believe had another cause.

APPENDIX A
Reporting Research Results

Communication of Scientific Knowledge
Face-to-Face Contact
Publication in Scientific Journals

The Research Report
Headings in APA Format
Title Page
Abstract
Introduction
Method
Results

Discussion
References
Footnotes and Author Notes
Tables and Figures

Tips on Writing the Research Report

Summary

Key Terms

Review and Discussion Questions

Research Project Ideas

STUDY QUESTIONS

- How do scientists share their research findings with others?

- Through what stages does a research report go as it is considered for publication in a scientific journal?

- What are the major sections of a research report, and what information is contained in each section?

- What are the important goals to keep in mind when writing a research report?

To this point we have discussed how researchers develop and test their research hypotheses and analyze and interpret the data they collect. Having accomplished these steps, the researcher may be in the enviable position of having collected data that support the proposed research hypothesis or that produce other unexpected but interesting results. In such cases the researcher will naturally want to communicate these findings to others. This is the ultimate goal of every scientist—contributing to the accumulation of scientific knowledge. In Appendix A we will consider how research is shared, with a particular emphasis on the practical aspects of writing a research report using American Psychological Association format.

Communication of Scientific Knowledge

Although a written research report will almost always be the final and definitive description of a scientific research project, the results of research are also shared through other media. Science is inherently a social enterprise, and information is often shared with other scientists in whatever ways are most convenient, enjoyable, fastest, and cheapest. This appendix will consider some of the ways that researchers share their ideas and their findings with others and will then discuss the format and style of written research reports.

Face-to-Face Contact

One way that scientists share their ideas is through direct contact with each other. It is a rather strange experience being a researcher working at a university because, unlike large corporations that have a corporate headquarters where many employees work together, the scientific colleagues of university professors are spread out around the world at different universities.

Professional Collaboration.   Scientists often collaborate with others on their research projects even when these colleagues are not nearby. Collaboration is efficient in the sense that more resources can be brought to bear on the problem of interest. Researchers working together share ideas, lab space, research funds, and their own time. However, because research collaborators are often located in different places around the world, communication is critical. The conduct of scientific research has been made much more efficient through recent technological advances in information transmission such as fax machines and e-mail. Because these sources of communication are inexpensive, quick, and readily available to researchers, they are used heavily. Although hard copies of journals are not yet out of date, much communication among scientists now occurs informally through electronic media, and many journals are now available electronically through libraries.

Scientific Meetings.   In addition to electronic communications, most researchers regularly attend professional meetings and conferences where they share their ideas and their research results in person with other scientists, both formally and informally. Formal presentations are made at conferences in the form of talks as well as at poster presentations in which the researcher displays data in a public forum and conference participants come around to look at and discuss them. These exchanges are extremely important to the advancement of science because they provide a forum in which colleagues can respond to and critique a scientist's work on the spot and while it is in progress. This feedback, which usually occurs in a friendly and helpful manner, can be extremely valuable in helping the scientist develop new ideas and determine new directions for future research. Informally, scientists spend time at conferences in restaurants and cafés, conversing and relaxing. These exchanges provide a chance to share ideas, and many important scientific ideas have been generated in such settings. Scientific meetings are particularly useful because they allow scientists to share the most up-to-date information about their research with each other.

Professional Organizations. Most researchers belong to one or more professional organizations that hold annual conferences. Within the field of psychology, these include the meetings of the *American Psychological Society (APS)* and the *American Psychological Association (APA)*. Sociologists attend the meetings of the *American Sociological Association (ASA)*. These meetings are large conferences, held during the summer months in major cities in the United States or Canada, where students and faculty members from all over North America present their latest research findings. The APA, APS, and ASA conventions, as well as many local conventions in your area, are open to undergraduate and graduate students.

If you are interested in a career in behavioral research, consider attending a scientific conference and perhaps submitting your research for potential inclusion in the program. Although attendance can sometimes be costly (you must pay for transportation, food, and lodging as well as a registration fee, although the latter is usually reduced for students), there is no substitute for learning what research is about and what types of people conduct it and for making contacts with these people.

Publication in Scientific Journals

Even though the avenues through which scientific knowledge is communicated are always changing, most research is still ultimately published in scientific journals, either in traditional book format or online. Scientists consider the publication of journal articles to be the ultimate test of success. If their work is published in important journals, and if other scientists read this work and cite it, they rightly feel that their work has had an impact on the field.

The process that leads to the ultimate publication of research results in a scientific journal involves a series of stages and takes a substantial amount of time. The first step is to write the research report—known at this stage as the "manuscript." It is not easy to write a research report. The work is painstaking and involves much specific knowledge and many skills. Because there are so many things to be done, problems can develop. It will probably take you at least twice as long to write your first research report as you think it will.

Scientists spend a good portion of their time writing professional papers, painstakingly going over every detail to make sure that each report is accurate, complete, persuasive, and fair. I often spend several months working on a manuscript, verifying that everything is correct. I read the paper again and again, checking the report with the data I have collected and making changes that I think result in a more informative and easier-to-read paper.

APA Format. Research reports in the behavioral sciences are written in one or more standard formats, as specified by the basic conventions of the scientific method. Before beginning to write a report, you should determine the appropriate guidelines for the journal or other outlet that you plan to use for your paper. Journal editors and publishers are quite serious about following the appropriate format. If you submit a manuscript that does not follow the guidelines, they may not read it at all.

One formal set of guidelines that has been used almost exclusively in psychological research, and frequently in other areas of behavioral science research, is the format outlined in the sixth edition of the *Publication Manual of the American Psychological Association* (2009). If you are planning to submit a research report to a journal, and if that journal requests that submitted manuscripts use APA format, it is well worth the investment to purchase a copy of this paperback. Because of its popularity and extensive use in social science journals, the APA format will form the basis of this discussion of the format of research reports. Other formats will be very similar. In addition to the publication manual, the APA also publishes a computer program called *APA-Style Helper.* This program works with your word processor to help you format an APA-style paper. There is also a workbook and training guide for the *APA Publication Manual* (Gelfand & Walker, 2001). These materials can be purchased from the APA website: *www.apa.org,* and you can link to this site from the textbook web page.

You may think that following the details of the APA format makes for a lot of work and results in boring reading, but scientists see the format as an important method for acquiring, organizing, and sharing knowledge (Madigan, Johnson, & Linton, 1995). It is true that the rules specified in the APA manual do not allow the researcher much leeway—writing a journal article is not like writing poetry. As we have seen, science is an organized discipline, and just as the scientific method determines how data are collected, analyzed, and interpreted, it also determines how they are reported. Everyone does reporting in the same way, and this makes for regularity and objectivity, if some monotony. Use of the standard format is thus one part of the scientific process and makes it easy for readers to quickly find the information they are looking for in your report. Furthermore, many aspects of the APA format are designed to help typesetters and proofreaders as the manuscript is prepared for publication.

Submission of the Manuscript. Once the research manuscript is completed, it is sent to a scientific journal for consideration for publication. There are many different journals that publish behavioral science research, and the decision of which journal to send a manuscript to is made on the basis of both the content and the quality of the research. In terms of content, an article on child development would be sent to a developmental psychology journal, whereas a paper on organizational behavior would be suited for an industrial organizational journal. Sometimes the data have not worked out as well as the researcher might have hoped, or maybe the researcher decides that the research hypothesis was not as interesting as he or she had thought when data collection began. If this is the case, then the researcher might choose to send the manuscript to a journal that publishes shorter articles or those of lesser quality. Other times the data have worked out well, and the researcher believes the paper is suitable for publication in a top-notch journal.

After having chosen a journal, the researcher will locate the name and address of the journal's editor in a recent edition of the journal. The editor is a senior scientist in the area who serves as the final decision maker regarding which articles are suitable for publication in the journal. Once the manuscript is submitted to the editor (and this is often done electronically now), the researcher may just as well forget about the paper for about three months or even more while the paper is under peer review.

Peer Review.   When the journal editor receives the submitted manuscript, he or she will choose three or four scientists to serve as peer reviewers. **Peer review** is the process by which the people who can best judge the quality of the research—other people in the scientist's field—read and comment on the manuscript. Often these people come from the group of scientists who constitute the editorial board of the journal. The submitted manuscript is sent to each of these reviewers, who read and study the paper and return their comments to the editor. Among other things, the reviewers assess the importance of the research, its scientific rigor, and the writing style. Usually reviewers are fair and objective, but just as in any other stage of the research process, personal values and biases may at times come into play.

Once the editor has received two or three reviews of the manuscript and has read it carefully, he or she writes an "action letter" to the author. In this letter the editor summarizes his or her own reactions to the paper, informed by the comments of the reviewers, and also communicates a decision about the fate of the paper. In most cases the author also receives copies of the reviewers' comments, although the identities of the reviewers are usually withheld from the author. In the best case the editor will decide that the paper makes an important enough contribution to be accepted for publication. Even in this happy case, the author will usually have to make some revisions first. More likely, the editor will not be happy with the manuscript as it stands and will require the author to make many revisions before publication. Sometimes the editor will request the author to collect more data to rule out potential alternative explanations of the results or to further demonstrate the findings. This revision may be sent out for further peer review.

Unfortunately, the most common outcome of the peer review process is rejection. The editor has decided that the manuscript is not suitable for publication in the journal. He or she may have found alternative explanations for the results or may have decided that the results are not strong enough or interesting enough to warrant publication. The problem is not always only one of quality. There are a limited number of journal pages available, and often even high-quality research cannot be published for lack of space. At this point the author may decide to submit the manuscript to another journal, where the entire peer review process begins over again, or to collect new data. Although sending the manuscript to another journal after it has been rejected from one is entirely appropriate, the author should submit the manuscript to only one journal at a time. In every case, however, the author should carefully consider the comments of the editor and reviewers and thoroughly revise the manuscript before resubmitting it.

Publication Lag.   You probably now realize why scientists rely so much on e-mail and personal communication to share their research results with others. By the time a paper is published in a journal (even if it is accepted on the first round), over a year will likely have elapsed since the manuscript was first submitted. Publishing research in scientific journals is a long and arduous process, which is frequently rewarded with rejection and infrequently rewarded with publication. Although the peer review process takes a long time, it helps ensure that high-quality papers are published and that these papers are improved before publication through the input from knowledgeable experts in the field. The rewards of publication include a personal sense of achievement and the knowledge that you have contributed to the accumulation of scientific knowledge. With this glad news in mind, let's turn to the details of the research report.

The Research Report

Developing an idea for research, collecting the data, and analyzing them to draw appropriate conclusions are only one part of the research process. It is safe to say that most researchers struggle over writing up their research as much as they do over designing or conducting it. Writing research reports takes plenty of effort and practice—it is not something that comes naturally to most people. As you write your first research report, you will struggle to organize the information in a coherent manner, to make sure that the reader can understand your procedures, and to present your data accurately and fairly. Becoming proficient requires perseverance.

In the next sections I will outline APA publication format, consider some issues of style, and then present some suggestions for writing good research reports.[1] As summarized in the figure on the inside of the front cover of this book, there are five major sections to the research report written in APA format:

Abstract

Introduction

---

[1] For even more information, you might want to look at an article by Bem (1987) and a book by Sternberg (1993), as well as the American Psychological Association's manual (2010).

Methods

Results

Discussion

Although these five sections form the bulk of the report, there are also five other sections that contain important information:

Title Page

References

Endnotes and Author Notes

Tables and Figures

Appendices

Although the major goal of the format is to allow efficient presentation of the data, the format can also facilitate the writing of an interesting and informative story in the sense that all of the pieces of the research report fit together to create a coherent whole. One method of helping accomplish this is to write the manuscript in an "hourglass" shape in which the report begins at a general level, progresses to more specific details, and then returns to a broad level in the final section. The hourglass approach is diagrammed in Figure A.1.

There are many specific details of the APA format, and one of the most useful ways to learn about these details is to carefully study a draft manuscript that has already been written in APA style. An annotated sample of a manuscript is provided at the end of this chapter, and a checklist for avoiding some common errors is shown in Table A.1.

Although the APA format provides many details about how the research report is to be written, it cannot be used to make every decision for you. There are no absolute rules for writing research reports, only general guidelines, and thus you will have to use your own good sense to create a high-quality report. You must strive for clarity and organization, but you will also need to be concise. The latter will involve making many decisions about what is important enough to include and what needs to be left out.

Headings in APA Format

One of the important aspects of the APA format is that it arranges all of the information in the report in a logical manner. The sections follow in a specified order, and each section contains a certain set of information. Each section should contain only the information appropriate to that section.

To help organize the paper, APA format makes use of a system of headings. First, the research report has a *page heading* that is printed at the top of each page, along with the page number. This heading normally is the first two or three words of the title of the research report. Furthermore, each section, and subsection, of the research report has its own heading. As shown in Figure A.2, in most cases three or four levels of headings are sufficient. If you need only

FIGURE A.1   "Using the "Hourglass Shape" to Write an Effective Research Report

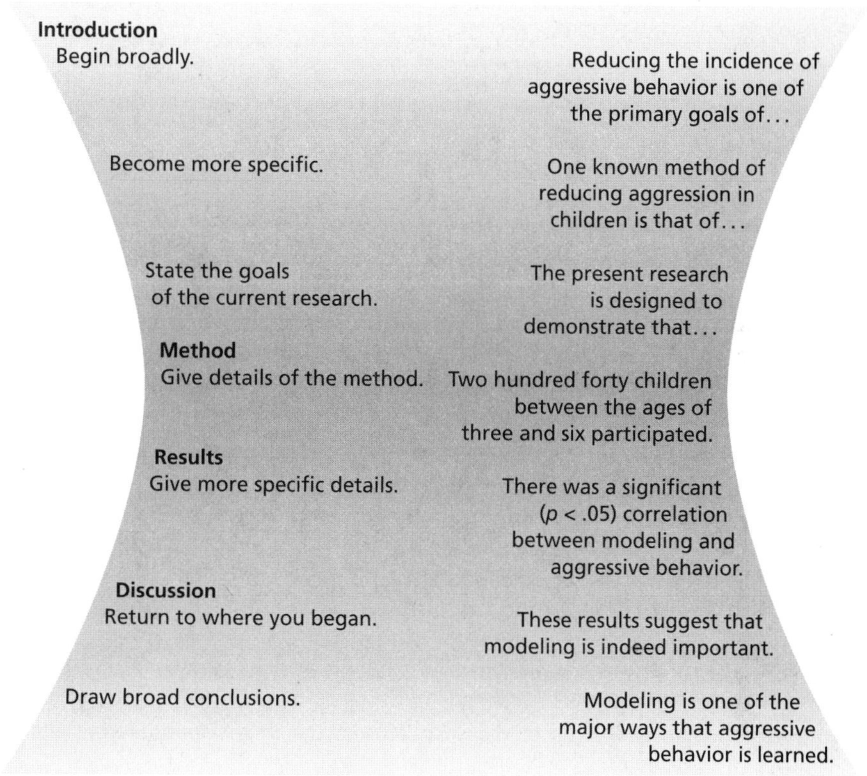

Introduction
Begin broadly.

Reducing the incidence of aggressive behavior is one of the primary goals of…

Become more specific.

One known method of reducing aggression in children is that of…

State the goals of the current research.

The present research is designed to demonstrate that…

Method
Give details of the method.

Two hundred forty children between the ages of three and six participated.

Results
Give more specific details.

There was a significant ($p < .05$) correlation between modeling and aggressive behavior.

Discussion
Return to where you began.

These results suggest that modeling is indeed important.

Draw broad conclusions.

Modeling is one of the major ways that aggressive behavior is learned.

two, use the Level 1 and Level 3 headings. If you need only three, use Levels 1, 3, and 4. If you need more than four, consult the APA publication manual.

Figure A.3 shows a schematic diagram of a sample research report with the appropriate headings.

Title Page

The research report begins with a title page, numbered as page 1 of the manuscript. Along with the title of the paper, this page also contains the names and the institutional affiliations of the author or authors, as well as a **running head** of not more than fifty characters. The running head identifies the research topic and will appear on the top of every other page of the journal article when it is published, just as the running head "Appendix A REPORTING RESEARCH RESULTS" is printed at the top of this page.

Describing the Nature of the Research.   The title of the research report should accurately describe the nature of the research in about ten to twelve words.

TABLE A.1 APA Format Checklist

Overall

Use 1-inch margins on all sides.

Use left justification on your word processor, not full justification.

Place footnotes at the end of the manuscript, not at the bottom of the page.

Place figures and tables at the end of the manuscript.

Title Page

The running head should be left justified and typed in capitals. Number the title page as page 1.

Abstract

The first line of the abstract is *not* indented.

Introduction

Begin the Introduction section on a new page. Center the title of the manuscript (upper and lower case) at the top of the first page. Do *not* label this section as Introduction.

Method

Do *not* begin on a new page.

Use the past tense to describe a study that has already been completed (e.g., "I ran 100 participants.")

Results

Do *not* begin on a new page.

Some common abbreviations should always be used. The abbreviations are the same in singular and plural, and do not have periods after them:

cm = centimeter	dB = decibel
g = gram	hr = hour
m = meter	mg = milligram
min = minutes	ml = milliliter
mm = millimeter	ms = millisecond
s = seconds	

References in the Text

Use the word *and* to separate authors when the reference is not in parentheses, but use the symbol & to separate authors when the reference is in parentheses.

Use only the last name, not the initials, of the authors.

List of references are alphabetized by the last name of the author, and separated by semicolons.

Indicate the year of publication every time you cite the work.

Reference List

Begin the reference list on a new page.

FIGURE A.2 Manuscript Headings in APA Format

APA Style Headings: 6th Edition

Level	Format
1	**Centered, Boldface, Uppercase and Lowercase Heading** Then your paragraph begins below, indented like a regular paragraph.
2	**Flush Left, Boldface, Uppercase, and Lowercase Heading** Then your paragraph begins below, indented like a regular paragraph.
3	**Indented, boldface, lowercase paragraph heading ending with a period.** Your paragraph begins right here, in line with the heading.[a]
4	***Indented, boldface, italicized, lowercase paragraph heading ending with a period.*** Your paragraph begins right here, in line with the heading.
5	*Indented, italicized, lowercase paragraph heading ending with a period.* Your paragraph begins right here, in line with the heading.

---

[a]For headings at Levels 3–5, the first letter of the first word in the heading is uppercase, and the remaining words are lowercase (except for proper nouns and the first word to follow a colon).

Because most research hypotheses involve an independent and dependent variable and the finding of a specific relationship between them, this relationship can usually be the basis of the title. Consider the following titles:

"Positive Mood Makes Judgments of Others' Emotions More Positive"
"Saccharine Enhances Concept Learning in Pigeons"

These titles are precise because they specify the independent and dependent variables as well as the specific relationship found between them. In contrast, the title "A Study of Learning and Forgetting" is poor because it wastes space by stating the obvious (that the research report describes a study) and because it does not say much about how learning and forgetting are measured or about how they are found to be related.

Listing the Authors.   A decision must also be made regarding who should be an author on the paper and what order the authors' names should follow if there are more than one. These decisions are made in terms of the magnitude of each person's contribution to the research project, and only those individuals who have made substantial contributions are listed as authors. The American Psychological Association publication manual offers some guidelines in this regard, but there are no hard and fast rules. When there is more than one author and each has contributed equally, the order of authorship may be determined randomly.

Abstract

The second page of the research report contains the Abstract, which provides a short summary of the entire research report. The Abstract is limited to a maximum of 120 words. Particular care should be taken in writing the

FIGURE A.3   Page Sequence for a Report in APA Format

Page Heading 1	Page Heading 2	Page Heading 3	Page Heading 4
Running head: ____ Title Author Name Affiliation Author Name Affiliation	Abstract —————— —————— —————— —————— (not more than 150 words)	Title —————— —————— —————— —————— ——————	—————— —————— —————— —————— —————— —————— —————— ——————

Page Heading 5	Page Heading 6	Page Heading 7	Page Heading 8
Method *Overview* —————— —————— —————— —————— ——————	*Participants* —————— —————— —————— *Stimulus Materials* —————— —————— ——————	*Procedure* —————— —————— —————— —————— —————— —————— ——————	—————— —————— —————— Results —————— ——————

Page Heading 9	Page Heading 10	Page Heading 11	Page Heading 12
—————— —————— Discussion —————— —————— —————— —————— ——————	References —————— —————— —————— —————— —————— ——————	Appendix —————— —————— —————— —————— —————— ——————	Author Note —————— —————— —————— —————— —————— ——————

Page Heading 13	Page Heading 14	Page Heading 15	
Footnotes —————— —————— —————— —————— —————— ——————	Table 1 *Table Title* [table] Table Notes _____	Figure Caption(s) *Figure 1.* _____ —————— ——————. *Figure 2.* _____ —————— ——————.	(Figures are placed last, one per page. Indicate figure number on back.)

The abstract, introduction, references, author notes, footnotes, table, figure captions, and figures each start on a new page.

Abstract because it, along with the title, will be contained in computer data-bases, such as those discussed in Chapter 2, and thus will be used by those deciding whether to read the entire paper.

I usually write the Abstract last after I know what I have to summarize. I try to take one or two sentences each from the Introduction, Methods, and Results sections to form the Abstract. Because the Abstract should use similar words to describe the research as are used in the research report itself, it is relatively easy to write. It is not usually a good idea to review the Discussion section in the Abstract—there is not enough space, and the Method and Results are more important.

Introduction

The body of the research report begins on the third page of the manuscript with the Introduction section. The title of the research report is centered at the top of this page. The general tasks of this section are to outline the goals and purposes of your research, to inform the reader about past research that is relevant to your research, and to link your research to those earlier findings. You must also explain why your research is interesting and important and try to get readers interested in the research project.

Engaging the Reader. In many ways the Introduction serves as the warm-up band for the headliner show that is going to follow—the Introduction is designed to get people's attention and prepare them for the research. One of my favorite examples of an opening paragraph in a research report is the following, from a paper by Lord and Gilbert (1983, p. 751):

> A graduate student and a professor were discussing evidence that California sunshine puts people in a good mood. "When I moved across the country," said the graduate student, "I noticed that the people who waited on me in stores and restaurants in California were more pleasant than those on the East Coast." "I have a better story than that," countered the professor. "When the moving men picked up our furniture on the East Coast they were thoroughly obnoxious. We drove across the country to California and arrived to find the moving men sitting on the front lawn in the sunshine, eating fried chicken. They greeted us warmly and were quite genial and accommodating in delivering our furniture. These were the *same men,* mind you." The graduate student and the professor agreed that the latter evidence was more compelling.

Who wouldn't be interested in reading such a paper?

Highlighting Relevant Existing Research. Once the general problem being investigated has been presented, the existing literature relevant to the current project is discussed, with an emphasis on how the present research is designed to build on the earlier findings and thus contribute to the accumulation of scientific knowledge. Only literature that is relevant to the current hypothesis is cited. The reader doesn't need a whole lot of information about this existing literature, only enough to indicate what it has shown, how it is limited, and how the new research is going to relate to it. The literature review must not stand separate from your research; rather, it becomes an integral part of the story that your research is designed to relate. The literature is always presented in a way that sets up your project as a logical extension of previous work.

After reviewing the literature, you can tie it into your research with sentences such as the following:

"Although the results of the previous research are consistent with the proposed hypothesis, an alternative explanation is still possible."

"Despite this research, very little is known about ..."

"One basic limitation with this research is that it has not ..."

Stating the Research Hypothesis.   Another major goal of the Introduction section is to explicitly define the conceptual variables that you will be investigating (see Chapter 4). For instance, if the study involves the assessment of "concept formation," you must be certain to define what concept formation is. Relating the conceptual variable to definitions used in past research can be useful in this regard.

By the end of the Introduction section, the writing begins to become more focused. We are now reaching the narrow part of the hourglass in Figure A.1. At this point the general ideas and limitations of previous work have been clearly made, and the goals of the present research have been outlined. The goal now is to give the reader more specifics about the research that is to follow. The general ideas are refined into the specific operational definitions of the independent and dependent variables, and the research hypothesis is stated. At this point it may be useful to consider potential problems that might be encountered in the research, as well as discuss how you hope to avoid them.

"Rewriting the Introduction."   One problem that frequently occurs in research is that the collected data do not exactly support the original research hypothesis that led to the creation of the research design. Perhaps the data only confirmed one part of the predictions and not another part, or maybe the researcher has discovered other interesting but unexpected relationships between the variables. In these cases the question becomes whether to write the Introduction section in terms of the original predictions, and then explain in the discussion the ways in which the results were unexpected, or to "rewrite" the Introduction as if the results that were found had been predicted all along.

It may seem that reframing and rewriting the research hypothesis are not very scientific, but this is not true. Although research is always designed to test a specific research hypothesis, that hypothesis is only one of the many possible hypotheses that could have been proposed, and in the end the observed data are more important than the original hypothesis. In fact, it can be argued that collected data are really no more important when they support a predicted research hypothesis than when they support an equally interesting but completely unexpected hypothesis. Of course, if your research has tested but failed to support a hypothesis derived from an important theory, it will be of interest to readers to mention this.

Because the collected data almost never exactly support the original research hypothesis, it is frequently useful to reframe or recast the Introduction of the report in terms of the findings that were actually significant. In some cases this may even involve reformulating the original research hypothesis. Although you may not find this procedure to be elegant, it has the inherent advantage of making the research report easier to understand and reducing the complexity of the paper. In the long run, rest assured that what is important is that the data you report be interesting and replicable, not necessarily that they exactly support your original research hypothesis (Madigan et al., 1995).

Method

The goal of the Method section is to precisely describe how the research was conducted from beginning to end. Precision is required in this regard so that the readers can follow exactly what was done, allowing them to draw appropriate conclusions about the data and to conduct an exact replication of the study should they so desire. At the same time, however, the Method section must also be concise, and only those details that are important need to be reported. In contrast to the other sections, which normally stand on their own, the Method section is normally made up of several subsections. The most common of these are reviewed here, although you may decide to use others as well, depending on the needs of your research report.

Participants.   This subsection provides a detailed description of the individuals who participated in the research, including the population from which the individuals were drawn, the sample size (N), and the sampling techniques used to select the sample (see Chapter 7). If any participants were deleted before the statistical analyses were conducted, this should be mentioned (see Appendix B). Any other information that you think is relevant to the research should also be included. For instance, if the research project involves college students, it is probably not necessary to report their average age or IQ. But if the participants were drawn from a special population, such as those with a particular personality disorder, the characteristics of the population and the sample will need to be described in detail. If the research is a survey study, then detailed information about the sampling procedures is necessary, whereas if it is an experimental study involving a convenience sample of college students, only this needs to be mentioned.

It is standard practice to indicate the number of men and women who participated in the research, but other potential differences among participants, such as age, race, or ethnicity, are not normally reported unless they are deemed relevant. What you report will also depend on whether you choose to look for or to report any differences you may have found between men and women or among different ethnic groups.

Materials and Apparatus.   This subsection provides details about the stimulus materials used as the independent and dependent variables. Stimulus materials may include videotapes, transparencies, computer programs, or questionnaires. In the latter case, the procedures used to develop the items in the scale would be described, as well as the number of questions and the response format. In many cases details about the scale have been reported in previous research reports, and it is only necessary to direct the reader to these existing papers. Again, the goal is to provide enough information to allow an exact replication but to avoid irrelevant details.

If you have used any special equipment, such as for collecting physiological responses or reaction times, you will need to describe the equipment. Appropriate descriptions will allow another person who wants to run the study to use the same or equivalent equipment.

Procedure.   The Procedure subsection is designed to completely describe the experience of being a participant in the research project and should include enough details that the reader can understand exactly what happened to the participant and conduct an exact replication of the research. The depth and length of this description will vary depending on the research design. In survey research, for instance, it may only be necessary in the Procedure to briefly describe when and where the measures were completed. Experimental designs, in contrast, will generally involve a longer description.

In a laboratory experiment involving the manipulation of the independent variable, the Procedure will provide details about the order in which all of the events occurred, beginning with the greeting of the participants by the experimenter and ending with the mention of their debriefing (see Chapter 3). It is usually most convenient to describe the Procedure following the order in which the events occurred, but in some cases it is more efficient to first describe the parts of the research that were common to all of the participants (for instance, the greeting, instructions, dependent measures, and debriefing) and then later to specify the changes that produced the different levels of the independent variable.

Results

The Results section presents the statistical analyses of the data. It is the most fine-grained of all of the sections and is therefore a place where the flow of the research report can bog down. The writer needs to think carefully about how to keep the paper smoothly moving along in a concise manner, while being certain to include all of the necessary statistical tests. This flow of the results can usually be enhanced if the order in which they are presented is arranged either in terms of (1) importance, (2) what the researcher expected to find, or (3) the sequence in which the variables were collected.

One technique is to write the Results section first without any statistics and then to add the statistical tests. You should try to write this section so that it would be understandable for someone who didn't read the rest of the report. You can do this by beginning the Results section with a brief restatement of the experimental hypothesis and the names of the independent and dependent variables (for instance, "The reader will recall that this research tested the hypothesis that reaction times would be influenced by both previous exposure and word content").

Determining What to Include. One of the major difficulties at this point is to determine what information should be put in the Results and what must be saved for the Discussion. Although the Results section should formally include only the statistical analyses of the data, it is often tempting and frequently useful to briefly discuss the meaning of the results as they are presented rather than waiting to do so. One solution that can be used if the paper is relatively short is to combine the Results and Discussion sections into a single section entitled "Results and Discussion."

In most cases, an initial goal of the Results section will be to document the effectiveness of the manipulated and measured variables. The reliability of the measured variables and the outcomes of any manipulation checks that were collected should be reported. Only after the measurement issues have been addressed are the results of the tests of the research hypothesis presented. Generally, it is friendlier to the reader if the findings are first stated in everyday language and then the statistical tests are reported. For instance, we might state, "The expected differences were found: 94 percent of animals who had ingested saccharine completed the task, whereas only 71 percent of those who had ingested the placebo did so." Then we would continue on to report the statistical test that confirmed the significance of the difference between the groups.

Knowing what *not* to include in the Results can be just as important as knowing what to include. For instance, you do not need to include statistical formulas or the name of the statistical software used to analyze the data unless these are new or likely to be unknown. You do need to make clear what statistical tests you used in the analysis, but you can assume that readers are familiar with these tests, and you do not have to describe what they are or how they are to be used. The appropriate results of the statistical tests, such as Ns or degrees of freedom, means and standard deviations, p-values and effect sizes, must of course be reported.

Deciding Whether to Use Tables and Figures. Another decision concerns whether to use tables and figures to present the data. If the analysis is relatively simple, they are not necessary, and the means and the statistical tests can be reported in the text. However, if there are a large number of correlations or means to report, then a table should be used. A general rule is that any information should be placed either in the text or in a figure or table but not in more than one place. When tables or figures are used, the reader should always be referred to them (for instance, "The mean ratings in each of the experimental conditions are shown in Table 1").

Discussion

In the Discussion section you will (1) review your major findings and provide your own interpretation of their meaning, (2) attempt to integrate the findings with other research, and (3) note possible qualifications and limitations of the results. The Discussion also presents an opportunity to focus on the unique responses of the participants. A description, for instance, of how specific individuals responded to the suspicion check or debriefing procedure might be appropriate.

The Discussion normally begins with a brief summary of the major findings. Because the findings have usually been stated in a piecemeal fashion in the Results, this is an opportunity to integrate them into a coherent whole. This summary section should be brief, however, and no new statistical tests should be reported either here or anywhere in the Discussion.

After the summary, the Discussion will turn to your interpretation of the results and your attempt to integrate them with those of previous research. Because your expectations in this regard have already been framed in the Introduction, the discussion can frequently be organized in a way that systematically answers the questions that have been proposed in the Introduction and that your research has (at least partially) answered. It is a good idea to check that every claim that you make about how the data have supported your research hypothesis is supported by an appropriate statistic, as reported in the Results. The Discussion may also be used to discuss alternative interpretations of your results.

Interpreting the Data.   In interpreting your data, emphasize what is new and important about the findings. It is entirely appropriate, and indeed expected, that you will use the Discussion section to draw the most interesting and positive conclusions about the data. It is not appropriate to be overly negative about the importance of the research. Just because there are some limitations in the findings, or because not all of the predictions were supported, this does not mean that the data are uninteresting. Indeed, all research has both strengths and weaknesses, and the Discussion should be focused on the strengths.

Framing the discussion positively does not, however, mean either that the importance of the findings should be overstated or that their limitations should be ignored. Rather, you must attempt to make sure that the conclusions match the true import of the data. It is not appropriate to state that the research is the definitive study in an area, showing all others to be in error, or to proclaim that the findings are going to change the world. To do so ignores the basic principle that science proceeds through the gradual accumulation of knowledge. Any weaknesses or limitations of the research that you may be aware of should be mentioned. The general goal is fairness, and being honest about these limitations may reduce the likelihood that less scientifically sophisticated readers will draw erroneous conclusions about the data.

In general, the better the results have worked out, the shorter the Discussion needs to be. If the predictions were entirely confirmed, all you really need to do is to say that they were and then briefly discuss their implications. If, however, the research hypotheses have not been supported, the Discussion section needs to consider why this might have been. Although interpreting data that do not allow rejection of the null hypothesis is always difficult, keep in mind that even nonsignificant results can contribute to the advancement of scientific knowledge.

If it has turned out that the measured variables were not reliable or construct valid, the appropriate conclusion will necessarily be to question the operational definitions of the conceptual variables. If the measured variables seem to have adequately assessed the conceptual variables, the relevant conclusion is either that the research hypothesis was incorrect or that a Type 2 error was made. Although the latter is always a possibility when results are non-significant (see Chapter 8), it should never be made the primary focus of the discussion of the limitations of a research report.

Considering the Broader Implications. After considering both the strengths and weaknesses of the research in some detail, you may be tempted to end the research report with a call for further research on the topic area, potentially with some suggestions in this regard. Although it is not inappropriate to do so, it is usually even better to end the paper where it began—with a discussion of the implication of the results for the topic area in the broadest possible context. The last paragraphs, which again represent the broad end of the hourglass format, present a chance for you to make some general statements about the impact of the research.

References

APA style uses the "author-year" format in which the last name of the author or authors and the year of publication of the research report are placed in parentheses within the body of the text. The information in the text is sufficient to allow the reader to locate the full citation of the paper in the References section of the article. The entries in the References section are formatted according to APA guidelines. There is a specific format for virtually any type of article, book, book chapter, software package, or other information that needs to be listed in the References. The most frequently used of these text and reference formats are shown in Table A.2. More information about reference styles is available in the *Publication Manual of the American Psychological Association* (American Psychological Association, 2010) and online at www.apastyle.org.

TABLE A.2   APA Reference Format (Revised)

The following are the most commonly used reference formats from the fifth edition of the *Publication Manual of the American Psychological Association* (American Psychological Association, 2001).

Single-Author Journal Article

Cited in text as (Stangor, 1988).

Listed in references as:

Stangor, C. (1988). Stereotype accessibility and information processing. *Personality and Social Psychology Bulletin, 14,* 694–708.

Journal Article with Two Authors

Cited in text as (Stangor & Duan, 1991).

Listed in references as:

Stangor, C, & Duan, C. (1991). Effects of multiple task demands upon memory for information about social groups. *Journal of Experimental Social Psychology 27,* 357–378.

Journal Article with More Than Two Authors

Cited in text as (Stangor, Sullivan, & Ford, 1992) the first time the work is cited, and as (Stangor et al., 1992) every other time.

Listed in references as:

Stangor, C, Sullivan, L. S., & Ford, T. E. (1992). Affective and cognitive determinants of prejudice. *Social Cognition, 9,* 359–380.

Written Book

Cited in text as (Stangor, 2003).

Listed in references as:

Stangor, C. (2007). *Research methods for the behavioral sciences* (3rd ed.). Boston: Houghton Mifflin.

Edited Book

Cited in text as (Macrae, Stangor, & Hewstone, 1996).

Listed in references as:

Macrae, C. N., Stangor, C, & Hewstone, M. (Eds.). (1996). *Foundations of stereotypes and stereotyping.* New York: Guilford Press.

Book Chapter in an Edited Book

Cited in text as (Stangor & Schaller, 1996).

Listed in references as:

Stangor, C, & Schaller, M. (1996). Stereotypes as individual and collective representations. In C. N. Macrae, C. Stangor, & M. Hewstone (Eds.), *Foundations of stereotypes and stereotyping* (pp. 3–37). New York: Guilford Press.

Online Document

Stangor, C. (2009). **Stereotyping, Prejudice and Intergroup Relations Laboratory.** Retrieved August 20, 2009 from http://sites.google.com/site/charlesstangor/SPIRL.

TABLE A.2 APA Reference Format (Continued)

Online document

A DOI (Digital Objective Identifier) is a unique string of numbers assigned to online periodicals to identify their content and provide a consistent link to their location on the Internet. If the DOI is present on the online article, then include it. If the DOI is not present, include the URL.

The References section is a list of all of the literature cited in your paper, alphabetized by the last name of the author. When the same person is the first author on more than one publication, those in which he or she is the only author come first. When two publications have exactly the same author or authors, the ordering is by the year of publication, with earlier publications first.

Footnotes and Author Notes

Footnotes are numbered consecutively in the text and are placed on one or more pages immediately after the References. Footnotes are not placed at the bottom of the pages in the manuscript copy. Footnotes should be kept to a minimum, but are sometimes used to report important information that would bog down the flow of the story if included in the text itself.

Author Notes include the mailing address, telephone number, and e-mail address of one of the authors for future correspondence. The Author Notes may also include any other information that the author wishes to communicate, including the sources of any funds that were obtained to conduct the research, collaborators who are not included as authors, and thanks to individuals who contributed to the project but who are not authors. The Author Notes are placed in the manuscript on a separate page following the Footnotes and will be printed on the first page of the journal article.

Tables and Figures

The tables and figures are numbered consecutively in the text (for instance, Figure 1 and Table 1) and are themselves included as the last pages of the manuscript rather than being inserted within the text. Although this may seem inconvenient to the reader, the procedure groups them together and contributes to the ease of preparing the manuscript for publication. The formats for tables are detailed in the APA publication manual. Each table has a brief title that explains what is included in it, and figures also have captions explaining them, which are printed on a separate page with the heading "Figure Captions" at the top. Write the figure number on the back of each figure to identify it.

Tips on Writing the Research Report

Writing a research report is not something that can easily be taught—it must be learned through experience. However, there are a few basic rules that may be useful to you.

1. *Be organized.* Think about what you're going to say before you start. Organize both across and within the sections of the report. Before you start writing, make an outline of what you plan to say and where you plan to say it. Be sure that the Discussion addresses all of the questions that were raised in the Introduction.

2. *Be precise.* Say exactly what you mean and exactly what you did. Define your conceptual variables exactly, so that readers know what you are studying, and describe the operational definitions in enough detail that an exact replication is possible. Use the most specific word you can think of to describe the participants and procedures (for instance, *three* rather than *some* and *college students* rather than *people*). Be careful to say only what you know happened to the participants, not what you think happened. For instance, unless you know for sure that they did, do not say that the participants "experienced a good mood." Say instead that they were "exposed to information designed to place them in a good mood." Use accepted scientific terminology wherever possible.

3. *Be concise.* Do not cite literature that is not directly relevant to your research. Assume that the reader has a basic knowledge of statistical principles. For instance, you don't need to explain why your results need to be reliable, only that they are reliable. Remember that you may not have space to tell everything. However, all information that is relevant to the research *must* be mentioned. You need to decide what is relevant.

4. *Be compulsive.* Follow APA format exactly. Check everything two or three times. Proofread the manuscript carefully yourself, and use the spell-checker on your word processor before you print it. Be prepared to rewrite the manuscript many times, moving paragraphs around and even starting over if you need to. Read the paper out loud to yourself, and ask others to read it, too. Allow yourself plenty of time, so that you have the opportunity to put the paper away for a day or two and then read it again. This break will often allow you to see things in a new light and to find new ways of expressing your ideas.

5. *Be clear and interesting.* Although your readers will be most interested in your data, you must try to frame those data in a compelling and interesting manner. Explain why what you did is important and why readers should care about what you are doing. Readers prefer simple, rather than complex, writing. Write your report so that an intelligent friend, who is a major in art history, or perhaps even your grandmother, could understand what you did and why.

Use the active voice when possible (e.g., "I demonstrated" rather than "It was found" or "This study demonstrated"). If you feel that the reader may have lost the thread of your story, repeat crucial aspects ("Recall from the Introduction that it was expected..."). The use of examples can be helpful, as can tables and figures if there would otherwise be too many numbers in the text. Make sure that your points flow in an orderly fashion from section to section. Transition words, such as *furthermore, nevertheless,* and *however,* can help in this regard.

6. *Be fair.* In addition to being nice to your readers, be fair to them. Avoid language that may be offensive, and do not be overly harsh in your critique of the work of others. It is better (and almost always more accurate) to say that you have "added" to previous work than to say that you've "destroyed" it or "proved it wrong." Also be particularly careful that the ideas you express are your own. If you have borrowed from others, be sure to give them credit by referencing their work.

SUMMARY

Communicating scientific ideas and research findings is one of the most important aspects of scientific progress because it contributes to the accumulation of scientific knowledge. Scientists share information with each other in person at scientific conventions, through electronic communication such as fax and e-mail, and through the publication of written research reports.

Research reports, many of which are eventually published in a scientific journal, are the definitive descriptions of a research project. The research report is prepared according to a formal set of guidelines, such as that provided by the American Psychological Association. The goals for writing the research report include being organized, precise, concise, compulsive, interesting, and fair.

There are five major sections within the APA format: Abstract, Introduction, Methods, Results, and Discussion, as well as other sections that contain supplementary information. Each section contains important information about the research, but only the information appropriate to that section. Although constrained to follow a specific format, the research report must also read smoothly and be interesting to the reader. Creating a research report that is both technically informative and easy to read takes a substantial amount of work and will generally require much rewriting.

KEY TERMS

peer review 294
running head 299

REVIEW AND DISCUSSION QUESTIONS

1. Why is it important for scientists to share their ideas and research findings with each other, and how do they do so?

2. Why is scientific knowledge communicated at scientific conventions and through electronic communications in addition to the formal publication of research reports in scientific journals?

3. Describe the progress of the research manuscript as it is considered for publication in a scientific journal. What are the strengths and weaknesses of the peer review process?

4. Describe the basic objectives of the research report written in APA style. What information goes in each of the five major sections?

5. What information is contained in each of the supplementary sections of the research report?

6. How are the levels of the headings of a research report determined?

7. Summarize the writing and stylistic goals that can help a person write an effective research report.

RESEARCH PROJECT IDEAS

1. Each of the following sentences violates a basic rule of report writing. Indicate the relevant difficulty in each case.

   a. "The scale was coded to assess optimism, or lack thereof, in the participants."
   b. "Seven of the twenty-one participants were male, and fourteen of the twenty-one were female."
   c. "To be significant, the p-value of the test had to be less than the alpha level of .05."
   d. "The majority of students were between twenty and twenty-six years old."
   e. "The professor required that we code the independent variables two different ways."
   f. "Results of the correlational analysis are presented in Table A."
   g. "The procedure in Experiment 2 was just about the same as in Experiment 1."

Sample Research Report

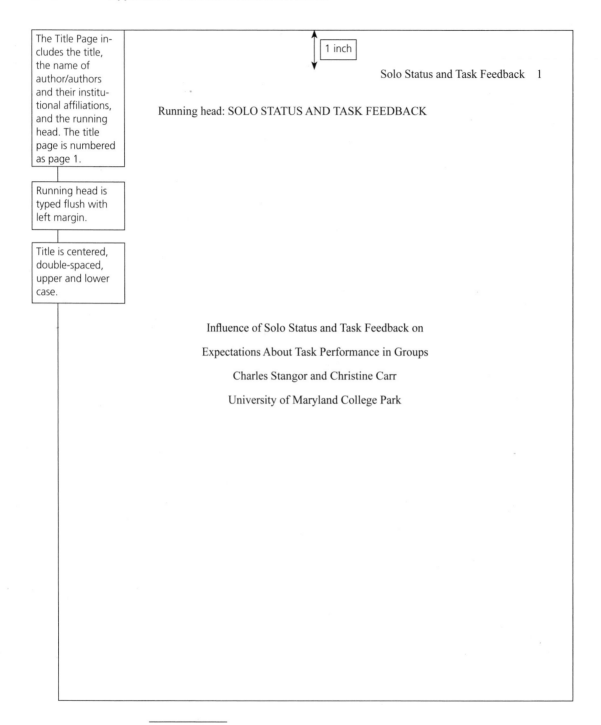

The Title Page includes the title, the name of author/authors and their institutional affiliations, and the running head. The title page is numbered as page 1.

Running head is typed flush with left margin.

Title is centered, double-spaced, upper and lower case.

1 inch

Solo Status and Task Feedback   1

Running head: SOLO STATUS AND TASK FEEDBACK

Influence of Solo Status and Task Feedback on

Expectations About Task Performance in Groups

Charles Stangor and Christine Carr

University of Maryland College Park

The manuscript should be double-spaced on 8½-by-11-inch paper. Preferred font is 12-point Times New Roman.

Use the "header" function in your word processor to have the header printed on each page. Leave five spaces between the last word in the header and the page number.

The Abstract appears on page 2. The first line of the Abstract is not indented.

Abstract is a single paragraph not exceeding 120 words.

Abstract contains key elements of all sections of the manuscript.

Solo Status and Task Feedback   2

Abstract

Two studies investigated men and women's predictions of their performance on a word-finding task in groups in which they expected to be either the only member of their sex and major or in which the other group members were also of the same sex and had similar majors. The data supported a feedback-undermining hypothesis: Individuals who were led to expect that they had high (versus ambiguous) abilities on a task expected to perform better in the future when working on the task alone and in similar groups but not in dissimilar groups. These differences seem to have occurred because working in a dissimilar group undermined an individual's task confidence rather than because of expected negative affective reactions in the groups.

The Introduction starts on page 3. The title of the paper is centered at the top of the page.

Begin with a general introduction to the topic of the manuscript.

c.f. is a Latin abbreviation meaning "to compare" and is used only in parentheses.

References are in the author/year format (see Table A.2). Full references are found in the References section at the end of the manuscript.

References in lists are ordered by the last name of the first author and separated by semicolons in the list.

Solo Status and Task Feedback   3

Influence of Solo Status and Task Feedback on

Expectations About Task Performance in Groups

Social psychologists have recently begun to expand their study of stereotyping and prejudice from a more traditional interest in how majority or powerful groups perceive and respond to minorities or less powerful groups, to an interest in how members of stigmatized groups perceive, interpret, cope, and attempt to change the stereotyping, prejudice, and discrimination they encounter or expect to encounter (cf. Cohen & Swim, 1995; Crocker, Major, & Steel, 1998; Miller & Kaiser, 1991; Saenz, 1994; Steele & Aronson, 1994; Swim & Stangor, 1998). Such an interest is driven not only by the theoretical goal of providing a more complete understanding of the nature of intergroup relations, but also by the practical goal of better understanding the potential outcomes of prejudice on the everyday life of stigmatized group members.

Although the target individual's experience of prejudice and discrimination may in some cases be direct (such as employment and housing discrimination, sexual harassment, or racial slurs), in other cases potential targets of stereotyping, prejudice, or discrimination may be indirectly affected by their own perceptions of how likely they are to be the victim of stereotyping, prejudice, or

Solo Status and Task Feedback   4

e.g. is a Latin abbreviation meaning "for example."

Provide more specific information about what is being studied.

Use et al. (not italicized) to indicate multiple authors in second and later citations of a paper with more than two authors, and every time for papers with more than five authors.

Here is a general overview of the research.

discrimination (e.g., Kleck & Strenta, 1980), even in the absence of such behavior.

Such perceptions may lead an individual to alter his or her task choices or task interests. He or she may avoid engaging in certain tasks, expect to have difficulty performing those tasks, or attempt to change the task situation before entering it. For instance, women concerned about being stereotyped by instructors or other students in mathematics, engineering, and science courses may be particularly unlikely to enroll in them (cf. Eccles, 1994), or African Americans with similar concerns may avoid academic pursuits altogether (Crocker et al., 1998).

The present research studies one particular situation in which individuals might expect to be vulnerable to stereotyping--namely, when they find themselves as the only member of their social group (for instance, the only woman within a larger group of men). In this case, the lone woman is known as a solo (Heilman, 1979; Kanter, 1977). Our general expectation is that individuals will be less certain about their abilities to perform well on relevant tasks when they are solos. This prediction is derived from the results of several existing lines of research. For one, there is literature to suggest that solos are likely to be stereotyped by other group members. For instance, Taylor, Fiske, Etcoff, and Ruderman (1978) had perceivers view discussion groups in which a solo man or woman interacted within a larger group of women or men. Taylor et al. found that the observers paid disproportionate attention to the solos, preferentially recalled their contributions to the discussion, and frequently described them using stereotypical traits.

Research showing that solos expect to be stereotyped is even more relevant to the present thesis. In one study, Cohen and Swim (1995) told male and female participants that they would be working with a group of students who were either of the same sex as they were or of the other sex. Cohen and Swim found that their participants reported expecting to be stereotyped by the other group members to a greater degree when they were to be a solo.

Taken together, then, there is at least some evidence to suggest that solos are aware that they may be stereotyped and that being a solo can impact task performance. However, a question not heretofore addressed concerns whether such individuals are aware of the potential impact that being in solo status may have on their task performance prior to engaging in the task. This question is important from a practical perspective because if individuals realize that being in solo status can have a negative impact on task performance, they may expect to perform more poorly than they would as majority group members, and this perception may lead them to avoid such situations.

> Cite only references that relate to the proposed hypothesis.

> Discuss how your research is different and what it is expected to add.

Solo Status and Task Feedback   6

State the research hypothesis.

We expected that perceived task ability would have an impact in the form of feedback undermining, such that for individuals who expected to work with similar others, those who received positive feedback would predict better performance than those who received ambiguous feedback, but that individuals expecting to be solos would predict poor task performance regardless of feedback. In short, this possibility suggests that solo status would create so much uncertainty about future task performance that it would undermine any effects of positive feedback on expectancies about task performance.

Heading is centered, upper case and lower case. Do not start these headings on a new page.

Method

Heading is flush left, italicized, upper case and lower case.

Overview

The Overview section is a common (but not required) way to set up the goals of the research and to let the reader know what to expect.

We approached our research question by providing our participants with evaluative feedback about their skills on a word-finding task that suggested either that they were clearly good at the task or that their skills were ambiguous. Furthermore, we manipulated the group with which they expected to subsequently work on the task to be either very similar to or very different from them. We then asked the participants to estimate their likely performance on the task on which they had been given feedback and their preferences for working on the same task again (or changing the task).

Solo Status and Task Feedback   7

We expected that solos would be aware of the potential negative impact of being in minority status on task performance and that this knowledge would make them unsure of their future performance. As a result, we expected that judgments about future performance in dissimilar groups would be different from those about future performance in similar groups. As another control, we also asked participants to predict their likely future performance on the task were they to work on it alone.

Participants

Participants were 63 white female and 31 white male undergraduates between the ages of 18 and 23 who participated in exchange for course credit in an introductory psychology course.[1] Participants were recruited by telephone on the basis of their college major to allow us to create potential work groups of either similar or dissimilar others. No individuals who did not have a declared college major were selected for participation. Participants were randomly assigned to one of four conditions: similar group, positive feedback; similar group, ambiguous feedback; dissimilar group, positive feedback; and dissimilar group, ambiguous feedback.

See page 285 for information about what to include in the Participants section.

Use digits for numbers 10 and greater.

Place text of the footnotes at the end of the manuscript, not at the bottom of the page.

Procedure and Stimulus Materials

In this case, because they are relatively short, two sections are combined together.

The Procedure must provide sufficient information for a reader to be able to conduct an exact replication.

Participants were greeted by a female experimenter and told that they would be participating in research comparing task performance in individual versus group situations. They were told that they would take part in four sessions during which they would be working alone, in groups, or in both. It was further explained that in each session they would be working on a word-finding task. They were asked if they had any questions, and they then signed an experimental consent form.

At this point participants were told that before the experiment could continue, the researchers needed to have an initial baseline measure of their performance, and they completed the word-finding task for the first time. As shown in Appendix A, the task consisted of two puzzles, each of which contained letters displayed in blocks of 14 columns and 14 rows. The experimenter showed the task to the participants and explained that the goal was to find as many words as possible in any direction. The experimenter left the room for 7 minutes while the participants worked on the two puzzles. The experimenter then returned and, explaining to the participants that their words would now be scored by an assistant in the next room, again left the room. The experimenter returned in 4 minutes to give the feedback, which consisted of a sheet that indicated ratings in four categories:

Solo Status and Task Feedback 9

number of words, diversity of words, originality of words, and length of words, each rated on a scale from 1 = *poor* to 7 = *excellent*.

Participants in the positive-feedback condition received scores of 6 or 7 on each of the four dimensions and were told by the experimenter that they had done "very well on all aspects of the task" and that they were "in the top 10% of the students who had previously done the task." Participants in the ambiguous-feedback condition received scores of 2, 6, 6, and 1 on the four respective dimensions and were told that they had done "very well on some aspects of the task and not so well on others." These participants were also told that, although they had scored "in the top 10% of the students who had previously done the task on two dimensions, they had scored in the bottom 10% of the students who had previously done the task" on the other two dimensions.

Participants were then told that there would be three more sessions of similar tasks and that we needed volunteers to work both alone and in groups. Furthermore, they were told that for the next session the researchers were attempting to place individuals in the environment of their choice and that we would need to get some information from them about their preferences for working both alone and in groups.

> Use digits for numbers less than 10 if they refer to scores or times.

We manipulated the supposed group that participants might be joining to be either similar or dissimilar by providing a sheet of demographic information about each of the potential group members. In the similar conditions, the participants learned that the group members were two men and two women of college age who had (as determined via pretesting) a very similar major to the participant. For instance, similar majors for psychology majors were sociology and criminal justice. In the dissimilar condition, all four of the other group members were described as being college-age men who had majors that were (again on the basis of pretesting) known to be perceived as very different to those of the participant (for instance, dissimilar majors for psychology students were engineering and physics).

At this point participants completed questionnaires assessing their estimated performance on the task if they were to work in the group and alone (1 = *poor*, 8 = *excellent*) and their desire to change the task before the next session began (1 = *not at all*, 8 = *very much*). Participants also indicated how well they had performed on the task in the last session (1 = *poor*, 7 = *excellent*) and rated the similarity of the people in the group they might be joining (1 = *different from me*, 7 = *like me*). At this point the experimenter asked the participants to write any thoughts that they had about the experiment so far, and the participants were debriefed.

Results

Manipulation Checks

We tested the effectiveness of the feedback manipulation and whether the students had indeed perceived the group as similar or dissimilar to them. The manipulation checks were analyzed in terms of 2 (task feedback: positive, ambiguous) $\times$ 2 (group composition: similar, dissimilar) ANOVAs. Both manipulations were successful. Those who had received ambiguous feedback ($M = 4.61$) rated their performance on the original task as having been significantly less positive than those who had received positive feedback ($M = 5.96$), $F(1,86) = 22.25$, $p < .001$. Furthermore, the participants who expected to join the similar group rated the group members as being significantly more similar to them ($M = 5.32$) in comparison to those who expected to join a dissimilar group ($M = 2.26$), $F(1,86) = 146.73$, $p < .001$. There were no other significant effects in these analyses.

Estimated Task Performance

We investigated estimated task performance while working alone and in groups using a 2 (task feedback: positive, ambiguous) $\times$ 2 (group composition:

Report first the results of the manipulation checks (and reliability of measures).

Round numbers to two digits to the right of the decimal, except for very small *p*-values. See Chapter 8 for information on reporting *p*-values.

In this case, headers are used to order the results according to which dependent variable is being analyzed.

> Mention the specific data analysis.

> Report the results of the *F* tests and the condition means.

similar, dissimilar) $\times$ 2 (judgments: alone, group) ANOVA with repeated measures on the last factor. The expected 3-way interaction was significant $F(1,84) = 4.68$, $p < .05$, and the means, as shown in Table 1, were in exactly the predicted direction. When the alone judgments were analyzed separately, only a main effect of feedback was observed, $F(1,84) = 16.61$, $p < .001$. Participants who received positive feedback ($M = 5.60$) estimated that they would perform better while working alone than did those who received ambiguous feedback ($M = 4.40$) regardless of group similarity. The simple interaction between feedback and group composition was not significant, $F(1,84) = 1.62$. On the group judgments the pattern was different. As shown in Table 1, the impact of feedback was stronger in the similar-group condition than in the dissimilar-group condition, although this simple interaction did not quite reach significance, $F(1,84) = 3.46$, $p < .07$.

There was one other significant effect—a main effect of judgment, $F(1,84) = 11.39$, $p < .001$, such that participants predicted better performance in the group conditions ($M = 5.91$) than they did in the alone conditions ($M = 5.06$). Although this was not expected, it seems reasonable to assume that this effect was due to the fact that the group sessions

> Attempt to explain unexpected results.

Solo Status and Task Feedback   13

were expected to be public. It is possible, for instance, that the participants

expected to receive help from the other group members.

Desire to Change the Task

We next looked at the influence of the manipulations on the desire to

change the task. This analysis produced a significant interaction $F(1,83) = 5.66$,

$p < .05$. The means took the form of a cross-over interaction. As shown in Figure

1, for individuals in the dissimilar-group condition ambiguous feedback

increased the desire to change the task—it would be undesirable to be in a situa-

tion in which failure could be seen by dissimilar others. For those in the similar-

group condition, positive feedback slightly increased the desire to change

the task.

Discussion

The basic finding of this study is that participants made different judgments

about their likely performance on and their desire to engage again in the same

word-finding task depend-ing on their expectations about their ability at the task

and the type of group with which they expected to work. In their estimation of

their future performance on the task while working alone, prior feedback had the

expected

> Begin the Discus-
> sion with a short
> overview of the
> research findings.

effect. Those who received positive feedback predicted better performance. On ratings of group performance, however, feedback and group composition produced an interactive effect, such that the impact of positive feedback was undermined in prediction of performance in dissimilar groups. Although those expecting to work in similar groups expected better performance when they had received positive feedback, those who expected to work in a dissimilar group predicted relatively poor performance regardless of feedback.

In terms of desire to change the task, we found that, as expected, individuals who were unsure of their expected task performance were more likely to want to change the task when they expected to work in a dissimilar group. However, individuals who had received positive feedback and who expected to work in a similar group were also more likely to want to change the task than those who received negative feedback and expected to work in a similar group. Although the latter was not expected, this might suggest that the participants found it undesirable to perform extremely well in the company of similar others—perhaps because doing so would seem embarrassing.

Our findings are consistent with the idea that performance expectations are simply more uncertain when an individual is expecting to work with others

Solo Status and Task Feedback   15

Compare the current results to other research findings, and relate the results to the questions raised in the Introduction.

who are dissimilar. As a result, generalization from past performance to future performance is thus less sure and more influenced by other factors. We are not completely sure that these other factors include the perceived likelihood of being stereotyped by others, but past research suggests that solos do expect to be stereotyped, and this perception could contribute to the observed differences.

The present research has a few limitations. First, our manipulation, in which both the sex of the group members and their major were simultaneously varied to create similar and dissimilar groups, has some problems. Although this approach provides a strong manipulation of similar or dissimilar groups, we cannot know for sure whether it was changes in sex or in major that produced the observed differences. Future research could vary each dimension separately. Also, it might be informative to vary the task itself to be either stereotypical of men or women.

Discuss the potential limitations of the research.

Second, it is not clear whether the present results, which were found for solos, would be the same for numerical minorities. We used solo status because it produces a strong manipulation of being different. Whether being in minority status, meaning individuals have at least one other member of their group, would prevent the effects from occurring could be studied in future research.

In any case, the present results suggest that individuals are aware of the composition of the groups in which they are likely to work and that this awareness can influence their perceptions of their own likely task performance and their desire to engage in the task. Such effects may account, in part, for how individuals choose college majors and occupations.

Close very broadly, addressing the issues that began the paper.

Solo Status and Task Feedback   17

References

Cohen, L. L., & Swim, J. K. (1995). The differential impact of gender ratios on women and men: Token-ism, self-confidence, and expectations. *Personality and Social Psychology Bulletin, 21,* 876–884.

Crocker, J., Major, B., & Steele, C. M. (1998). Social stigma. In S. T. Fiske, D. Gilbert, & G. Lindzey (Eds.), *Handbook of social psychology* (4th ed.). Boston: McGraw-Hill.

Eccles, J. S. (1994). Understanding women's educational and occupational choices. *Psychology of Women Quarterly, 18,* 585–609.

Heilman, M. E. (1979). High school students' occupational interest as a function of projected sex ratios in male-dominated occupations. *Journal of Applied Psychology, 64,* 275–279.

Kanter, R. M. (1977). Some effects of proportions on group life: Skewed sex ratios and responses to token women. *American Journal of Sociology, 82,* 965–990.

Kleck, R., & Strenta, A. (1980). Perceptions of the impact of negatively valued physical characteristics on social interaction. Journal of Personality and Social Psychology, 39, 861–873.

Miller, C. T., & Kaiser, C. R. (2001). A theoretical perspective on coping with stigma. Journal of Social Issues, 56, 73–92.

See page 307 for information about the References section.

Saenz, D. S. (1994). Token status and problem-solving deficits: Detrimental effects of distinctiveness and performance monitoring. *Social Cognition, 12,* 61–74.

Steele, C. M., & Aronson, J. (1994). Stereotype threat and the intellectual test performance of African Americans. *Journal of Personality and Social Psychology, 69,* 797–811.

Swim, J. T., & Stangor, C. (Eds.). (1998). Prejudice from the target's perspective. Santa Barbara, CA: Academic Press.

Taylor, S. E., Fiske, S. T., Etcoff, N. L., & Ruderman, A. J. (1978). Categorical and contextual bases of person memory and stereotyping. Journal of Personality and Social Psychology, 36, 778–793.

Solo Status and Task Feedback 19

Appendix

Samples of Word Puzzles Used to Provide

Performance Feedback

O	Q	Z	A	L	V	S	K	G	S	X	E	N	D	F
L	F	A	O	R	S	D	W	H	S	J	C	K	U	H
M	Q	Y	G	E	Z	C	A	R	R	L	L	Y	T	F
K	R	I	A	H	C	R	I	O	J	I	F	Y	U	A
R	V	N	Y	R	P	Q	T	S	C	G	S	K	R	P
O	R	E	S	E	G	A	D	N	S	L	K	T	Q	Z
W	D	P	N	X	L	E	E	N	R	O	T	O	Z	V
E	J	E	Z	U	S	P	F	E	U	B	R	A	W	I
M	R	O	C	K	T	B	L	X	B	E	Q	S	O	I
O	I	L	W	G	Z	P	G	G	B	T	U	D	T	L
H	A	J	R	W	A	E	L	H	E	C	Z	S	A	A
C	X	T	H	T	P	O	U	Q	R	F	L	E	H	S
Q	U	T	S	O	G	Z	E	V	S	B	O	O	K	Z
Y	W	U	R	H	O	L	E	P	U	N	C	H	D	C
B	K	E	K	O	Z	D	R	A	M	A	X	Q	R	K

DESK
CHAIR
RUBBER
PEN
PENCIL
BOOK
SHELF
SCISSORS
HOLEPUNCH
STAPLER
SHARPENER
GLUE
GLOBE
CALCULATOR
HOMEWORK
ART
DRAMA

F	W	P	T	V	C	C	L	A	E	G	D	U	J	T
I	A	I	S	I	P	W	B	C	T	H	Q	K	Q	R
R	A	V	V	D	Z	U	F	C	S	L	R	C	R	E
E	F	P	H	G	I	N	T	O	I	E	Q	H	V	Y
M	Q	M	Y	L	U	O	P	U	T	C	W	E	E	W
A	N	W	D	R	R	L	T	N	N	K	P	F	I	A
N	O	E	S	F	U	E	I	T	E	O	P	J	W	L
W	R	E	R	M	Q	A	E	A	D	X	J	K	Y	M
R	W	X	B	O	P	R	E	N	A	E	L	C	R	Y
E	R	E	H	C	T	U	B	T	I	O	P	E	K	G
I	R	C	H	W	S	C	X	I	U	G	K	M	U	J
H	U	H	Z	W	G	I	O	B	G	A	N	P	T	E
S	N	P	J	A	E	D	A	D	B	Y	K	E	X	C
A	B	E	L	E	C	T	R	I	C	I	A	N	R	C
C	H	L	K	N	C	A	R	P	E	N	T	E	R	C

ACCOUNTANT
BAKER
BUILDER
BUTCHER
CARPENTER
CASHIER
CHEF
CLEANER
DENTIST
DOCTOR
ELECTRICIAN
ENGINEER
FIREMAN
JUDGE
LAWYER
NURSE
PAINTER
PLUMBER

Author Note

This is an edited version of a manuscript that has been submitted for

publication.

Correspondence concerning this article should be addressed to Charles

Stangor, Department of Psychology, University of Maryland, College Park, MD

20742. Electronic mail: Stangor@psyc.umd.edu.

Author Note
appears on a
separate page
after the Refer-
ences. Author
Note is not num-
bered or refer-
enced in the text.

Footnotes

[1]Ninety-nine participants were originally run. However, five of these were deleted from analysis because they expressed suspicion about the validity of the task feedback.

Footnotes are listed together, starting on a new page.

Table 1

Estimated Task Performance as a Function of Task

Feedback and Group Composition

Task feedback	Alone judgments		Group judgments	
	Similar	Different	Similar	Different
Positive	6.06	5.92	6.75	5.23
Ambiguous	4.14	4.53	4.86	4.53
Difference	1.92	1.39	1.89	0.70

Note: Cell sizes range from 11 to 13.

Tables are inserted at the end of the manuscript, each on a separate page. The table number and a descriptive title are listed flush left. Notes can be added to explain information included in the table.

Figure Caption

Figure 1. Desire to change task as a function of task feedback and group composition.

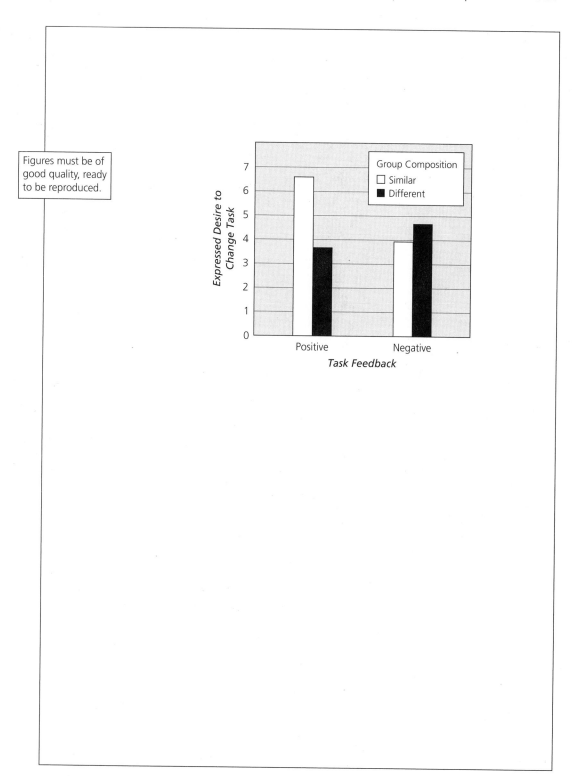

Figures must be of good quality, ready to be reproduced.

APPENDIX B
Data Preparation and Univariate Statistics

STUDY QUESTIONS

- How are computers used in data collection and analysis?

- How are collected data prepared for statistical analysis?

- How are missing data treated in statistical analyses?

- When is it appropriate to delete data before they are analyzed?

- What are descriptive statistics and inferential statistics?

- What determines how well the data in a sample can be used to predict population parameters?

Appendices B, C, and D are designed as a guide to the practical use of statistical procedures used to understand the implications of collected data. In most cases these statistics will be computed with statistical software programs. The use of computers is encouraged not only because it saves time but also because it reduces computational errors. Nevertheless, understanding how the statistical tests are computed and computing at least some by hand are essential for a full understanding of their underlying logic.

Appendices B and C will serve as a review of elementary statistical calculations for students who have previously had an introductory statistics course and are familiar with statistical methods. These appendices provide many formulas for computing these statistics by hand. Appendix D provides information about more advanced statistical procedures, and because these procedures are normally conducted on computers, we will focus on interpreting computer printouts. Together the three appendices will serve as a basic research reference.

We will begin our discussion of statistical techniques in this appendix by considering the selection of statistical software programs to analyze data and the preparation of data for statistical analysis. We will also discuss methods for graphically and numerically studying the distributions of scores on sample variables, as well as reviewing the elementary concepts of statistical inference.

Preparing Data for Analysis

An adequate discussion of data analysis necessarily involves a consideration of the role of computers. They are increasingly being used both to collect data from participants and to analyze data. The dramatic recent increases in computing power have provided new ways of collecting data and have also encouraged the development of many statistical analyses that were not heretofore available.

Collecting the Data

In many cases the individuals who participate in behavioral science research can directly enter their data into a computer using data collection software packages. These programs allow the researcher to create displays of stimulus information, including text, charts, and graphic images, for presentation to the research participants. The software can be programmed to select and present displays and can record responses from a keyboard, a mouse, or other devices such as physiological recording equipment; the software can also record reaction times. The use of computers to collect data can both save time and reduce errors. For instance, when the responses to a questionnaire are completed on a paper copy, the data must later be entered into the computer for analysis. This takes time and may result in errors. Appendix F considers the use of computers to collect data in more detail.

Analyzing the Data

In addition to providing new ways of collecting data, the increased use of computers has resulted in dramatic changes in how data are analyzed. Up until the 1970s, every statistical analysis was calculated by hand with a mechanical adding machine. These calculations often took days to complete and check. In the 1970s and 1980s, analyses were computed by large mainframe computers, which reduced the processing time to hours. Today, data are entered into the computer, the relevant statistical analyses and variables are selected, and the results of most analyses are calculated within seconds.

There are many statistical software packages available for analyzing behavioral science data. Which one you use will depend on the availability of different programs and the requirements of your research project. We will focus our discussion in Appendices B, C, and D on the program that is most commonly used in the behavioral sciences—the *IBM Statistical Package for the Social Sciences* (*IBM SPSS*). This program can be used to compute all of the statistical analyses that we will be discussing and is available for student use at many colleges and universities. A student version is available for purchase at a moderate price.

Like any good statistical program, IBM SPSS contains a spreadsheet data editor, the ability to easily make transformations on the variables (such as adding them together or reverse-scoring them), and subprograms to compute the statistical analyses that you will need. IBM SPSS contains, among many others, the following subprograms:

Frequency distributions

Descriptive statistics

Correlations

Regression

Analysis of variance

Reliability

Loglinear analysis

Factor analysis

Entering the Data Into the Computer

The raw data are normally entered in a matrix format into the data editor of the statistical software package. In this format the data can be saved and edited. In most cases the data matrix is arranged so that the participants make up the rows of the matrix, the variables are represented in the columns, and the entries are the scores on the variables.

Figure B.1 shows the data from the first fifteen participants in Table 6.1 after they have been entered into the IBM SPSS data editor. The variables are

FIGURE B.1 Data in the IBM SPSS Data Editor

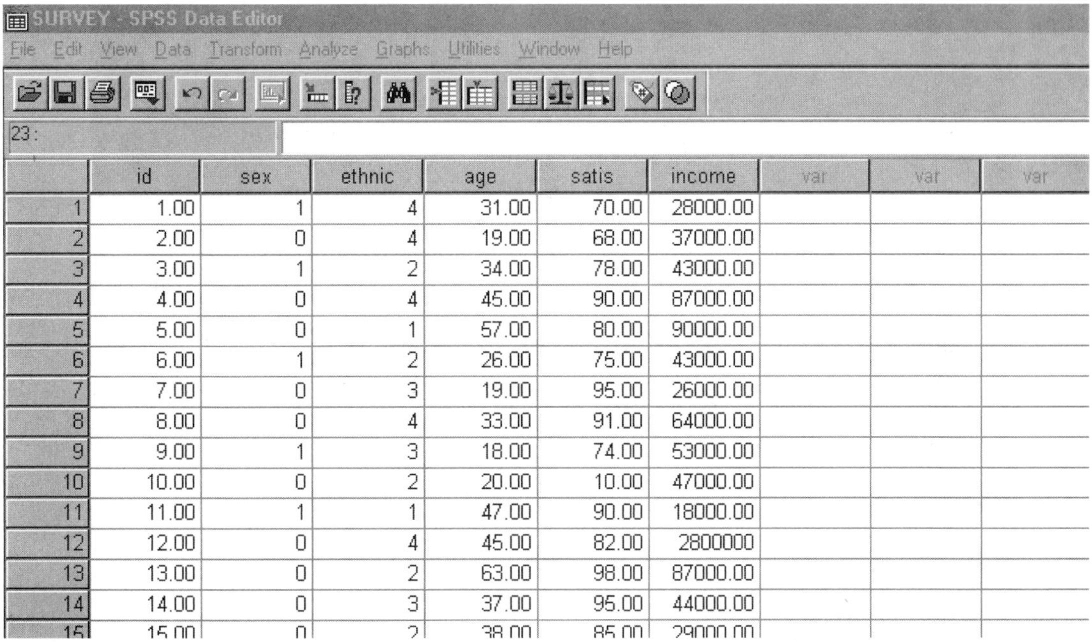

	id	sex	ethnic	age	satis	income	var	var	var
1	1.00	1	4	31.00	70.00	28000.00			
2	2.00	0	4	19.00	68.00	37000.00			
3	3.00	1	2	34.00	78.00	43000.00			
4	4.00	0	4	45.00	90.00	87000.00			
5	5.00	0	1	57.00	80.00	90000.00			
6	6.00	1	2	26.00	75.00	43000.00			
7	7.00	0	3	19.00	95.00	26000.00			
8	8.00	0	4	33.00	91.00	64000.00			
9	9.00	1	3	18.00	74.00	53000.00			
10	10.00	0	2	20.00	10.00	47000.00			
11	11.00	1	1	47.00	90.00	18000.00			
12	12.00	0	4	45.00	82.00	2800000			
13	13.00	0	2	63.00	98.00	87000.00			
14	14.00	0	3	37.00	95.00	44000.00			
15	15.00	0	2	38.00	85.00	29000.00			

listed across the top of the matrix and have names of up to eight letters. The first variable, labeled "id," provides a unique identification number for each participant.

Using Coding Systems. The two nominal variables ("sex" and "ethnic") are listed next. These variables are coded with numbers. The coding system is arbitrary, but consecutive integers are normally used. In this case, sex is coded as follows:

0 = female
1 = male

Ethnic is coded according to the following scheme:

1 = African American
2 = Asian
3 = Hispanic
4 = White
5 = Other

The experimental conditions in an experimental research design would also be coded with integers—for instance:

1 = experimental condition
0 = control condition

Three quantitative variables are also entered: "age," "satis," and "income."

The participants are listed down the left side of the matrix, and the data for each person take up one row of the matrix. The variable "id" provides a unique number for each participant, and this number can be used to match the data matrix with the original questionnaires if need be. It does not matter in which order the variables or the participants are entered. It may be convenient, however, to enter all of the independent variables first, followed by the dependent variables.

Keeping Notes.   It is important to keep good notes about how the data were entered into the computer. Although you may think you will be able to remember which variable name refers to which variable and how you coded each of the variables, it is easy to forget important details (for instance, did the code number 2 indicate African Americans or Asian Americans?). In most statistical packages, including IBM SPSS, it is possible to enter labels to indicate what the numbers used to code the nominal variables refer to.

Saving the Data.   As you enter the data into the data editor, save them regularly to disk in case there is a computer problem. Also be sure to have at least one backup copy of your data files. It is also a good idea to enter all of the data that you have collected into the computer, even if you do not plan to use them in the analysis. It does take some work to enter each variable, but it takes even more work later to find and enter the data for a variable that you thought you wouldn't need but then decided you did.

It is extremely easy to make mistakes when you are entering data. Work slowly and carefully, being sure to guard against every conceivable error. If the data were originally recorded on paper, you should save the original questionnaires at least until the analyses are completed. If you plan to publish the research, some publishers will require you to save all of your data for at least five years after the article is published.

Checking and Cleaning the Data

Once the data have been entered, the first goal is always to check that they have been entered properly. One approach is to compare all of the entered data with the original questionnaires. This is time-consuming and may not always be necessary. It is always, however, a good idea to spot-check a small sample of the data. For instance, you might compare the entered data for the first participant, the last participant, and a couple of the participants in the middle with their original questionnaires. If you find many mistakes, this will indicate that the whole data set should be checked.

The most basic procedure for checking the accuracy of data coding is to search for obvious errors. Begin (as we have discussed in Chapter 6) by calculating descriptive statistics and printing a frequency distribution or a stem and leaf plot for each of the variables. Inspecting the mean, N, and the maximum and minimum values of the variables is a helpful check on the data coding.

For instance, for the variable *sex* in our data set, the minimum and maximum values should be 0 and 1 and *N* should equal 25, the total number of participants. Once the data are checked, any errors should be corrected.

Even though these actions seem obvious, and even though you can't imagine making such mistakes, you would be surprised how many errors are made by experimenters failing to initially check the data once they have been entered. Generally, statistical analyses are not affected to a great extent if one or two data points within a data set are off by a number or two. For instance, if a coder mistakenly enters a "2" instead of a "3" on a seven-point Likert scale for one participant, the data analysis will not be greatly affected. However, if the coder enters "22" instead of "2" or "+6" instead of "−6," the statistical tests can be dramatically changed. Checking the maximum and minimum values of all the variables before beginning other analyses can help you avoid many of these problems.

Dealing with Missing Data

One of the most commonly occurring headaches in data analysis occurs when some of the data are not available. In general, the basic rule is to avoid missing data at all costs because they can pose a threat to the validity of the research and may lead to the necessity of additional data collection.

When data are missing, the entry in the data matrix that would contain the value is usually left blank. This means that not all analyses can be performed on all participants. In some cases, such as when the information about the individual's experimental condition is missing, it will mean that the individual cannot be used in any analyses. In other cases (for instance, when data are missing only on some dependent measures), the data from the individual can be used, but not in analyses involving that variable. Statistical software packages usually allow the user to specify how missing values should be treated in the statistical analyses, and it is worth becoming familiar with these procedures.

Reasons for Missing Data.   There are two types of missing data, and they will usually be treated differently. One type occurs when the respondent has decided not to answer a question, perhaps because it is inappropriate or because the respondent has other, personal reasons for not doing so. For instance, if a questionnaire asks an individual to rate the attractiveness of his or her boyfriend or girlfriend, a person who doesn't currently have a partner will have to leave the question blank. Thinking carefully about whether all questions are appropriate ahead of time can help you alleviate this type of missing data, as well as potentially saving respondents from embarrassing situations.

A second and more serious problem occurs when data are missing because although the information could and should be available, it is for some other reason not there. Perhaps the individual forgot to answer the question or completely missed an entire page of the questionnaire. Data can also be missing because equipment failed, pertinent information about the respondent (such as his or her demographic information) was not recorded by the experimenter, or it cannot be determined which person contributed the data. Many of these problems can be avoided through careful data collection and pilot testing. When questionnaires are completed in the presence of the experimenter, their completeness can be checked before the respondent leaves. If more than one page of dependent measures are used, it is a good idea to staple them together when they are collected and to mark each page with a code number to avoid confusion. Equipment problems can often be reduced through pilot testing.

Attrition Problems.   When the research requires that data be collected from the respondents at more than one time, it is virtually certain that some of them will drop out. This represents the basic problem of participant attrition, as we have discussed in Chapter 14. In this case, the question becomes not only what to do with those who are missing at later sessions (they may have to be discarded from the study altogether) but also how to determine whether those who did not return are somehow different from those who did.

Although there is no good solution to this problem, one possibility is to create a variable that indicates whether the person returned for the second session or not. Then this variable can be used as an independent variable in an analysis that compares the scores from the first session of the participants who did return to the later session with those who did not return. If there are no differences, the researcher can be more certain that there are no important differences between the two groups and thus that differential attrition is not a problem.

Deleting and Retaining Data

One of the more difficult decisions in data analysis concerns the possibility of deleting some data from the final statistical analyses. In general, the researcher is obligated to use all of the data that have been collected unless there is a valid reason to discard any. Thus a decision to discard data must always be carefully considered before it is made. Discarding of data might occur for several reasons and at various levels of analysis. We might, for instance, wish to delete variables that do not seem to be measuring what they were expected to measure. Or we might want to discard the responses from one or more individuals because they are extreme or unusual, because they did not follow or understand the directions, or because they did not take the task seriously. Let us consider each of these possibilities.

Deleting Variables.   We have already considered in Chapter 5 cases in which although they were designed to measure the same conceptual variable, one or more variables are deleted because a reliability analysis indicates that they do not measure the same thing that other variables are measuring. Doing so is usually acceptable, particularly when a new measured variable is being developed. The decision to delete a variable is more difficult, however, in cases where one variable (for instance, a self-report measure) shows the expected relationship with the independent variable but another variable (for instance, a behavioral measure) does not. In such cases it is usually not appropriate to delete a variable simply because it does not show the expected results. Rather, the results of both variables should be reported, but the researcher should try to explain in the Discussion section of the research report why the different variables might have shown different relationships.

Deleting Responses.   Another reason for deleting data is because one or more responses given by one or more participants are considered to be outliers. As we have seen in Chapter 6, an *outlier* is a very extreme score on a variable. Consider as an example a scientist who is testing the hypothesis that because anxiety-related words are highly emotionally charged, they will be pronounced more slowly. A computer program is designed to show participants a series of words, some of which are related to anxiety and some of which are comparable neutral words, and to measure how long it takes the participants to pronounce them. The scientist determines that the average pronunciation time across the participants was 765 milliseconds for the high-anxiety words, but only 634 milliseconds for the control words, a statistically significant difference. However, there is one individual who took over 10 seconds (that is, 10,000 milliseconds) to make a response to one of the high-anxiety words, and this response clearly contributed to the observed difference.

The difficult question the researcher faces in this situation is whether to keep or delete the outlier. In such a case the scientist would probably first question the measurement or coding of the data. Perhaps the computer failed to record the response correctly, or a mistake was made when the score was entered into the data matrix. If this does not appear to be the case, the possibility that something unique happened on this response for this person must be considered. Perhaps she or he was not paying attention, or maybe this person could not see or comprehend the word. Although these possibilities all suggest that the score should be deleted, it is also possible that the participant may simply have taken that long to pronounce the word.

Trimming the Data.   Although there are no hard and fast rules for determining whether a score should or should not be deleted, one common approach is to delete scores that are more than three standard deviations above or below the variable's mean. In this case the 10,000 milliseconds score would probably be found to be extreme enough to be deleted. However, deletion of extreme responses from only one end of the distribution is usually considered inappropriate. Rather, with a procedure known as **trimming** (Tukey, 1977), the most extreme response given by the individual on the other end of the distribution (even if it is not an outlier) is also removed before analysis.

Deleting Participants.   In some cases the participant may have contributed such a large number of unusual scores that the researcher decides to delete all of that participant's data. This might occur, for instance, if the average response time for the individual across all of the responses is very extreme, which might be taken to indicate that the person was not able to perform the task or did not understand the instructions. It is also advisable to delete individuals who have failed a suspicion check (see Chapter 3) from further analysis. Any person who has guessed the research hypothesis or who did not take the research seriously may contribute invalid data.

Whenever variables, scores, or participants have been deleted from analysis, these deletions must be noted in the research report. One exception to this rule involves cases where whole studies might not be reported, perhaps because the initial first tests of the research hypothesis were unsuccessful. Perhaps the best guideline in these cases is to report all decisions that would affect a reader's interpretation of the reported data, either in a footnote or in the text of the research report. In general, whenever data are deleted for any reason, some doubt is cast on the research itself. As a result, it is always better to try avoiding problems ahead of time.

Transforming the Data

Once the data have been entered and cleaned and decisions have been made about deleting and retaining them, the data often have to be transformed before the statistical analyses are conducted. For instance, on a Likert scale some of the variables must be reverse-scored, and then a mean or a sum across the items must be taken. In other cases the experimenter may want to create composite measures by summing or averaging variables together. Statistical software packages allow the user to take averages and sums among variables and to make other transformations as desired.

In general, a good rule of thumb is to always let the computer make the transformations for you rather than doing them yourself by hand. The computer is less likely to make errors, and once you learn how to use it to make the transformations, you will find this technique is also much faster.

Conducting Statistical Analysis

Once the data have been entered into the data editor, you will want to begin conducting statistical analyses on them. **Statistics** are mathematical methods for systematically organizing and analyzing data.

Descriptive Statistics, Parameters, and Inferential Statistics

A **descriptive statistic** is a number that represents the characteristics of the data in a sample, whereas a **parameter** is a number that represents the characteristics of a population.[1] Each descriptive statistic has an

---

[1]Samples and populations are discussed in detail in Chapter 6 of this book.

associated parameter. Descriptive statistics are symbolized with Arabic letters, whereas parameters are symbolized with Greek letters. For instance:

	Descriptive Statistic	Population Parameter
Mean	$\bar{x}$	μ (mu)
Standard deviation	s	σ (sigma)
Correlation coefficient	r	ρ (rho)

One important difference between a descriptive statistic and a parameter is that a descriptive statistic can be calculated exactly because it is based on the data collected from a sample, whereas a parameter can only be estimated because it describes a population and the entire population cannot be measured. However, as we will see later, we can use descriptive statistics to estimate population parameters. For instance, we can use $\bar{x}$ to estimate μ and r to estimate ρ.

An **inferential statistic** is a number, such as a p-value or a *confidence interval,* that is used to estimate the value of a parameter on the basis of a descriptive statistic. For instance, we can use inferential statistics to make statements about the probability that $\rho > 0$ or that $\mu = 100$. The techniques of statistical inference are discussed in detail in Chapter 8. In this appendix we will cover the mathematical computations of some inferential statistics.

Statistical Notation

The following notational system is used in Appendices B, C, and D:

X and Y refer to the names of measured variables in a sample.

N refers to the sample size (usually the number of participants from whom data have been collected).

Subscripts on variable names refer to the score of a given individual on a given variable. For instance, X_1 refers to the score of the first person on variable X, and Y_N refers to the score of the Nth (that is, the last) person on variable Y.

Summation Notation. The summation sign (Σ) indicates that a set of scores should be summed. For instance, consider the following five scores on a variable, X:

$$X_1 = 6$$
$$X_2 = 5$$
$$X_3 = 2$$
$$X_4 = 7$$
$$X_5 = 3$$

$\Sigma(X_1, X_2, X_3, X_4, X_5)$ indicates the sum of the five scores, that is, $(6 + 5 + 2 + 7 + 3) = 23$. We can represent these operations in *summation notation* as follows:

$$\sum_{i=1}^{N} X_i = 23$$

The notations above and below the summation sign indicate that i takes on the values from 1 (X_1) to $N (X_N)$. For convenience, because the summation is usually across the whole sample (from 1 to N), the subscript notation is often dropped, and the following simplification is used:

$$\sum X = 23$$

Rounding.   A common practice in the reporting of the results of statistical analysis is to round the presented figures (including both descriptive and inferential statistics) to two decimal places. This rounding should be done only when the computation is complete. Intermediate stages in hand calculations should not be rounded.

Computing Descriptive Statistics

The goal of statistics is to summarize a set of scores. As we have seen in Chapter 6, perhaps the most straightforward method of doing so is to indicate how frequently each score occurred in the sample.

Frequency Distributions

When the variables are nominal, a presentation of the frequency of the scores is accomplished with a *frequency distribution,* and the data can be shown graphically in a *bar chart.* An example of each can be found in Table 6.1. For quantitative variables, there are often so many values that listing the frequency of each one in a frequency distribution would not provide a very useful summary. One solution, as we have discussed in Chapter 6, is to create a *grouped frequency distribution.* The adjacent values are grouped into a set of categories, and the frequencies of the categories are examined. A grouped frequency distribution is shown in Figure 6.2. In this case the ages have been grouped into five categories: "Less than 21," "21–30," "31–40," "41–50," "greater than 50."

The grouped frequency distribution may be displayed visually in the form of a *histogram,* as shown in Figure 6.2(b). A histogram is slightly different from a bar chart because the bars touch each other to indicate that the original variable is continuous. If the frequencies of the groups are indicated with a line, rather than bars, as shown in Figure 6.2(c), the display is called a frequency curve. Another alternative to the display of continuous data, as shown in Figure 6.3, is the stem and leaf plot. However, although frequency distributions can provide important information about the distributions of quantitative variables, it is also useful to describe these distributions with descriptive statistics.

Measures of Central Tendency

Central tendency refers to the point in the distribution of a variable on which the data are centered. There are three primary measures of central tendency—the *mean,* the *median,* and the *mode*—and the uses of each are discussed in Chapter 6. Let us consider how these measures would be calculated for the following ten scores on a variable *X:*

$$X_1 = 6$$
$$X_2 = 5$$
$$X_3 = 2$$
$$X_4 = 7$$
$$X_5 = 3$$
$$X_6 = 4$$
$$X_7 = 6$$
$$X_8 = 2$$
$$X_9 = 1$$
$$X_{10} = 8$$

The Mean.   The mean (also known as the arithmetic average) is symbolized as $\overline{X}$ (read "X-bar") and is calculated as the sum of all of the scores divided by the sample size.

$$\overline{X} = \frac{X_1 + X_2 + X_3 + \ldots X_N}{N} = \frac{\Sigma X}{N}$$

In our case the mean of *X* is

$$\overline{X} = \frac{6 + 5 + 2 + 7 + 3 + 4 + 6 + 2 + 1 + 8}{13} = \frac{44}{10} = 4.4$$

The Median.   The sample median represents the score at which half of the observations are greater and half are smaller. Another way of saying this is that the median is the score at the fiftieth percentile rank, where **percentile rank** refers to the percentage of scores on the variable that are lower than the score itself. To calculate the median, the scores are first ranked from lowest to highest. If the sample size is odd, the median is the middle number. If the sample size is even, the median is the mean of the two center numbers. In our case the ranked scores are 1, 2, 2, 3, 4, 5, 6, 6, 7, 8, and the median is the average of 4 and 5, or 4.5.

The Mode.   The mode is the most frequently occurring value in a variable and can be obtained by visual inspection of the scores themselves or a frequency distribution of the scores. In some cases the distribution is **multimodal** (having more than one mode). This is true in our case, where (because there are two of each score) the modes are 2 and 6.

Measures of Dispersion

Dispersion refers to the extent to which the observations are spread out around the measure of central tendency.

The Range.   One simple measure of dispersion is to find the largest (the *maximum*) and the smallest (the *minimum*) observed values of the variable and to compute the range of the variable as the maximum score minus the minimum score. In our case the range of X is the maximum value (8) minus the minimum value (1) = 7.

The Variance and the Standard Deviation.   Dispersion can also be measured through calculation of the distance of each of the scores from a measure of central tendency, such as the mean. Let us consider the calculation of a measure of central tendency known as the *standard deviation,* as shown in Table B.1. The first column in Table B.1 represents the scores on X, and the second column, labeled $X - \overline{X}$, represents the mean deviation scores.

The **mean deviation scores** are calculated for each individual as the person's score (X) minus the mean ($\overline{X} = 4.4$). If the score is above the mean, the mean deviation is positive, and if the score is below the mean, the mean deviation is negative. It turns out that the sum of the mean deviation scores is always zero:

$$\sum (X - \overline{X}) = 0$$

Not only is this particular property true only for the mean (and no other value), but it also provides a convenient way to check your calculations.

TABLE B.1   Calculation of Descriptive Statistics

X	$(X - \overline{X})$	$(X - \overline{X})^2$	X^2	z
1	−3.40	11.56	1	−1.43
2	−2.40	5.76	4	−1.01
2	−2.40	5.76	4	−1.01
3	−1.40	1.96	9	−.59
4	−0.40	0.16	16	−.17
5	0.60	0.36	25	.25
6	1.60	2.56	36	.68
6	1.60	2.56	36	.68
7	2.60	6.76	49	1.10
8	3.60	12.96	64	1.52
$\Sigma = 44$	$\Sigma = 0.00$	$\Sigma = 50.40$	$\Sigma = 244$	$\overline{X} = 4.4$

TABLE B.2 Descriptive Statistics: IBM SPSS Output

	N					Std.				
	Valid	Missing	Mean	Median	Mode	Deviation	Variance	Range	Minimum	Maximum
AGE	25	0	33.5200	32.0000	18.00ª	12.5104	156.5100	45.00	18.00	63.00
SATIS	25	0	74.1600	80.0000	80.00	23.4462	549.7233	89.00	10.00	99.00
INCOME	25	0	159920	43000.0	43000.00	550480.2	3.0E+11	2782000	18000.00	2800000

ªMultiple modes exist. The smallest value is shown.

This is a printout from the Frequencies Procedure in IBM SPSS. (See footnote below for an explanation of scientific notation.)

Next, the deviation scores are each squared, as shown in the column in Table B.1 marked $(X - \overline{X})^2$. The sum of the squared deviations is known as the **sum of squares,** symbolized as **SS.**

$$SS = \sum (X - \overline{X})^2 = 50.4$$

The variance (symbolized as s^2) is the sum of squares divided by N:

$$s^2 = \frac{SS}{N} = \frac{50.4}{10} = 5.04$$

The standard deviation (s) is the square root of the variance:

$$s = \sqrt{s^2} = 2.24$$

There is a shortcut to computing the sum of squares that does not involve creating the mean deviation scores:

$$SS = \sum (X^2) - \frac{(\sum X^2)}{N} = 244 - \frac{1,936}{10} = 50.4$$

Note in this case that $\Sigma(X^2)$ is the sum of the X^2 scores (as shown in the fourth column in Table B.1), whereas $(\Sigma X)^2$ is the sum of the scores squared ($44^2 = 1,936$).

Computer Output

When the sample size is large, it will be easier to use a computer to calculate the descriptive statistics. A sample printout from IBM SPSS is shown in Table B.2.[2]

---

[2]SPSS and other statistical programs often use scientific notation when they print their results. If you see a printout that includes a notation such as "8.6E + 02" or "8.6E − 02," this means that the number is in scientific notation. To convert the figure to decimal notation, first write the number to the *left* of the E (in this case it is 8.6). Then use the number on the *right* side of the E to indicate which way to move the decimal point. If the number is positive, move the decimal point the indicated number of positions to the right. If the number is negative, move the decimal point the indicated number of positions to the left. Examples:

$8.6 - 02 = .086$ $9.4E - 04 = .00094$
$8.6 + 02 = 860$ $9.4E + 04 = 94,000$

Standard Scores

As we have discussed in Chapter 6, most distributions of quantitative variables, regardless of whether they are the heights of individuals, intelligence test scores, memory errors, or ratings of supervisor satisfaction, are found to fall into a bell-shaped curve known as the *normal distribution* (there are some exceptions to this general rule, as we have discussed in Chapter 6). Nevertheless, even though the shape of the distributions of many variables is normal, these distributions will usually have different means and standard deviations. This presents a difficulty if we wish to compare the scores on different variables with each other.

For instance, consider Bill and Susan, who were taking a research methods class but had different instructors who gave different exams. Susan and Bill wanted to know who had done better:

Susan had received a score of 80 on a test with $\overline{X} = 50$ and $s = 15$.

Bill had received a score of 75 on a test with $\overline{X} = 60$ and $s = 10$.

The solution to this problem is to transform each of the scores into a standard score or a z score using the following formula:

$$z = \frac{X - \overline{X}}{s}$$

A **standard score (z score)** represents the distance of a score from the mean of the variable (the mean deviation) expressed in standard deviation units. The last column in Table B.1 presents the standard scores for the variable X that we have been using as an example. One important property of standard scores is that once all of the original scores have been converted to standard scores, the mean of the standard scores will always be zero and the standard deviation of the standard scores will always be equal to 1.

The advantage of standard scores is that because the scores from each of the variables now have the same mean and standard deviation, we can compare the scores:

$$Z_{\text{Susan}} = \frac{X - \overline{X}}{s} = \frac{80 - 50}{15} = 2.0$$

$$Z_{\text{Bill}} = \frac{X - \overline{X}}{s} = \frac{75 - 60}{10} = 1.5$$

On the basis of these calculations, we can see that Susan ($z = 2.0$) did better than Bill ($z = 1.5$) because she has a higher standard score.

The Standard Normal Distribution

If we assume that the original scores are normally distributed, once they have been converted to standard scores, they will approximate the shape of a hypothetical population distribution of standard scores known as the **standard normal distribution.** Because the standard normal distribution is made up of standard scores, it will have a mean (μ) = 0 and a standard deviation (σ) = 1. Furthermore, because the standard normal distribution is so well defined, we can calculate the proportion of scores that will fall at each point in the distribution. And we can use this information to calculate the percentile rank of a person with a given standard score (as we have seen, the percentile rank of a score refers to the percentage of scores that are lower than it is).

The standard normal distribution is shown in Figure B.2, along with the percentage of scores falling in various areas under the frequency curve. You can see that in the hypothetical distribution, 34.13 percent of the scores lie between $z = 0$ and $z = 1$, 13.59 percent of the scores lie between $z = 1$ and $z = 2$, and 2.15 percent of the scores lie between $z = 2$ and $z = 3$. There are also some scores greater than $z = 3$, but not very many. In fact, only .13 percent of the scores are greater than $z = 3$.

Keep in mind that because the standard normal distribution is symmetrical, the percentage of scores that lie between the mean and a positive z score is exactly the same as the percentage of scores between the mean and the same negative z score. Furthermore, exactly 50 percent of the scores are less than the mean (0), and 50 percent are greater than the mean.

The exact percentile rank of a given standard score can be found with Statistical Table B in Appendix E. The table gives the proportion of scores within the standard normal distribution that fall between the mean (0) and a given z value. For instance, consider Bill, who had a standard score of $z = 1.5$ on his test. The table indicates that 43.32 percent of the scores lie between $z = 0$ and $z = 1.5$. Therefore, Bill's score is higher than all of the scores below the mean (50 percent) and also higher than the 43.32 percent of the scores that lie between $z = 0$ and $z = 1.5$. Bill's percentile rank is thus $50.00 + 43.32 = 93.32$. Similarly, Susan's percentile rank is 97.72.

FIGURE B.2 The Standard Normal Distribution

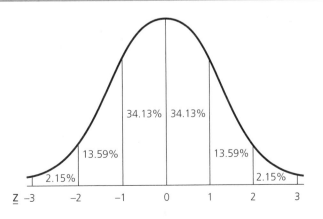

Working with Inferential Statistics

Consider for a moment a researcher who is interested in estimating the average grade-point average (GPA) of all of the psychology majors at a large university. He begins by taking a simple random sample of one hundred psychology majors and calculates the following descriptive statistics:

$$\overline{X} = 3.40$$
$$s = 2.23$$

Although the sample mean $(\overline{X})$ and standard deviation (s) can be calculated exactly, the corresponding population parameters μ and σ can only be estimated. This estimation is accomplished through probabilistic statements about the likelihood that the parameters fall within a given range.

Unbiased Estimators

It can be demonstrated mathematically that the sample mean $(\overline{X})$ is an **unbiased estimator** of the population mean (μ). By unbiased, we mean that $\overline{X}$ will not consistently overestimate or underestimate the population mean and thus that it represents the best guess of μ.

The sample standard deviation (s), however, is not an unbiased estimator of the population standard deviation, sigma (σ). However, an unbiased estimate of sigma, known as "sigma-hat" $(\hat{s})$, can be derived with the following formula:

$$\hat{s} = \sqrt{\frac{SS}{N-1}}$$

The Central Limit Theorem

Although these estimates of μ and σ are unbiased, and thus provide the best guess of the parameter values, they are not likely to be precise estimates. It is possible, however, through the use of a mathematical statement known as the central limit theorem, to determine how precisely the sample mean, $\overline{X}$, estimates the population mean, μ.[3] The **central limit theorem** shows that descriptive statistics calculated on larger samples provide more precise estimates of population parameters than do descriptive statistics calculated on smaller samples. This is true because small samples are more likely to be unusual than are larger samples and thus are less likely to provide an accurate description of the population.

The Standard Error

It can be demonstrated that if one were to take all possible samples of $N = 100$ from a given population, not only would the resulting distribution

---

[3]It is also possible to estimate how well s estimates σ, but because that estimate is not frequently needed, we will not discuss that procedure here.

of the sample means (known as the **sampling distribution of the mean**) have $\overline{X} = \mu$, but also that the distribution would be normally distributed with a standard deviation known as the **standard error of the mean** (or simply the **standard error**). The standard error is symbolized as $s_{\overline{X}}$ and calculated as follows:

$$s_{\overline{X}} = \frac{s}{\sqrt{N-1}} = \frac{2.23}{\sqrt{99}} = .22$$

Confidence Intervals

Because we can specify the sampling distribution of the mean, we can also specify a range of scores, known as a **confidence interval,** within which the population mean is likely to fall. However, this statement is probabilistic, and the exact width of the confidence interval is determined with a statistic known as **Student's t.** The exact distribution of the t statistic changes depending on the sample size, and these changes are specified with the degrees of freedom associated with the t statistic. The confidence interval is specified as the range between a lower limit:

$$\text{Lower limit } \mu = \overline{X} - t(s_{\overline{X}}) = 3.40 - 1.99(.22) = 2.96$$

and an upper limit:

$$\text{Upper limit } \mu = \overline{X} + t(s_{\overline{X}}) = 3.40 + 1.99(.22) = 3.84$$

where t is the value of the t statistic for a given alpha as found in Statistical Table C in Appendix E, with $df = N - 1$. In our case if we set alpha = .05, then the appropriate t value (with $df = 99$) is $t = 1.99$. The confidence interval allows us to state with 95 percent certainty that the GPA in the college population, as estimated by our sample, is between 2.96 and 3.84.

SUMMARY

Once the data from a research project have been collected, they must be prepared for statistical analysis. Normally this is accomplished by the user entering the data into a computer software program. Once they are entered and saved, the data are checked for accuracy. Decisions must also be made about how to deal with any missing values and whether it is appropriate to delete any of the data.

Statistical analyses of the sample data are based on descriptive statistics, whereas population parameters are estimated using inferential statistics. Frequency distributions are normally used to summarize nominal variables, whereas measures of central tendency and dispersion are normally used to summarize quantitative variables.

Use of inferential statistics involves making estimates about the values of population parameters based on the sampling distribution of the sample statistics. Although the sample mean $(\overline{X})$ is an unbiased estimator of the population mean (μ), the sample standard deviation (s) must be corrected to provide an unbiased estimator of the population mean (σ).

The ability to accurately predict population parameters is based to a large extent on the size of the sample that has been collected, since larger samples provide more precise estimates. Statistics such as the standard error of the mean and confidence intervals around the mean are used to specify how precisely the parameters have been estimated.

KEY TERMS

central limit theorem 354
confidence interval 355
descriptive statistic 346
inferential statistic 347
mean deviation scores 350
multimodal 350
parameter 346
percentile rank 349
sampling distribution of the
    mean 355

standard error 355
standard error of the mean 355
standard normal distribution 353
standard score (z score) 352
statistics 346
Student's t 355
sum of squares (SS) 351
trimming 345
unbiased estimator 354
z score 352

REVIEW AND DISCUSSION QUESTIONS

1. What aspects of data analysis can be performed by computers, and what are the advantages of using them to do so?

2. Review the procedures used to verify that collected data are coded and entered correctly before they are analyzed through statistical software packages. What mistakes can be made when these steps are not properly followed?

3. What are the most common causes of missing data, and what difficulties do missing data cause? What can be done if data are missing?

4. Comment on the circumstances under which a researcher would consider deleting one or more responses, participants, or variables from analysis.

5. What is the difference between descriptive and inferential statistics?

6. Describe the most common descriptive statistics.

7. What are standard scores, and how are they calculated?

8. What is meant by an unbiased estimator of a population parameter?

9. How does the sample size influence the extent to which the sample data can be used to accurately estimate population parameters?

10. What statistics are used to indicate how accurately the sample data can predict population parameters?

RESEARCH PROJECT IDEAS

1. Compute a frequency distribution and draw by hand a bar chart for the variable *sex* using the data in Table 6.1. If you have access to a computer program, enter the data and compute the same statistics using the computer.

2. With a computer program, compute a grouped frequency distribution, a histogram, and a frequency curve for the life satisfaction variable in Table 6.1.

3. Compute by hand the mean, median, mode, range, variance, and standard deviation for the quantitative variables in Table 6.1. Check your calculations with the printout in Table B.2.

APPENDIX C
Bivariate Statistics

STUDY QUESTIONS

- What statistical tests are used to assess the relationships between two nominal variables, two quantitative variables, and one nominal and one quantitative variable?

- How is the Pearson correlation coefficient calculated and tested for significance?

- How is the relationship between two nominal variables in a contingency table statistically measured with χ^2?

- How is Cohen's kappa computed?

- How is bivariate regression used to predict the scores on an outcome variable given knowledge of scores on a predictor variable?

- What do the regression equation, the regression line, and the sum of squares refer to in bivariate regression?

- How is the One-Way Analysis of Variance computed?

In this appendix we continue with discussion of statistical analysis by considering **bivariate statistics**—statistical methods used to measure the relationships between two variables. These statistical tests allow assessment of the relationships between two quantitative variables (the Pearson correlation coefficient and bivariate regression), between two nominal variables (the analysis of contingency tables), and between a nominal independent and a quantitative dependent variable (the One-Way Analysis of Variance).

The Pearson Correlation Coefficient

The *Pearson product-moment correlation coefficient* (Pearson's *r*) is used to specify the direction and magnitude of linear association between two quantitative variables. The correlation coefficient can range from $r = -1.00$ to $r = +1.00$. Positive values of *r* indicate that the relationship is positive linear, and negative values indicate that it is negative linear. The strength of the correlation coefficient (the effect size) is indexed by the absolute value of the correlation coefficient. The use and interpretation of *r* are discussed in detail in Chapter 9.

Let us consider the calculation of *r* on the basis of mean deviation scores using the data in Table C.1 (the data are the same as in Table 9.1). Each of twenty individuals has contributed scores on both a Likert scale measure of optimism that ranges from 1 to 9 where higher numbers indicate greater optimism and a measure of health behavior that ranges from 1 to 25 where higher numbers indicate healthier behaviors. The third and fourth columns in the table present the standard (*z*) scores for the two variables.

Calculating *r*

We can calculate an index of the direction of relationship between the two variables (referred to as *x* and *y*) by multiplying the standard scores for each individual. The results, known as the cross-products, are shown in the fifth column. The cross-products will be mostly positive if most of the students have either two positive or two negative mean deviation scores. In this case the relationship is positive linear. If most students have a positive mean deviation on one variable and a negative mean deviation on the other variable, the cross-products will be mostly negative, indicating that the relationship is negative linear.

Pearson's *r* is computed as the sum of the cross-products divided by the sample size minus 1:

$$r = \frac{\Sigma(Z_x Z_y)}{N - 1} = \frac{9.88}{19} = .52$$

In essence, *r* represents the extent to which the participants have, on average, the same *z* score on each of the two variables. In fact, the correlation between the two variables will be $r = 1.00$ if and only if each individual has identical *z* scores on each variable. In this case the sum of the cross-products is equal to $N - 1$ and $r = 1.00$.

TABLE C.1 Computation of Pearson's r

Optimism	Health	$z_{Optimism}$	z_{Health}	$z_{Optimism} \times z_{Health}$
6	13	.39	.33	.13
7	24	.76	2.34	1.77
2	8	−1.09	−.58	.64
5	7	.02	−.77	−.01
2	11	−1.09	−.04	.04
3	6	−.72	−.95	.69
7	21	.76	1.79	1.36
9	12	1.50	.15	.22
8	14	1.13	.51	.58
9	21	1.50	1.79	2.68
6	10	.39	−.22	−.09
1	15	−1.46	.69	−1.01
9	8	1.50	−.58	−.88
2	7	−1.09	−.77	.84
4	9	−.35	−.40	.14
2	6	−1.09	−.95	1.04
6	9	.39	−.40	−.16
2	6	−1.09	−.95	1.04
6	12	.39	.15	.06
3	5	−.72	−1.13	.82

$\overline{X} = 4.95$ $\overline{X} = 11.20$
$s = .86$ $s = 2.70$
The sum of the cross-products is 9.88; $r = .52$.

Because r involves the relationship between the standard scores, the original variables being correlated do not need to have the same response format. For instance, we can correlate a Likert scale that ranges from 1 to 9 with a measure of health behavior that ranges from 1 to 25.

We can also calculate Pearson's r without first computing standard scores using the following formula:

$$r = \frac{\sum XY - \dfrac{(\sum X)(\sum Y)}{N}}{\sqrt{\left[\sum X^2 - \dfrac{(\sum X)^2}{N}\right]\left[\sum Y^2 - \dfrac{(\sum Y)^2}{N}\right]}}$$

In our example the calculation is:

$$r = \frac{1255 - \frac{(99)(224)}{20}}{\sqrt{\left[629 - \frac{(99)^2}{20}\right]\left[3,078 - \frac{(224)^2}{20}\right]}} = .52$$

Obtaining the *p*-Value

The significance of a calculated *r* can be obtained using the critical values of *r* as shown in Statistical Table D in Appendix E. Because the distribution of *r* varies depending on the sample size, the critical *r* ($r_{critical}$) is found with the degrees of freedom (*df*) for the correlation coefficient. The *df* are always $N - 2$. In our case it can be determined that the observed *r* (.52), with *df* = 18, is greater than the $r_{critical}$ of .444, and therefore we can reject the null hypothesis that *r* = 0, at *p* < .05.

The effect size for the Pearson correlation coefficient is *r*, the correlation coefficient itself, and the proportion of variance measure is r^2, which is frequently referred to as the *coefficient of determination.*

As you will recall from Chapter 9, when there are more than two correlation coefficients to be reported, it is common to place them in a *correlation matrix.* Table C.2 presents a computer printout of the correlation matrix shown in Table 9.3. Note that in addition to the correlation coefficient, *r*, the two-tailed significance level (*p*-value) and the sample size (*N*) are also printed.

TABLE C.2   Correlations: IBM SPSS Output

		SAT	SUPPORT	STUDY	GPA
Pearson Correlation	SAT	1.000	-.015	.243**	.254**
	SUPPORT	-.015	1.000	.020	.138
	STUDY	.243**	.020	1.000	.241**
	GPA	.254**	.138	.241**	1.000
Sig. (2-tailed)	SAT		.852	.002	.001
	SUPPORT	.852		.804	.087
	STUDY	.002	.804		.003
	GPA	.001	.087	.003	
N	SAT	155	155	155	155
	SUPPORT	155	155	155	155
	STUDY	155	155	155	155
	GPA	155	155	155	155

**. Correlation is significant at the 0.01 level (2-tailed).

This is a printout from the Bivariate Correlation Procedure in IBM SPSS. It includes the Pearson *r,* the sample size (*N*), and the *p*-value. Different printouts will place these values in different places.

Contingency Tables

As you will recall from Chapter 9, *contingency tables* display the number of individuals who have each value on each of two nominal variables. The size of the contingency table is determined by the number of values on the variable that represents the rows of the matrix and the number of values on the variable that represents the columns of the matrix. For instance, if there are two values of the row variable and three values of the column variable, the table is a 2 × 3 contingency table.

Although there are many different statistics that can be used to analyze contingency tables, in the following sections we will consider two of the most commonly used measures—the *chi-square test for independence* and a measure of interrater reliability known as *Cohen's kappa.*

The Chi-Square Test for Independence

As we have seen in Chapter 9, the *chi-square statistic,* symbolized as χ^2, is used to assess the degree of association between two nominal variables. The null hypothesis is that there is no relationship between the two variables. Table C.3 presents a IBM Statistical Package for the Social Sciences (IBM SPSS) computer output of the χ^2 analysis of the study shown in Table 9.2. The data are from a study assessing the attitudes of 300 community residents toward construction of a new community center in their neighborhood. The 4 × 2 contingency table displays the number of individuals in each of the combinations of the two nominal variables.

The number of individuals in each of the ethnic groups (for instance, 160 whites and 62 African Americans) is indicated to the right of the contingency table, and the numbers who favor and oppose the project are indicated at the bottom of the table. These numbers are known as the *row marginal frequencies* and the *column marginal frequencies,* respectively. The contingency table also indicates, within each of the boxes (they are called the *cells*), the *observed frequencies* or *counts* (that is, the number of each ethnic group who favor or oppose the project).

Calculating χ^2. Calculation of the chi-square statistic begins with a determination, for each cell of the contingency table, of the number of each ethnic group who would be expected to favor or oppose the project if the null hypothesis were true. These *expected frequencies,* or f_e, are calculated on the expectation that if there were no relationship between the variables, the number in each of the categories would be determined by the marginal frequencies.

For instance, since 152 out of the 300 total respondents favored the project, we would expect that $\frac{152}{300}$ of the 62 African American respondents would agree. So the expected frequency in the African American/agree cell is 152 × 62/300 = 31.4. More generally:

$$f_e = \frac{\text{Row Marginal} \times \text{Column Marginal}}{N}$$

TABLE C.3 Contingency Table: IBM SPSS Output

ETHNIC * OPINION Crosstabulation

			OPINION		
			Favor	Oppose	Total
ETHNIC	African American	Count	51	11	62
		Expected Count	31.4	30.6	62.0
	Asian	Count	31	29	60
		Expected Count	30.4	29.6	60.0
	Hispanic	Count	14	4	18
		Expected Count	9.1	8.9	18.0
	White	Count	56	104	160
		Expected Count	81.1	78.9	160.0
Total		Count	152	148	300
		Expected Count	152.0	148.0	300.0

Chi-Square Tests

	Value	df	Asymp. Sig. (2-tailed)
Pearson Chi-Square	45.780	3	.000

This is a printout from the Crosstabs procedure in IBM SPSS. Notice that on computer output, a p-value such as $p = .000$ means that the p-value is very small and thus highly significant!

The expected frequencies (counts) are also listed in Table C.3.

Once the f_e have been computed, the chi-square statistic can be, too:

$$\chi^2 = \sum \frac{(f_o - f_e)^2}{f_e}$$

where the summation is across all of the cells in the contingency table, f_o is the observed frequency in the cell, and f_e is the expected frequency for the cell. In our case, the calculation is

$$\chi^2 = \frac{(51 - 31.40)^2}{31.40} + \frac{(11 - 30.60)^2}{30.60} \cdots + \frac{(104 - 78.90)^2}{78.90} = 45.78$$

Calculating the p-value. Because the sampling distributions of χ^2 differ depending on the number of cells in the contingency table, the appropriate p-value is obtained with the use of the degrees of freedom (df) associated with χ^2, which are calculated as follows:

$$f = (\text{Number of rows} - 1) \times (\text{Number of columns} - 1) = (4 - 1) \times (2 - 1) =$$

Statistical Table E in Appendix E presents a listing of the critical values of χ^2 with df from 1 to 30 for different values of α. If the observed χ^2 is greater than the critical χ^2 as listed in the table at the appropriate df, the test is statistically significant. In our case $\chi^2_{observed}$ (45.78) is greater than the $\chi^2_{critical}$ (11.341) at alpha = .01.

Calculating the Effect Size Statistics. The chi-square test has a different associated effect size statistic depending on the number of rows and columns in the table. For 2 × 2 tables, the appropriate effect size statistic is **phi (ϕ).** Phi is calculated as:

$$\phi = \sqrt{\frac{X^2}{N}} = \sqrt{\frac{45.78}{300}} = .39$$

For tables other than 2 × 2, the associated effect size statistic is **Cramer's statistic (V_c),** calculated as

$$V_c = \sqrt{\frac{\chi^2}{N(L - 1)}}$$

where L is the lesser of either $r - 1$ or $c - 1$.

Kappa

As we have discussed in Chapter 5, in some cases the variables that form the basis of a reliability analysis are nominal rather than quantitative, and in these cases a statistic known as kappa (κ) is the appropriate test for reliability. Because in this situation the data are represented as a contingency table, and because the calculation of κ is quite similar to the calculation of χ^2, we consider it here.

Let us take as an example a case where two trained judges (Ana and Eva) have observed a set of children for a period of time and categorized their play behavior into one of the following three categories:

Plays alone

Plays in a pair

Plays in a group

We can create a contingency table indicating the coding of each judge for each child's behavior, as shown in Table C.4 (ignore the values in the parentheses for a moment).

TABLE C.4 Coding of Two Raters

	Ana's Coding			
Eva's Coding	Alone	Pair	Group	Total
Alone	18 (7.25)	4	7	29
Pair	5	25 (12.87)	9	39
Group	2	4	26 (13.44)	32
Total	25	33	42	100

We are interested in how often the two judges agree with each other. Agreements are represented on the diagonal. For instance, we can see that Ana and Eva agreed on "alone" judgments eighteen times; "pair" judgments, twenty-five times; and "group" judgments, twenty-six times. We can calculate the frequency that the two coders agreed with each other as the number of codings that fall on the diagonal:

$$\Sigma f_0 = 18 + 25 + 26 = 69$$

Thus the *proportion of agreement* between Eva and Ana is $\frac{69}{100} = .69$. Although this might suggest that agreement was quite good, this estimate inflates the actual agreement between the judges because it does not take into consideration that the coders would have agreed on some of the codings by chance.

One approach to correcting for chance agreement is to correct the observed frequency of agreement by the frequency of agreement that would have been expected by chance (see Cohen, 1960). As in a chi-square analysis, we compute f_e (but only for the cells on the diagonal) as

$$f_e = \frac{\text{Row Marginal} \times \text{Column Marginal}}{N}$$

where N is the total number of judgments. We can then calculate the sum of the expected frequencies:

$$\Sigma f_e = \frac{(29 \times 25)}{100} + \frac{(33 \times 39)}{100} + \frac{(32 \times 42)}{100} = 7.25 + 12.87 + 13.44 = 33.56$$

and compute κ:

$$\kappa = \frac{\Sigma f_o - \Sigma f_e}{N - \Sigma f_e} = \frac{69 - 33.56}{100 - 33.56} = .53$$

Notice that the observed kappa (.53), which corrects for chance agreement, is considerably lower than the proportion of agreement that we calculated previously (.69), which does not. Although there is no statistical test, in general kappa values greater than .7 are considered satisfactory. In this case the computed value, $\kappa = .53$, suggests that the coders will wish to improve their coding methods.

Bivariate Regression

We have seen that the correlation coefficient indexes the linear relationship between two quantitative variables, and we have seen that the coefficient of determination (r^2) indicates the extent to which we can predict for a person from the same population but who is not in the sample the likely score on the dependent variable given that we know that person's score on the independent variable. Larger values of r (and thus r^2) indicate a better ability to predict. Bivariate regression allows us to create an equation to make the prediction.

The Regression Equation

The actual prediction of the dependent variable from knowledge of one or more independent variables is accomplished through the creation of a **regression equation.** When there is only a single predictor (independent) variable, the formula for the regression equation is as follows:

$$\hat{Y} = \overline{Y} + r\frac{s_Y}{s_X}(X - \overline{X})$$

Of course, r is the Pearson correlation coefficient, and s_X and s_Y are the standard deviations of X and Y, respectively. $\hat{Y}$ ("Y hat") is the predicted score of an individual on the dependent variable, Y, given that person's score on the independent variable, X.

Let us return for a moment to the data in Table C.1. We can create a regression equation that can be used to predict the likely health behavior of a person with a given optimism score. Using the knowledge that the correlation between the two variables is $r = .52$, as well as information from Table C.1, we can predict that a person with an optimism score of 6 ($X = 6.0$) will have a health behavior score of $\hat{Y} = 12.91$.

$$\hat{Y} = 11.20 + .52\frac{2.70}{.86}(6 - 4.95) = 12.91$$

As discussed in Chapter 9, the regression equation has many applied uses. For instance, an employer may predict a job candidate's likely job performance ($\hat{Y}$) on the basis of his or her score on a job screening test (X).

The Regression Line

Unless the correlation between X and Y is either $r = 1.00$ or $r = -1.00$, we will not be able to perfectly predict the score on the dependent measure for an individual who is not in the sample. However, the regression equation does produce the *best possible* prediction of $\hat{Y}$ in the sense that it minimizes the sum of squared deviations (the sum of squares) around the line described by the regression equation—the regression line or line of best fit.

Figure C.1 presents a scatterplot of the standard scores of the optimism and health behavior variables using the scores from Table C.1. Two lines have

FIGURE C.1 Scatterplot

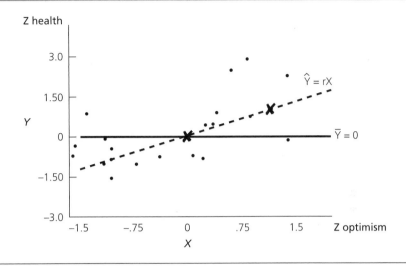

This figure is a scatterplot of the standard scores of optimism and health behavior. The data are from Table C.1. The correlation between the two variables is $r = .52$. In addition to the points, two lines have been plotted on the graph. The solid line represents $X = \bar{Y}$, our best guess of Y if we did not know X. The dashed line is the regression line or line of best fit: $\hat{Y} = rX$.

The line of best fit is drawn by plotting a line between two points that are on the line. We substitute two values of X:

$$\text{If } X = 0, \text{ then } \hat{Y} = .52 \times 0 = 0$$

$$\text{If } X = 0, \text{ then } \hat{Y} = .52 \times 1 = .52$$

The deviation of the points around the line of best fit $\sum(Y - \hat{Y})^2$ is less than the deviation of the points around the mean of $Y \sum(Y - \bar{Y})^2$.

also been plotted. The solid line is the equation $X = \bar{Y}$. This line indicates that the best guess of the value of Y (health behavior) *if we didn't have any knowledge of X* (optimism) would be $\bar{Y}$. The dashed line represents the line of best fit, which is our best guess of health behavior *given that we know the individual's optimism score.*

Partitioning of the Sum of Squares

Unless $r = 1.00$ or $r = -1.00$, the points on the scatterplot will not fall exactly on the line of best fit, indicating that we cannot predict the $\hat{Y}$ scores exactly. We can calculate the extent to which the points deviate from the line by summing the squared distances of the points from the line. It can be shown that whenever r is not equal to 0, the sum of the squared deviations of the points from the line of best fit (known as the *unexplained or residual sum of squares*) will always be smaller than the sum of the squared deviations of the points from the line that represents $\hat{Y}$ (this is, the *total sum of squares*). Thus the total SS of Y can be broken up into two parts—Total SS = Unexplained SS + Explained SS— or more formally:

$$\Sigma(Y - \bar{Y})^2 = \Sigma(Y - \hat{Y})^2 + \Sigma(\hat{Y} - \bar{Y})^2$$

Thus the improvement in prediction that comes from use of the regression equation to predict $\hat{Y}$, rather than simply predicting the mean of Y, is the explained SS divided by the total SS:

$$r^2 = \frac{\text{Explained } SS}{\text{Total } SS}$$

Of course, we won't ever need to calculate r^2 this way because r^2 is the correlation coefficient squared (the coefficient of determination)!

If X and Y are first converted to standard scores, the regression equation takes a simpler form and also becomes symmetrical. That is:

$$Z_{\hat{y}} = rz_x$$

and

$$Z_{\hat{x}} = rz_y$$

One-Way Analysis of Variance

As discussed in Chapter 10, One-Way Analysis of Variance (ANOVA) is used to compare the means on a dependent variable between two or more groups of participants who differ on a single independent variable.[1] The number of

---

[1] As we have seen in Chapter 10, the t test is a specialized case of the ANOVA that can be used to compare the means of two groups. The formula for the t test in a between-participants design is:

$$t = \frac{\bar{x}_1 - \bar{x}_2}{s_p\sqrt{\dfrac{1}{n_1} + \dfrac{1}{n_2}}}$$

where x_1 and x_2 are the means of groups 1 and 2, respectively, n_1 and n_2 are the sample sizes in groups 1 and 2, and s_p is the pooled variance estimate, calculated as:

$$s_p^2 = \frac{(n_1 - 1)s_1^2 + (n_2 - 1)s_2^2}{n_1 + n_2 - 2}$$

where s_1^2 is the variance of group 1 and s_2^2 is the variance of group 2. The significance of the t test is calculated using Statistical Table C in Appendix E. The degrees of freedom are $n_1 + n_2 - 2$. The test is significant if the obtained t value is equal to or greater than the tabled critical value.

groups is symbolized by k. The k groups may represent the different conditions in an experimental research design, or they may represent naturally occurring groupings in a quasi-experimental study. In each case the null hypothesis is that the groups have been drawn from the same population and thus that the mean on the dependent variable is the same for all of the groups except for differences due to random error:

$$H_0 : \mu_1 = \mu_2 = \mu_3 \cdots = \mu_k$$

The ANOVA is based on the assumption that if the means of the k groups are equal, then there should be no variability among them except that due to chance. If the groups differ, then the group means should not all be the same, and thus there will be significantly more variability among them than would be expected by chance.

ANOVA compares two estimates of variance. One comes from differences among the scores within each group. This estimate, known as the within-group variance, is considered random error. The second estimate, known as the between-groups variance, comes from differences among the group means. If these two estimates do not differ appreciably, we conclude that all of the group means come from the same population and that the differences among them are due to random error. If the group means differ more than expected, the null hypothesis that the differences are due only to chance is rejected.

Computation of a One-Way Between-Participants ANOVA

Let us consider the use of the ANOVA to analyze a hypothetical experimental research design in which scores on a dependent measure of aggressive behavior are compared for fifteen children, five of whom have previously viewed a set of violent cartoons, five of whom have viewed a set of nonviolent cartoons, and five of whom have viewed no cartoons.

Cartoons Viewed

Violent	Nonviolent	None
9	5	3
7	8	6
9	7	3
8	4	5
8	5	5
$\overline{X}_{violent} = 8.20$	$\overline{X}_{nonviolent} = 5.80$	$\overline{X}_{none} = 4.40$

$\overline{X}_{total} = 6.13$

We first calculate the *grand mean* $(\overline{X}_{total})$, which is the mean across all fifteen participants, as well as the means within each of the three groups. We then calculate the sum of squares of the scores for the participants within each of the three groups using the equation on page 351. The SS for the nonviolent cartoon group is

$$SS_{\text{within(nonviolent cartoons)}} = \left(179 - \frac{841}{5}\right) = 10.80$$

and the SS for the other two groups are

$$SS_{\text{within(no cartoons)}} = 7.20$$
$$SS_{\text{within(violent cartoons)}} = 2.80$$

The within-group sum of squares, or SS_{within}, is the total SS across the three groups:

$$SS_{\text{within}} = SS_1 + SS_2 \cdots + SS_k = 10.8 + 7.2 + 2.8 = 20.80$$

The SS_{within} is converted to an estimate of the within-group variability through division of it by a number that relates to the number of scores on which it is based. In the ANOVA the division is by the degrees of freedom. The within-group degrees of freedom (df_{within}) are equal to $N - k$ where N is the total number of participants and k is the number of groups. In our case the $df_{\text{within}} = 15 - 3 = 12$. This variability estimate is called the within-group mean square, or MS_{within}:

$$MS_{\text{within}} = \frac{SS_{\text{within}}}{df_{\text{within}}} = \frac{20.80}{12} = 1.73$$

The next step is to estimate the variability of the means of the k groups around the grand mean, the between-groups sum of squares, or SS_{between}. We subtract each condition mean from the grand mean and square these deviations. Then we multiply each by the number of participants in the condition and sum them all together:

$$SS_{\text{between}} = \Sigma N_i (\overline{X}_i - \overline{X}_{total})^2$$

where N_i is the number of participants in each group and $\overline{X}_i$ represents the means of each group. In our example

$$SS_{\text{between}} = 5(5.8 - 6.13)^2 + 5(4.4 - 6.13)^2 + 5(8.2 - 6.13)^2 = 36.93$$

The between-conditions sum of squares is then divided by the between-groups degrees of freedom (df_{between}), which are $k - 1$. The result is the between-conditions variability estimate, the between-groups mean square (MS_{between}):

$$MS_{\text{between}} = \frac{SS_{\text{between}}}{df_{\text{between}}} = \frac{36.93}{2} = 18.47$$

The ANOVA Summary Table

The following is a summary of all of the calculations:

$SS_{within} = 20.80$

$df_{within} = N - N = 12$

$MS_{within} = SS_{within}/df_{within} = 1.73$

$SS_{between} = 36.93$

$df_{between} = k - 1 = 2$

$MS_{between} = SS_{between}/df_{between} = 18.47$

These calculations are summarized in the ANOVA summary table, as shown in Table C.5.

The F Statistic. Also included in the table is the F value, which is the ratio of the between- to the within-variability estimates:

$$F_{obtained} = \frac{MS_{between}}{MS_{within}} = \frac{18.47}{1.73} = 10.65$$

TABLE C.5 One-Way ANOVA: IBM SPSS Output

Descriptives

			N	Mean	Std. Deviation
AGGRESS	CARTOON	1.00	5	8.2000	.8367
		2.00	5	5.8000	1.6432
		3.00	5	4.4000	1.3416
		Total	15	6.1333	2.0307

ANOVA

		Sum of Squares	df	Mean Square	F	Sig.
AGGRESS	Between Groups	36.933	2	18.467	10.654	.002
	Within Groups	20.800	12	1.733		
	Total	57.733	14			

This is a printout from the one-way ANOVA Procedure in IBM SPSS.

The $F_{obtained}$ is compared to the sampling distribution of the F statistic, which indicates the expected F value if the null hypothesis of no differences among the group means was true. Because the sampling distribution of F takes on different shapes depending on the $df_{between}$ and the df_{within}, the $F_{critical}$ is found through Statistical Table F in Appendix E with these two values. The $F_{obtained}$ is compared to the $F_{critical}$ value from the table. If $F_{obtained}$ is greater than or equal to $F_{critical}$ at the chosen alpha, the null hypothesis (that all the condition means are the same) is rejected. The means must then be examined to see if they are in the direction predicted by the research hypothesis.

The *p*-Value.   In our case, because $F_{obtained}$ (10.65) is greater than the $F_{critical}$ with $df_{between} = 2$ and $df_{within} = 12$ as found in Statistical Table F at alpha $= .05(6.93)$, the null hypothesis is rejected.

Eta

The effect size for the one-way ANOVA is eta (η), and the proportion of variance statistic is η^2. The former can be calculated from the information in the ANOVA summary table:

$$\eta^2 = \frac{SS_{between}}{(SS_{between} + SS_{within})} = \frac{36.93}{(36.93)} = .80$$

Because eta is not always given in research reports, it is useful to know that it can be calculated from the degrees of freedom and the F value as follows:

$$\eta = \sqrt{\frac{F(df_{between})}{F(df_{between}) + df_{within}}} = \sqrt{\frac{10.65(2)}{10.65(2) + 12}} = .80$$

SUMMARY

Bivariate statistics are used to assess the relationships between two nominal variables (the χ^2 test for independence), between two quantitative variables (the Pearson correlation coefficient and bivariate regression), or between a nominal and a quantitative variable (one-way ANOVA).

KEY TERMS

bivariate statistics 359
Cramer's statistic (V_c) 364

phi (ϕ) 364
regression equation 366

REVIEW AND DISCUSSION QUESTIONS

1. List all of the different bivariate statistical tests covered in this chapter, and indicate how they are used.

2. How is Statistical Table D used to assess the significance of the correlation coefficient? What are the appropriate *df*?

3. Interpret in your own words the meaning of the computer printout in Table C.2.

4. Interpret in your own words the meaning of the computer printout in Table C.3.

5. Explain the meaning of the regression equation and the regression line as shown in Figure C.1.

6. What is meant by "partitioning the sum of squares" in a regression analysis?

7. Interpret in your own words the meaning of the computer printout in Table C.5.

RESEARCH PROJECT IDEAS

1. Compute Pearson's *r* between the life satisfaction variable and the family income variable in Table 6.1. Test the *r* for statistical significance, and draw conclusions about the meaning of the test.

2. Compute a Pearson correlation coefficient between the age and the family income variable using the data in Table 6.1. Then compute the correlation again, deleting the individual with the very extreme income of $2,800,000. Notice how the presence of outliers can influence the correlation coefficient.

3. Compute the correlation between age and family income again using only the individuals in Table 6.1 who have an income less than $30,000. Again, notice how the correlation coefficient changes.

APPENDIX D
Multivariate Statistics

Multiple Regression
Regression Coefficients
The Multiple Correlation Coefficient (R)
Hierarchical and Stepwise Analyses
Multiple Regression and ANOVA

Loglinear Analysis

Means Comparisons
A Priori Contrast Analysis
Post Hoc Means Comparisons

Multivariate Statistics
Coefficient Alpha
Exploratory Factor Analysis

Canonical Correlation and MANOVA
Structural Equation Analysis

How to Choose the Appropriate Statistical Test

Summary

Key Terms

Review and Discussion Questions

Research Project Ideas

STUDY QUESTIONS

- What are simultaneous, hierarchical, and stepwise multiple regression analyses?

- What is a loglinear analysis?

- Which statistical procedures are used to compare group means?

- What are multivariate statistics?

- How are factor analyses used in research?

- What are the Multivariate Analysis of Variance (MANOVA) and canonical correlation?

- What is structural equation analysis?

- What procedures are used to choose the appropriate statistical test for a given research design?

As we have discussed at many points throughout this book, most research designs in the behavioral sciences involve a study of the relationships among more than two variables. In this appendix we will consider statistical techniques that are used to analyze such designs. The first part of the appendix will review analyses in which there is more than one independent variable. These designs are primarily analyzed through multiple regression analysis and factorial ANOVA. We will also consider the selection and computation of means comparisons tests as well as the use of *loglinear analyses* to analyze factorial designs in which the dependent measure is nominal rather than quantitative. In the second part of the appendix we will consider cases where there is more than one dependent variable. These analyses include the Multivariate Analysis of Variance (MANOVA), canonical correlation analysis, factor analysis, and structural equation analysis. Finally, we will also address another fundamental aspect of data analysis—determining which statistical procedures are most appropriate for analyzing which types of data.

Multiple Regression

As we have discussed in Chapter 9, many relational research designs take the form of multiple regression, in which more than one independent variable is used to predict a single dependent variable. Like bivariate regression (discussed in Appendix C), the goal of multiple regression is to create a mathematical equation that allows us to make the best prediction of a person's score on a dependent or outcome variable given knowledge of that person's scores on a set of independent or predictor variables.

Multiple regression is perhaps the most useful and flexible of all of the statistical procedures that we discuss in this book, and it has many applications in behavioral science research. For instance, as we have seen in Chapter 12, multiple regression can be used to reduce error by controlling for scores on baseline measures in before-after research designs. Multiple regression is also used to create path-analytic diagrams that allow specifying causal relationships among variables (see Chapter 9).

The goal of a multiple regression analysis is to find a linear combination of independent variables that makes the best prediction of a single quantitative dependent variable in the sense that it minimizes the squared deviations around a line of best fit. The general form of the multiple regression equation is

$$\hat{Y} = A + B_1 + X_1 + B_2 + X_2 + B_3 + X_3 \cdots + B_i + X_i$$

where the X's represent scores on independent variables, A is a constant known as the *intercept,* and the B's, known as the *regression coefficients,* represent the linear relationship between each independent variable and the dependent variable, taking into consideration or *controlling for* each of the other independent variables.

If the predictor variables are first converted to standard (z) scores, the regression equation can be written as

$$\hat{Y}_z = \beta_1 z_1 + \beta_2 z_2 + \beta_3 z_3 \cdots \beta_i z_i$$

In the standardized equation the intercept is always zero and is therefore no longer in the equation. The betas (β_1, β_2, and β_3), which are not the same as the B's in the previous equation, are known as the *standardized regression coefficients* or *beta weights*.

Regression Coefficients

Consider as an example the multiple regression analysis that was presented in Chapter 9 and displayed in Figure 9.4. The goal of the analysis is to predict the current grade-point average (GPA) of a group of 155 college students using knowledge about their scores on three predictor variables—Scholastic Aptitude Test (SAT) score, study time, and rated social support. The input to the regression analysis is the correlation matrix among the predictor and outcome variables, as shown in Table 9.3. Because the actual calculation of the regression coefficients involves many mathematical calculations, it is best performed by computer. The computer printout from the IBM Statistical Package for the Social Sciences (IBM SPSS) is shown in Table D.1.

The unstandardized regression coefficients and the intercept are listed in the bottom panel of the printout, in the column labeled "B." This information can be used to create a regression equation that would allow us to predict the college GPA of a student who is not in the sample if we know his or her scores on the predictor variables. For instance, a student who was known to have the following scores on the predictor variables:

Study hours = 12

SAT = 1120

Social support = 7

would be expected to have a college GPA of 2.51:

$$\text{GPA} = .428 + .00086 \times 1120 + .086 \times 7 + .043 \times 12 = 2.51$$

Unless the goal is to actually make the prediction of an individual's score, the standardized regression coefficients are more commonly used and are usually presented in the research report (see as an example Figure 9.4). In our case, the solution to the standardized regression comes from the column labeled "beta" in the bottom panel of Table D.1:

$$\hat{z}_{\text{GPA}} = .210 \times z_{\text{SAT}} + .137 \times z_{\text{SUPPORT}} + .187 \times z_{\text{STUDY}}$$

As discussed in Chapter 9, the standardized regression coefficients indicate the extent to which any one independent variable predicts the dependent variable, taking account of or controlling for the effects of all of the other independent variables.

TABLE D.1   Output from a Multiple Regression Analysis

Model Summary[a,b]

Model	Variables		R	R Square	Adjusted R Square	Std. Error of the Estimate
	Entered	Removed				
1	STUDY, SUPPORT, SAT[c,d]	.	.342	.117	.100	.6256

a. Dependent Variable: GPA

b. Method: Enter

c. Independent Variables: (Constant), STUDY, SUPPORT, SAT

d. All requested variables entered.

ANOVA[a]

Model		Sum of Squares	df	Mean Square	F	Sig.
1	Regression	7.841	3	2.614	6.679	.000[b]
	Residual	59.089	151	.391		
	Total	66.930	154			

a. Dependent Variable: GPA

b. Independent Variables: (Constant), STUDY, SUPPORT, SAT

Coefficients[a]

Model		Unstandardized Coefficients		Standardized Coefficients	t	Sig.
		B	Std. Error	Beta		
1	(Constant)	.428	.533		.804	.423
	SAT	8.6E-04	.000	.210	2.666	.009
	SUPPORT	8.6E-02	.048	.137	1.795	.075
	STUDY	4.3E-02	.018	.187	2.368	.019

a. Dependent Variable: GPA

This is a printout from the multiple regression procedure in IBM SPSS (see footnote on page 351 for an explanation of scientific notation).

Each of the regression coefficients can be tested for statistical significance (the test is the same for the unstandardized and the standardized coefficient). The appropriate statistical test is a t statistic, along with an associated p-value, as shown in the right-most two columns in the coefficients section of Table D.1.

The Multiple Correlation Coefficient (*R*)

The *multiple correlation coefficient, R,* indicates the extent to which the predictor variables as a group predict the outcome variable. R is thus the effect size for the multiple regression analysis, and R^2 indicates the proportion of variance in the outcome variable that is accounted for by all of the predictor variables together. The multiple R is printed in the first section of the printout in Table D.1. The statistical test for the significance of R is an F ratio, and this is also found on the computer printout. As shown in the middle section of Table D.1, the F value in our example is highly statistically significant. The F value should be reported in the research report, much as it would be in an ANOVA, but with the "regression" and the "residual" degrees of freedom. In this case the appropriate way to report the F value is: $F(3,151) = 6.68$, $p < .01$.

Hierarchical and Stepwise Analyses

To this point we have considered the case in which all of the predictor variables are simultaneously used to predict the outcome variable and the multiple R is used to indicate how well they do so. This procedure is known as **simultaneous multiple regression.** In other cases, however, it is possible to enter the predictor variables into the multiple regression analysis in steps or stages. The goal is to examine the extent to which the entering of a new set of variables increases the multiple correlation coefficient.

In some cases the variables are entered in a predetermined theoretical order. For instance, when predicting job satisfaction, the researcher might first enter demographic variables such as the employee's salary, age, and number of years on the job. Then, in a second stage the researcher might enter the individual's ratings of his or her supervisors and work environment. This approach would allow the researcher to see if the set of variables that measured the person's perceptions of the job (set 2) increased the ability to predict satisfaction above and beyond the demographic variables (set 1). When the predictor variables are added in a predetermined order, the analysis is known as a **hierarchical multiple regression.**

In other cases there is no particular order selected ahead of time, but the variables are entered into the analysis such that those that produce the biggest increase in the multiple R are entered first. For instance, if our researcher did not have a particular theory, but only wanted to see what variables predicted job satisfaction, she or he might let the computer determine which of the variables best predicted according to the extent to which they increased the multiple R. This approach is known as a **stepwise multiple regression.** A fuller discussion of these procedures can be found in Cohen and Cohen (1983), and in Aiken and West (1991).

Multiple Regression and ANOVA

Although we have only considered the use of quantitative predictor variables to this point, it is also possible to use nominal variables as the predictors in either bivariate or multiple regression analyses. Consider, for instance, an experimental research design in which there were two levels of the independent variable. Instead of conducting a one-way ANOVA on the dependent variable, we could analyze the data using regression. Individuals who were in one condition of the experiment would receive a score of 0 on the predictor variable, and those who were in the other condition would receive a score of 1 (it does not matter which score is assigned to which group).

This predictor variable would be entered into a bivariate regression analysis along with the measured dependent variable from the experiment. It turns out that the associated p-value of the regression equation will be exactly the same as the p-value associated with the F in a one-way between-participants ANOVA (you can test this yourself—see Research Project Ideas problem 1 at the end of this appendix).

Although the relationship between correlation and the means tests in ANOVA analysis is clear from this example, in cases of factorial ANOVA the coding of the different levels of the independent variables and the interaction tests is more complicated (see Cohen & Cohen, 1983). However, any test that can be conducted as an ANOVA can also be conducted as a multiple regression analysis. In fact, both multiple regression and ANOVA are special cases of a set of mathematical procedures called the **general linear model (GLM).** Because the GLM is almost always used by computer programs to compute ANOVAs, you may find this term listed in your statistical software package.

When the prediction involves both nominal and quantitative variables, the analysis allows the means of the dependent variable in the different experimental conditions to be adjusted or controlled for the influence of the quantitative variables. This procedure, called the **Analysis of Covariance,** can be used in some cases to control for the effects of potential confounding variables (see Cohen & Cohen, 1983).

Loglinear Analysis

As we have discussed the use of factorial ANOVA in detail in Chapter 11, including the interpretation of the ANOVA summary table, we will not review these procedures here. However, one limitation of factorial ANOVA is that it should be used only when the dependent variable is approximately normally distributed. Although this can usually be assumed for quantitative dependent measures, the ANOVA should never be used to analyze nominal dependent measures. For instance, if the dependent measure is a dichotomous response, such as a "yes" or a "no" decision or an indication of whether someone "helped" or "did not help," an ANOVA analysis is not appropriate.

As we have seen in Appendix C, if there is only one nominal independent-variable and one nominal dependent variable, the χ^2 test for independence is the appropriate test of association. However, when more than one nominal variable is used to predict a nominal dependent variable, a statistical analysis known as loglinear analysis can be used. The **loglinear analysis** basically represents a χ^2 analysis in which contingency tables that include more than two variables are created and the association among them is tested. A full discussion of loglinear analysis can be found in statistical textbooks such as Hays (1988).

Means Comparisons

As we have discussed in Chapter 11, whenever there are more than two conditions in an ANOVA analysis, the F value or values alone do not provide enough information for the scientist to fully understand the differences among the condition means. For instance, a significant main effect of a variable that has more than two levels indicates that the group means are not all the same but does not indicate which means are statistically different from each other. Similarly, a significant F value can indicate that an interaction is significant, but it cannot indicate which means are different from each other.

In these cases *means comparisons* are used to test the differences between and among particular group means. As we have discussed in Chapter 11, means comparisons can be either *pairwise comparisons* in which any two means are compared or *complex comparisons* in which more than two means are simultaneously compared. Furthermore, the approach to comparing means is different depending on whether the specific means comparisons were planned ahead of time (*a priori means comparisons*) or are chosen after the data have been collected (*post hoc means comparisons*). There are a variety of different statistical tests that can be used to compare means, and in this section we will consider some of the most popular means comparison statistics (see Keppel & Zedeck, 1989, for more information).

A Priori Contrast Analysis

The most general method of conducting means comparisons that have been planned a priori (this method can be used for either pairwise or complex comparisons) is known as **contrast analysis** (see Rosenthal & Rosnow, 1985, for a detailed investigation of this topic). A contrast analysis involves computing an F value, which is the ratio of two variance estimates (mean squares). The mean square that is entered into the numerator of the F ratio is known as the $MS_{comparison}$ and is calculated as follows:

$$MS_{comparison} = n(c_1 + \overline{X}_1 + c_2\overline{X}_2c = \cdots c_k\overline{X}_k)^2$$

where n is the number of participants in each of the k groups, the $\overline{X}_1$ are the group means for each of the groups, and the c_i are the contrast weights.

Setting the Contrast Weights.   The **contrast weights** are set by the researcher to indicate how the group means are to be compared. The following rules apply in the setting of contrast weights:

Means that are not being compared are given contrast weights of $c_i = 0$.

The sum of the contrast weights $(\sum c_i)$ must equal 0.

The F involves a ratio between the $MS_{comparison}$ and the MS_{within} from the ANOVA analysis:

$$F = \frac{MS_{comparison}}{MS_{within}}$$

The significance of F is tested with $df_{comparison} = 1$ and the df_{within} from the ANOVA analysis.

Computing the Contrasts.   To take a specific example, let us return for a moment to the ANOVA summary table and the observed group means from the data in Table C.5. Assume that the researcher wishes to compare aggressive play behavior in the violent-cartoon condition with aggressive play in the nonviolent-cartoon condition. He or she therefore sets the following contrast weights:

$c_{violent} = 1$

$c_{nonviolent} = -1$

$c_{none} = 0$

and then calculates the $MS_{comparison}$:

$$MS_{comparison} = \frac{5[(1)8.20 + (-1)5.80 + (0)4.44]^2}{(1)^2 + (1)^2 + (0)^2} = \frac{28.80}{2.00} = 14.40$$

and the associated F value:

$$F_{comparison} = \frac{MS_{comparison}}{MS_{within}} = \frac{14.4}{1.78} = 8.24$$

The critical F value $(F_{critical})$ is found from Statistical Table F in Appendix E with $df_{numerator} = 1$ and $df_{denominator} = 12$. This value is 4.75. Because the $F_{comparison}$ (8.24) is greater than the $F_{critical}$ (4.75), we conclude that aggressive play for the children in the violent-cartoon condition is significantly greater than that in the nonviolent-cartoon condition.

It is also possible to use contrast analysis to conduct complex comparisons in which more than two means are compared at the same time. For instance, if the researcher wished to compare aggressive play in the violent-cartoon condition with aggressive play in the nonviolent and no-film conditions combined, the following contrast weights would be used:

$c_{violent} = 1$

$c_{nonviolent} = -1/2$

$c_{none} = -1/2$

Note that (as it should be) the sum of the comparison weights is zero. In this case, the $F_{comparison}$ (18.28) is again greater than $F_{critical}$ (4.75) and thus is significant. Contrast analysis can also be used to compare means from factorial and repeated measures experimental designs.

Post Hoc Means Comparisons

As we have discussed in Chapter 11, one of the dangers of means comparisons is that there can be a lot of them, and each test increases the likelihood of a Type 1 error. The increases in experimentwise alpha are particularly problematic when the researcher desires to make pairwise comparisons that have not been planned ahead of time. *Post hoc means comparisons tests* are designed to control the experimentwise alpha level in means comparisons that are made after the data have been conducted.

The Fisher LSD Test.   One approach to reducing the probability of a Type 1 error is to use the overall F test as a type of initial filter on the significance of the mean differences. In this procedure, known as the **Fisher Least Significant Difference (LSD) Test,** regular contrast analyses (as discussed previously) are used, but with the following provisos:

1. Only pairwise comparisons are allowed.
2. Pairwise comparisons can be made only if the initial ANOVA F value is significant.

The Fisher test thus protects to some extent against increases in Type 1 errors by limiting the number of comparisons that can be made, and only allowing them to be made after an initially significant F test.

The Scheffé Test.   A second approach to conducting post hoc means comparisons, and one that can be used for either pairwise or complex comparisons, is to reduce the alpha level to statistically reduce the likelihood of a Type 1 error. One such approach is known as the **Scheffé Means Comparison Test.** The Scheffé test involves comparing the $F_{comparison}$ to a critical F value that is adjusted to take into consideration the number of possible comparisons. This is done through computation of a Scheffé F value:

$$F_{Scheffé} = (k - 1)F_{critical}$$

where k is the number of groups in the research design being compared. The contrast test is considered significant only if the $F_{comparison}$ is greater than or equal to $F_{Scheffé}$. In our example, the contrast analysis comparing aggression in the violent versus the nonviolent films would not be considered significant because the $F_{comparison}$ (8.24) is less than $F_{Scheffé}$ ($2 \times 4.75 = 9.50$).

The Tukey HSD Test.   One disadvantage of the Scheffé test is that it is very conservative, and thus although it reduces the probability of Type 1 errors, it also increases the possibility of Type 2 errors. However, many researchers do not feel that the Fisher LSD Test sufficiently protects against the possibility of Type 1 errors. Therefore, alternative means comparisons tests are sometimes used. One popular alternative, which is often considered to be the most appropriate for post hoc comparisons, is the **Tukey Honestly Significant Difference (HSD) Test.** This means comparison statistic can be calculated by most statistical software programs (see Keppel & Zedeck, 1989).

Multivariate Statistics

To this point in the book we have primarily considered cases in which data have been collected on more than one independent variable but there is only a single dependent variable. Such statistical procedures are called **univariate statistics.** However, in many research projects more than one dependent variable is collected. Inclusion of a combination of variables that measure the same or similar things together increases the reliability of measurement and thus the likelihood that significant relationships will be found.

Multivariate statistics are data analysis procedures that are specifically designed to analyze more than one dependent variable at the same time.[1] Most basically, the goal of multivariate statistics is to reduce the number of measured variables by analyzing the correlations among them and combining them together to create a smaller number of new variables that adequately summarize the original variables and can be used in their place in subsequent statistical analyses (see Harris, 1985; Stevens, 1996; Tabachnick & Fidell, 1989).

The decisions about which variables to combine together in multivariate statistical procedures can be made both on the basis of theoretical expectations about which variables should be measuring the same conceptual variables and on an empirical analysis of how the measures actually correlate among one another. These procedures are mathematically complex and are calculated by computers.

Coefficient Alpha

We have already discussed one type of multivariate statistical analysis in Chapter 5. Measures that are expected to be assessing the same conceptual variable are usually entered into a *reliability analysis,* and if they are found to be intercorrelated, they are combined together into a single score. And we have seen that the most frequently used measure of reliability among a set of quantitative variables is *coefficient alpha*. Although it is usually better to compute coefficient alpha using a computer program (a sample computer output

---

[1]Although we will focus on the case in which the multiple measures are dependent variables, multivariate statistics can actually be used whenever there are multiple measured variables. They are therefore appropriate for descriptive, correlational, or experimental research designs, depending on the specific needs of the research project.

TABLE D.2   Output from a Reliability Analysis

```
R E L I A B I L I T Y   A N A L Y S I S   -   S C A L E   (A L P H A)

Item-total Statistics

                  Scale         Scale      Corrected
                  Mean         Variance       Item-           Alpha
                 if Item       if Item        Total          if Item
                 Deleted       Deleted     Correlation       Deleted

    ESTEEM1      30.7309       39.0992        .3330           .8289
    ESTEEM2      30.5785       39.3036        .4272           .8191
    ESTEEM3      31.5998       38.0226        .5548           .8087
    ESTEEM4      30.8318       39.2916        .4105           .8204
    ESTEEM5      31.7253       37.3330        .5043           .8119
    ESTEEM6      30.9731       35.8242        .6625           .7967
    ESTEEM7      31.0908       35.9659        .6256           .7999
    ESTEEM8      32.6143       34.9959        .5133           .8128
    ESTEEM9      32.6973       35.1990        .5426           .8084
    ESTEEM10     32.2287       34.4056        .6031           .8011


Reliability Coefficients

N of Cases =    892.0                    N of Items = 10


Alpha =    .8268
```

This is a printout from the reliability procedure in IBM SPSS. The data represent the scores from 892 students who completed the ten-item Rosenberg self-esteem scale, as shown in Figure 4.2. Items 3, 5, 8, 9, and 10 have been reverse-scored before analysis. As shown at the bottom of the printout, coefficient alpha, based on all ten items, is .83. The last column, labeled "Alpha if item deleted," is particularly useful because it indicates the coefficient alpha that the scale would have if the item on that line was deleted. This information can be used to delete some items from the scale in order to increase alpha (see Chapter 5).

is shown in Table D.2), it is also possible to do so by hand using the following formula:

$$\text{Coefficient alpha} = \frac{k}{k-1} \times \left(\frac{\sigma^{2}{}_{y} - \Sigma\sigma_i^2}{\sigma_y^2} \right)$$

y where k is the number of items, σ_y^2 is the variance of the scale sum, and σ_i^2 are the variances of the k items. (The interpretation of coefficient alpha is discussed in Chapter 5.)

Exploratory Factor Analysis

When the measured dependent variables are all designed to assess the same conceptual variable, reliability analysis is most appropriate. In other cases, however, the measured variables might be expected to assess similar but not necessarily identical conceptual variables. Consider, for instance, a researcher who is interested in assessing the effects of a therapy program on the mood states of a sample of patients who have just completed the therapy in comparison to a control group of patients who have not had therapy. Both groups are asked to rate, using seven-point Likert scales, how much they have experienced each of the twenty-one emotions listed in Table D.3 over the past week. The researcher's hypothesis is that the group that has completed therapy will report more positive emotion. However, because the ratings

TABLE D.3 Output from a Factor Analysis: The Rotated Factor Matrix

	Factor 1	Factor 2	Factor 3	Factor 4
Happy	.87	—	—	—
Satisfied	.85	—	—	—
Pleased	.84	—	—	—
Delighted	.83	—	—	—
Glad	.83	—	—	—
Content	.77	—	—	—
Excited	.71	—	—	—
Sad	−.68	.41		
Droopy	—	.84	—	—
Gloomy	—	.79	—	—
Depressed	—	.75	—	—
Miserable	—	.67	—	—
Distressed	—	.60	—	—
Tired	—	.58	—	—
Sleepy	—	.58	—	—
Angry	—	—	.69	—
Frustrated	—	—	.65	—
Tense	—	—	.63	—
Annoyed	—	—	.62	—
Relaxed	—	−.48	—	.74
Calm	—	—	—	.63

This rotated factor matrix presents the loadings of each of the original twenty-one emotion variables on each of the four factors. Negative loadings indicate that the variable is negatively related to the factor. Loadings less than .30 are not reported. The four factors seem to indicate the emotions of "satisfaction," "depression," "anger," and "relaxation," respectively. The factor rotation is satisfactory because, with only a few exceptions, each of the original variables loads on only one of the factors. The factor analysis has successfully reduced the twenty-one original items to only four factors.

measure a variety of different emotional responses, the researcher does not think that it would be appropriate to combine all of the twenty-one emotion ratings into a single score. Instead, she or he decides to conduct an exploratory factor analysis.

Exploratory factor analysis is a multivariate statistical technique used to analyze the underlying pattern of correlations among a set of measured variables and to develop a simplified picture of the relationships among these variables. This approach is generally used when the researcher does not already have an expectation about which variables will be associated with each other but rather wishes to learn about the associations by examining the collected data.

Creation of the Factors.   In our example the researcher begins with the correlation matrix among the sixteen emotion variables. The factor analysis is used to reduce the number of variables by creating or *extracting* a smaller set of **factors,**[2] each of which is a linear combination of the scores on the original variables. In the first stage of the factor analysis the number of factors needed to adequately summarize the original variables is determined. In this part of the analysis the factors are ordered such that the first factor is the combination of the original variables that does the best job of summarizing the data and each subsequent factor does less well in doing so.

In the second stage the linear combinations of the original variables are created through a process known as *rotation*. The goal of the rotation is to achieve a set of factors where, as much as possible, each of the original variables contributes to only one of the underlying factors. In practice there are a number of different techniques for determining the number of factors and developing the linear combinations. For instance, the factors themselves may be constrained to be either correlated or uncorrelated (see Tabachnick & Fidell, 1989).

The Factor Loading Matrix.   The primary output of an exploratory factor analysis, as shown in Table D.3, is a matrix indicating how each of the original measured variables contributes to each of the factors after the extraction and rotation. In our example four factors, represented in the four columns, were extracted from the correlation matrix. The numbers in the columns are called the *factor loadings* of the twenty-one original emotion variables on each of the four factors. Factor loadings range from -1.00 to $+1.00$ and are interpreted in the same manner as a correlation coefficient would be. Higher loadings (either positive or negative) indicate that the variable is more strongly associated with the factor. The variables that correlate most highly with each other, because they have something in common with each other, end up loading on the same factor.

---

[2]Be careful not to confuse the use of the term *factor* in a factor analysis with the term *factor* as an independent variable in a factorial experimental design. They are not the same.

One important limitation of an exploratory factor analysis is that it does not provide an interpretation of what the factors mean—this must be done by the scientist. However, a "good" factor analysis is one that is interpretable in the sense that the factors seem to comprise theoretically meaningful variables. The factor analysis in Table D.3 is interpretable because the four factors appear to represent the broader emotions of "satisfaction," "depression," "anger," and "relaxation," respectively.

Factor Scores. Once the factors have been extracted, a new set of variables, one for each factor, can be created. The participants' scores on each of these variables are known as the **factor scores.** Each factor score is a combination of the participants' scores on all of the variables that load on the factor and represents, in essence, what the person would have scored if it had been possible to directly measure the factor. The advantage of the factor analysis is that the factor scores can be used as dependent variables in subsequent analyses to substitute, often without much loss of information, for the original variables.

In our example, the researcher could then compare the therapy group with the control group not on each of the twenty-one original variables but on the four factor scores representing satisfaction, depression, anger, and relaxation. You can see that great economy has been gained through the factor analysis because the original twenty-one variables have now been reduced to the four factor score variables. Although some information is lost, there is a great savings in the number of variables that need to be analyzed.

Canonical Correlation and MANOVA

Although exploratory factor analysis is frequently used to create a simplified picture of the relationships among the dependent measures, and the factor scores are then used as dependent measures in subsequent analyses, there is another method of analyzing data that can be used when there is a set of dependent variables to be analyzed. This approach involves computing statistical associations between the independent variable or variables in the research design and the set of dependent variables, taken as a group.

When the independent variable or variables in the research design are nominal, the **Multivariate Analysis of Variance (MANOVA)** can be used. The MANOVA is essentially an ANOVA that assesses the significance of the relationship between one or more nominal independent variables and a set of dependent variables. For instance, rather than computing an exploratory factor analysis, our researcher could have used a MANOVA analysis to directly test whether there was a significant difference between the therapy group and the control group on all of the sixteen emotion variables taken together.

The statistical test in a MANOVA analysis is known as a *multivariate F.* Like an *F* test in an ANOVA, the multivariate *F* has associated degrees of freedom as well as a *p*-value. If the multivariate *F* is significant, the researcher can draw the conclusion that the groups are different on some linear combination of the dependent variables.

Canonical correlation is a statistical procedure similar to a MANOVA that is used when the independent variable or variables are quantitative rather than nominal. The **canonical correlation** assesses the association between either a single independent variable and a set of dependent variables or between sets of independent and dependent variables. The goal of the statistical analysis is to determine whether there is an overall relationship between the two sets of variables. The resulting statistical test is significant if there is a linear combination that results in a significant association between the independent and the dependent variables.

Practical Uses.   The major advantage of MANOVA and canonical correlation is that they allow the researcher to make a single statistical test of the relationship between the independent and dependent variables. Thus these tests are frequently used as a preliminary step to control the likelihood of Type 1 errors—if the multivariate statistical test is significant, then other follow-up tests (ANOVAs, correlations, or regressions) are made on the individual dependent variables, but if the multivariate statistic is not significant, the null hypothesis is not rejected and no further analyses are made.

Disadvantages.   Although MANOVA and canonical correlation are sometimes used as initial tests in cases where there is a set of dependent variables, they do not provide information about how the independent and dependent variables are associated. For instance, a significant multivariate F test in a MANOVA analysis means that there is some pattern of differences across the groups on the dependent variables, but it does not provide any information about what these differences are. For this reason, many researchers avoid using MANOVA and canonical correlation and rely on factor analysis instead.

Structural Equation Analysis

In the preceding examples, because there was no preexisting hypothesis about the expected relationships among the variables, the researcher used multivariate statistical tests to help determine this relationship. In other cases, however, the expected relationships among the dependent variables and between the independent and dependent variables can be specified ahead of time. In these cases another multivariate approach, known as structural equation analysis, can be used. As we have seen in Chapter 9, a **structural equation analysis** is a multivariate statistical procedure that tests whether the observed relationships among a set of variables conform to a theoretical prediction about how those variables should be related.

Confirmatory Factor Analysis.   One type of structural equation analysis is known as a confirmatory factor analysis. Like exploratory factor analysis, the goal of **confirmatory factor analysis** is to explore the correlations among a set of measured variables. In a structural equation analysis, however, the summary variables are called **latent variables** rather than factors.

Consider, for instance, a scientist who has developed a new thirty-item scale to assess creativity. However, the items were designed to assess different conceptual variables, each of which represents a subcomponent of creativity. For instance, some of the items were designed to measure "musical creativity," some were designed to measure "artistic creativity," and still others were designed to assess "social creativity," such as having a good sense of humor.

Because there is an expected relationship among the measured variables, confirmatory factor analysis can be used to test whether the actual correlations among the items conform to the theoretical expectations about how the items should be correlated. In a confirmatory factor analysis an expected theoretical relationship among the variables, in the form of a hypothesized factor loading matrix, is inputted into the program. In our case the scientist would specify that three factors (musical creativity, artistic creativity, and social creativity) were expected, as well as indicating which of the items were expected to load on each of the factors. As we will see further on, the confirmatory factor analysis would be used to test whether the observed relationships among the items on the creativity scale matched the relationships that were expected to be observed among them.

Testing of Relationships Among Variables.

One particular advantage of structural equation analyses is that, in addition to the relationships between the measured variables and the latent variables (the factor loadings), the relationships among the latent variables can be studied. And the latent variables can include both independent and dependent variables. Consider as an example an industrial psychologist who has conducted a correlational study designed to predict the conceptual variable of "job performance" from three conceptual variables of "supervisor satisfaction," "coworker satisfaction," and "job interest."

As shown in Figure D.1, the researcher has used three measured variables (represented as squares) to assess each of the four latent variables (supervisor satisfaction, coworker satisfaction, job interest, and job performance). Rather than computing a separate reliability analysis on the three independent variables and the dependent variable, combining each set of three scores together, and then using a regression analysis with three independent variables and one dependent variable, the scientist could use a structural equation analysis to test the entire set of relationships at the same time. In the structural equation analysis all of the relationships among the variables—some of which involve the relationship between the measured variables and the latent variables and others of which involve the relationships among the latent variables themselves—are simultaneously tested.

The Goodness of Fit Index.

In addition to estimating the actual relationships among the variables, the structural equation analysis tests whether these observed relationships fit a proposed set of theoretical relationships

FIGURE D.1 Structural Equation Model

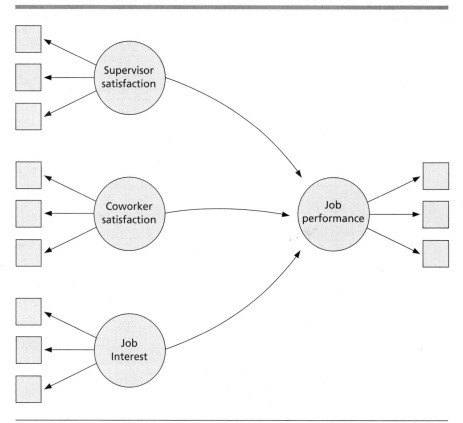

This hypothetical structural equation analysis uses nine measures of job satisfaction, which are combined into three latent variables, to predict a single latent variable of job performance, as measured by three dependent variables. The value of the overall fit of the model to the collected data can be estimated. The structural equation analysis tests both the measurement of the latent variables and the relationships among them.

among the variables. A measure known as a **goodness of fit statistic** is used to test how well the collected data fit the hypothesized relationship, and in many cases the fit of the data is also tested with a chi-square test of statistical significance. If the pattern of observed relationships among the measured variables matches the pattern of expected relationships, then the goodness of fit statistic is large (usually above .90) and the chi-square test is small and nonsignificant. In this case the data are said to "fit" the hypothesized model.

In summary, structural equation analysis, of which confirmatory factor analysis is one example, is a procedure used to test hypotheses about the relationships among variables. If the observed relationships among the variables fit the proposed relationships among the variables, the data can be taken as supporting the research hypothesis. Although most often used in correlational designs, structural equation modeling can also be used in experimental research designs where there is more than one measured dependent variable.

How to Choose the Appropriate Statistical Test

This book has been devoted to outlining the general procedures for creating research designs, collecting data, and analyzing those data to draw appropriate conclusions. In many cases the research design itself specifies which set of statistical techniques will be used to analyze the collected data. For instance, experimental designs are usually analyzed with ANOVA, and correlational research

FIGURE D.2 Choosing a Statistical Analysis

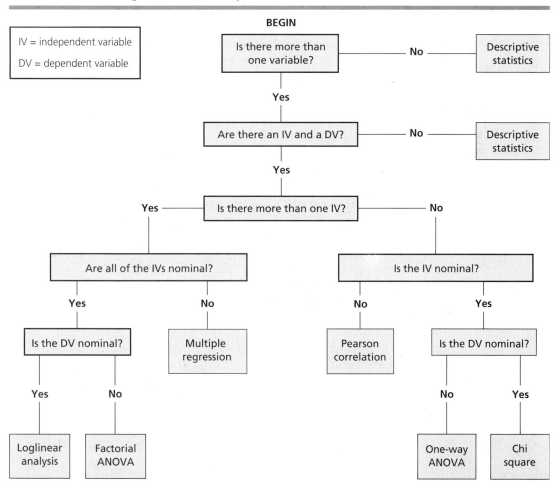

designs are best analyzed with correlational techniques such as multiple regression analysis. Nevertheless, these basic rules are virtually always limited in some sense because the collected data are almost always more complicated than was expected, and therefore creative application of statistical techniques to the data is required to fully understand them. Thus the art of data analysis goes beyond a mere understanding of research designs and statistical analysis and involves the creative selection of statistical tools to better understand collected data.

Experts in data analysis are able to get a "feel" for the data, and this understanding leads them to try different approaches to data analysis. One approach that can help get you started when you are considering a data analysis strategy is to determine the format of the independent and dependent variables in the research design and then to choose an appropriate statistical technique by following the flow chart shown in Figure D.2. Nevertheless, experience with data analysis will be your best teacher when you are learning the complex art of data analysis.

SUMMARY

In most research projects the relationships among more than two variables are assessed at the same time. When there are more than two independent variables but only a single dependent variable, multiple regression is the most appropriate data analysis procedure. The independent variables in a multiple regression can be entered simultaneously, hierarchically, or by using a stepwise approach. The factorial Analysis of Variance is really a type of regression analysis in which the independent variables are nominal. When there is more than one independent variable and the dependent measure is nominal, loglinear analysis, rather than ANOVA, is the appropriate statistical test.

One difficulty in ANOVA designs that have more than two conditions is that the F values do not always provide information about which groups are significantly different from each other. A number of means comparison procedures, including contrast analysis, the Fisher LSD test, the Scheffé test, and the Tukey HSD test, can be used to help make this determination.

In cases where more than one dependent measure has been assessed, multivariate statistics may be used to analyze the relationships among the variables and to reduce their complexity. Examples of multivariate procedures include exploratory factor analysis, MANOVA, and canonical correlation. When a theoretical relationship among the variables is specified ahead of time, structural equation modeling can be used to test whether the observed data fit the expected pattern of relationships.

One of the important aspects of research is learning how to use the complex array of available statistical procedures to analyze the data that have been collected. There is no substitute for experience in learning to do so.

KEY TERMS

Analysis of Covariance 379
canonical correlation 388
confirmatory factor analysis 388
contrast analysis 380
contrast weights 381
exploratory factor analysis 386
factor scores 387
factors 386
Fisher Least Significant Difference
    (LSD) Test 382
general linear model (GLM) 379
goodness of fit statistic 390
hierarchical multiple regression 378
latent variables 389

loglinear analysis 380
Multivariate Analysis of Variance
    (MANOVA) 387
multivariate statistics 383
Scheffé Means Comparison
    Test 382
simultaneous multiple
    regression 378
stepwise multiple regression 378
structural equation analysis 388
Tukey Honestly Significant
    Difference (HSD) Test 383
univariate statistics 383

REVIEW AND DISCUSSION QUESTIONS

1. Why is it possible to consider ANOVA as a special case of regression?

2. Give an example of when simultaneous, hierarchical, and stepwise multiple regression analyses might be used in research.

3. How is a loglinear analysis used?

4. Consider the various means comparison procedures that have been discussed in this appendix, and indicate the advantages and disadvantages of each.

5. What is the difference between exploratory factor analysis and confirmatory factor analysis, and under what conditions would each be used?

6. What are the Multivariate Analysis of Variance (MANOVA) and canonical correlation, and what are their advantages and disadvantages?

7. How is structural equation analysis used to test the measurement of, and the relationships among, conceptual variables?

8. Interpret in your own words the meaning of the computer printouts in Tables D.1, D.2, and D.3.

RESEARCH PROJECT IDEAS

1. Compute a Pearson correlation coefficient between the independent variable and the dependent variable in Research Project Ideas problem 7 in Appendix C. If you have access to a computer software package, demonstrate that the p-value for the correlation coefficient is exactly the same as that for a one-way ANOVA on the data.

APPENDIX E
Statistical Tables

Statistical Table A: Random Numbers

Statistical Table A contains a list of random numbers that can be used to draw random samples from populations or to make random assignment to conditions. Consider the table as a list of single digits ranging from 0 to 9 (the numbers are spaced in pairs to make them easier to read).

Selecting a Random Sample

To select a simple random sample, you must first number the participants in your population (the sampling frame). Let's say that there are 7,000 people in the frame, numbered from 0001 to 7000, and assume you wish to draw a sample 100 of these individuals.

Beginning anywhere in the table, you will create 100 four-digit numbers. For instance, let's say that you began at the top of the second column and worked down that column. The numbers would be:

6065

~~7106~~

4821

5963

3166 …

If the number that you select is above 7,000, just ignore it and move on. Continue this process until you have obtained 100 numbers. These 100 individuals will be in your sample.

Selecting Orders for Random Assignment Conditions

The table can also be used to create the orders for running participants in experiments that use random assignment to conditions. Assume, for instance, that you needed to order four conditions.

First, number the conditions from 1 to 4 in any order. Then, begin somewhere in the table, and go through the numbers until you find either a 1, a 2, a 3, or a 4. This condition will go first. Then, continue through the table until you find a number that you haven't already found, and so on. For instance, if I began in the third row and worked across, I would first find a 1, a 3, a 2, and then a 4.

STATISTICAL TABLE A   Random Number Table

75 60 37 09 88	08 94 46 87 98	60 11 49 68 29	91 68 93 79 29
74 65 24 12 93	82 38 69 43 63	99 07 95 72 56	39 27 34 09 41
05 71 83 25 48	22 98 16 44 51	33 60 93 47 94	34 26 06 81 28
00 06 63 57 92	74 03 53 71 47	86 47 28 55 92	33 20 28 45 49
82 48 75 70 05	42 06 73 76 39	95 68 12 12 01	59 25 42 51 61
91 21 86 40 18	55 13 72 51 93	40 26 32 64 47	67 55 89 27 34
68 59 86 51 28	44 32 21 90 74	32 89 56 87 22	42 62 27 52 03
37 63 58 24 60	57 57 56 05 07	48 01 24 05 70	13 45 34 83 41
64 31 87 14 42	52 53 04 64 62	21 03 47 63 08	09 65 62 98 61
10 66 04 59 46	77 32 46 82 73	49 79 75 78 34	84 20 95 32 74
42 61 10 93 15	80 48 50 52 28	00 64 88 81 30	53 60 33 40 72
46 39 66 23 15	74 45 72 13 08	81 84 55 86 49	32 59 63 73 08
95 38 26 74 33	89 63 67 85 47	33 47 51 29 92	07 92 69 22 69
72 63 08 33 81	67 51 98 65 17	81 43 55 10 13	41 63 46 10 53
11 89 89 53 65	34 44 29 19 66	74 32 87 32 97	45 42 63 22 11
31 08 04 92 30	72 42 89 30 41	97 03 48 61 04	40 42 22 25 28
85 54 58 35 98	48 60 52 31 93	94 86 13 25 14	01 57 23 18 67
50 14 24 78 20	34 23 56 61 98	35 93 50 30 12	52 39 75 24 49
47 07 98 78 06	75 19 03 89 17	06 92 78 16 83	16 13 55 22 63
57 35 95 84 44	40 29 90 96 96	38 83 83 55 14	98 75 15 58 25
28 26 38 44 81	19 26 99 74 29	84 40 58 35 71	58 04 95 86 74
69 94 40 62 70	15 60 93 22 79	40 81 62 56 66	35 89 17 25 62
99 39 31 18 56	11 13 76 48 26	33 36 24 20 97	03 83 22 75 83
64 60 67 78 86	17 75 04 93 28	19 82 55 21 43	07 73 24 85 87
53 04 78 98 41	53 93 98 05 30	51 37 24 13 10	48 13 15 04 06
21 34 59 88 31	48 65 00 09 44	34 44 99 98 40	07 72 44 25 32
46 42 92 66 20	13 36 41 57 25	47 01 45 32 30	61 51 33 16 51
06 23 75 56 43	90 71 23 98 01	74 43 81 52 73	37 95 48 58 58
94 94 28 25 52	18 16 04 27 72	49 82 48 79 21	31 48 80 37 75
34 37 97 77 31	10 07 46 68 85	83 30 69 01 34	51 31 00 22 44
91 54 65 30 10	10 55 48 87 61	14 47 69 60 09	74 89 13 00 69
60 38 19 14 13	42 90 06 60 66	31 42 02 86 83	09 05 42 83 76
20 95 74 36 04	82 92 97 80 68	11 84 97 74 07	67 30 76 38 89
83 66 13 27 42	70 54 97 51 25	92 50 60 96 83	70 28 77 83 14
87 31 13 51 04	66 11 59 84 87	47 68 00 74 66	45 82 04 00 84
16 49 57 88 27	42 15 84 12 62	25 75 13 98 55	45 98 71 12 05
74 57 52 70 10	79 70 25 97 51	67 80 36 56 52	20 41 69 75 71
19 53 80 24 06	15 14 04 26 67	94 17 91 58 24	00 16 80 65 01
31 14 50 02 91	93 11 59 73 33	41 69 50 85 58	34 68 42 01 36
29 26 11 72 42	81 40 46 42 03	76 27 03 83 69	73 14 76 44 21
55 46 22 40 67	36 12 92 27 00	12 80 53 13 33	82 21 91 49 30
28 90 15 49 26	42 02 11 58 82	42 38 74 47 27	48 50 20 84 16
42 62 49 73 33	77 25 67 06 66	38 04 98 66 44	72 26 92 07 28
35 86 42 40 36	91 41 43 50 24	42 23 04 09 02	44 76 04 34 99
45 62 85 78 11	33 52 35 24 87	72 15 63 59 10	00 94 57 10 94
42 39 38 74 05	78 91 43 88 95	06 99 11 78 17	17 77 10 52 71
11 17 55 73 83	41 60 28 81 15	73 15 22 48 94	86 69 72 21 68

Statistical Table B: Distribution of *z* in the Standard Normal Distribution

This table represents the proportion of the area under the standard normal distribution. The distribution has a mean of 0 and a standard deviation of 1.00. The total area under the curve is also equal to 1.00. (You can convert the listed proportions to percentages by multiplying by 100.)

Because the distribution is symmetrical, only the areas corresponding to positive *z* values are listed. Negative *z* values will have exactly the same areas.

Column B represents the percentage of the distribution that falls between the mean and the tabled *z* value:

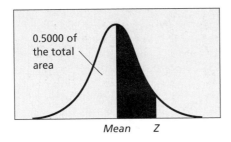
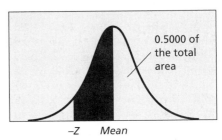

Column C represents the proportion of area beyond *z*:

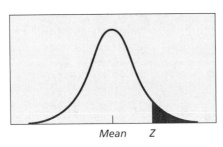
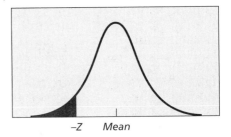

When you calculate proportions with positive *z* scores, remember that .50 of the scores lie below the mean.

STATISTICAL TABLE B　Distribution of z in the Standard Normal Distribution

(A) z	(B) Area Between Mean and z	(C) Area Beyond z	(A) z	(B) Area Between Mean and z	(C) Area Beyond z	(A) z	(B) Area Between Mean and z	(C) Area Beyond z
0.00	.0000	.5000	0.40	.1554	.3446	0.80	.2881	.2119
0.01	.0040	.4960	0.41	.1591	.3409	0.81	.2910	.2090
0.02	.0080	.4920	0.42	.1628	.3372	0.82	.2939	.2061
0.03	.0120	.4880	0.43	.1664	.3336	0.83	.2967	.2033
0.04	.0160	.4840	0.44	.1700	.3300	0.84	.2995	.2005
0.05	.0199	.4801	0.45	.1736	.3264	0.85	.3023	.1977
0.06	.0239	.4761	0.46	.1772	.3228	0.86	.3051	.1949
0.07	.0279	.4721	0.47	.1808	.3192	0.87	.3078	.1922
0.08	.0319	.4681	0.48	.1844	.3156	0.88	.3106	.1894
0.09	.0359	.4641	0.49	.1879	.3121	0.89	.3133	.1867
0.10	.0398	.4602	0.50	.1915	.3085	0.90	.3159	.1841
0.11	.0438	.4562	0.51	.1950	.3050	0.91	.3186	.1814
0.12	.0478	.4522	0.52	.1985	.3015	0.92	.3212	.1788
0.13	.0517	.4483	0.53	.2019	.2981	0.93	.3238	.1762
0.14	.0557	.4443	0.54	.2054	.2946	0.94	.3264	.1736
0.15	.0596	.4404	0.55	.2088	.2912	0.95	.3289	.1711
0.16	.0636	.4364	0.56	.2123	.2877	0.96	.3315	.1685
0.17	.0675	.4325	0.57	.2157	.2843	0.97	.3340	.1660
0.18	.0714	.4286	0.58	.2190	.2810	0.98	.3365	.1635
0.19	.0753	.4247	0.59	.2224	.2776	0.99	.3389	.1611
0.20	.0793	.4207	0.60	.2257	.2743	1.00	.3413	.1587
0.21	.0832	.4168	0.61	.2291	.2709	1.01	.3438	.1562
0.22	.0871	.4129	0.62	.2324	.2676	1.02	.3461	.1539
0.23	.0910	.4090	0.63	.2357	.2643	1.03	.3485	.1515
0.24	.0948	.4052	0.64	.2389	.2611	1.04	.3508	.1492
0.25	.0987	.4013	0.65	.2422	.2578	1.05	.3531	.1469
0.26	.1026	.3974	0.66	.2454	.2546	1.06	.3554	.1446
0.27	.1064	.3936	0.67	.2486	.2514	1.07	.3577	.1423
0.28	.1103	.3897	0.68	.2517	.2483	1.08	.3599	.1401
0.29	.1141	.3859	0.69	.2549	.2451	1.09	.3621	.1379
0.30	.1179	.3821	0.70	.2580	.2420	1.10	.3643	.1357
0.31	.1217	.3783	0.71	.2611	.2389	1.11	.3665	.1335
0.32	.1255	.3745	0.72	.2642	.2358	1.12	.3686	.1314
0.33	.1293	.3707	0.73	.2673	.2327	1.13	.3708	.1292
0.34	.1331	.3669	0.74	.2704	.2296	1.14	.3729	.1271
0.35	.1368	.3632	0.75	.2734	.2266	1.15	.3749	.1251
0.36	.1406	.3594	0.76	.2764	.2236	1.16	.3770	.1230
0.37	.1443	.3557	0.77	.2794	.2206	1.17	.3790	.1210
0.38	.1480	.3520	0.78	.2823	.2177	1.18	.3810	.1190
0.39	.1517	.3483	0.79	.2852	.2148	1.19	.3830	.1170
1.20	.3849	.1151	1.60	.4452	.0548	2.00	.4772	.0228
1.21	.3869	.1131	1.61	.4463	.0537	2.01	.4778	.0222

STATISTICAL TABLE B (continued)

(A) z	(B) Area Between Mean and z	(C) Area Beyond z	(A) z	(B) Area Between Mean and z	(C) Area Beyond z	(A) z	(B) Area Between Mean and z	(C) Area Beyond z
1.22	.3888	.1112	1.62	.4474	.0526	2.02	.4783	.0217
1.23	.3907	.1093	1.63	.4484	.0516	2.03	.4788	.0212
1.24	.3925	.1075	1.64	.4495	.0505	2.04	.4793	.0207
1.25	.3944	.1056	1.65	.4505	.0495	2.05	.4798	.0202
1.26	.3962	.1038	1.66	.4515	.0485	2.06	.4803	.0197
1.27	.3980	.1020	1.67	.4525	.0475	2.07	.4808	.0192
1.28	.3997	.1003	1.68	.4535	.0465	2.08	.4812	.0188
1.29	.4015	.0985	1.69	.4545	.0455	2.09	.4817	.0183
1.30	.4032	.0968	1.70	.4554	.0446	2.10	.4821	.0179
1.31	.4049	.0951	1.71	.4564	.0436	2.11	.4826	.0174
1.32	.4066	.0934	1.72	.4573	.0427	2.12	.4830	.0170
1.33	.4082	.0918	1.73	.4582	.0418	2.13	.4834	.0166
1.34	.4099	.0901	1.74	.4591	.0409	2.14	.4838	.0162
1.35	.4115	.0885	1.75	.4599	.0401	2.15	.4842	.0158
1.36	.4131	.0869	1.76	.4608	.0392	2.16	.4846	.0154
1.37	.4147	.0853	1.77	.4616	.0384	2.17	.4850	.0150
1.38	.4162	.0838	1.78	.4625	.0375	2.18	.4854	.0146
1.39	.4177	.0823	1.79	.4633	.0367	2.19	.4857	.0143
1.40	.4192	.0808	1.80	.4641	.0359	2.20	.4861	.0139
1.41	.4207	.0793	1.81	.4649	.0351	2.21	.4864	.0136
1.42	.4222	.0778	1.82	.4656	.0344	2.22	.4868	.0132
1.43	.4236	.0764	1.83	.4664	.0336	2.23	.4871	.0129
1.44	.4251	.0749	1.84	.4671	.0329	2.24	.4875	.0125
1.45	.4265	.0735	1.85	.4678	.0322	2.25	.4878	.0122
1.46	.4279	.0721	1.86	.4686	.0314	2.26	.4881	.0119
1.47	.4292	.0708	1.87	.4693	.0307	2.27	.4884	.0116
1.48	.4306	.0694	1.88	.4699	.0301	2.28	.4887	.0113
1.49	.4319	.0681	1.89	.4706	.0294	2.29	.4890	.0110
1.50	.4332	.0668	1.90	.4713	.0287	2.30	.4893	.0107
1.51	.4345	.0655	1.91	.4719	.0281	2.31	.4896	.0104
1.52	.4357	.0643	1.92	.4726	.0274	2.32	.4898	.0102
1.53	.4370	.0630	1.93	.4732	.0268	2.33	.4901	.0099
1.54	.4382	.0618	1.94	.4738	.0262	2.34	.4904	.0096
1.55	.4394	.0606	1.95	.4744	.0256	2.35	.4906	.0094
1.56	.4406	.0594	1.96	.4750	.0250	2.36	.4909	.0091
1.57	.4418	.0582	1.97	.4756	.0244	2.37	.4911	.0089
1.58	.4429	.0571	1.98	.4761	.0239	2.38	.4913	.0087
1.59	.4441	.0559	1.99	.4767	.0233	2.39	.4916	.0084
2.40	.4918	.0082	2.72	.4967	.0033	3.04	.4988	.0012
2.41	.4920	.0080	2.73	.4968	.0032	3.05	.4989	.0011
2.42	.4922	.0078	2.74	.4969	.0031	3.06	.4989	.0011
2.43	.4925	.0075	2.75	.4970	.0030	3.07	.4989	.0011
2.44	.4927	.0073	2.76	.4971	.0029	3.08	.4990	.0010

STATISTICAL TABLE B   (continued)

(A) *z*	(B) Area Between Mean and z	(C) Area Beyond z	(A) *z*	(B) Area Between Mean and z	(C) Area Beyond z	(A) *z*	(B) Area Between Mean and z	(C) Area Beyond z
2.45	.4929	.0071	2.77	.4972	.0028	3.09	.4990	.0010
2.46	.4931	.0069	2.78	.4973	.0027	3.10	.4990	.0010
2.47	.4932	.0068	2.79	.4974	.0026	3.11	.4991	.0009
2.48	.4934	.0066	2.80	.4974	.0026	3.12	.4991	.0009
2.49	.4936	.0064	2.81	.4975	.0025	3.13	.4991	.0009
2.50	.4938	.0062	2.82	.4976	.0024	3.14	.4992	.0008
2.51	.4940	.0060	2.83	.4977	.0023	3.15	.4992	.0008
2.52	.4941	.0059	2.84	.4977	.0023	3.16	.4992	.0008
2.53	.4943	.0057	2.85	.4978	.0022	3.17	.4992	.0008
2.54	.4945	.0055	2.86	.4979	.0021	3.18	.4993	.0007
2.55	.4946	.0054	2.87	.4979	.0021	3.19	.4993	.0007
2.56	.4948	.0052	2.88	.4980	.0020	3.20	.4993	.0007
2.57	.4949	.0051	2.89	.4981	.0019	3.21	.4993	.0007
2.58	.4951	.0049	2.90	.4981	.0019	3.22	.4994	.0006
2.59	.4952	.0048	2.91	.4982	.0018	3.23	.4994	.0006
2.60	.4953	.0047	2.92	.4982	.0018	3.24	.4994	.0006
2.61	.4955	.0045	2.93	.4983	.0017	3.25	.4994	.0006
2.62	.4956	.0044	2.94	.4984	.0016	3.30	.4995	.0005
2.63	.4957	.0043	2.95	.4984	.0016	3.35	.4996	.0004
2.64	.4959	.0041	2.96	.4985	.0015	3.40	.4997	.0003
2.65	.4960	.0040	2.97	.4985	.0015	3.45	.4997	.0003
2.66	.4961	.0039	2.98	.4986	.0014	3.50	.4998	.0002
2.67	.4962	.0038	2.99	.4986	.0014	3.60	.4998	.0002
2.68	.4963	.0037	3.00	.4987	.0013	3.70	.4999	.0001
2.69	.4964	.0036	3.01	.4987	.0013	3.80	.4999	.0001
2.70	.4965	.0035	3.02	.4987	.0013	3.90	.49995	.00005
2.71	.4966	.0034	3.03	.4988	.0012	4.00	.49997	.00003

Source: From R. A. Fisher and F. Yates (1974). *Statistical Tables for Biological, Agricultural and Medical Research* (6th ed.). Edinburgh Gate, Harlow, Essex: Addison Wesley Longman. Copyright © 1963 R. A. Fisher and F. Yates. Reprinted by permission of Pearson Education Limited.

Statistical Table C: Critical Values of t

The obtained t value with the listed degrees of freedom (down the side) is significant at the listed alpha (across the top) if it is equal to or greater than the value shown in the table. Negative t values have the equivalent p-values as their positive counterparts.

STATISTICAL TABLE C   Critical Values of t

df	$\alpha = .10$	$\alpha = .05$	$\alpha = .02$	$\alpha = .01$	$\alpha = .001$
1	6.314	12.706	31.821	63.657	636.619
2	2.920	4.303	6.965	9.925	31.598
3	2.353	3.182	4.541	5.841	12.941
4	2.132	2.776	3.747	4.604	8.610
5	2.015	2.571	3.365	4.032	6.859
6	1.943	2.447	3.143	3.707	5.959
7	1.895	2.365	2.998	3.499	5.405
8	1.860	2.306	2.896	3.355	5.041
9	1.833	2.262	2.821	3.250	4.781
10	1.812	2.228	2.764	3.169	4.587
11	1.796	2.201	2.718	3.106	4.437
12	1.782	2.179	2.681	3.055	4.318
13	1.771	2.160	2.650	3.012	4.221
14	1.761	2.145	2.624	2.977	4.140
15	1.753	2.131	2.602	2.947	4.073
16	1.746	2.120	2.583	2.921	4.015
17	1.740	2.110	2.567	2.898	3.965
18	1.734	2.101	2.552	2.878	3.922
19	1.729	2.093	2.539	2.861	3.883
20	1.725	2.086	2.528	2.845	3.850
21	1.721	2.080	2.518	2.831	3.819
22	1.717	2.074	2.508	2.819	3.792
23	1.714	2.069	2.500	2.807	3.767
24	1.711	2.064	2.492	2.797	3.745
25	1.708	2.060	2.485	2.787	3.725
26	1.706	2.056	2.479	2.779	3.707
27	1.703	2.052	2.473	2.771	3.690
28	1.701	2.048	2.467	2.763	3.674
29	1.699	2.045	2.462	2.756	3.659
30	1.697	2.042	2.457	2.750	3.646
40	1.684	2.021	2.423	2.704	3.551
60	1.671	2.000	2.390	2.660	3.460
120	1.658	1.980	2.358	2.617	3.373
∞	1.645	1.960	2.326	2.576	3.291

Note: All p-values in this table are two-sided.
Source: From R. A. Fisher and F. Yates (1974). *Statistical Tables for Biological, Agricultural and Medical Research* (6th ed.). Edinburgh Gate, Harlow, Essex: Addison Wesley Longman. Copyright © 1963 R. A. Fisher and F. Yates. Reprinted by permission of Pearson Education Limited.

Statistical Table D: Critical Values of *r*

The obtained *r* value with the listed degrees of freedom (down the side) is significant at the listed alpha (across the top) if it is equal to or greater than the value shown in the table. The appropriate *df* for testing the significance of *r* is *N* − 2.

STATISTICAL TABLE D   Critical Values of *r*

(N − 2)	α = .10	α = .05	α = .02	α = .01	α = .001
1	.988	.997	.9995	.9999	1.000
2	.900	.950	.980	.990	.999
3	.805	.878	.934	.959	.991
4	.729	.811	.882	.917	.974
5	.669	.754	.833	.874	.951
6	.622	.707	.789	.834	.925
7	.582	.666	.750	.798	.898
8	.550	.632	.716	.765	.872
9	.521	.602	.685	.735	.847
10	.497	.576	.658	.708	.823
11	.476	.553	.634	.684	.801
12	.458	.532	.612	.661	.780
13	.441	.514	.592	.641	.760
14	.426	.497	.574	.623	.742
15	.412	.482	.558	.606	.725
16	.400	.468	.542	.590	.708
17	.389	.456	.528	.575	.693
18	.378	.444	.516	.561	.679
19	.369	.433	.503	.549	.665
20	.360	.423	.492	.537	.652
22	.344	.404	.472	.515	.629
24	.330	.388	.453	.496	.607
25	.323	.381	.445	.487	.597
30	.296	.349	.409	.449	.554
35	.275	.325	.381	.418	.519
40	.257	.304	.358	.393	.490
45	.243	.288	.338	.372	.465
50	.231	.273	.322	.354	.443
55	.220	.261	.307	.338	.424
60	.211	.250	.295	.325	.408
65	.203	.240	.284	.312	.393
70	.195	.232	.274	.302	.380
75	.189	.224	.264	.292	.368
80	.183	.217	.256	.283	.357
85	.178	.211	.249	.275	.347
90	.173	.205	.242	.267	.338
95	.168	.200	.236	.260	.329
100	.164	.195	.230	.254	.321
125	.147	.174	.206	.228	.288

STATISTICAL TABLE D   (continued)

(N − 2)	α = .10	α = .05	α = .02	α = .01	α = .001
150	.134	.159	.189	.208	.264
175	.124	.148	.174	.194	.248
200	.116	.138	.164	.181	.235
300	.095	.113	.134	.148	.188
500	.074	.088	.104	.115	.148
1000	.052	.062	.073	.081	.104
2000	.037	.044	.052	.058	.074

Note: All p-values in this table are two-sided.

Source: From R. A. Fisher and F. Yates (1974). *Statistical Tables for Biological, Agricultural and Medical Research* (6th ed.). Edinburgh Gate, Harlow, Essex: Addison Wesley Longman. Copyright © 1963 R. A. Fisher and F. Yates. Reprinted by permission of Pearson Education Limited.

Statistical Table E: Critical Values of Chi Square

The obtained χ^2 value with the listed degrees of freedom (down the side) is significant at the listed alpha (across the top) if it is equal to or greater than the value shown in the table.

STATISTICAL TABLE E Critical Values of Chi Square

df	$\alpha = .10$	$\alpha = .05$	$\alpha = .02$	$\alpha = .01$
1	2.706	3.841	5.412	6.635
2	4.605	5.991	7.824	9.210
3	6.251	7.815	9.837	11.341
4	7.779	9.488	11.668	13.277
5	9.236	11.070	13.388	15.086
6	10.645	12.592	15.033	16.812
7	12.017	14.067	16.622	18.475
8	13.362	15.507	18.168	20.090
9	14.684	16.919	19.679	21.666
10	15.987	18.307	21.161	23.209
11	17.275	19.675	22.618	24.725
12	18.549	21.026	24.054	26.217
13	19.812	22.362	25.472	27.688
14	21.064	23.685	26.873	29.141
15	22.307	24.996	28.259	30.578
16	23.542	26.296	29.633	32.000
17	24.769	27.587	30.995	33.409
18	25.989	28.869	32.346	34.805
19	27.204	30.144	33.687	36.191
20	28.412	31.410	35.020	37.566
21	29.615	32.671	36.343	38.932
22	30.813	33.924	37.659	40.289
23	32.007	35.172	38.968	41.638
24	33.196	36.415	40.270	42.980
25	34.382	37.652	41.566	44.314
26	35.563	38.885	42.856	45.642
27	36.741	40.113	44.140	46.963
28	37.916	41.337	45.419	48.278
29	39.087	42.557	46.693	49.588
30	40.256	43.773	47.962	50.892

Source: From R. A. Fisher and F. Yates (1974). *Statistical Tables for Biological, Agricultural and Medical Research* (6th ed.). Edinburgh Gate, Harlow, Essex: Addison Wesley Longman. Copyright © 1963 R. A. Fisher and F. Yates. Reprinted by permission of Pearson Education Limited.

Statistical Table F: Critical Values of *F*

The obtained *F* value with the listed numerator and denominator degrees of freedom is significant at alpha = .05 if it is equal to or greater than the value shown in the light row of the table. The obtained *F* value is significant at alpha = .01 if it is equal to or greater than the value shown in the dark row of the table.

STATISTICAL TABLE F   Critical Values of *F*

Degrees of Freedom

		1	2	3	4	5	6	7	8	9	10	11
	1	161	200	216	225	230	234	237	239	241	242	243
		4052	4999	5403	5625	5764	5859	5928	5981	6022	6056	6082
	2	18.51	19.00	19.16	19.25	19.30	19.33	19.36	19.37	19.38	19.39	19.40
		98.49	99.01	99.17	99.25	99.30	99.33	99.34	99.36	99.38	99.40	99.41
	3	10.13	9.55	9.28	9.12	9.01	8.94	8.88	8.84	8.81	8.78	8.76
		34.12	30.81	29.46	28.71	28.34	27.91	27.67	27.49	27.34	27.23	27.13
	4	7.71	6.94	6.59	6.39	6.26	6.16	6.09	6.04	6.00	5.96	5.93
		21.20	18.0	16.69	15.98	15.52	15.21	14.98	14.80	14.66	14.54	14.45
	5	6.61	5.79	5.41	5.19	5.05	4.95	4.88	4.82	4.78	4.74	4.70
		16.26	13.27	12.06	11.39	10.97	10.67	10.45	10.27	10.15	10.05	9.96
Degrees of Freedom for Denominator	6	5.99	5.14	4.76	4.53	4.39	4.28	4.21	4.15	4.10	4.06	4.03
		13.74	10.92	9.78	9.15	8.75	8.47	8.26	8.10	7.98	7.87	7.79
	7	5.59	4.74	4.35	4.12	3.97	3.87	3.79	3.73	3.68	3.63	3.60
		12.25	9.55	8.45	7.85	7.46	7.19	7.00	6.84	6.71	6.62	6.54
	8	5.32	4.46	4.07	3.84	3.69	3.58	3.50	3.44	3.39	3.34	3.31
		11.26	8.65	7.59	7.01	6.63	6.37	6.19	6.03	5.91	5.82	5.74
	9	5.12	4.26	3.86	3.63	3.48	3.37	3.29	3.23	3.18	3.13	3.10
		10.56	8.02	6.99	6.42	6.06	5.80	5.62	5.47	5.35	5.26	5.18
	10	4.96	4.10	3.71	3.48	3.33	3.22	3.14	3.07	3.02	2.97	2.94
		10.04	7.56	6.55	5.99	5.64	5.39	5.21	5.06	4.95	4.85	4.78
	11	4.84	3.98	3.59	3.36	3.20	3.09	3.01	2.95	2.90	2.86	2.82
		9.65	7.20	6.22	5.67	5.32	5.07	4.88	4.74	4.63	4.54	4.46
	12	4.75	3.88	3.49	3.26	3.11	3.00	2.92	2.85	2.80	2.76	2.72
		9.33	6.93	5.95	5.41	5.06	4.82	4.65	4.50	4.39	4.30	4.22
	13	4.67	3.80	3.41	3.18	3.02	2.92	2.84	2.77	2.72	2.67	2.63
		9.07	6.70	5.74	5.20	4.86	4.62	4.44	4.30	4.19	4.10	4.02

for Numerator

12	14	16	20	24	30	40	50	75	100	200	500	∞
244	245	246	248	249	250	251	252	253	253	254	254	254
6106	6142	6169	6208	6234	6258	6286	6302	6323	6334	6352	6361	6336
19.41	19.42	19.43	19.44	19.45	19.46	19.47	19.47	19.48	19.49	19.49	19.50	19.50
99.42	99.43	99.44	99.45	99.46	99.47	99.48	99.48	99.49	99.49	99.49	99.50	99.50
8.74	8.71	8.69	8.66	8.64	8.62	8.60	8.58	8.57	8.56	8.54	8.54	8.53
27.05	26.92	26.83	26.69	26.60	26.50	26.41	26.30	26.27	26.23	26.18	26.14	26.12
5.91	5.87	5.84	5.80	5.77	5.74	5.71	5.70	5.68	5.66	5.65	5.64	5.63
14.37	14.24	14.15	14.02	13.93	13.83	13.74	13.69	13.61	13.57	13.52	13.48	13.46
4.68	4.64	4.60	4.56	4.53	4.50	4.46	4.44	4.42	4.40	4.38	4.37	4.36
9.89	9.77	9.68	9.55	9.47	9.38	9.29	9.24	9.17	9.13	9.07	9.04	9.02
4.00	3.96	3.92	3.87	3.84	3.81	3.77	3.75	3.72	3.71	3.69	3.68	3.67
7.72	7.60	7.52	7.39	7.31	7.23	7.14	7.09	7.02	6.99	6.94	6.90	6.88
3.57	3.52	3.49	3.44	3.41	3.38	3.34	3.32	3.29	3.28	3.25	3.24	3.23
6.47	6.35	6.27	6.15	6.07	5.98	5.90	5.85	5.78	5.75	5.70	5.67	5.65
3.28	3.23	3.20	3.15	3.12	3.08	3.05	3.03	3.00	2.98	2.96	2.94	2.93
5.67	5.56	5.48	5.36	5.28	5.20	5.11	5.06	5.00	4.96	4.91	4.88	4.86
3.07	3.02	2.98	2.93	2.90	2.86	2.82	2.80	2.77	2.76	2.73	2.72	2.71
5.11	5.00	4.92	4.80	4.73	4.64	4.56	4.51	4.45	4.41	4.36	4.33	4.31
2.91	2.86	2.82	2.77	2.74	2.70	2.67	2.64	2.61	2.59	2.56	2.55	2.54
4.71	4.60	4.52	4.41	4.33	4.25	4.17	4.12	4.05	4.01	3.96	3.93	3.91
2.79	2.74	2.70	2.65	2.61	2.57	2.53	2.50	2.47	2.45	2.42	2.41	2.40
4.40	4.29	4.21	4.10	4.02	3.94	3.86	3.80	3.74	3.70	3.66	3.62	3.60
2.69	2.64	2.60	2.54	2.50	2.46	2.42	2.40	2.36	2.35	2.32	2.31	2.30
4.16	4.05	3.98	3.86	3.78	3.70	3.61	3.56	3.49	3.46	3.41	3.38	3.36
2.60	2.55	2.51	2.46	2.42	2.38	2.34	2.32	2.28	2.26	2.22	2.22	2.21
3.96	3.85	3.78	3.67	3.59	3.51	3.42	3.37	3.30	3.27	3.18	3.18	3.16

STATISTICAL TABLE F (continued)

Degrees of Freedom

		1	2	3	4	5	6	7	8	9	10	11
Degrees of Freedom for Denominator	14	4.60	3.74	3.34	3.11	2.96	2.85	2.77	2.70	2.65	2.60	2.56
		8.86	6.51	5.56	5.03	4.69	4.46	4.28	4.14	4.03	3.94	3.86
	15	4.54	3.68	3.29	3.06	2.90	2.79	2.70	2.64	2.59	2.55	2.51
		8.68	6.36	5.42	4.89	4.56	4.32	4.14	4.00	3.89	3.80	3.73
	16	4.49	3.63	3.24	3.01	2.85	2.74	2.66	2.59	2.54	2.49	2.45
		8.53	6.23	5.29	4.77	4.44	4.20	4.03	3.89	3.78	3.69	3.61
	17	4.45	3.59	3.20	2.96	2.81	2.70	2.62	2.55	2.50	2.45	2.41
		8.40	6.11	5.18	4.67	4.34	4.10	3.93	3.79	3.68	3.59	3.52
	18	4.41	3.55	3.16	2.93	2.77	2.66	2.58	2.51	2.46	2.41	2.37
		8.28	6.01	5.09	4.58	4.25	4.01	3.85	3.71	3.60	3.51	3.44
	19	4.38	3.52	3.13	2.90	2.74	2.63	2.55	2.48	2.43	2.38	2.34
		8.18	5.93	5.01	4.50	4.17	3.94	3.77	3.63	3.52	3.43	3.36
	20	4.35	3.49	3.10	2.87	2.71	2.60	2.52	2.45	2.40	2.35	2.31
		8.10	5.85	4.94	4.43	4.10	3.87	3.71	3.56	3.45	3.37	3.30
	21	4.32	3.47	3.07	2.84	2.68	2.57	2.49	2.42	2.37	2.32	2.28
		8.02	5.78	4.87	4.37	4.04	3.81	3.65	3.51	3.40	3.31	3.24
	22	4.30	3.44	3.05	2.82	2.66	2.55	2.47	2.40	2.35	2.30	2.26
		7.94	5.72	4.82	4.31	3.99	3.76	3.59	3.45	3.35	3.26	3.18
	23	4.28	3.42	3.03	2.80	2.64	2.53	2.45	2.38	2.32	2.28	2.24
		7.88	5.66	4.76	4.26	3.94	3.71	3.54	3.41	3.30	3.21	3.14
	24	4.26	3.40	3.01	2.78	2.62	2.51	2.43	2.36	2.30	2.26	2.22
		7.82	5.61	4.72	4.22	3.90	3.67	3.50	3.36	3.25	3.17	3.09
	25	4.24	3.38	2.99	2.76	2.60	2.49	2.41	2.34	2.28	2.24	2.20
		7.77	5.57	4.68	4.18	3.86	3.63	3.46	3.32	3.21	3.13	3.05
	26	4.22	3.37	2.89	2.74	2.59	2.47	2.39	2.32	2.27	2.22	2.18
		7.72	5.53	4.64	4.14	3.82	3.59	3.42	3.29	3.17	3.09	3.02
	27	4.21	3.35	2.96	2.73	2.57	2.46	2.37	2.30	2.25	2.20	2.16
		7.68	5.49	4.60	4.11	3.79	3.56	3.39	3.26	3.14	3.06	2.98
	28	4.20	3.34	2.95	2.71	2.56	2.44	2.36	2.29	3.24	2.19	2.15
		7.64	5.45	4.57	4.07	3.76	3.53	3.36	3.23	3.11	3.03	2.95
	29	4.18	3.33	2.93	2.70	2.54	2.43	2.35	2.28	2.22	2.18	2.14
		7.60	5.52	4.54	4.04	3.73	3.50	3.32	3.20	3.08	3.00	2.92

for Numerator

12	14	16	20	24	30	40	50	75	100	200	500	∞
2.53	2.48	2.44	2.39	2.35	2.31	2.27	2.24	2.21	2.19	2.16	2.14	2.13
3.80	3.70	3.62	3.51	3.43	3.34	3.26	3.21	3.14	3.11	3.06	3.02	3.00
2.48	2.43	2.39	2.33	2.29	2.25	2.21	2.18	2.15	2.12	2.10	2.08	2.07
3.67	3.56	3.48	3.36	3.29	3.20	3.12	3.07	3.00	2.97	2.92	2.89	2.87
2.42	2.37	2.33	2.28	2.24	2.20	2.16	2.13	2.09	2.07	2.04	2.02	2.01
3.55	3.45	3.37	3.25	3.18	3.10	3.01	2.96	2.89	2.86	2.80	2.77	2.75
2.38	2.33	2.29	2.23	2.19	2.15	2.11	2.08	2.04	2.02	1.99	1.97	1.96
3.45	3.35	3.27	3.16	3.08	3.00	2.92	2.86	2.79	2.76	2.70	2.67	2.65
2.34	2.29	2.25	2.19	2.15	2.11	2.07	2.04	2.00	1.98	1.95	1.93	1.92
3.37	3.27	3.19	3.07	3.00	2.91	2.83	2.78	2.71	2.68	2.62	2.59	2.57
2.31	2.26	2.21	2.15	2.11	2.07	2.02	2.00	1.96	1.94	1.91	1.90	1.88
3.30	3.19	3.12	3.00	2.92	2.84	2.76	2.70	2.63	2.60	2.54	2.51	2.49
2.28	2.23	2.18	2.12	2.08	2.04	1.99	1.96	1.92	1.90	1.87	1.85	1.84
3.23	3.13	3.05	2.94	2.86	2.77	2.69	2.63	2.56	2.53	2.47	2.44	2.42
2.25	2.20	2.15	2.09	2.05	2.00	1.96	1.93	1.80	1.87	1.84	1.82	1.81
3.17	3.07	2.99	2.88	2.80	2.72	2.63	2.58	2.51	2.47	2.42	2.38	2.36
2.23	2.18	2.13	2.07	2.03	1.98	1.93	1.91	1.87	1.84	1.81	1.80	1.78
3.12	3.02	2.94	2.83	2.75	2.67	2.58	2.53	2.46	2.42	2.37	2.33	2.31
2.20	2.14	2.10	2.04	2.00	1.96	1.91	1.88	1.84	1.82	1.79	1.77	1.76
3.07	2.97	2.89	2.78	2.70	2.62	2.53	2.48	2.41	2.37	2.32	2.28	2.26
2.18	2.13	2.09	2.02	1.98	1.94	1.89	1.86	1.82	1.80	1.76	1.74	1.73
3.03	2.93	2.85	2.74	2.66	2.58	2.49	2.44	2.36	2.33	2.27	2.23	2.21
2.16	2.11	2.06	2.00	1.96	1.92	1.87	1.84	1.80	1.77	1.74	1.72	1.71
2.99	2.89	2.81	2.70	2.62	2.54	2.45	2.40	2.32	2.29	2.23	2.19	2.17
2.15	2.10	2.05	1.99	1.95	1.90	1.85	1.82	1.78	1.76	1.72	1.70	1.69
2.96	2.86	2.77	2.66	2.58	2.50	2.41	2.36	2.28	2.25	2.19	2.15	2.13
2.13	2.08	2.03	1.97	1.93	1.88	1.84	1.80	1.76	1.74	1.71	1.68	1.67
2.93	2.83	2.74	2.63	2.55	2.47	2.38	2.33	2.25	2.21	2.16	2.12	2.10
2.12	2.06	2.02	1.96	1.91	1.87	1.81	1.78	1.75	1.72	1.69	1.67	1.65
2.90	2.80	2.71	2.60	2.52	2.44	2.35	2.30	2.22	2.18	2.13	2.09	2.06
2.10	2.05	2.00	1.94	1.90	1.85	1.80	1.77	1.73	1.71	1.68	1.65	1.64
2.87	2.77	2.68	2.57	2.49	2.41	2.32	2.27	2.19	2.15	2.10	2.06	2.03

STATISTICAL TABLE F   (continued)

							Degrees of Freedom				
	1	2	3	4	5	6	7	8	9	10	11
30	4.17	3.32	2.92	2.69	2.53	2.42	2.34	2.27	2.21	2.16	2.12
	7.56	5.39	4.51	4.02	3.70	3.47	3.30	3.17	3.06	2.98	2.90
32	4.15	3.30	2.90	2.67	2.51	2.40	2.32	2.25	2.19	2.14	2.10
	7.50	5.34	4.46	3.97	3.66	3.42	3.25	3.12	3.01	2.94	2.86
34	4.13	3.28	2.88	2.65	2.49	2.38	2.30	2.23	2.17	2.12	2.08
	7.44	5.29	4.42	3.93	3.61	3.38	3.21	3.08	2.97	2.89	2.82
36	4.11	3.26	2.86	2.63	2.48	2.36	2.28	2.21	2.15	2.10	2.06
	7.39	5.25	4.38	3.89	3.58	3.35	3.18	3.04	2.94	2.86	2.78
38	4.10	3.25	2.85	2.62	2.46	2.35	2.26	2.19	2.14	2.09	2.05
	7.35	5.21	4.34	3.86	3.54	3.32	3.15	3.02	2.91	2.82	2.75
40	4.08	3.23	2.84	2.61	2.45	2.34	2.25	2.18	2.12	2.07	2.04
	7.31	5.18	4.31	3.83	3.51	3.29	3.12	2.99	2.88	2.80	2.73
42	4.07	3.22	2.83	2.59	2.44	2.32	2.24	2.17	2.11	2.06	2.02
	7.27	5.15	4.29	3.80	3.49	3.26	3.10	2.96	2.86	2.77	2.70
44	4.06	3.21	2.82	2.58	2.43	2.31	2.23	2.16	2.10	2.05	2.01
	7.24	5.12	4.26	3.78	3.46	3.24	3.07	2.94	2.84	2.75	2.68
46	4.05	3.20	2.81	2.57	2.42	2.30	2.22	2.14	2.09	2.04	2.00
	7.21	5.10	4.24	3.76	3.44	3.22	3.05	2.92	2.82	2.73	2.66
48	4.04	3.19	2.80	2.56	2.41	2.30	2.21	2.14	2.08	2.03	1.99
	7.19	5.08	4.22	3.74	3.42	3.20	3.04	2.90	2.80	2.71	2.64
50	4.03	3.18	2.79	2.56	2.40	2.29	2.20	2.13	2.07	2.02	1.98
	7.17	5.06	4.20	3.72	3.41	3.18	3.02	2.88	2.78	2.70	2.62
55	4.02	3.17	2.78	2.54	2.38	2.27	2.18	2.11	2.05	2.00	1.97
	7.12	5.01	4.16	3.68	3.37	3.15	2.98	2.85	2.75	2.66	2.59
60	4.00	3.15	2.76	2.52	2.37	2.25	2.17	2.10	2.04	1.99	1.95
	7.08	4.98	4.13	3.65	3.34	3.12	2.95	2.82	2.75	2.63	2.56
65	3.99	3.14	2.75	2.51	2.36	2.24	2.15	2.08	2.02	1.98	1.94
	7.04	4.95	4.10	3.62	3.31	3.09	2.93	2.79	2.70	2.61	2.54
70	3.98	3.13	2.74	2.50	2.35	2.32	2.14	2.07	2.01	1.97	1.93
	7.01	4.92	4.08	3.60	3.29	3.07	2.91	2.77	2.67	2.59	2.51
80	3.96	3.11	2.72	2.48	2.33	2.21	2.12	2.05	1.99	1.95	1.91
	6.96	4.88	4.04	3.56	3.25	3.04	2.87	2.74	2.64	2.55	2.48

Degrees of Freedom for Denominator

for Numerator

12	14	16	20	24	30	40	50	75	100	200	500	∞
2.09	2.04	1.99	1.93	1.89	1.84	1.79	1.76	1.72	1.69	1.66	1.64	1.62
2.84	2.74	2.66	2.55	2.47	2.38	2.29	2.24	2.16	2.13	2.07	2.03	2.01
2.07	2.02	1.97	1.91	1.86	1.82	1.76	1.74	1.69	1.67	1.64	1.61	1.59
2.80	2.70	2.62	2.51	2.42	2.34	2.25	2.20	2.12	2.08	2.02	1.98	1.96
2.05	2.00	1.95	1.89	1.84	1.80	1.74	1.71	1.67	1.64	1.61	1.59	1.57
2.76	2.66	2.58	2.47	2.38	2.30	2.21	2.15	2.08	2.04	1.98	1.94	1.91
2.03	1.89	1.93	1.87	1.82	1.78	1.72	1.69	1.65	1.62	1.59	1.56	1.55
2.72	2.62	2.54	2.43	2.35	2.26	2.17	2.12	2.04	2.00	1.94	1.90	1.87
2.02	1.96	1.92	1.85	1.80	1.76	1.71	1.67	1.63	1.60	1.57	1.54	1.53
2.69	2.59	2.51	2.40	2.32	2.22	2.14	2.08	2.00	1.97	1.90	1.86	1.84
2.00	1.95	1.90	1.84	1.79	1.74	1.69	1.66	1.61	1.59	1.55	1.53	1.51
2.66	2.56	2.49	2.37	2.29	2.20	2.11	2.05	1.97	1.94	1.88	1.84	1.81
1.90	1.94	1.89	1.82	1.78	1.73	1.68	1.64	1.60	1.57	1.54	1.51	1.49
2.64	2.54	2.46	2.35	2.26	2.17	2.08	2.02	1.94	1.91	1.85	1.80	1.78
1.98	1.92	1.88	1.81	1.76	1.72	1.66	1.63	1.58	1.56	1.52	1.50	1.48
2.62	2.52	2.44	2.32	2.24	2.15	2.06	2.09	1.92	1.88	1.82	1.78	1.75
1.97	1.91	1.87	1.80	1.75	1.71	1.65	1.62	1.57	1.54	1.51	1.48	1.46
2.60	2.50	2.42	2.30	2.22	2.13	2.04	1.98	1.90	1.86	1.80	1.76	1.72
1.96	1.90	1.86	1.79	1.74	1.70	1.64	1.61	1.56	1.53	1.50	1.47	1.45
2.58	2.48	2.40	2.28	2.20	2.11	2.02	1.96	1.88	1.84	1.78	1.73	1.70
1.95	1.90	1.85	1.78	1.74	1.69	1.63	1.60	1.55	1.52	1.48	1.46	1.44
2.56	2.46	2.39	2.26	2.18	2.10	2.00	1.94	1.86	1.82	1.76	1.71	1.68
1.93	1.88	1.83	1.76	1.72	1.67	1.61	1.58	1.52	1.50	1.46	1.43	1.41
2.53	2.43	2.35	2.23	2.15	2.06	1.96	1.90	1.82	1.78	1.71	1.66	1.64
1.92	1.86	1.81	1.75	1.70	1.65	1.59	1.56	1.50	1.48	1.44	1.41	1.39
2.50	2.40	2.32	2.20	2.12	2.03	1.93	1.87	1.79	1.74	1.68	1.63	1.60
1.90	1.85	1.80	1.73	1.68	1.63	1.57	1.54	1.49	1.46	1.42	1.39	1.37
2.47	2.37	2.30	2.18	2.09	2.00	1.90	1.84	1.76	1.71	1.64	1.60	1.56
1.89	1.84	1.79	1.72	1.67	1.62	1.56	1.53	1.47	1.45	1.40	1.37	1.35
2.45	2.35	2.28	2.15	2.07	1.98	1.88	1.82	1.74	1.69	1.62	1.56	1.53
1.88	1.82	1.77	1.70	1.65	1.60	1.54	1.51	1.45	1.42	1.38	1.35	1.32
2.41	2.32	2.24	2.11	2.03	1.94	1.84	1.78	1.70	1.65	1.57	1.52	1.49

STATISTICAL TABLE F   (continued)

Degrees of Freedom

		1	2	3	4	5	6	7	8	9	10	11
Degrees of Freedom for Denominator	100	3.94	3.09	2.70	2.46	2.30	2.19	2.10	2.03	1.97	1.92	1.88
		6.90	4.82	3.98	3.51	3.20	2.99	2.82	2.69	2.59	2.51	2.43
	125	3.92	3.07	2.68	2.44	2.29	2.17	2.08	2.01	1.95	1.90	1.86
		6.84	4.78	3.94	3.47	3.17	2.95	2.79	2.65	2.56	2.47	2.40
	150	3.91	3.06	2.67	2.43	2.27	2.16	2.07	2.00	1.94	1.89	1.85
		6.81	4.75	3.91	3.44	3.13	2.92	2.76	2.62	2.53	2.44	2.37
	200	3.89	3.04	2.65	2.41	2.26	2.14	2.05	1.98	1.92	1.87	1.83
		6.76	4.71	3.38	3.41	3.11	2.90	2.73	2.60	2.50	2.41	2.34
	400	3.86	3.02	2.62	2.39	2.23	2.12	2.03	1.96	1.90	1.85	1.81
		6.70	4.66	3.83	3.36	3.06	2.85	2.69	2.55	2.46	2.37	2.29
	1000	3.85	3.00	2.61	2.38	2.22	2.10	2.02	1.95	1.89	1.84	1.80
		6.66	4.62	3.80	3.34	3.04	2.82	2.66	2.53	2.43	2.34	2.26
	∞	3.84	2.99	2.60	2.37	2.21	2.09	2.01	1.94	1.88	1.83	1.79
		6.64	4.60	3.78	3.32	3.02	2.80	2.64	2.51	2.41	2.32	2.24

for Numerator

12	14	16	20	24	30	40	50	75	100	200	500	∞
1.85	1.79	1.75	1.68	1.63	1.57	1.51	1.48	1.42	1.39	1.34	1.30	1.28
2.36	2.26	2.19	2.06	1.98	1.89	1.79	1.73	1.64	1.59	1.51	1.46	1.43
1.83	1.77	1.72	1.65	1.60	1.55	1.49	1.45	1.39	1.36	1.31	1.27	1.25
2.33	2.23	2.15	2.03	1.94	1.85	1.75	1.68	1.59	1.54	1.46	1.40	1.37
1.82	1.76	1.71	1.64	1.59	1.54	1.47	1.44	1.37	1.34	1.29	1.25	1.22
2.30	2.20	2.12	2.00	1.91	1.83	1.72	1.66	1.56	1.51	1.43	1.37	1.33
1.80	1.74	1.69	1.62	1.57	1.52	1.45	1.42	1.35	1.32	1.26	1.22	1.19
2.28	1.17	2.09	1.97	1.88	1.79	1.69	1.62	1.53	1.48	1.39	1.33	1.28
1.78	1.72	1.67	1.60	1.54	1.49	1.42	1.38	1.32	1.28	1.22	1.16	1.13
2.23	2.12	2.04	1.92	1.84	1.74	1.64	1.57	1.47	1.42	1.32	1.24	1.19
1.76	1.70	1.65	1.58	1.53	1.47	1.41	1.36	1.30	1.26	1.19	1.13	1.08
2.20	2.09	2.01	1.89	1.81	1.71	1.61	1.54	1.44	1.38	1.28	1.19	1.11
1.75	1.69	1.64	1.57	1.52	1.46	1.40	1.35	1.28	1.24	1.17	1.11	1.00
2.18	2.07	1.99	1.87	1.79	1.69	1.59	1.52	1.41	1.36	1.25	1.15	1.00

Source: From R. A. Fisher and F. Yates (1974). *Statistical Tables for Biological, Agricultural and Medical Research* (6th ed.). Edinburgh Gate, Harlow, Essex: Addison Wesley Longman. Copyright © 1963 R. A. Fisher and F. Yates. Reprinted by permission of Pearson Education Limited.

Statistical Table G: Statistical Power

This table represents the number of participants needed in various research designs to produce a power of .80 with alpha = .05. For ANOVA designs, the number of participants per condition is the tabled number divided by the number of conditions in the design. Small, medium, and large effect sizes are .10, .30 and .50, except for one-way and factorial ANOVA, where they are .10, .25, and .40, respectively.

STATISTICAL TABLE G Statistical Power

	Estimated Effect Size		
	Small	Medium	Large
Correlation coefficient (r)			
	783	85	28
One-way (between participants) ANOVA (F)			
2 groups	786	128	52
3 groups	966	156	63
6 groups	1290	210	84
Factorial (between-participants) ANOVA (F)			
2 × 2	788	132	56
2 × 3	972	162	66
3 × 3	1206	198	90
2 × 2 × 2	792	136	64
Contingency table (χ2)			
1 df	785	87	31
2 df	964	107	39
3 df	1090	121	44
4 df	1194	133	48
Multiple regression (R)			
2 IVs	481	67	30
3 IVs	547	76	34
5 IVs	645	91	42
8 IVs	757	107	50

Source: From Cohen, J. (1992). A power primer. *Psychological Bulletin, 112,* 155–159. Copyright © 1992 by the American Psychological Association. Adapted with permission.

APPENDIX F
Using Computers to Collect Data

As we have seen throughout this book, computers are commonly used in the behavioral sciences to perform statistical analyses and to write and edit research reports. But computers are also being used to a greater and greater extent to collect data from research participants. This Appendix presents a brief summary of the use of computers to collect data, both in the lab and over the Internet.

Collecting data with computers has several important advantages. For one, computers can help standardize conditions by ensuring that each participant receives the exact same stimuli, in the exact same order, and for the exact same amount of time. The computer can also be programmed to automatically assign participants to experimental conditions—for instance, by using blocked random assignment—and to present different information to the participants in the different conditions. In many cases this allows the experimenter to leave the lab room after the research participant starts the procedure, thereby reducing the possibility of distraction, demand characteristics, and experimenter bias.

Another advantage of computers is that they allow researchers to present and collect information in ways that would be difficult or impossible to do without them. In terms of presenting information, computers can randomly select stimuli from lists, allowing counterbalancing across research participants. They can also keep track of which stimuli have been presented, and in which order. Moreover, computers can present a wide variety of stimuli, including text, graphics, audio, and video. Computers also allow researchers to present stimuli at exactly timed durations, which may be extremely short. For instance, in priming experiments, it may desired that the stimulus (such as an image) be presented for exactly 50 milliseconds (1/20 of a second), so that although participants may react to it at an unconscious level, they are not aware of seeing it.

In terms of the dependent variables, computers can collect virtually any data that could be collected in other ways, including free- and fixed-format responses, reaction times, and even in some cases physiological measures. Furthermore, the computer can be programmed so that the participant must answer each item before he or she continues, thus reducing the amount of missing data. When participants complete measures on computers, the data can normally be transferred directly to the statistical software package, alleviating the need to enter the data manually.

Despite these many advantages, using computers also has some disadvantages. For one, although they become cheaper every year, computers are still more expensive than paper-and-pencil measures. Furthermore, because each participant must have his or her own computer, the number of participants that can be run at the same time will be limited. It is also possible that some people will not pay attention to or will not follow the instructions given by the computer, and the experimenter may not be able to check up on whether they have. In some cases the computer may malfunction.

A number of software packages are available for use in collecting data; these are summarized in Table F.1. All of these packages perform the following basic functions:

1. Allow the experimenter to indicate which stimuli are to be presented, in which order, and which measures are to be collected. In some cases the experimental setup uses a graphical interface; in other cases the setup is more like a programming language.

2. Randomly assign participants to experimental conditions and present different instructions and stimuli in the different conditions.

3. Present a variety of stimuli, including text, graphics, video, and audio. These stimuli can be chosen randomly from lists, grouped into blocks, and placed in specific locations on the screen.

4. Collecting responses, including free- and fixed-format self-report measures. These responses can be assessed through keyboard, mouse, voice, or button-box input.

5. Precisely time the duration at which stimuli are displayed as well as the elapsed time between the presentation of a stimulus and the participant's response.

6. Write all collected data to a file suitable for importing into software packages.

Other functions that are available on some packages are the ability to collect visual and physiological data and to collect data over the Internet. If you are planning to use computers to conduct research, you may wish to check with your instructor to see if any of these programs are available at your college or university.

STATISTICAL TABLE F.1   Some Computer Software Packages for Collecting Data from Research Participants

Program	Platforms/Comments	Website
DirectRT	Windows	*www.empirisoft.com/directrt*
E-prime	Windows	*www.pstnet.com/e-prime/ default.htm*
Inquisit	Windows	*www.millisecond.com*
Matlab	Windows & Mac	*www.mathworks.com/products/ matlab/*
Medialab	Windows	*www.empirisoft.com/medialab*
Presentation	Windows freeware; collects physiological measures	*www.neurobehavioralsystems.com*
Psyctoolbox	Works with Matlab to collect visual data such as gaze tracking	*http://psychtoolbox.org*
PsyScope	Mac freeware	*http://psyscope.psy.cmu.edu*
RSVP	Mac freeware	*www.cog.brown.edu/~tarr/rsvp.html*
Superlab	Windows & Mac	*www.superlab.com*
Perseus Survey Solutions	Windows; web-based survey collection	*www.perseus.com*

Glossary

A priori comparisons See *Planned comparisons*.

A-B-A design A research design in which measurements are made before, during, and after the change in the independent variable occurs.

Abstracts Written summaries of research reports.

Acquiescent responding (yeah-saying bias) A form of reactivity in which people tend to agree with whatever questions they are asked.

Alpha (α) The probability of making a Type 1 error.

Alternative explanations The possibility that a confounding variable, rather than the independent variable, caused the differences in the dependent measure.

Analysis of Covariance (ANCOVA) An analysis in which the means of the dependent variable in the different experimental conditions are adjusted or controlled for the influence of one or more quantitative variables on the dependent variable.

Analysis of Variance (ANOVA) A statistical procedure designed to compare the means of the dependent variable across the conditions of an experimental research design.

ANCOVA See *Analysis of Covariance*.

ANOVA See *Analysis of Variance*.

ANOVA summary table A table that displays the ANOVA calculations including F and its associated p-value.

Applied research Research designed to investigate issues that have implications for everyday life and to provide solutions to real-world problems.

Archival research Research that uses existing records of public behavior as data.

Arithmetic mean ($\bar{x}$) A measure of central tendency equal to the sum of the scores on the variable divided by the sample size (N).

Artifacts Aspects of the research methodology that may produce confounding.

Attrition A threat to internal validity in longitudinal research when participants who stay in the research are different from those who drop out.

Bar chart A visual display of a frequency distribution.

Baseline measure An initial measurement of the dependent variable in a before-after research design.

Basic research Research designed to answer fundamental questions rather than to address a specific real-world problem.

Before-after research designs Designs in which the dependent measure is assessed both prior to and after the experimental manipulation has occurred.

Behavioral categories The specific set of observations that are recorded in systematic observational research.

Behavioral measures Measured variables designed to directly measure an individual's actions.

Behavioral research Research designed to study the thoughts, feelings, and behavior of human beings and animals.

Beta (β) The probability of making a Type 2 error.

Beta weights See *Regression coefficients*.

Between-groups variance In ANOVA, a measure of the variability of the dependent variable across the experimental conditions.

Between-participants designs Experiments in which the comparison of the scores on the dependent variable is between the participants in the different levels of the independent variable and each individual is in only one level.

Binomial distribution The sampling distribution of events that have two equally likely outcomes.

Bivariate statistics Statistical procedures used to analyze the relationship between two variables.

Blocked random assignment A method of random assignment in which participants are assigned to conditions in sequential blocks, each of which contains all of the conditions.

Canonical correlation A statistical procedure used to assess the relationships between one or more quantitative independent variables and a set of quantitative dependent variables.

Carryover   A situation that can occur in a repeated-measures design when the effects of one level of the manipulation are still present when the dependent measure is assessed for another level of the manipulation.

Case studies   Descriptive records of one or more individual's experiences and behavior.

Cells   The conditions in factorial designs.

Census   A survey of an entire population.

Central limit theorem   A mathematical statement that demonstrates that as the sample size increases, the sample mean provides a more precise estimate of the population mean.

Central tendency   The point in the distribution of a quantitative variable around which the scores are centered.

Chi-square (χ^2) statistic   A statistic used to assess the relationship between two nominal variables.

Cluster sampling   A probability sampling technique in which a population is divided into groups (called *clusters*) for which there are sampling frames and then some of the clusters are chosen to be sampled.

Coefficient of determination (r^2)   The proportion of variance accounted for by the correlation coefficient.

Common-causal variables   In a correlational research design, variables that are not part of the research hypothesis but that cause both the predictor and the outcome variable and thus produce a spurious correlation between them.

Comparison group   A group that is expected to be similar to the experimental group but that (because random assignment has not been used) is not expected to be equivalent to the experimental group.

Comparison-group before-after design   Research in which more than one group of individuals is studied and the dependent measure is assessed for all groups before and after the intervening event.

Comparison-group design   Research that uses more than one group of individuals that differ in terms of whether they have had or have not had the experience of interest.

Complex comparisons   Means comparisons in which more than two means are compared at the same time.

Conceptual replication   A replication that investigates the relationship between the same conceptual variables that were studied in previous research but tests the hypothesis using different operational definitions of the independent variable and/or the dependent variable.

Conceptual variables   Abstract ideas that form the basis of research designs and that are measured by measured variables.

Concurrent validity   A form of criterion validity that involves evaluation of the relationship between a self-report and a behavioral measure that are assessed at the same time.

Conditions   A term used to describe the levels of an experimental manipulation in one-way experimental designs, or the cells in a factorial design.

Confidence interval   A range of scores within which a population parameter is likely to fall.

Confirmatory factor analysis   A type of structural equation analysis that tests whether a set of collected data is consistent with a hypothesized set of factor loadings.

Confound checks   Measures used to determine whether the manipulation has unwittingly caused differences on confounding variables.

Confounding   A situation that occurs when one or more variables are mixed up with the independent variable, thereby making it impossible to determine which of the variables has produced changes in the dependent variable.

Confounding variables   Variables other than the independent variable on which the participants in one experimental condition differ systematically from those in other conditions.

Construct validity   The extent to which a measured variable actually measures the conceptual variable that it is designed to assess.

Constructive replication   A replication that investigates the same hypothesis as the original experiment (either in the form of an exact or a conceptual replication) but also adds new conditions to the original experiment to assess the specific variables that might change the previously observed relationship.

Content analysis   The systematic coding of free-format data.

Content validity   The degree to which a measured variable appears to have adequately sampled from the potential domain of topics that might relate to the conceptual variable of interest.

Contingency table   A table that displays the number of individuals who have each value on each of two nominal variables.

Contrast analysis   A method of conducting a priori means comparisons that can be used for either pairwise or complex comparisons.

Contrast tests   Statistical procedures used to make complex means comparisons.

Contrast weights   Numbers set by the researcher in a contrast analysis that indicate how the group means are to be compared.

Control condition   The level of the independent variable in which the situation of interest was not created. (Compare with *Experimental condition*.)

Convenience samples   Nonprobability samples containing whatever individuals are readily available, with no attempt to make the samples representative of a population.

Convergent validity   The extent to which a measured variable is found to be related to other measured variables designed to measure the same conceptual variable.

Converging operations   Using more than one measurement or research approach to study a given topic, with the hope that all of the approaches will produce similar results.

Correlation matrix   A table showing the correlations of many variables with each other.

Correlational research   Research that involves the measurement of two or more relevant variables and an assessment of the relationship between or among those variables.

Counterbalancing   A procedure in which the order of the conditions in a repeated-measures design is arranged so that each condition occurs equally often in each order.

Cover story   A false or misleading statement by the experimenter about what is being studied that is used to reduce the possibility of demand characteristics.

Cramer's statistic (V_c)   The effect size statistic in contingency tables other than 2×2.

Criterion validity   An assessment of validity calculated though the correlation of a self-report measure with a behavioral measured (criterion) variable.

Criterion variable   The behavioral variable that is predicted when testing for criterion validity.

Cronbach's coefficient alpha (α)   A measure of internal consistency that estimates the average correlation among all of the items on a scale.

Cross-sectional research designs   Research in which comparisons are made across different age groups, but all groups are measured at the same time (Compare with *Longitudinal research designs*).

Crossover interaction   An interaction in a 2×2 factorial design in which the two simple effects are opposite in direction.

Curvilinear relationships   Nonlinear relationships that change in direction and, thus, cannot be described with a single straight line.

Data   Information collected through formal observation or measurement.

Debriefing   Information given to a participant immediately after an experiment has ended that is designed to both explain the purposes and procedures of the research and remove any harmful aftereffects of participation.

Deception   The practice of not completely and fully informing research participants about the nature of a research project before they participate in it; sometimes used when the research could not be conducted if participants knew what was really being studied.

Deductive method   The use of a theory to generate specific ideas that can be tested through research.

Degrees of freedom (*df*)   The number of values that are free to vary given restrictions that have been placed on the data.

Demand characteristics   Aspects of the research that allow participants to guess the research hypothesis.

Dependent variable   In an experiment, the variable that is caused by the independent variable.

Descriptive research   Research designed to answer questions about the current state of affairs.

Descriptive statistics   Numbers, such as the *mean*, the *median*, the *mode*, the *standard deviation*, and the *variance*, that summarize the distribution of a measured variable.

Discriminant validity   The extent to which a measured variable is found to be unrelated to other measured variables designed to assess different conceptual variables.

Dispersion   The extent to which the scores in a sample are all tightly clustered around the central tendency or are more spread out away from it. Dispersion is normally measured using the *standard deviation* and the *variance*.

Distribution   The pattern of scores observed on a measured variable.

Ecological validity   The extent to which research is conducted in situations that are similar to the everyday life experiences of the participants.

Effect size   A statistic that indexes the size of a relationship.

Empirical   Based on systematic collection of data.

Equivalent-forms reliability   A form of test-retest reliability in which two different but equivalent versions of the same measure are given at different times and the correlation between the scores on the two versions is assessed.

Eta (η)   The effect size measure in the ANOVA.

Event sampling   In systematic observation, the act of focusing in on specific behaviors to be observed.

Exact replication   Research that repeats a previous research design as exactly as possible, keeping almost everything about the research the same as it was the first time around.

Experimental condition   The level of the independent variable in which the situation of interest was created. (Compare with *Control condition.*)

Experimental control   The extent to which the experiment has eliminated effects on the dependent variable other than the effects of the independent variable.

Experimental manipulations   The independent variable, created by the experimenter, in an experimental design.

Experimental realism   The extent to which the experimental manipulation involves the participants in the research.

Experimental research   Research that includes the manipulation of a given situation or experience for two or more groups of individuals who are initially created to be equivalent, followed by a measurement of the effect of that experience.

Experimental script   A precise description of all aspects of the research procedure.

Experimenter bias   A source of internal validity that occurs when an experimenter who knows the research hypothesis unknowingly communicates his or her expectations to the research participants.

Experimentwise alpha   The probability of the researcher having made a Type 1 error in at least one of the statistical tests conducted during the research.

Exploratory factor analysis   A multivariate statistical technique used to analyze the underlying pattern of correlations among a set of measured variables and to develop a simplified picture of the relationships among these variables.

External validity   The extent to which the results of a research design can be generalized beyond the specific settings and participants used in the experiment to other places, people, and times.

Extraneous variables   Variables other than the predictor variable that cause the outcome variable but that do not cause the predictor variable.

F   In the ANOVA, a statistic that assesses the extent to which the means of the experimental conditions differ more than would be expected by chance.

Face validity   The extent to which a measured variable appears to be an adequate measure of the conceptual variable.

Factor   An independent variable in a factorial experimental design.

Factor scores   In a factor analysis, the new summarizing variables that are created out of the original variables.

Factorial experimental designs   Experimental research designs that have more than one independent variable.

Factors   In a factor analysis, the sets of variables that are found to be correlated with each other.

Facts   Information that is objectively true.

Falsifiable   A characteristic of a theory or research hypothesis such that the variables of interest can be adequately measured and the expected relationship between the variables can be shown through research to be incorrect.

Field experiments   Experimental research designs that are conducted in a natural environment such as a library, a factory, or a school rather than in a research laboratory.

Fisher least significant difference (LSD) test   A post hoc means comparison test in which pairwise means comparisons are made only if the initial ANOVA *F* value is significant.

Fixed-format self-report measures   Measured variables in which the respondent indicates his or her thoughts or feelings by answering a structured set of questions.

Focus group   A type of unstructured interview in which a number of people are interviewed at the same time and share ideas with the interviewer and with each other.

Free-format self-report measures   Measured variables in which respondents are asked to freely list their thoughts or feelings as they come to mind.

Frequency curve   A visual display of a grouped or ungrouped frequency distribution that uses a line to indicate the frequencies.

Frequency distribution   A statistical table that indicates how many individuals in a sample fall into each of a set of categories.

General   In relation to a theory, summarizing many different outcomes.

General linear model (GLM)   A set of mathematical procedures used by computer programs to compute multiple regression and ANOVA.

Generalization   The extent to which relationships among conceptual variables can be demonstrated in a wide variety of people and with a wide variety of manipulated or measured variables.

Goodness of fit statistic   In a structural equation analysis, a test that indicates how well the collected data fit the hypothesized relationships among the variables.

Grouped frequency distribution   A statistical table that indicates how many individuals in a sample fall into each of a set of categories on a quantitative variable.

Guttman scale   A fixed-format self-report scale in which the items are arranged in a cumulative order such that it is assumed that if a respondent answers one item correctly, he or she will also answer all previous items correctly.

Hierarchical multiple regression   A multiple regression analysis in which the predictor variables are added into the regression equation in a predetermined order.

Hindsight bias   The tendency to think that we could have predicted something that we probably could not have predicted.

Histogram   A visual display of a grouped frequency distribution that uses bars to indicate the frequencies.

History threats   Threats to internal validity that result from the potential influence of changes in the social climate during the course of a study.

Impact   The extent to which the experimental manipulation creates the hoped-for changes in the conceptual independent variable.

Inclusion criteria   The rules that determine whether a study is to be included in a metaanalysis.

Independent   Two variables are said to be independent if there is no association between them.

Independent variable   In an experiment, the variable that is manipulated by the researcher.

Individual sampling   In systematic observation, the act of choosing which individuals will be observed.

Inductive method   The observation of specific facts to get ideas about more general relationships among variables.

Inferential statistics   Numbers, such as a p-value, that are used to specify the characteristics of a population on the basis of the data in a sample.

Informed consent   The practice of providing research participants with information about the nature of the research project before they make a decision about whether or not to participate.

Institutional review board (IRB)   A panel of at least five individuals, including at least one whose primary interest is in nonscientific domains, that determines the ethics of proposed research.

Interaction   A pattern of means that may occur in a factorial experimental design when the influence of one independent variable on the dependent variable is different at different levels of another independent variable or variables.

Internal analysis   In an experiment, an analysis in which the scores on the manipulation check measure are correlated with the scores on the dependent variable as an alternative test of the research hypothesis.

Internal consistency   The extent to which the scores on the items of a scale correlate with each other and thus are all measuring true score rather than random error.

Internal validity   The extent to which changes in the dependent variable can confidently be attributed to the influence of the independent variable rather than to the potential influence of confounding variables.

Interrater reliability   The internal consistency of the ratings made by a group of judges.

Interval scale   A measured variable in which equal changes in the measured variable are known to correspond to equal changes in the conceptual variable being measured.

Interview   A survey that is read to a respondent either in person or over the telephone.

Items   Questions on a scale.

kappa (κ)   A statistic used to measure interrater reliability.

Latent variables   The conceptual variables or factors in a structural equation analysis.

Latin square design   A repeated-measures research design that is counterbalanced such that each condition appears equally often in each order and also follows equally often after each of the other conditions.

Laws Principles that are so general that they are assumed to apply to all situations.

Levels The specific situations created by the experimental manipulation.

Likert scale A fixed-format self-report scale that consists of a series of items that indicate agreement or disagreement with the issue that is to be measured, each with a set of responses on which the respondents indicate their opinions.

Linear relationship A relationship between two quantitative variables that can be approximated with a straight line.

Loglinear analysis A statistical analysis that assesses the relationship between more than one nominal predictor variable and a nominal dependent variable.

Longitudinal research designs (panel studies) Research in which the same individuals are measured more than one time and the time period between the measurements is long enough that changes in the variables of interest could occur (Compare with *Cross-sectional research designs*).

Main effect Differences on the dependent measure across the levels of any one factor when all other factors in the experiment are controlled for.

Manipulated See *Experimental manipulation*.

Manipulation checks Measures used to determine whether the experimental manipulation has had the intended impact on the conceptual independent variable of interest.

Margin of error See *Confidence interval*.

Marginal means The means of the dependent variable within the levels of any one factor, which are combined across the levels of one or more other factors in the design.

Matched-group research design A research design in which participants are measured on a variable of interest before the experiment begins and are then assigned to conditions on the basis of their scores on that variable.

Maturation threats Threats to internal validity that involve potential changes in the research participants over time that are unrelated to the independent variable.

Mean See *Arithmetic mean*.

Mean deviation See *Mean deviation scores*.

Mean deviation scores People's scores on the variable (X) minus the mean of the variable $(X-\bar{x})$.

Means comparisons Statistical tests used when there are more than two condition means to determine which condition means are significantly different from each other.

Measured variables Numbers that represent conceptual variables and that can be used in data analysis.

Measurement The assignment of numbers to objects or events according to specific rules.

Measures See *Measured variables*.

Median A measure of central tendency equal to the score at which half of the scores are higher and half of the scores are lower.

Mediating variable (mediator) A variable that is caused by one variable and that in turn causes another variable.

Mediator See *Mediating variable*.

Meta-analysis A statistical technique that uses the results of existing studies to integrate and draw conclusions about those studies.

Mixed factorial designs Experimental designs that use both between-participants and repeated measures factors.

Mode A measure of central tendency equal to the score or scores that occur most frequently on the variable.

Moderator variable A variable that produces an interaction of the relationship between two other variables such that the relationship between them is different at different levels of the moderator variable.

Mortality See *Attrition*.

Multimodal A distribution that has more than one mode.

Multiple correlation coefficient (*R*) A statistic that indicates the extent to which all of the predictor variables in a regression analysis are able together to predict the outcome variable.

Multiple regression A statistical technique for analyzing a research design in which more than one predictor variable is used to predict a single outcome variable.

Multivariate analysis of variance (MANOVA) A statistical procedure used to assess the relationships between one or more nominal independent variables and a set of quantitative dependent variables.

Multivariate statistics Data analysis procedures designed to analyze more than one dependent variable at the same time.

Mundane realism. See *Ecological validity*.

Naive experimenters Researchers who do not know the research hypothesis.

Naturalistic research Research designed to study the behavior of people or animals in their everyday lives.

Nominal variable A variable that names or identifies a particular characteristic.

Nomological net The pattern of correlations among a group of measured variables that provides evidence for the convergent and discriminant validity of the measures.

Nonlinear relationships Relationships between two quantitative variables that cannot be approximated with a straight line.

Nonreactive behavioral measures Behavioral measures that are designed to avoid reactivity because the respondent is not aware that the measurement is occurring, does not realize what the measure is designed to assess, or cannot change his or her responses.

Normal distribution Bell-shaped and symmetrical pattern of scores that is expected to be observed on most measured quantitative variables.

Null hypothesis (H_0) The assumption that observed data reflect only what would be expected from the sampling distribution.

Objective Free from personal bias or emotion.

Observational research Research that involves observing behavior and recording those observations objectively.

One-sided *p*-values *P*-values that consider only the likelihood that a relationship occurs in the predicted direction.

One-way experimental design An experiment that has one independent variable.

Operational definition A precise statement of how a conceptual variable is measured or manipulated.

Ordinal scale A measured variable in which the numbers indicate whether there is more or less of the conceptual variable but do not indicate the exact interval between the individuals on the conceptual variable.

Outliers Scores that are so extreme that their validity is questioned.

Oversampling A procedure used in stratified sampling in which a greater proportion of individuals are sampled from some strata than from others.

Pairwise comparisons Means comparisons in which any one condition mean is compared with any other condition mean.

Parameter A number that represents the characteristics of a population. (Compare with *Descriptive statistic*).

Parsimonious In relation to a theory, providing the simplest possible account of an outcome or outcomes.

Participant replication A replication that tests whether the findings of an existing study will hold up in a different population of research participants.

Participant variable A variable that represents differences among individuals on a demographic characteristic or a personality trait.

Participant-variable design A research design in which one of the variables represents measured differences among the research participants, such as demographic characteristics or personality traits.

Path analysis A form of multiple regression that assesses the relationships among a number of variables.

Path diagram A graphic display of the relationships among a number of variables.

Pearson product-moment correlation coefficient (*r*) A statistic used to assess the direction and the size of the relationship between two variables.

Peer review The process by which experts in a field judge whether a research report is suitable for publication in a scientific journal.

Percentile rank The percentage of scores on the variable that are lower than the score itself.

Phi (ϕ) The effect size statistic for 2×2 contingency tables.

Pilot test An initial practice test of a research procedure to see if it is working as expected.

Placebo effect An artifact that occurs when participants' expectations about what effect an experimental manipulation is supposed to have influence the dependent measure independently of the actual effect of the manipulation.

Planned comparisons Means comparisons in which specific differences between means, as predicted by the research hypothesis, are analyzed.

Population The entire group of people about whom a researcher wants to learn.

Post hoc comparisons Means comparisons that were not planned ahead of time. Usually these comparisons take into consideration that many comparisons are being made and thus control the experimentwise alpha.

Postexperimental interview Questions asked of participants after research has ended to probe for the effectiveness of the experimental manipulation and for suspicion.

Power The probability that the researcher will, on the basis of the observed data, be able to reject the null hypothesis given that the null hypothesis is actually false and thus should be rejected. Power is equal to $1 - \beta$.

Predictive validity A form of criterion validity in which a self-report measure is used to predict future behavior.

Probability sampling A sampling procedure used to ensure that each person in a population has a known chance of being selected to be part of the sample.

Probability value (*p*-value) The statistical likelihood of an observed pattern of data, calculated on the basis of the sampling distribution of the statistic.

Process debriefing A debriefing that involves an active attempt by an experimenter to undo any changes that might have occurred in participants during the research.

Program evaluation research Research designed to study intervention programs, such as after-school programs or prenatal care clinics, with the goal of determining whether the programs are effective in helping the people who make use of them.

Projective measure A measure of personalities in which an unstructured image, such as an inkblot, is shown to participants, who are asked to list what comes to mind as they view the image.

Proportion of explained variability The amount of the dependent (or outcome) variable accounted for by the independent (or predictor) variable.

Protocol See *Experimental script*.

Psychophysiological measures Measured variables designed to assess the physiological functioning of the nervous or endocrine system.

Qualitative research Descriptive research that is focused on observing and describing events as they occur, with the goal of capturing all of the richness of everyday behavior.

Quantitative research Descriptive research in which the collected data are subjected to formal statistical analysis.

Quantitative variable A variable that is used to indicate the extent to which a person possesses a characteristic.

Quasi-experimental research designs Research designs in which the independent variable involves a grouping but in which equivalence has not been created between the groups.

Questionnaire A set of self-report items that is completed by respondents at their own pace, often without supervision.

Random assignment to conditions A method of ensuring that the participants in the different levels of the independent variable are equivalent before the experimental manipulation occurs.

Random error Chance fluctuations in measurement that influence scores on measured variables.

Range A measure of dispersion equal to the maximum observed score minus the minimum observed score on a variable.

Ratio scales Interval scales in which there is a zero point that is known to represent the complete lack of the conceptual variable.

Raw data The original collected data in a research project.

Reactivity Changes in responding that occur as a result of measurement.

Reciprocal causation In a correlational research design, the possibility that the predictor variable causes the outcome variable and the outcome variable also causes the predictor variable.

Regression coefficients Statistics that indicate the relationship between one of the predictor variables and the outcome variable in a multiple regression analysis.

Regression equation The equation that makes the best possible prediction of scores on the outcome variable using scores on one or more predictor variables.

Regression line On a scatterplot, the line that minimizes the squared distance of the points from the line.

Regression to the mean A statistical artifact such that whenever the same variable is measured more than once, if the correlation between the two measures is less than $r = 1.00$ or greater than $r = -1.00$, then the individuals will tend to score more toward the average score of the group on the second measure than they did on the first measure, even if nothing has changed between the two measures.

Reliability The extent to which a measured variable is free from random error.

Repeated-measures designs Experiments in which the same people participate in more than one condition of an experiment, thereby creating equivalence, and the differences across the various levels are assessed within the same participants.

Replication   The repeating of research, either exactly or with modifications.

Representative sample   A sample that is approximately the same as the population in every respect.

Research design   A specific method used to collect, analyze, and interpret data.

Research hypothesis   A specific and falsifi-able prediction regarding the relationship between or among two or more variables.

Research programs   Collections of experiments in which a topic of interest is systematically studied through conceptual and constructive replications over a period of time.

Research report   A document that presents scientific findings using a standardized written format.

Response rate   The percentage of people who actually complete a questionnaire and return it to the investigator.

Restriction of range   A circumstance that occurs when most participants have similar scores on a variable that is being correlated with another variable. Restriction of range reduces the absolute value of the correlation coefficient.

Retesting effects   Reactivity that occurs when the responses on the second administration are influenced by respondents having been given the same or similar measures before.

Reversal design   See *A-B-A design*.

Reverse causation   In a correlational research design, the possibility that the outcome variable causes the predictor variable rather than vice versa.

Review paper   A document that discusses the research in a given area with the goals of summarizing the existing findings, drawing conclusions about the conditions under which relationships may or may not occur, linking the research findings to other areas of research, and making suggestions for further research.

Running head   A short label that identifies the research topic and that appears at the top of the pages of a journal article.

Sample   The group of people who actually participate in a research project.

Sampling   Methods of selecting people to participate in a research project, usually with the goal of being able to use these people to make inferences about a population.

Sampling bias   What occurs when a sample is not actually representative of the population because the probability with which members of the population have been selected for participation is not known.

Sampling distribution   The distribution of all the possible values of a statistic.

Sampling distribution of the mean   The set of all possible means of samples of a given size taken from a population.

Sampling frame   A list indicating an entire population.

Scales   Fixed-format self-report measures that contain more than one item (such as an intelligence test or a measure of self-esteem).

Scaling   Specification of the relationship between the numbers on the measured variable and the values of the conceptual variable.

Scatterplot   A graph showing the relationship between two quantitative variables in which a point for each individual is plotted at the intersection of their scores on the predictor and the outcome variables.

Scheffé means comparison test   A post hoc means comparison test in which the critical *F* value is adjusted to take into consideration the number of possible comparisons.

Scientific fraud   The intentional alteration or fabrication of scientific data.

Scientific method   The set of assumptions, rules, and procedures that scientists use when conducting research.

Selection threats   Threats to internal validity that occur whenever individuals select themselves into groups rather than being randomly assigned to the groups.

Self-promotion   A type of reactivity in which the research participants respond in a way that they think will make them look intelligent, knowledgeable, caring, healthy, and nonprejudiced.

Self-report measures   Measures in which individuals are asked to respond to questions posed by an interviewer or on a questionnaire.

Semantic differential   A fixed-format self-report scale in which the topic being evaluated is presented once at the top of the page and the items consist of pairs of adjectives located at the two endpoints of a standard response format.

Significance level   See *Alpha*.

Simple effect   The effect of one factor within one level of another factor.

Simple random sampling   A probabilistic sampling technique in which each person in the population has an equal chance of being included in the sample.

Simulation study   Research in which participants are fully informed about the nature of the research and asked to behave "as if" they were in a social setting of interest.

Simultaneous multiple regression   A multiple regression analysis in which all of the predictor variables are simultaneously used to predict the outcome variable.

Single-group before-after design   Research that uses a single group of participants who are measured before and after they have had the experience of interest.

Single-group design   Research that uses a single group of participants who are measured after they have had the experience of interest.

Single-participant research designs   Research in which a single individual, or a small group of individuals, is studied over a period of time.

Skewed   In relation to a distribution of scores, not symmetrical.

Snowball sampling   A nonprobabilistic sampling technique in which one or more members of a population are located and used to lead the researchers to other members of the population.

Social desirability   A type of reactivity in which research participants present themselves in a positive or socially acceptable way to the researcher.

Split-half reliability   A measure of internal consistency that involves correlating the respondents' scores on one half of the items with their scores on the other half of the items.

Spurious relationship   A relationship between two variables that is produced by a common-causal variable.

Standard deviation (s)   A measure of dispersion equal to the square root of the variance.

Standard error   See *Standard error of the mean*.

Standard error of the mean   The theoretical standard deviation of the means in the sampling distribution of the mean.

Standard normal distribution   A hypothetical population distribution of standard scores.

Standard score   A number that represents the distance of a score from the mean of the variable (the mean deviation) expressed in standard deviation units:

$$\frac{x - \bar{x}}{s}$$

Standardization of conditions   The goal of treating all experimental participants in exactly the same way, with the single exception of the manipulation itself.

States   Personality variables that are expected to change within the same person over a short period of time.

Statistically nonsignificant   The conclusion to not reject the null hypothesis, made when the p-value is greater than alpha ($p > .05$).

Statistically significant   The conclusion to reject the null hypothesis, made when the p-value is smaller than alpha ($p < .05$).

Statistics   Mathematical methods used to systematically organize and analyze data.

Stem and leaf plot   A method of graphically summarizing raw data such that the original data values can still be seen.

Stepwise multiple regression   A multiple regression analysis in which the predictor variables are entered into the analysis according to the extent to which they increase the multiple R.

Strata   Population subgroups used in stratified sampling.

Stratified sampling   A probability sampling technique that involves dividing a sample into subgroups (or *strata*) and then selecting samples from each of these groups.

Structural equation analysis   A multivariate statistical procedure that tests whether the actual relationships among a set of collected variables conform to a theoretical prediction about how those variables should be related.

Structured interview   An interview that uses fixed-format, self-report questions.

Student's *t*   A statistic, derived from a theoretical set of sampling distributions that become smaller as the degrees of freedom increase, that is used in testing differences between means and in creating confidence intervals.

Sum of squares (SS)   The sum of the squared mean deviations of a variable: $\sum (X - x)^2$.

Survey   A series of self-report measures administered through either an interview or a written questionnaire.

Suspicion check   One or more questions asked of participants at the end of research to determine whether they believed the experimental manipulation or guessed the research hypothesis.

Systematic error The influence on a measured variable of other conceptual variables that are not part of the conceptual variable of interest.

Systematic observation Observation following a fixed set of decisions about which observations are to be made on which people and in which times and places.

Systematic random sampling A probability sampling technique that involves selecting every nth person from a sampling frame.

***T* test** A statistical test used to determine whether two observed means are statistically different. T is a special case of the F statistic.

Tautological A characteristic of a theory or research hypothesis such that it cannot be dis-confirmed.

Test-retest reliability The extent to which scores on the same measured variable correlate with each other on two different measurements given at two different times.

Theory An integrated set of principles that explains and predicts many, but not all, observed relationships within a given domain of inquiry.

Think-aloud protocol A free-response measure in which participants verbalize the thoughts they are having as they complete a task.

Time sampling In systematic observation, the act of observing individuals for certain amounts of time.

Time-series designs Longitudinal research designs in which the dependent measure is assessed for one or more groups more than twice, at regular intervals, both before and after the experience of interest occurs.

Traits Personality variables that are not expected to vary (or at most to vary only slowly) within people over time.

Trimming A method of deleting outliers from the distribution of a variable in which the most extreme scores on each end of the distribution are simultaneously deleted.

True score The part of a scale score that is not random error.

Tukey honestly significant difference (HSD) test A post hoc means comparison test that controls for experimentwise alpha.

Two-sided *p*-values *P*-values that consider the likelihood that a relationship can occur either in the expected or the unexpected direction.

Type 1 error Rejection of the null hypothesis when it is really true; Type 1 errors occur with probability equal to alpha.

Type 2 error Failure to reject the null hypothesis when the null hypothesis is really false. Type 2 errors occur with probability equal to beta.

Unbiased estimator A statistic, such as the sample mean, that does not consistently overestimate or underestimate the population parameter.

Univariate statistics Data analysis procedures that use one dependent variable.

Unrelated-experiments technique An experimental technique in which participants are told that they will be participating in two separate experiments. In reality, there is only one experiment, and the experimental manipulation is created in the "first experiment," and the dependent measure is collected in the "second experiment."

Unstructured interview An interview that uses free-format, self-report questions.

Values Personal beliefs of an individual.

Variable Any attribute that can assume different values—for instance, among different people or across different times or places.

Variance (s^2) A measure of dispersion equal to the sum of squares divided by the sample size (N).

Within-groups variance A measure of the variability of the dependent variable across the participants within the experimental conditions in ANOVA.

Within-participants (within-subjects) design See *Repeated-measures designs*.

Z score See *Standard score*.

References

Adair, J. G., Dushenko, T. W., & Lindsay, R. C. L. (1985). Ethical regulations and their impact on research practice. *American Psychologist, 40,* 59–72.

Aiken, L., & West, S. (1991). *Multiple regression: Testing and interpreting interactions.* Newbury Park, CA: Sage.

Ainsworth, M. D. S., Blehar, M. C., Waters, E., & Wall, S. (1978). *Patterns of attachment.* Hillsdale, NJ: Lawrence Erlbaum.

American Psychological Association (2002). Ethical principles of psychologists. *American Psychologist, 57,* 1060–1073.

American Psychological Association (2010). *Publication manual of the American Psychological Association* (6th ed.). Washington, DC: American Psychological Association.

Anderson, C. A. (1989). Temperature and aggression: Ubiquitous effects of heat on occurrence of human violence. *Psychological Bulletin, 106,* 74–96.

Applebaum, M. I., & McCall, R. B. (1983). Design and analysis in developmental psychology. In P. H. Mussen & W. Kessen (Eds.), *Handbook of child psychology: Vol. 1. History, theory and methods* (pp. 415–476). New York, NY: Wiley.

Aronson, E., & Carlsmith, J. M. (1968). Experimentation in social psychology. In G. Lindzey & E. Aronson (Eds.), *Handbook of social psychology* (2nd ed., Vol. 2, pp. 1–79). Reading, MA: Addison-Wesley.

Aronson, E., & Mills, J. (1959). The effect of severity of initiation on liking for a group. *Journal of Abnormal and Social Psychology, 59,* 177–181.

Baddeley, A. D. (1990). *Human memory: Theory and practice.* Boston, MA: Allyn and Bacon.

Bakeman, R., & Gottman, J. M. (1986). *Observing interaction.* Cambridge, England: Cambridge University Press.

Banaji, M. R., & Crowder, R. G. (1989). The bankruptcy of everyday memory. *American Psychologist, 44,* 1185–1193.

Baron, R. M., & Kenny, D. A. (1986). The moderator-mediator variable distinction in social psychological research: Conceptual, strategic and statistical considerations. *Journal of Personality and Social Psychology, 51,* 1173–1182.

Baron, R. A., & Ransberger, V. M. (1978). Ambient temperature and the occurrence of collective violence: The "long, hot summer" revisited. *Journal of Personality and Social Psychology, 36,* 351–360.

Bartholow, B. D., Fabiana, M., Gratton, G., & Battencourt, B. A. (2001). A psychophysiological examination of cognitive processing of and affective responses to social expectancy violations. *Psychological Science, 12,* 197–204.

Basso, D., Beattie, M., & Bresnahan, J. (1995). A sensitive and reliable locomotion rating scale for open field testing in rats. *Journal of Neurotrauma, 12,* 1–21.

Baumrind, D. (1985). Research using intentional deception: Ethical issues revisited. *American Psychologist, 40,* 165–174.

Bem, D. J. (1987). Writing the empirical journal article. In M. P. Zanna & J. M. Darley (Eds.), *The complete academic: A practical guide for the beginning social scientist.* New York, NY: Random House.

Berkowitz, L., & Donnerstein, E. (1982). External validity is more than skin deep: Some answers to criticisms of laboratory experiments. *American Psychologist, 37,* 245–257.

Berkowitz, L., & Macaulay, J. (1971). The contagion of criminal violence. *Sociometry, 34,* 238–260.

Berscheid, E., Baron, K. S., Dermer, M., & Libman, M. (1973). Anticipating informed consent: An empirical approach. *American Psychologist, 28,* 913–925.

Bissonnette, V., Ickes, W., Bernstein, I., & Knowles, E. (1990). Personality moderating variables: A warning about statistical artifacts and a comparison of analytic techniques. *Journal of Personality, 58,* 567–587.

Bower, G. H. (1981). Mood and memory. *American Psychologist, 36,* 129–148.

Bramel, D. (1962). A dissonance theory approach to defensive projection. *Journal of Abnormal and Social Psychology, 64,* 121–129.

Brendl, C. M., Chattopadhyay, A., Pelham, B. W., & Carvallo, M. (2005). Name letter branding: Valence transfers when product specific needs are active. *Journal of Consumer Research, 32*(3), 405–415.

Brierley, B., Shaw, P., & David, A. S. (2002). The human amygdala: A systematic review and meta-analyses of volumetric magnetic resonance imaging. *Brain Research Reviews, 39,* 84–105.

Cacioppo, J. T., & Petty, R. E. (1983). *Social psychophysiology: A sourcebook.* New York, NY: Guilford.

Cacioppo, J. T., Petty, R. E., & Morris, K. J. (1983). Effects of need for cognition on message evaluation, recall, and persuasion. *Journal of Personality and Social Psychology, 45,* 805–818.

Cacioppo, J. T., Tassinary, L. G., & Berntson, G. G. (Eds.). (2000). *Handbook of psychophysiology* (2nd ed.). Cambridge, England: Cambridge University Press.

Campbell, D. T. (1969). Reforms as experiments. *American Psychologist, 24,* 409–429.

Campbell, D. T., & Stanley, J. C. (1963). *Experimental and quasi-experimental designs for research.* Chicago, IL: Rand McNally.

Carlsmith, J. M., & Anderson, C. A. (1979). Ambient temperature and the occurrence of collective violence: A new analysis. *Journal of Personality and Social Psychology, 37,* 337–344.

Clark, D. M., Salkovskis, P. M., Ost, L.-G., Breitholtz, E., Koehler, K. A., Westling, B. E., et al. (1997). Misinterpretation of body sensations in panic disorder. *Journal of Consulting and Clinical Psychology, 65*(2), 203–213.

Clubb, J. M., Austin, E. W., Geda, C. L., & Traugott, M. W. (1985). Sharing research data in the social sciences. In S. E. Fienber, M. E. Martin, & M. L. Straff (Eds.), *Sharing Research Data.* Washington, DC: National Academy Press.

Cohen, J. (1977). *Statistical power analysis for the behavioral sciences.* New York, NY: Academic Press.

Cohen, J., & Cohen, P. (1983). *Applied multiple regression/correlation analysis for the behavioral sciences* (2nd ed.). Hillsdale, NJ: Lawrence Erlbaum.

Cohen, S., Tyrrell, D. A. J., & Smith, A. P. (1993). Negative life events, perceived stress, negative affect and susceptibility to the common cold. *Journal of Personality and Social Psychology, 64,* 131–140.

Cook, T. D., & Campbell, D. T. (1979). *Quasi-experimentation: Design and analysis issues for field settings.* Chicago, IL: Rand McNally.

Coombs, C. H. (1964). *A theory of data.* New York, NY: Wiley.

Cooper, H. M., & Rosenthal, R. (1980). Statistical versus traditional procedures for summarizing research findings. *Psychological Bulletin, 87*(3), 442–449.

Crowne, D. P., & Marlowe, D. (1964). *Studies in evaluative dependence.* New York, NY: Wiley.

Davis, J. A., & Smith, T. W. (1994). *General social surveys, 1972–1994: Cumulative code-book.* Chicago, IL: National Opinion Research Center.

Davis, J., Smith, T., & Marsden, P. (2000). General Social Surveys, 1972–2000, from http://www.icpsr.umich.edu:8080/GSS/homepage.htm.

Denzin, N, & Lincoln, Y. (2003). *Collecting and interpreting qualitative materials.* (2nd ed.). Thousand Oaks, CA: Sage.

Dickerson, C. A., Thibodeau, R., Aronson, E., & Miller, D. (1992). Using cognitive dissonance to encourage water conservation. *Journal of Applied Social Psychology, 22*(11), 841–854.

Diener, E., & Crandall, R. (1978). *Ethics in social and behavioral research.* Chicago, IL: University of Chicago Press.

Diener, E., Fraser, S. C, Beaman, A. L., & Kelem, R. T. (1976). Effects of deindividuation variables on stealing among stealing Halloween trick-or-treaters. *Journal of Personality and Social Psychology, 33,* 178–183.

Dillman, D. A. (1978). *Mail and telephone surveys: The total design method.* New York, NY: Wiley.

DiMatteo, M. R., Morton, S. C, Lepper, H. S., & Damush, T. M. (1996). Cesarean childbirth and psychosocial outcomes: A meta-analysis. *Health Psychology, 15,* 303–314.

Dowden, C, & Brown, S. L. (2002). The role of substance abuse factors in predicting recidivism: A meta-analysis. *Psychology, Crime and Law, 8,* 243–264.

Durkheim, E. (1951). *Suicide.* (J. A. Spaudling & G. Simpson, Trans.). New York, NY: Free Press.

Eagly, A. H., & Chravala, C. (1986). Sex differences in conformity: Status and gender-role interpretations. *Psychology of Women Quarterly, 10,* 203–220.

Eisenberger, R., & Cameron, J. (1996). Detrimental effects of reward: Reality or myth? *American Psychologist, 51,* 1151–1166.

Eisenberger, N. I., Lieberman, M. D., & Williams, K. D. (2003). Does rejection hurt? An fMRI study of social exclusion. *Science, 302*(5643), 290–292.

Ekman, P., Friesen, W. V., & Scherer, K. R. (1976). Body movement and voice pitch in deceptive interaction. *Semiotica, 16,* 23–27.

Ellsworth, P. C, & Langer, E. J. (1976). Staring and approach: An interpretation of the stare as a nonspecific activator. *Journal of Personality and Social Psychology, 33,* 117–122.

Ericsson, K. A., & Simon, H. A. (1980). Verbal reports as data. *Psychological Review, 87,* 215–251.

Eron, L. D., Huesmann, L. R., Lefkowitz, M. M., & Walder, L. O. (1972). Does television watching cause aggression? *American Psychologist, 27,* 253–263.

Fazio, R. H., Effrein, E. A., & Falender, V. J. (1981). Self-perceptions following social interaction. *Journal of Personality and Social Psychology, 41(2),* 232–242.

Festinger, L., Riecken, H. W., & Schachter, S. (1956). *When prophecy fails: A social and psychological study of a modern group that predicted the destruction of the world,* Minneapolis, MN: University of Minnesota Press.

Fiske, S. T., Bersoff, D. N., Borgida, E., Deaux, K., & Heilman, M. E. (1991). Social science research on trial: The use of sex stereotyping research in *Price Waterhouse* vs. *Hopkins. American Psychologist, 46,* 1049–1060.

Fiske, S. T, Neuberg, S. L., Beattie, A. E., & Milberg, S. J. (1987). Category-based and attribute-based reactions to others: Some informational conditions of stereotyping and individuating processes. *Journal of Experimental Social Psychology, 23,* 399–427.

Fiske, S. T., & Taylor, S. E. (2007). *Social cognition, from brains to culture.* New York, NY: McGraw-Hill.

Fowler, K. A., Lilienfeld, S. O., & Patrick, C. J. (2009). Detecting psychopathy from thin slices of behavior. *Psychological Assessment, 21(1),* 68–78.

Freud, S. (1959). Analysis of a phobia in a 5-year-old boy. In A. Strachey & J. Strachey (Eds.), *Collected Papers* (Vol. 3). New York, NY: Basic Books.

Gelfand, H., & Walker, C. (Eds.). (2001). *Mastering APA style: Instructor's resource guide.* Washington, DC: American Psychological Association.

Gerard, H. B., & Matthewson, G. C. (1966). The effects of severity of initiation on liking for a group: A replication. *Journal of Experimental Social Psychology, 2,* 278–287.

Gosling, S., Ko, S. J., Mannarelli, T., & Morris, M. (2002). A room with a cue: Personality judgments based on offices and bedrooms. *Journal of Personality and Social Psychology, 82,* 379–398.

Greenberg, B. S. (1980). *Life on television: Current analyses of U.S. TV drama.* Norwood, NJ: Ablex.

Greenwald, A. G., McGhee, D. E., & Schwartz, J. L. K. (1998). Measuring individual differences in implicit cognition: The Implicit Association Test. *Journal of Personality and Social Psychology, 74,* 1464–1480.

Gully, S. M., Incalcaterra, K. A., Joshi, A., & Beaubien, J. M. (2002). A meta-analysis of team-efficacy, potency, and performance: Interdependence and level of analysis as moderators of observed relationships. *Journal of Applied Psychology, 87,* 819–832.

Guttman, L. (1944). A basis of scaling quantitative data. *American Sociological Review, 9,* 139–150.

Haney, C., Banks, C., & Zimbardo, P. (1973). Interpersonal dynamics in a simulated prison. *International Journal of Criminology and Penology, 1,* 69–87.

Harackiewicz, J. M., Manderlink, G., & Sansone, C. (1984). Rewarding pinball wizardry: Effects of evaluation and cue value on intrinsic interest. *Journal of Personality and Social Psychology, 47,* 287–300.

Hardy, D. J., & Hinkin, C. H. (2002). Reaction time slowing in adults with HIV: Results of a meta-analysis using brinley plots. *Brain and Cognition, 50,* 25–34.

Harmon-Jones, E., & Sigelman, J. (2001). State anger and prefrontal brain activity: Evidence that insult-related relative left prefrontal activation is associated with experienced anger and aggression. *Journal of Personality and Social Psychology, 80,* 797–803.

Harris, R. J. (1985). *A primer of multivariate statistics* (2nd ed.). Orlando, FL: Academic Press.

Hays, W. L. (1988). *Statistics* (4th ed.). New York, NY: Holt, Rinehart and Winston.

Heider, F. (1958). *The psychology of interpersonal relations.* Hillsdale, NJ: Lawrence Erlbaum.

Herrnstein, R. J., & Murray, C. (1994). *The bell curve: Intelligence and class structure in American life.* New York, NY: Free Press.

Hillyer, J. E., & Joynes, R. L. (2009). A new measure of hindlimb stepping ability in neonatally spinalized rats. *Behavioural Brain Research, 202(2),* 291–302.

Hsee, C. K., & Hastie, R. (2006). Decision and experience: Why don't we choose what makes us happy? *Trends in Cognitive Sciences, 10(1),* 31–37.

Huck, S. W., & Sandler, H. M. (1979). *Rival hypotheses: Alternative interpretations of data-based conclusions.* New York, NY: Harper and Row.

Hull, J. G., & Young, R. D. (1983). Self-consciousness, self-esteem, and success-failure as determinants of alcohol consumption in male social drinkers. *Journal of Personality and Social Psychology, 44,* 1097–1109.

Humphreys, L. (1975). *Tearoom trade: Impersonal sex in public places* (Enl. ed.). Chicago, IL: Aldine.

Ickes, W. (1984). Compositions in black and white: Determinants of interaction in interracial dyads. *Journal of Personality and Social Psychology, 47,* 330–341.

Isen, A. M., & Levin, P. F (1972). The effect of feeling good on helping: Cookies and kindness. *Journal of Personality and Social Psychology, 21,* 384–388.

Isen, A. M., Nygren, T. E., & Ashby, F G. (1988). Influence of positive affect on the subjective utility of gains and losses: It is just not worth the risk. *Journal of Personality and Social Psychology, 55,* 710–717.

Johnson, R. D., & Downing, L. L. (1979). Deindividuation and the valence of cues: Effects on prosocial and antisocial behavior. *Journal of Personality and Social Psychology, 37,* 1532–1538.

Jorgensen, R. S., Johnson, B. T., Kolodziej, M. E., & Schreer, G. E. (1996). Elevated blood pressure and personality: A meta-analytic review. *Psychological Bulletin, 120,* 293–320.

Kahle, L. R. (1980). Stimulus condition self-selection by males in the interaction of locus of control and skill-chance situations. *Journal of Personality and Social Psychology, 38,* 50–56.

Kassin, S. M., & Kiechel, K. L. (1996). The social psychology of false confessions: Compliance, internalization and confabulation. *Psychological Science, 7,* 125–128.

Kelley, H. H. (1967). Attribution theory in social psychology. In D. Levine (Ed.), *Nebraska symposium on motivation, 15,* (pp. 192–238). Lincoln, NE: University of Nebraska Press.

Kenny, D. A. (1979). *Correlation and causality.* New York, NY: Wiley-Interscience.

Keppel, G., & Zedeck, S. (1989). *Data analysis for research designs.* New York, NY: Freeman.

Kim, H., & Marcus, H. (1999). Deviance or uniqueness, harmony or conformity: A cultural analysis. *Journal of Personality and Social Psychology, 77,* 785–800.

Kimmel, A. (1998). In defense of deception. *American Psychologist, 53,* 803–805.

Kish, L. (1965). *Survey sampling.* New York, NY: Wiley.

Knight, L. J., Barbaree, H. E., & Boland, F. J. (1986). Alcohol and the balanced-placebo design: The role of experimenter demands in expectancy. *Journal of Abnormal Psychology, 95,* 335–340.

Kohlberg, L. (1969). Stage and sequence: The cognitive-developmental approach to socialization. In D. A. Goslin (Ed.), *Handbook of socialization theory and research* (pp. 347–480). Chicago, IL: Rand McNally.

Lewin, K. (1944). Constructs in psychology and psychological ecology. *University of Iowa Studies in Child Welfare, 20,* 23–27.

Lieberman, J., Solomon, S., Greenberg, J., & McGregor, H. (1999). A hot new way to measure aggression: Hot sauce allocation. *Aggressive Behavior, 25,* 331–348.

Likert, R. (1932). A technique for the measurement of attitudes. *Archives of Psychology, 140,* 5–53.

Lord, C. G., & Gilbert, D. T. (1983). The "same person" heuristic: An attributional procedure based on an assumption about person similarity. *Journal of Personality and Social Psychology, 45,* 751–762.

Macrae, C. N., Bodenhausen, G. V., Milne, A. B., & Jetten, J. (1994). Out of mind but back in sight: Stereotypes on the rebound. *Journal of Personality and Social Psychology, 67,* 808–817.

Madey, S. F., Simo, M., Dillworth, D., & Kemper, D. (1996). They do get more attractive at closing time, but only when you are not in a relationship. *Basic and Applied Social Psychology, 18,* 387–393.

Madigan, R., Johnson, S., & Linton, P. (1995). The language of psychology: APA style as epistemology. *American Psychologist, 50(6),* 428–436.

Mann, C. (1994). Can meta-analysis make policy? *Science, 266,* 960–962.

Markus, H. (1978). The effect of mere presence on social facilitation: An unobtrusive test. *Journal of Experimental Social Psychology, 4, 14,* 389–397.

Marks, I. M., & Mathews, A. M. (1979). Brief standard self-rating for phobic patients. *Behaviour Research and Therapy, 17(3),* 263–267.

McCall, M., & Belmont, H. J. (1996). Credit card insignia and restaurant tipping: Evidence for an associative link. *Journal of Applied Psychology, 81(5),* 609–613.

McCann, I. L., & Holmes, D. S. (1984). Influence of aerobic exercise on depression. *Journal of Personality and Social Psychology, 46,* 1142–1147.

Milgram, S. (1974). *Obedience to authority: An experimental view.* New York, NY: Harper and Row.

Mill, J. S. (1930). *A system of logic.* London, England: Longmans Green.

Miller, N. E. (1985). The value of behavioral research on animals. *American Psychologist, 40,* 423–440.

Mills, J. (1976). A procedure for explaining experiments involving deception. *Personality and Social Psychology Bulletin, 2,* 3–13.

Modin, B. (2002). Birth order and mortality: A life-long follow-up of 14,200 boys and girls born in early 20th century Sweden. *Social Science and Medicine, 54,* 1051–1064.

Morgan, C. D., & Murray, H. A. (1935). A method for investigating fantasies: The thematic apperception test. *Archives of Neurological Psychiatry, 34,* 289–306.

Mori, D., Chaiken, S., & Pliner, P. (1987). "Eating lightly" and the self-presentation of femininity. *Journal of Personality and Social Psychology, 53(4),* 693–702.

Nettles, M. T, Thoeny, A. R., & Gosman, E. J. (1986). Comparative and predictive analyses of black and white students' college achievement and experiences. *Journal of Higher Education, 57,* 289–318.

Nisbett, R. E., & Ross, L. (1980). *Human inference: Strategies and shortcomings of social judgment.* Englewood Cliffs, NJ: Prentice-Hall.

Nisbett, R. E., & Wilson, T. D. (1977). Telling more than we can know: Verbal reports on mental processes. *Psychological Review, 84,* 231–259.

Nunnally, J. C. (1978). *Psychometric theory.* New York, NY: McGraw-Hill.

Orne, M. T. (1962). On the social psychology of the psychological experiment. *American Psychologist, 17,* 776–783.

Ortmann, A., & Hertwig, R. (1997). Is deception acceptable? *American Psychologist, 52,* 746–747.

Osgood, C. E., Suci, G. J., & Tannenbaum, P. H. (1957). *The measurement of meaning.* Urbana, IL: University of Illinois Press.

Parr, J. M., Kavanagh, D. J., Cahill, L., Young, R. M., & Mitchell, G. (2009). Effectiveness of current treatment approaches for benzodiazepine discontinuation: A meta-analysis. *Addiction, 104*(1), 13–24.

Pennebaker, J. W., Dyer, M. A., Caulkins, R. S., Litowitz, D. L., Ackerman, P. L., & Anderson, D. B. (1979). Don't the girls get prettier at closing time: A country and western application to psychology. *Personality and Social Psychology Bulletin, 5,* 122–125.

Piaget, J. (1952). *The origins of intelligence in children.* New York, NY: International University Press.

Piliavin, I. M., Rodin, J., & Piliavin, J. A. (1969). Good samaritanism: An underground phenomenon? *Journal of Personality and Social Psychology, 8,* 121–133.

Plous, S. (1996). Attitudes toward the use of animals in psychological research and education. *Psychological Science, 7,* 352–358.

Pomerantz, E. M., Ruble, D. N, Frey, K. S., & Greulich, F. (1995). Meeting goals and confronting conflict: Children's changing perceptions of social comparison. *Child Development, 66,* 723–738.

Popper, K. R. (1959). *The logic of scientific discovery.* New York, NY: Basic Books.

Prentice, D. A., & Miller, D. T. (1992). When small effects are impressive. *Psychological Bulletin, 112,* 160–164.

Price, L. (1984). Art, science, faith, and medicine: The implications of the placebo effect. *Sociology of Health and Illness, 6,* 61–73.

Ratcliff, R., & McKoon, G. (1996). Bias effects in implicit memory tasks. *Journal of Experimental Psychology: General, 125,* 403–421.

Reed, J. G., & Baxter, P. M. (1983). *Library use: A handbook for psychology.* Washington, DC: American Psychological Association.

Reiss, S., Peterson, R. A., Gursky, D. M., & McNally, R. J. (1986). Anxiety sensitivity, anxiety frequency and the predictions of fearfulness. *Behaviour Research and Therapy, 24*(1), 1–8.

Robinson, J. P., Shaver, P. R., & Wrightsman, L. S. (1991). *Measures of personality and social psychological attitudes.* San Diego, CA: Academic Press.

Rokeach, M. (1964). *The three Christs of Ypsilanti: A psychological study.* New York, NY: Knopf.

Rosenberg, M. (1965). *Society and the adolescent self-image.* Princeton, NJ: Princeton University Press.

Rosenhan, D. L. (1973). On being sane in insane places. *Science, 179,* 250–258.

Rosenthal, R. (1994). Science and ethics in conducting, analyzing, and reporting psychological research. *Psychological Science, 5,* 127–134.

Rosenthal, R., & Fode, K. L. (1963). The effect of experimenter bias on the performance of the albino rat. *Behavioral Science, 8,* 183–189.

Rosenthal, R., & Rosnow, R. L. (1975). *The volunteer subject.* New York, NY: Wiley.

Rosenthal, R., & Rosnow, R. L. (1985). *Contrast analysis: Focused comparison in the Analysis of Variance.* Cambridge, England: Cambridge University Press.

Rosenthal, R., & Rosnow, R. L. (1991). *Essentials of behavioral research: Methods and data analysis* (2nd ed.). New York, NY: McGraw-Hill.

Ross, L., Lepper, M. R., & Hubbard, M. (1975). Perseverance in self-perception and social perception: Biased attributional processes in the debriefing paradigm. *Journal of Personality and Social Psychology, 32,* 880–892.

Rossi, P. H., & Freeman, H. E. (1993). *Evaluation: A systematic approach* (5th ed.). Newbury Park, CA: Sage.

Roy, D. F. (1959–1960). Banana time. *Human Organization, 18,* 158–168.

Rubin, Z. (1973). Designing honest experiments. *American Psychologist, 28,* 445–448.

Saxe, L., Dougherty, D., & Cross, T. (1985). The validity of polygraph testing: Scientific analysis and public controversy. *American Psychologist, 40,* 355–366.

Saywitz, K. J., & Snyder, L. (1996). Narrative elaboration: Test of a new procedure for interviewing children. *Journal of Constructive and Clinical Research, 64,* 1347–1357.

Scheier, M. F, Carver, C. S., & Bridges, M. W. (1994). Distinguishing optimism from neuroticism (and trait anxiety, self-mastery, and self-esteem): A reevaluation of the life orientation test. *Journal of Personality, 67,* 1063–1078.

Schlenker, B. R., & Forsyth, D. R. (1977). On the ethics of psychological research. *Journal of Experimental Social Psychology, 13,* 369–396.

Schmitt, D. P. (2000). A meta-analysis of sex differences in romantic attraction: Do rating contests moderate tactic effectiveness judgments? *British Journal of Social Psychology, 41,* 387–402.

Schuman, H., & Presser, S. (1981). *Questions and answers: Experiments on question form, wordings, and content in surveys.* New York, NY: Academic Press.

Schwarz, N., & Strack, F (1991). Context effects in attitude surveys: Applying cognitive theory to social research. In W. Stroebe & M. Hewstone (Eds.), *European review of social psychology* (Vol. 2, pp. 31–50). New York, NY: Wiley and Sons.

Sears, D. O. (1986). College sophomores in the laboratory: Influences of a narrow data base on social psychology's view of human nature. *Journal of Personality and Social Psychology, 51,* 515–530.

Selltiz, C, Jahoda, M., Deutsch, M., & Cook, S. W. (1966). *Research methods in social relations.* New York, NY: Holt, Rinehart and Winston.

Serketich, W. J., & Dumas, J. E. (1996). The effectiveness of behavioral parent training to modify antisocial behavior in children. A meta-analysis. *Behavior Therapy, 27,* 171–186.

Shear, M. K., Brown, T. A., Barlow, D. H., Money, R., Sholomskas, D. E., Woods, S. W., et al. (1997). Multicenter collaborative panic disorder severity Scale. *American Journal of Psychiatry, 154*(11), 1571–1575.

Shrout, P. E. (1997). Should significance tests be banned? Introduction to a special section exploring the pros and cons. *Psychological Science, 8,* 1–2.

Sigall, H., & Mills, J. (1998). Measures of independent variables and mediators are useful in social psychology experiments: But are they necessary? *Personality and Social Psychology Review, 2,* 218–226.

Simonton, D. K. (1988). Presidential style: Personality, biography, and performance. *Journal of Personality and Social Psychology, 55,* 928–936.

Slaby, R. G., & Frey, K. S. (1975). Development of gender constancy and selective attention to same-sex models. *Child Development, 46,* 849–856.

Smith, M. L., Glass, G. V., & Miller, R. L. (1980). *The benefits of psychotherapy.* Baltimore, MD: Johns Hopkins University Press.

Smith, S. S., & Richardson, D. (1983). Amelioration of deception and harm in psychological research. *Journal of Personality and Social Psychology, 44,* 1075–1082.

Snyder, M. (1974). Self-monitoring of expressive behavior. *Journal of Personality and Social Psychology, 30,* 526–537.

Sperry, R. W. (1982). Some effects of disconnecting the cerebral hemispheres. *Science, 217,* 1223–1226.

Stangor, C., & Carr, C. (2002). Influence of solo status and task performance feedback on ex dimensions pectations about task performance in groups. Manuscript submitted for publication.

Stangor, C., Jonas, K., Stroebe, W., & Hewstone, M. (1996). Development and change of national stereotypes and attitudes. *European Journal of Social Psychology, 26,* 663–675.

Stangor, C., & Ruble, D. N. (1987). Development of gender-role knowledge and gender constancy. In L. Liben & M. Signorella (Eds.), *Children's gender schemata* (pp. 5–22). San Francisco, CA: Jossey-Bass.

Stangor, C., Sullivan, L. A., & Ford, T. E. (1991). Affective and cognitive determinants of prejudice. *Social Cognition, 9,* 359–380.

Steele, H., Steele, M., & Croft, C. (2008). Early attachment predicts emotion recognition at 6 and 11 years old. *Attachment & Human Development, 10*(4), 379–393.

Sternberg, R. J. (1993). *The psychologist's companion* (3rd ed.). New York, NY: Cambridge University Press.

Stevens, J. (1996). *Applied multivariate statistics for the social sciences.* Mawah NJ: Lawrence Erlbaum.

Sullivan, G. L., & O'Connor, P.J. (1988). Women's role portrayals in magazine advertising: 1958–1983. *Sex Roles, 18,* 181–188.

Tabachnick, B. G., & Fidell, L. S. (1989). *Using multivariate statistics* (2nd ed.). New York, NY: Harper and Row.

Teachman, B. A., Smith-Janik, S. B., & Saporito, J. (2007). Information processing biases and panic disorder: Relationships among cognitive and symptom measures. *Behaviour Research and Therapy, 45*(8), 1791–1811.

Thomas, G., & Blackman, D. (1992). The future of animal studies in psychology. *American Psychologist, 47,* 1678.

Trappey, C. (1996). A meta-analysis of consumer choice and subliminal advertising. *Psychology and Marketing, 13,* 517–530.

Tukey, J. W. (1977). *Exploratory data analysis.* Reading, MA: Addison-Wesley.

Twenge, J. M., & Nolen-Hoeksema, S. (2002). Age, gender, race, socioeconomic status, and birth cohort difference on the children's depression inventory: A meta-analysis. *Journal of Abnormal Psychology, 111,* 578–588.

U.S. Department of Health and Human Services. (2001). OPRR Reports: Protection of human subjects, Title 45, Code of Federal Regulations Part 46, as amended December 13, 2001. Washington, DC: Government Printing Office.

Vaughan, T. R. (1967). Governmental intervention in social research: Political and ethical in the Wichita jury recordings. In G. Sjoberg (Ed.), *Ethics, politics, and social research* (pp. 50–77). Cambridge, MA: Schenkman.

Webb, E. J., Campbell, D. T., Schwartz, R. D., Sechrest, L., & Grove, J. B. (1981). *Unobtrusive measures: Nonreactive research in the social sciences* (2nd ed.). Boston, MA: Houghton Mifflin.

Weber, S. J., & Cook, T. D. (1972). Subject effects in laboratory research: An examination of subject roles, demand characteristics, and valid inference. *Psychological Bulletin, 77,* 273–295.

Weick, K. E. (1985). Systematic observational methods. In G. Lindzey & E. Aronson (Eds.), *Handbook of social psychology* (3rd ed., Vol. 1, pp. 567–634). New York, NY: Random House.

Wells, G. L., Leippe, M. R., & Ostrom, T. M. (1979). Guidelines for empirically assessing the fairness of a line-up. *Law and Human Behavior, 11,* 113–130.

Whyte, W. F. (1993). *Street corner society: The social structure of an Italian slum* (4th ed.). Chicago, IL: University of Chicago Press.

Wisneski, D., Lytle, B., & Skitka, L. (2009). Gut reactions: Moral conviction, religiosity, and trust in authority. *Psychological Science, In press.*

Word, C. O., Zanna, M. P., & Cooper, J. (1974). The nonverbal mediation of self-fulfilling prophecies in interracial interaction. *Journal of Experimental Social Psychology, 10,* 109–120.

Zajonc, R. B. (1965). Social facilitation. *Science, 149,* 269–274.

Zajonc, R. B. (1980). Compresence. In P. B. Paulus (Ed.), *Psychology of group influence* (pp. 35–60). Hillsdale, NJ: Lawrence Erlbaum.

Zimbardo, P. G. (1970). The human choice: Individuation, reason, and order versus deindividuation, impulse, and chaos. In W. J. Arnold & D. Levine (Eds.), *Nebraska Symposium on Motivation, 1969.* Lincoln, NE: University of Nebraska Press.

Index